Advanced Information and Knowledge Processing

Series Editors
Professor Lakhmi Jain
lakhmi.jain@unisa.edu.au

Professor Xindong Wu
xwu@cs.uvm.edu

T0139983

Also in this series

Dirk Husmeier, Richard Dybowski and Stephen Roberts (Eds)
Probabilistic Modeling in Bioinformatics and Medical Informatics
1-85233-778-8

Ajith Abraham, Lakhmi Jain and Robert Goldberg (Eds)
Evolutionary Multiobjective Optimization
1-85233-787-7

K.C. Tan, E.F. Khor and T.H. Lee
Multiobjective Evolutionary Algorithms and Applications
1-85233-836-9

Nikhil R. Pal and Lakhmi Jain (Eds)
Advanced Techniques in Knowledge Discovery and Data Mining
1-85233-867-9

Amit Konar and Lakhmi Jain
Cognitive Engineering
1-85233-975-6

Miroslav Kárný (Ed.)
Optimized Bayesian Dynamic Advising
1-85233-928-4

Yannis Manolopoulos, Alexandros Nanopoulos, Apostolos N. Papadopoulos and
Yannis Theodoridis
R-trees: Theory and Applications
1-85233-977-2

Sanghamitra Bandyopadhyay, Ujjwal Maulik, Lawrence B. Holder and Diane J. Cook (Eds)
Advanced Methods for Knowledge Discovery from Complex Data
1-85233-989-6

Marcus A. Maloof (Ed.)
Machine Learning and Data Mining for Computer Security
1-84628-029-X

Sifeng Liu and Yi Lin
Grey Information
1-85233-995-0

Vasile Palade, Cosmin Danut Bocaniala
and Lakhmi Jain (Eds)

Computational Intelligence in Fault Diagnosis

With 154 Figures

 Springer

Vasile Palade, PhD
Oxford University Computing Laboratory
Oxford
UK

Lakhmi Jain, PhD
KES Center
University of South Australia
Australia

Cosmin Danut Bocaniala, Phd
Department of Communication Systems
Lancaster University
Lancaster
UK

British Library Cataloguing in Publication Data
A catalogue record for this book is available from the British Library

Advanced Information and Knowledge Processing ISSN 1610-3947

ISBN-13: 978-1-84996-583-5   e-ISBN-13: 978-1-84628-631-5

© Springer-Verlag London Limited 2010

Printed in the United States of America   (MVY)

9 8 7 6 5 4 3 2 1

Springer Science+Business Media
springer.com

Contributors

Viorel Ariton
"Danubius" University of Galati
Lunca Siretului no. 3, 800416
Galati, Romania
Email: variton@univ-danubius.ro

Cosmin Danut Bocaniala
Computer Science and Engineering Department
"Dunarea de Jos" University of Galati
Domneasca 47, Galati, Romania
Email: cosmin.bocaniala@ugal.ro

João Calado
IDMEC/ISEL, Polytechnic Institute of Lisbon
Mechanical Engineering Studies Centre
Rua Conselheiro Emídio Navarro, 1950-062
Lisbon, Portugal
Email: jcalado@dem.isel.ipl.pt

Kok Yeng Chen
School of Electrical and Electronic Engineering
University of Science Malaysia
Engineering Campus, 14300
Nibong Tebal, Penang, Malaysia

Florin Ionescu
Department of Mechatronics
University of Applied Sciences in Konstanz
Brauneggerstraße 55, 78462 – Konstanz, Germany
Email: ionescu@fh-konstanz.de

Weng Kin Lai
MIMOS Berhad
Technology Park Malaysia
57000 Kuala Lumpur, Malaysia

Chee Peng Lim
School of Electrical and Electronic Engineering
University of Science Malaysia
Engineering Campus, 14300
Nibong Tebal, Penang, Malaysia
Email: cplim@eng.usm.my

Arūnas Lipnickas
Kaunas University of Technology
Department of Control Technology
Studentų 48-317, Kaunas LT-51367, Lithuania
Email: arunas.lipnickas@ktu.lt

Luca Marinai
Department of Power, Propulsion & Aerospace Engineering
Cranfield University
Beds. MK43 0AL, United Kingdom
Email: l.marinai@cranfield.ac.uk

Luis Mendonça
Technical University of Lisbon
Dept. of Mechanical Engineering, GCAR/IDMEC
Pav. Eng. Mecânica III, Av. Rovisco Pais, 1049-001 Lisbon, Portugal
Email: mendonca@dem.ist.utl.pt

Stephen Ogaji
Department of Power, Propulsion and Aerospace Engineering
School of Engineering
Cranfield University
Beds. MK43 0AL, United Kingdom
E-mail: s.ogaji@cranfield.ac.uk

Vasile Palade
Oxford University
Computing Laboratory
Wolfson Building, Parks Road
Oxford, OX1 3QD, United Kingdom
Email: vasile.palade@comlab.ox.ac.uk

José Sá da Costa
Technical University of Lisbon
Department of Mechanical Engineering, GCAR/IDMEC
Pav. Eng. Mecânica III, Av. Rovisco Pais, 1049-001 Lisbon, Portugal
Email: sadacosta@ist.utl.pt

Riti Singh
Department of Power, Propulsion and Aerospace Engineering
School of Engineering
Cranfield University
Beds. MK43 OAL, United Kingdom

João Sousa
Technical University of Lisbon
Dept. of Mechanical Engineering, GCAR/IDMEC
Pav. Eng. Mecânica III, Av. Rovisco Pais, 1049-001 Lisbon, Portugal
Email: jsousa@dem.ist.utl.pt

Dan Stefanoiu
Department of Automatic Control and Computer Science
"Politehnica" University of Bucharest
313 Splaiul Independenţei, 060042–Bucharest, Romania
Email: danny@indinf.pub.ro

Foreword

With the increased complexity of industrial machines and processes, the task of fault diagnosis is becoming increasingly difficult and its complexity almost unmanageable using conventional techniques. Therefore, in the past decade, intense research was dedicated to find alternative solutions using methods that mirror human reasoning as well as involve complex problem solving techniques inspired from nature, to cope with the need for adaptation of the diagnostic methodology to the inherent changes occurring in the diagnosed process.

The automatic diagnosis requires the ability to identify the symptoms automatically and map them to their causes as well as, eventually, to prescribe solutions for repairing/restoring the good functionality of the device, machine or plant. Some methods can prove suitable for certain systems while being totally inappropriate for others.

Computational intelligence attempts to emulate human and biological reasoning, decision-making, learning and optimization via a series of techniques that mirror the adaptive evolutionary nature of living beings. Such techniques can be either used individually or combined into more complex hybrid methodologies, resulting in systems with enhanced capabilities, e.g., the same system can benefit from the decision-making under uncertainty enabled by fuzzy logic as well as from learning and adaptation that neural networks provide, or from the evolutionary optimization inherent in genetic algorithms.

Since the early 1990s, attempts to apply various computational intelligence methods to fault diagnosis, sometimes used to augment traditional methods, were made mainly in research laboratories. Given their success, these are now moving into industrial settings. Big companies such as Siemens and ABB have embraced such novel technologies very early.

Most successful attempts proved that fault diagnosis can greatly benefit from computational intelligence techniques. Neural networks can ease fault identification through model matching and learning of new symptoms. Fuzzy logic can improve the diagnostic decision-making under the uncertainty inherent in the diagnostic information: vague symptoms, ambiguous mapping of symptoms to their causes as well as capturing the gradual degradation of systems and processes in appropriate (fuzzy) models. Genetic algorithms are capable of optimizing the diagnostic models as well as the diagnostic process itself by tracking the (sometimes gradual) changes occurring in the diagnosed system in various ways.

We welcome this new book for offering us a very good overview of the state of the art in the development of computational intelligence techniques pertaining to fault diagnosis. Covering all computational intelligence techniques both in theory as well as illustrating how they work by clear examples and/or practical applications on a relatively broad range of problems, the book gradually exposes the reader to these various methods in its eleven chapters.

Structurally, the book is a comprehensive collection of works arranged in a progressive manner, to ease the gradual grasping of concepts. Starting with a very good overview of computational intelligence and its suitability to the difficult task of fault diagnosis, in Chapter 1, it continues (in Chapters 2 to 5) with four applications involving fuzzy logic to solve various real-world diagnosis problems, then Chapters 6 and 7 illustrate successful neural network-based diagnostic models, to progress in Chapter 8 to a generic computational intelligence approach. Hybrid neuro-fuzzy diagnostic approaches are further illustrated in Chapters 9 and 10. The last chapter presents a novel distributed causal model for diagnosing complex systems.

Overall, I salute this work for marking the progress made in this significant area of fault diagnosis, which can be very useful to a broad audience, ranging from industrial users to graduate students. Enabling the use of these techniques in industrial applications as well as for training and teaching purposes, the book can be regarded as both a repository of knowledge for practitioners and a basis for a course on computational intelligence in diagnosis.

Professor *Mihaela Ulieru*,
Canada Research Chair

Preface

In one of his recent commentaries, called "Integration automation", Mark Venables, editor of the *IEE Manufacturing Engineer Journal*, predicts that "there are five technologies that will drive the future of industrial automation. These are control and diagnosis, communication, software, electronics, and materials – with the former trio being the most important" (http://www.iee.org/oncomms/ sector/computing/commentary.cfm). Indeed, one of the main current trends in solving problems in manufacturing industry is developing fault-tolerant control schemes. Fault-tolerant control is concerned with making the controlled system able to maintain control objectives, despite the occurrence of a fault. Hence, fault diagnosis represents the main ingredient of a fault-tolerant control system. Diagnosing the faults that occurred in a system permits triggering control mechanisms to keep a plant working sufficiently well until the necessary maintenance may be performed. In practice, this feature results in a significant improvement in industrial plant safety, productivity and time in service.

There are two main categories of fault diagnosis techniques currently in use and each has its own basic support theory. The first class of methodologics used for fault diagnosis-related problems were based on *mathematical models* of the monitored plant. The differences between the plant model and its actual behaviour are called residuals and form the basis for deciding if a fault did or did not occur; and if a fault has occurred, deciding which particular fault occurred. Unfortunately, these techniques provide satisfactory results only when plants exhibit linear behaviour or when the modelling errors can be kept within acceptable limits. Accurate mathematical models can be obtained only for plants with low behavioural complexity.

Recent research efforts have concentrated on finding suitable techniques to model plants with high nonlinear behaviour, noise and uncertainty. These three characteristics have been successfully mastered by using *computational intelligence* methodologies. These solutions are based on models such as fuzzy systems, neural networks, and genetic algorithms, to name only the most important of them. The above methods are commonly combined to give the desired result. Besides using residuals for diagnosis purposes, the computational intelligence methods may also be used to directly map the sensor measurements to the faults' space. These methods allow an understanding of plant behaviour using rules obtained directly from sensor measurements. However, even if these techniques can solve the difficult problems posed by nonlinearity, noise and uncertainty, if the complexity of the plant behaviour is very high, the computational load becomes too large for practical purposes.

Finding consistent solutions for *large-scale complex systems diagnosis* problems is currently one of the major interests of industrial research. It presents a challenge to researchers in the field too. The preoccupation of the European researchers in the area of fault diagnosis is illustrated by the existence of three large projects, recently funded by the European Commission. One of these is MAGIC (Multi-Agents-Based Diagnostic Data Acquisition and Management in Complex Systems, http://magic.uni-duisburg.de/). The other two are IFATIS (Intelligent Fault Tolerant Control in Integrated Systems, http://ifatis.uni-duisburg.de/) and NeCST (Networked Control Systems Tolerant to faults, http://www.strep-necst.org/). The usual approach to the problem is by distributing the diagnosis task over a set of subsystems of the monitoring system. The global diagnosis is then formulated by combining the output of the individual local diagnosis processes.

In this book we offer a collection of the latest contributions to the area of computational intelligence applications to fault diagnosis. These have been written by members of a number of well-established fault diagnosis research groups. There is also a special section which deals with the latest issues in fault diagnosis of complex systems. The book contains 10 chapters and is preceded by a review and state-of-the-art introductory chapter. Each of the chapters focuses on some theoretical aspects of computational intelligence methodologies applied to real-world fault diagnosis problems. Four of the chapters deal with fuzzy sets applications. Three chapters deal with neural network applications to fault diagnosis. Two chapters are concerned with neuro-fuzzy techniques for fault diagnosis. The last chapter considers the problem of diagnosing complex systems using local agents. These agents may be implemented by using computational intelligence-based fault diagnosis techniques.

The book has a unifying content as most of the chapters revolve around two main applications. These are aero-engines fault diagnosis, and the diagnosis benchmark proposed within the European Commission's FP5 DAMADICS project (http://www.eng.hull.ac.uk/research/control/damadics1.htm), respectively. The aeroengines applications, described in Chapters 2 and 6, have been developed by the research group at Cranfield University, UK, led by Professor Riti Singh. The applications to the DAMADICS diagnosis benchmark problem, which feature the flow control valve, are described in five chapters and have been developed by the research group at Instituto Superior Técnico, Lisbon, Portugal, led by Professor José Sá da Costa.

In Chapter 1, Bocaniala and Palade present an overview of the main computational intelligence techniques and their applications to the fault diagnosis field. The advantages and disadvantages of each methodology when applied to diagnosis of systems featuring lower or larger complexity are discussed. The methodologies reviewed include neural networks, fuzzy systems, neuro-fuzzy systems, and genetic algorithms, and are the methodologies employed for diagnosis in the remaining chapters. This chapter also introduces the benchmarks used throughout the book.

The next four chapters, from Chapter 2 to Chapter 5, deal with *fuzzy sets applications* to fault diagnosis. In Chapter 2, Marinai and Singh present an application of fuzzy sets to gas path diagnostics of aero-engines. The objective is to estimate the changes in engine components' performance resulting from the engine degradation over time. It uses only few measurable parameters, which are inevitably affected by noise. The use of fuzzy logic permits the noisy measurements to be successfully used. Fuzzy rules are used to map input sets of measurements into faulty output classes of performance parameters in a constrained search space. This enables problem reduction and is aimed at overcoming the difficulty of analytical formulation. The arrangement of the diagnostics model and its outcome can be attained in a relatively short time. This makes the technique suitable for on-board use.

Mendonça, Sousa and Sá da Costa describe in Chapter 3 the application of optimised fuzzy models to fault detection and isolation systems. In this approach, fuzzy models or observers are used for both normal operation and faulty operation. The fuzzy observers are obtained from simulated data driven by real data. The inputs of the fuzzy models are selected using a regularity criterion algorithm. The parameters of the fuzzy models are optimised using a real-coded genetic algorithm. The scheme uses these fuzzy observers to compute the residuals. The application of this approach to a pneumatic servomotor actuated industrial valve, which is the benchmark problem studied within the DAMADICS project, has the ability to detect and isolate a large number of faults. The data also contains noise, which increases the difficulty in detecting and isolating the faults.

In Chapter 4, Bocaniala and Sá da Costa present a fuzzy classifier employed for fault diagnosis purposes that is applied with good results to the DAMADICS diagnosis benchmark problem. The fuzzy classifier identifies the areas in the sensor measurements space corresponding to normal and faulty operating states by using fuzzy subsets. The main advantages of the developed fuzzy classifier are the high accuracy with which it delimits the areas corresponding to different system states, and the high precision of the discrimination within overlapping areas.

In Chapter 5, the last chapter concerned with fuzzy logic applications, Stefanoiu and Ionescu introduce a nonconventional method of fault diagnosis. It is based upon some statistical and fuzzy concepts. The intention is to automate a part of human reasoning when performing the detection and classification of defects by the use of vibrations. The defect classification maps obtained allow the user to perform reliable detection and isolation of defects, independent of their nature. Signal prefiltering is not mandatory; the fuzzy model is able to work with the raw vibration as well as with prefiltered data.

The following three chapters are concerned with *neural network applications* to fault diagnosis. In Chapter 6, Ogaji and Singh present a hierarchical approach to gas path diagnostic for aero-engines and use multiple neural networks. The networks involved are trained to detect, isolate and assess faults in some components of a single-spool gas turbine. The level of accuracy achieved by this decentralised application of ANNs shows benefits over techniques that require only a single network for fault detection, isolation and assessment.

In Chapter 7, Lipnickas gives the description of a two-stage neural network-based classifier system for the fault diagnosis of industrial processes. The first-stage neural network classifier operates as primary fault detection unit, and is used to distinguish between normal operating state and abnormal operating states. In order to reduce the number of false alarms, a penalty factor is introduced in the training error cost function. The second-stage neural network classifier is used to differentiate between different faults. The performance of the proposed approach is validated by application to the DAMADICS diagnosis benchmark problem.

In Chapter 8, Ariton focuses on fault diagnosis of artefacts occurring in industry that execute various tasks involving conductive flows of matter and energy. The proposed multifunctional conductive flow systems abstraction is close to that of a human diagnostician when conceiving entities and relations on physical, functional and behavioural structures, that is, reasoning that is intrinsically abductive. This chapter presents the use of abduction by its plausibility and relevance using a neural network-based approach. The case study on a hydraulic installation of a rolling mill plant exemplifies the knowledge elicitation process and diagnostic expert system building and running.

The subsequent two chapters discuss *neuro-fuzzy* applications to fault diagnosis. In Chapter 9, Chen, Lim and Lai apply Fuzzy Min-Max (FMM) neural networks to the diagnosis of heat transfer and tube blockage conditions of the circulating water system in a power generation plant. If the FMM neural network is integrated with a rule extraction algorithm, then it is able to overcome the "black-box" phenomenon by justifying its predictions with fuzzy if-then rules that are compatible with the domain information as well as the opinions of the experts involved in the maintenance process. To assess the effectiveness of the FMM network, real sensor measurements are collected and used for diagnosis. The FMM network parameters are systematically varied and tested.

In Chapter 10, Calado and Sá da Costa describe a fault diagnosis approach based on Hierarchical Fuzzy Neural Networks (HFNNs). In contrast to conventional feed-forward neural networks, the employed HFNN has an additional layer that converts the increment in each on-line measurement into fuzzy sets. Thus, on-line measurement data are compressed into qualitative values whose semantics are represented by fuzzy sets and, hence, the training of the HFNN and the diagnosis of the faults can be carried out more efficiently. The methodology is applied to the DAMADICS diagnosis benchmark.

Finally, in Chapter 11, Bocaniala and Sá da Costa describe a novel framework for using causal models in distributed fault diagnosis. The causal model associated with the monitored system is split into minimally separated and causally independent regions. The fact that each region is causally independent from the rest of the model allows performing the diagnosis of that region locally, without needing to communicate with the rest of the model. This property allows maintaining the diagnosis focus exclusively on those regions of the map that are affected by faults. Each local diagnosing agent can be implemented using computational intelligence approaches described in previous chapters or more traditional techniques, like observers. Hence, monitoring a complex system becomes a tractable problem.

In summary, the book contains an illustrative selection of chapters on fault diagnosis approaches using computational intelligence methodologies. The book is intended mainly for doctoral students and researchers who wish to find out the latest developments and research results in the area. They will need this book to enhance their knowledge and to provide a foundation for further study.

The editors wish to use this opportunity to thank all the authors for their valuable contributions to this book. Considerable thanks are due to reviewers for providing extremely useful comments that helped so much when deciding the final form of the book. Not lastly, special thanks go from Vasile Palade and Cosmin Danut Bocaniala to Professor Ron J. Patton, the Head of the DAMADICS project and one of the most respected and brilliant researchers worldwide in the area of fault diagnosis, for opening up to us this fascinating domain of fault diagnosis.

We very much enjoyed editing this book and hope that it will prove useful to its readers.

January 2005

Vasile Palade
Cosmin Danut Bocaniala
Lakhmi Jain

Contents

1. Computational Intelligence Methodologies in Fault Diagnosis: Review and State of the Art

Cosmin Danut Bocaniala and Vasile Palade

This first chapter of the book introduces the reader to the area of computational intelligence techniques and to their significant and abundant applications to fault diagnosis. Fault diagnosis represents an important contemporary research field, due to the ever-increasing need for safety, maintainability and reliability of industrial plants. The research in this field influences important areas of our day-to-day life by increasing security when using safety-critical devices, extending the lifetime of many expensive devices, and improving efficiency of manufacturing lines, which leads to smaller production expenses and lower prices for the end user.

The main problems raised by the processes taking place within modern industrial plants are their high nonlinearity, noisy signals, and uncertainty. Computational intelligence techniques – neural networks, fuzzy techniques, genetic algorithms, etc. – are the very answer of the fault diagnosis research community to these problems. This book represents a collection of recent results on applying various computational intelligence techniques to fault diagnosis. In this introductory chapter, the reader is presented with a short description of the main computational intelligence techniques together with a literature review on their applications to fault diagnosis.

Another major problem raised by the modern industrial plants is their high level of complexity. The complexity of a plant is understood here as the impossibility to model its global emergent behavior using state-of-the-art modeling techniques. Unfortunately, even if they offer better performance than mathematical models when modeling processes with reasonable complexity, the computational intelligence techniques cannot successfully model very complex processes.

The answer given by the research community to this problem is to develop distributed fault diagnosis methodologies. The main idea is to partition the monitored system in subsystems having a reasonable complexity level and, then, to successfully apply state-of-the-art methodologies on each one of them. The global diagnosis of the system is going to be based on all these local diagnosis processes. Implementing the local diagnosis processes using computational intelligence methodologies retains their ability to treat the local nonlinearities, noise and uncertainty. The book contains a special chapter dealing with distributed fault diagnosis methodologies.

1.1.   Fault Diagnosis, Techniques and Approaches

Fault diagnosis research deals with real-world problems as plant efficiency, maintainability and reliability. For safety-critical systems, such as nuclear plants and aircrafts, the problem of detecting the occurrence of faults is of high importance. The consequences of faults in such systems could be disastrous in terms of human mortality and environmental impact. To a lesser extent, fault detection in process and manufacturing industries is also crucial in order to improve production efficiency, quality of the product and cost of production.

There are two main directions for development of fault diagnosis systems: using *hardware redundancy* or using *analytical redundancy*. Hardware redundancy uses multiplication of physical devices and, usually, a voting system to detect the occurrence of a fault and its location in the system. The main problem in this approach is the significant cost for the necessary extra equipment. Analytical redundancy uses instead redundant functional relationships between variables of the system. The main advantage of this approach compared to hardware redundancy is that no extra equipment is necessary. This chapter reviews fault diagnosis schemes based on analytical redundancy.

The early 1970s mark the beginning of analytical redundancy-based fault diagnosis research. Beard (1971) developed at MIT an observer-based fault detection scheme. Jones (1973) continued his work. Their contribution is known as the *Beard-Jones Fault Detection Filter*. Mehra and Peschon (1971) and Willsky and Jones (1974) were the first to use statistical approaches to fault diagnosis. Clark and his colleagues (Clark, Fosth and Walton, 1975) applied for the first time Luenberger observers. Also, Mironovsky (1980) proposed a residual generation scheme based on consistency checking on the system input and output over a time window.

The 1980s and early 1990s represent a period of time during which the major approaches on quantitative fault diagnosis were developed: observer-based approach, parity relation method, parameter estimation method, etc. Some important tutorial papers from this period are Frank (1987), Isermann (1991), Basseville and Nikiforov (1993). It is to be noted that these methodologies are well-established theoretically. For this reason, in this book they are called the *classical* fault diagnosis methodologies. These methodologies have in common the use of a set of analytical redundancy relationships that represents the model of the system describing the desired performance of the monitored system. The system is monitored for possible digressions from this model, that indicate occurrences of faults and that may assist in isolating the faulty components. The research community grouped around this general approach is known as the Fault Detection and Isolation (FDI) community.

In 1991, a Steering Committee called SAFEPROCESS (Fault Detection, Supervision and Safety for Technical Processes) has been created within IFAC (International Federation of Automatic Control). Due to its importance, in 1993, SAFEPROCESS became a Technical Committee within IFAC. One important initiative of this committee was to define a common terminology in the FDI field (Isermann and Ballé, 1997).

During the last decade, the research focused on fault diagnosis for nonlinear systems. Computational intelligence techniques – neural networks, fuzzy logic, neuro-fuzzy systems, and genetic algorithms – have been extensively and successfully applied to fault diagnosis. A recent tutorial on the use of these methods in the FDI community is provided in (Patton *et al.*, 1999; 2000).

In the late 1980s a group of Artificial Intelligence researchers independently proposed a fault diagnosis theory based on First-Order Logic. The system is modeled using the set of basic components of the system and the connections between them. The diagnosis consists in identifying the possible faulty components via an inference process. The papers laying the foundations of this theory are (Reiter, 1987) and (de Kleer and Williams, 1987). A more recent survey on this approach may be found in (Hamscher *et al.*, 1992). The research community that follows this approach is known as the Model-Based Diagnosis (MBD) community. The relationship between the FDI approach and the MBD approach is studied in (Cordier *et al.*, 2000) and (de Kleer and Kurien, 2003).

The content of this introductory chapter is organised as follows. Section 1.1 contains a general discussion on fault diagnosis, including basic terminology and its relation to control systems. It also briefly surveys classical fault diagnosis methodologies. Section 1.2 provides a short description of the main computational intelligence techniques – neural networks, fuzzy techniques, neuro-fuzzy systems, genetic algorithms – together with a literature review on their applications to fault diagnosis. The section includes discussions on the advantages and disadvantages of each methodology, which can help the user to decide which method is the best for his specific case study. It is noteworthy that many times hybrids of computational intelligence methodologies are used in practice, in order to sum up their advantages and to overcome their disadvantages. For a recent review on hybrid intelligent systems, see (Negoita *et al.*, 2005). Section 1.3 contains concise descriptions of the benchmarks used in the book. Specific details regarding these benchmarks are discussed in individual chapters. The last section draws some conclusions on the practical benefits of the surveyed methodologies.

1.1.1. Basic Definitions

The basic notions presented in this subsection follow the IFAC Technical Committee – SAFEPROCESS – terminology in the field (Isermann and Ballé, 1997) as used by Chen and Patton (1999).

1.1.1.1. Fault Diagnosis. Fault-Tolerant Control

A *fault* represents an unexpected change of system function, although it may not represent a physical failure. The term *failure* indicates a serious breakdown of a system component or function that leads to a significantly deviated behavior of the whole system. The term *fault* rather indicates a malfunction that does not affect significantly the normal behavior of the system.

An *incipient* (*soft*) fault represents a small and often slowly developing continuous fault. Its effects on the system are in the beginning almost unnoticeable. A fault is called *hard* or *abrupt* if its effects on the system are larger and bring the system very close to the limit of acceptable behavior.

A fault is called *intermittent* if its effects on the system are hidden for discontinuous periods of time (Isermann, 1997). Although a fault is tolerable at the moment it occurs, it must be diagnosed as early as possible as it may lead to serious consequences in time.

A *fault diagnosis system* is a monitoring system that is used to detect faults and diagnose their location and significance in a system. The system performs the following tasks:

- **fault detection** – to indicate if a fault occurred or not in the system
- **fault isolation** – to determine the location of the fault
- **fault identification** – to estimate the size and nature of the fault

The first two tasks of the system - fault detection and isolation - are considered the most important. Fault diagnosis is then very often considered as fault detection and isolation (FDI).

A *fault-tolerant control system* is a controlled system that continues to operate acceptably following faults in the system or in the controller. An important feature of such a system is automatic *reconfiguration*, once a malfunction is detected and isolated. Fault diagnosis contribution to such a fault-tolerant control system is detection and isolation of faults in order to decide how to perform reconfiguration.

1.1.1.2. Diagnosis Based on Analytical Models

"The *model based fault diagnosis* can be defined as the determination of the faults in a system by comparing available system measurements with a priori information represented by the system's analytical/mathematical model, through generation of residuals quantities and their analyses. A *residual* is a fault indicator that reflects the faulty condition of the monitored system" (Chen and Patton, 1999).

The problem that occurs when using an analytical model for the given system is that it cannot perfectly model uncertainties due to disturbances and noise. This results in differences between the analytical model output and the system output due to nonmodeled dynamics and other uncertainties. These differences may cause the residuals to indicate erroneously faults. A *robust FDI scheme* represents a FDI scheme that provides satisfactory sensitivity to faults, while being robust (insensitive or even invariant) to modeling uncertainties (Frank, 1991; Patton and Chen, 1996; 1997) and to noise. One of the main challenges in designing a robust FDI scheme is to make it able to diagnose incipient faults. The effects of an incipient fault on a system are almost unnoticeable in the beginning, thus effects of uncertainties on the system could hide these small effects.

A fault diagnosis task consists of two main stages: *residual generation* and *decision-making* (Chow and Willsky, 1980) (Figure 1.1). Residual generation is a procedure for extracting fault symptoms from the system, using available input and output information. A *residual generator* represents an algorithm used to generate residuals (Chen and Patton, 1999). Decision-making represents examining the residual signals in order to establish if a fault occurred and isolate the fault.

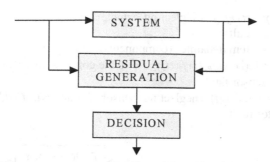

Figure 1.1. The two main stages of fault diagnosis.

1.1.2. Modeling Systems with Faults

This subsection provides the general analytical description of a system considered with all possible faults. The residual generation structure is given and analytical conditions for fault detectability and isolability discussed. For the sake of simplicity, it will be assumed that a linear model reproduces the system dynamics. In the case of a nonlinear dynamics, it is assumed that the model used will be a linearized model around a few operating points. The state space model presented in the first subsection stands only for the cases when a linear model can represent the system. The nonlinear systems can be modeled using a set of linear models built around a set of operating points. The transition between different operating regions is performed using for instance fuzzy logic. The technique has been introduced by Takagi and Sugeno (1985).

The information used for FDI is the measured input to the actuators and the output of the sensors (Figure 1.2). The measured output $y(t)$ is used by the feedback control, and the controller generates the measured input $u(t)$. If the input $u(t)$ is available, then FDI uses the open-loop model of the system, even if it is in a control loop. If the input is not available, then FDI needs to use, as input, the reference command $u_C(t)$. In this case, the system model used for FDI is the closed-loop model. In this situation, the controller plays an important role because a robust controller can hide the effects of the faults, therefore making FDI very difficult. This problem is addressed in (Patton, 1997).

1.1.2.1. General Structure of Faulty Systems

The state space model of the monitored system shown in Figure 1.2 is

$$\begin{cases} \dot{x}(t) = Ax(t) + Bu_R(t) \\ y_R(t) = Cx(t) + Du_R(t) \end{cases} \tag{1}$$

where $x \in R^n$ is the state vector, $u_R \in R^r$ is the input vector to the actuator and $y_R \in R^m$ is the system output vector; A, B, C and D are known matrices with known dimensions.

The faults in the system could occur due to actuators, system components and sensors. When considering faults, the dynamics of the system change as follows:

- actuator fault

$u_R(t)=u(t)+f_a(t)$ (neglecting actuator dynamics), $f_a \in R^r$ is the actuator vector fault

- system dynamics (components) fault

$x(t)=Ax(t)+Bu_R(t)+f_c(t), f_c \in R^n$ is the component vector fault

- sensor fault

$y(t)=y_R(t)+f_s(t)$ (neglecting sensor dynamics), $f_s \in R^m$ is the sensor vector fault

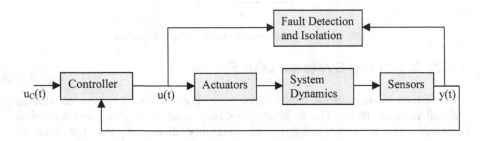

Figure 1.2.   The information used by a fault diagnosis system.

If the previous three fault categories are considered simultaneous, the system model changes to:

$$\begin{cases} \dot{x}(t) = Ax(t) + Bu(t) + Bf_a(t) + f_c(t) \\ y(t) = Cx(t) + Du(t) + Df_a(t) + f_s(t) \end{cases} \quad (2)$$

In a more general case, the state-space model describes a system with all possible faults as:

$$\begin{cases} \dot{x}(t) = Ax(t) + Bu(t) + R_1 f(t) \\ y(t) = Cx(t) + Du(t) + R_2 f(t) \end{cases} \quad (3)$$

where $f(t) \in R^g$ is a fault vector, whose elements $f_i(t)$ $(i=1,...,g)$ correspond to specific faults, and R_1 and R_2 are faults entry matrices which represent the effect of faults on the system.

Equation 3 gives the general model for a faulty system in the time domain. For the frequencies domain, the input - output model transfer matrix will consequently be:

$$y(s)=G_u(s)u(s)+G_f(s)f(s) \quad (4)$$

where

$$\begin{cases} G_u(s) = C(sI - A)^{-1}B + D \\ G_f(s) = C(sI - A)^{-1}R_1 + R_2 \end{cases} \quad (5)$$

1.1.2.2. General Structure of Residual Generation

The input values of a residual generator are the input and the output of the monitored system. This fact is expressed mathematically by Eq. 6, where $H_u(s)$ and $H_y(s)$ are transfer matrices realizable using stable linear systems:

$$r(s)=H_u(s)u(s)+H_y(s)y(s) \quad (6)$$

The residual must be designed (in the ideal case) to be zero for the fault-free case and non-zero when faults occur:

$$r(t) = 0 \text{ if and only if } f(t) = 0 \tag{7}$$

Therefore, the matrices $H_u(s)$ and $H_y(s)$ must satisfy next constraint condition:

$$H_u(s) + H_y(s)G_u(s) = 0 \tag{8}$$

The above equation is called the *generalized* representation of all residual generators (Patton and Chen, 1991). The design of a residual generator consists simply in choosing two matrices $H_u(s)$ and $H_y(s)$, which satisfy Eq. 8. According to the parameterization chosen for H_u and H_y, a different way to generate the residuals is obtained.

Fault detection is performed comparing the residual evaluation function $J(r(t))$ with a threshold function $T(t)$ using the next test:

$$
\begin{aligned}
J(r(t)) &\leq T(t) \quad \text{for} \quad f(t) = 0 \\
J(r(t)) &> T(t) \quad \text{for} \quad f(t) \neq 0
\end{aligned}
\tag{9}
$$

1.1.2.3. Fault Detectability. Fault Isolability

In the presence of system faults, the residual vector will be:

$$r(s) = H_y(s)G_f(s)f(s) = G_{rf}(s)f(s)$$

$$r(s) = \left[G_{rf}(s)\right]_1 f_1(s) + \left[G_{rf}(s)\right]_2 f_2(s) + \dots + \left[G_{rf}(s)\right]_g f_g(s) \tag{10}$$

where $G_{rf}(s) = H_y(s)G_f(s)$ represents the relation between residual and faults, $[G_{rf}(s)]_i$ is the i-th column of matrix G_{rf} and $f_i(s)$ is the i-th component of $f(s)$.

The fault f_i is *detectable* in the residual $r(s)$ if the corresponding column of $G_{rf}(s)$ is nonzero, $[G_{rf}(s)]_i \neq 0$; this is called the *fault detectability condition* of the residual $r(s)$ to the fault f_i (Chen and Patton, 1999). There are cases when a fault is present in the system, but a residual that satisfies the detectability condition does not indicate the fault as a continuous signal. This condition is not enough for detecting such faults, as noticed in (Patton and Kangethe, 1989) and (Frank et al., 1993).

The fault f_i is called *strongly detectable* in the residual $r(s)$ if the steady-state gain $[G_{rf}(0)]_i \neq 0$. This is called the *strong fault detectability condition* of the residual $r(s)$ to the fault f_i (Chen and Patton, 1999).

A fault is called *isolable* using a residual vector set, if it is distinguishable from other faults using this set. Usually, each residual from the considered set is designed to be sensitive to a subset of faults and insensitive to the others. There are three main approaches to design residual sets.

A residual set is called a *structured residual set*, if it has the required sensitivity to specific faults and insensitivity to the remaining faults (Gertler, 1991). If all the faults are to be isolated, the residual set is called a *dedicated residual set*, which was inspired by the *dedicated observer scheme* (Clark, 1978). A residual vector is called a *generalized residual set* if each residual component is sensitive to all faults but one.

Another approach to perform fault isolation is to design a *directional* residual vector, which lies in a fixed and fault-specified direction (or subspace) in the residual space, in response to a specific fault. In this case, each fault is assigned a constant vector called the *signature direction* of that fault (Chen and Patton, 1999).

1.1.3. Classical Diagnosis Methods

The central issue in model-based fault diagnosis is residual generation. Each residual generation method has its associated specific technique of computing the residual vector. In this section, three closely correspondent methods are briefly presented first: observer-based, parity relation and factorization. The parameter estimation method is also shortly presented.

The goal of an *observer-based* approach is to estimate system output using Luenberger observers in a deterministic setting (Frank, 1987; Patton and Kangethe, 1989), or Kalman filter in the stochastic case (Tzafestas and Watanabe, 1990). Then the output estimation error is used as a residual.

In the deterministic case, a functional Luenberger observer is used to estimate the output as a linear function of the state, *Lx(t)*:

$$\begin{cases} \dot{x}(t) = Fz(t) + Ky(t) + Ju(t) \\ w(t) = Gz(t) + Ry(t) + Su(t) \end{cases} \tag{11}$$

where $x(t) \in R^q$ is the state vector of this functional observer; F, K, J, R, G and S are matrices with appropriate dimensions. The output $w(t)$ of this observer is called an estimate of $Lx(t)$, for the system given in Eq. 11, in an *asymptotic sense*, if in the absence of faults (Chen and Patton, 1999):

$$\lim_{t \to \infty} \left[w(t) - Lx(t) \right] = 0 \tag{12}$$

The *parity relation* method consists in checking the consistency of the measurements of the monitored system (Chen and Patton, 1999). If we consider the measurements of an *n*-dimensional vector using *m* sensors, the equation is:

$$y(k) = Cx(k) + f(k) + e(k) \tag{13}$$

where $y(k) \in R^m$ is a measurement vector, $x(k) \in R^n$ is the state vector, $f(k)$ is the vector of sensor faults, $e(k)$ is the noise vector and C is an $m \times n$ measurement matrix.

In order to perform fault detection and isolation, the vector $y(k)$ can be combined into a set of linearly independent equations to generate the parity vector (residual) (Eq. 14). The residual $r(k)$ must have zero value for the fault-free case. Therefore, the matrix V must satisfy the constraint $VC=0$. If the constraint holds, the residual depends only on the faults and noise (Eq. 15),

$$r(k) = Vy(k) \tag{14}$$

$$r(k) = v_1[f_1(k) + e_1] + \cdots + v_m[f_m(k) + e_m] \tag{15}$$

where v_i is the *i*-th column of V, f_i is the *i*-th element of $f(k)$ which stands for the fault in the *i*-th sensor.

The *factorization* method synthesizes the residual generator in the frequency domain by factorization of the $G_u(s)$ matrix from the input-output model of the monitored system. The method was initiated by Viswanadham, Taylor and Luce (1987) and extended by Ding and Frank (1990). The factorization method proposed by Vidyasagar (1985) states that for any $m \times r$ proper rational matrix, in our case $G_u(s)$, there are two stable, rational and realizable matrices $M(s)$ and $N(s)$ so that

$$G_u(s) = M^{-1}(s)N(s) \tag{16}$$

The residual generator is considered as

$$r(s)=Q(s)[M(s)y(s)-N(s)u(s)] \tag{17}$$

The input-output model in the frequency domain is

$$y(s)=G_u(s)u(s)+G_f(s)f(s) \tag{18}$$

Using Eq. 17 in Eq. 18, the residual takes the form:

$$r(s)=Q(s)M(s)G_f(s)f(s) \tag{19}$$

that is only affected by faults.

The matrix $Q(s)$ could be used to improve the residual performance responding to faults in a particular frequency region.

System identification techniques could also be used in model-based FDI (Isermann, 1991; 1997). The premise in *parameter estimation* methods is that the faults are reflected in the physical system parameters. The system parameters are estimated using parameter estimation methods and afterwards compared to the parameters offered by the reference model obtained in fault-free condition. Any substantial difference between the two sets of parameters indicates a system fault.

The input-output model is used under the form:

$$y(t)=f(P,u(t)) \tag{20}$$

where P is the vector comprising information about system parameters and f is a function that could be both linear or nonlinear. If the estimation of the P vector at step $k-1$ is $\hat{P}_{k-1}$, then the residual can be defined as in Eq. 21. The isolation task cannot be easily performed (Isermann, 1984).

$$r(k) = y(k) - f(\hat{P}_{k-1}, u(k)) \tag{21}$$

The practice shows that the quantitative methodologies presented in this section perform well on reasonably small systems. The modeling errors in the case of small systems do not consistently affect the diagnosis process. Unfortunately, trying to model accurately enough a complex system proves to be a difficult task. The main problem is the large number of components of such a system and the even larger number of interactions between them. There is also a high probability of obtaining large modeling errors that will affect significantly the diagnosis process. In this case, it is either impossible to model the behavior of the system, or the model obtained is too large to be used in practice or even for research purposes.

1.2. Overview of Computational Intelligence Methodologies in Fault Diagnosis

In order to obtain good performance, analytical approaches to FDI systems require very accurate mathematical models of the monitored systems. As a result, modeling errors will affect the performances of the FDI systems; especially when the monitored system is nonlinear. Using computational intelligence approaches, i.e., neural networks, fuzzy logic-based systems, neuro-fuzzy hybrids, or evolutionary computing techniques, such as genetic algorithms, may compensate for modeling errors, as these methodologies offer good approximations of non-linear systems.

In their survey on soft computing approaches in fault diagnosis, Patton *et al.* (1999) recommend that "a robust FDI system should combine both numerical (quantitative) and symbolic (qualitative) information". The class of hybrid systems called neuro-fuzzy systems, combinations between neural networks and fuzzy systems, represents an example of such robust systems. Another class of robust FDI systems, in the previously defined sense, represents combinations between classical approaches, i.e., observer-based or parameter estimation, used for residual generation phase, on the one hand, and neural networks, fuzzy logic, or evolutionary computing techniques, used for decision-making phase, on the other hand.

The purpose of this section is to provide a review on the recent computational intelligence approaches to fault detection and isolation. The first subsection presents recent neural network applications. The second subsection brings in the latest fuzzy logic contributions. The neuro-fuzzy systems are discussed in the fourth subsection. The last subsection describes the way genetic algorithms – the most known and, at the same time, the most commonly used evolutionary computing technique – are employed for diagnosis purposes. Besides genetic algorithms, there are other emerging evolutionary computing techniques used, with very good results, for solving fault diagnosis problems. The most promising one is the particle swarm optimization (PSO) technique (Unland and Ulieru, 2005).

1.2.1. Neural Network Applications

Neural networks represent information processing systems formed by interconnecting simple processing units called *neurons*. Each neuron is an independent processing unit that transforms its input via a function called *activation function*. The connections between neurons are characterized by *weight* values that represent the memory of the network. There are three important characteristics of neural networks that make them a suitable tool for modeling the behavior of a system: *generalization ability*, *noise tolerance* and *fast response* once trained (Puscasu *et al.*, 2000). Generally, the input-output vectors of a system represent values measured by sensors, a fact that introduces a certain level of noise. Even if the training data are affected by noise, a neural network is still able to generalize the system behavior, the level of accuracy being proportional to the level of noise.

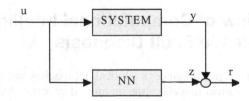

Figure 1.3.   Residual generation using a neural network.

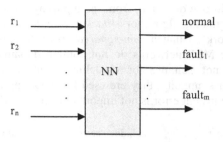

Figure 1.4. Residual vector $r=(r_1,...,r_n)$ mapping into a normal or faulty class.

Table 1.1. Frequently used neural network architectures in recent papers

Neural Networks for Modeling	Neural Networks for Classification
Multilayer Perceptron Networks	Multilayer Perceptron Network
Recurrent Neural Networks	Radial Basis Function Networks
Dynamic Neural Networks	SOM (Self-Organizing Map) Networks
Counter Propagation Networks	Probabilistic Neural Networks
GMDH (Group Method of Data Handling) Networks	
CMAC (Cerebellar Model Articulation Controller) Networks	

Neural networks may be applied in FDI systems for both detection and isolation. For the detection phase, the normal behavior of the monitored system is *modeled* using a neural network. Residual signals are generated by comparing the output of the neural network with the output of the system (Figure 1.3). For the isolation phase, a neural network is used to perform the *classification* of the residuals into the corresponding classes of faults (Figure 1.4).

There are FDI systems that employ neural networks for both detection and isolation, but also hybrid FDI systems that use neural networks for either detection or isolation phase only. A list of neural network architectures frequently used in recent fault diagnosis applications is given in Table 1.1, which shows that most of the recent research effort focused on the use of neural networks for system modeling purposes.

1.2.1.1. Multilayer Perceptron Networks
Multilayer Perceptron (MLP) Networks have a simple architecture shown in Figure 1.5 and they may be used for both modeling and classification tasks. The layers are

fully interconnected in one direction, from the input layer toward the output layer. The commonly used training algorithm is *backpropagation*, that seeks to update the weights of the network so that a *sum-squared-error* decreases toward a desired minimum value. The MLP networks do not contain dynamics in their structure. Therefore they are not suitable for modeling systems with large dynamics. However, due to their simplicity, they are used for modeling the monitored system behaviour when the transient error is not important (Paton *et al.*, 1999).

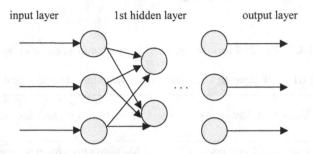

Figure 1.5.   Multilayer Perceptron Network architecture.

An MLP network used for classification encodes the mapping between the residual vector, which feeds the input of the network, and the faulty vector, which represents the output of the network. An MLP classifier establishes the boundaries between the areas occupied by the different states of the system (Haykin, 1999). Therefore, the performance of an MLP classifier, which represents the percentage of the well-classified inputs per state, will be influenced by the degree of overlapping between the states of the system. The current state of the system will be identified according to the area that the input symptoms vector belongs to. However, this approach is too rigid. Take, for instance, an incipient fault that, shortly after occurring in the system, can hardly be distinguished by the normal state. The temporal development of such a fault can be rather described as a gradual passing from normal operating conditions to the plain manifestation of the fault. That is, the trajectory of the input symptoms vector moves gradually from the area corresponding to the normal behavior to the area corresponding to that incipient faulty behavior.

In order to model the behavior of dynamic systems using an MLP network, one can extend its architecture adding *tapped delay lines*. The tapped delay lines used with an input of the neural network allow the network to consider not only the current value of an input, but also a given number of past values of that input. This allows modeling the behavior of the system by taking into consideration the dynamics of the considered input over a time window. Bendtsen and Izadi-Zamanabadi (2002) used an MLP network enhanced with tapped delay lines not only to model the monitored system, but also to estimate an adaptive threshold to be applied on the residual signals. The authors prove that, given a bounded perturbation of the input of the neural network, there are calculable bounds for all possible outputs.

An interesting neural network implementation of diagnosis tasks, based on MLP and Counterpropagation networks, is presented in (Ariton and Palade, 2005). Some details on this approach are presented in Chapter 8 of this book.

1.2.1.2. Recurrent Neural Networks

The class of Recurrent Neural Networks (RNNs), with the general structure shown in Figure 1.6, possesses internal dynamic constituents that allow them to model the dynamics of the monitored system. The dashed lines in the figure represent the internal recurrent connections of the network. Their role is to provide feedback from the next layers of neurons and, usually, their weights are set to unity value.

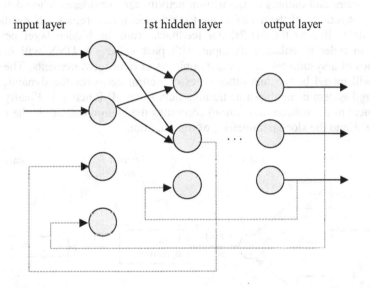

Figure 1.6.   Recurrent Neural Network architecture.

The RNNs can also be used to perform classification tasks. Roverso (2000) used *ensembles* of RNN classifiers to diagnose faults in a Pressurized Water Reactor (PWR) Nuclear Plant. The use of ensembles addresses the problem of output stability when using RNNs. The training algorithm for the same RNN architecture can end up in different local minima if trained with the same training data but randomly initialized weights. As a result, different versions of the same RNN can provide different outputs for the same inputs. In the mentioned paper, the ensemble of RNNs combines the outputs of its constituents into one single result using the bagging method (Breiman, 1996). The quality of the results obtained using an ensemble is directly proportional to the level of disagreement among its constituents (Krogh and Vedelsby, 1995).

Elman Neural Networks (ENNs) are a particular case of RNNs. An ENN has only one hidden layer fully interconnected with the input and output layers, with the addition of a feedback connection from the output of each neuron in the hidden layer to the input of the network. This special feedback feature allows

Elman networks to learn and recognize temporal or spatial patterns. Fuente and Saludes (2000) employ a bank of ENNs to perform fault isolation.

1.2.1.3. Dynamic Neural Networks

Dynamic Neural Networks (DNNs) have the same architecture as MLPs except that the usual neurons are replaced by dynamic neurons. The structure of a dynamic neuron (Ayoubi, 1994) is shown in Figure 1.7. The behavior of a dynamic neuron is described in Eq. 22 (Korbicz *et al.*, 1999). The output of the *adder* component, $x(k)$, represents the weighted summation of the input of the neuron. The *internal filter* is the component that introduces dynamics to the neuron transfer function. The past internal states and outputs of the neuron activity are considered when determining the current activity of the neuron. Due to this special feature, a DNN needs neither tapped delay line as the MLPs, nor feedback from the hidden layer neurons as RNNs, in order to enhance its input with past values. A DNN will model the dynamics of a system taking as inputs only its current measurements. Therefore, a DNN will model better than other types of neural networks the dynamics of the monitored system using the same training data as an MLP network. Finally, the last component of the neuron (*activation*) computes the neuron output via the nonlinear function F and the slope parameter g of this function.

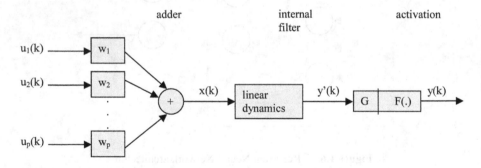

Figure 1.7.   Dynamic neuron structure.

$$x(k) = \sum_{i=1}^{p} w_i u_i(k)$$

$$y'(k) = -\sum_{i=1}^{n} a_i y'(k-i) + \sum_{i=1}^{n} b_i x(k-i) \qquad (22)$$

$$y(k) = F(g \cdot y'(k))$$

The unknown parameters of a DNN are, besides its weights, the vectors $a=[a_1,...,a_n]^T$ and $b=[b_1,...,b_n]^T$, and the slope g of each neuron (Eq. 22). Therefore, the training process of a DNN must incorporate methods for adjusting the weights as well as methods to estimate these parameters. Korbicz *et al.* (1999) discuss two training methods for DNNs in a fault diagnosis application, the Extended Dynamic Backpropagation (EDBP) algorithm and the Evolutionary Search with Soft Selection (ESSS) algorithm. In (Patan and Parisini, 2002), stochastic methods are applied to DNN training for fault diagnosis tasks. Compared to MLP networks or

RNNs, the training of a DNN requires more time, memory, and computational effort.

Marcu *et al.* (1999) study the mixing of three variations of DNNs and their application to generating residuals for a three-tank laboratory system. Marcu *et al.* (2000) apply two types of DNNs to model the evaporation station from the Lublin sugar factory using real process data. The two types of DNNs are the Dynamic Multilayer Perceptron Networks (DMLPs), previously described, and Dynamic Radial Basis Function (DRBF) Networks that have dynamics provided by the ARMA filters in the hidden layers structure (Ayoubi, 1994). A comparative study of the performance of the two types of networks has been done.

Mirea and Marcu (2002) present a neural network architecture for system identification, Functional-Link Neural Networks (FLNNs) with dynamic neurons in the hidden layer. The FLNNs are one-layer perceptron networks that contribute the inputs of each neuron on the hidden layer with functional transformations of the common inputs (Patra *et al.*, 1999). The performance of this architecture is demonstrated on a three-tank laboratory system and on real data from the evaporation station at the Lublin sugar factory in Poland.

1.2.1.4. Radial Basis Function Networks

These networks are single-layer perceptron networks and they are commonly used to perform classification tasks. The general architecture of an RBF classifier for FDI purposes is shown in Figure 1.8. The input of the network is the residual vector r. The output of the neural network, the faulty vector f, has the components $f_i = g(\| r - c_i \|)$, $i=0,\ldots,m$, where the domain of the g function is the $[0,1]$ interval. The first component of the faulty vector f, f_0, stands for the normal state. The interpretation of the output is that the input residual vector r is as close to the vector c_i as is the i-th component of f to 1, and as far from the vector c_j as the j-th component of f to 0 is close. The vectors c_i, $i=0,\ldots,m$, are called the *centers* of the neural network.

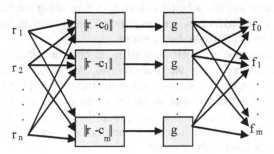

Figure 1.8.   The architecture of an RBF classifier for FDI purpose.

The most frequently used activation function for the hidden layer of RBFs has the general form given in Eq. 23.

$$g(u) = \exp(-\frac{u^2}{2\sigma^2}) \qquad (23)$$

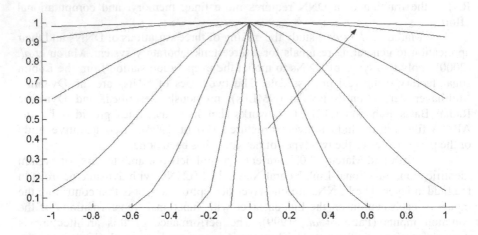

Figure 1.9.   The influence of σ parameter on the shape of the activation function.

The parameter σ represents the width factor, and its influence on the function is shown in Figure 1.9. The arrow shows the width of the graph of the function increasing as the σ parameter increases.

The components of the output of the RBF classifier can be seen as degrees of belongingness of the residual vector to clusters corresponding to the centers. Each center also corresponds to a system state and, therefore, the output vector represents the degrees of assignment of the residual vector to the system states. The degree of belongingness is gradual and its measure is given by a value in the [0,1] interval via the g function. As noted at the end of the discussion regarding the MLP classifiers, expressing the belongingness of the input residual vector to a system state gradually seems to offer a better description than using the belongingness to a classical set. Thus, an RBF classifier can express better than an MLP classifier the assignment of the residuals to the faulty states.

The performance of an RBF classifier depends on the success of tuning the weights and the centers using the training set. An RBF classifier performs a clustering operation on the residual vectors in the training set (Haykin, 1999). There are as many centers as the number of faulty states of the system. If the residual vectors corresponding to a state naturally group themselves in more than just one cluster, then the RBF classifier needs as many centers per state as the number of natural clusters associated with that state.

Another problem of the RBF networks is that they can cope only with faulty states specified during the training phase. However, if one of the faulty states that were not specified occurs, it also needs to be detected and isolated. In (Terstyánszky and Kovács, 2002; Dalmi et al., 2002), a general method is proposed for improving the fault diagnosis by taking into account these faults that are not specified during the training of the RBF network. When an unspecified fault occurs, the architecture of the RBF network used will be updated through introducing a new neuron on the hidden layer. The new neuron corresponds to the unspecified faulty behavior. Also, once a new neuron has been introduced, the parameters of the network must also be updated accordingly.

1.2.2. Fuzzy Logic Applications

Fuzzy logic is used for both fault detection via modeling, and fault isolation via classification for nonlinear systems. Mamdani (1976) proposed a *linguistic* tool to build the fuzzy model of a system. He proposed to model the system behavior using *if-then* rules connecting linguistic terms that captured the intuitive understanding of the available signals by human subjects. For instance, the values associated with a signal can be placed into three overlapping intervals: *small, medium* and *large*. Takagi and Sugeno (1985) proposed a *mathematical* tool to build the fuzzy model of a system. This type of models is more accurate than the Mamdani-type models for modeling real-world processes. In exchange, the transparency offered by the use of linguistic terms to human subjects is lost somehow. Another important advantage of the Takagi-Sugeno approach is the fact that nonlinear systems can be modeled using a set of linear models built around a set of operating points. The transition between different operating regions, defined by the previous set of operating points, is performed using fuzzy logic.

Fuzzy logic is very often used to perform fault isolation tasks. The relationships between residuals and the faulty states of the monitored system are expressed by a set of *if-then* rules. The Mamdani-type models are preferred for this task due to the transparency offered by using linguistic terms. The training phase has the purpose of adjusting the shape of the fuzzy membership functions of the fuzzy sets, by using residuals-faults associations present in the training set. During the test phase, the residuals presented at the input of the fuzzy classifier are mapped into the corresponding faulty state using fuzzy inference.

This subsection introduces first the Takagi-Sugeno (1985) fuzzy modeling technique. Next, it presents the Mamdani-like fuzzy classifier for residual evaluation used by Frank (1996). This classifier does not represent a practical choice when dealing with a complex system, as the number of rules that describe the relationships between residuals and faults is very large. The solution proposed in (Koscielny *et. al.*, 1999) to overcome the *curse of dimensionality* is discussed at the end of this subsection.

1.2.2.1. Fuzzy Modeling of Systems with Faults

Takagi and Sugeno (1985) use fuzzy rules, with the general form given by Eq. 24, to build the fuzzy model of a system.

$$R: IF\ x_1\ is\ A_1\ and\ ...\ and\ x_k\ is\ A_k\ THEN\ y=p_0+p_1x_1+\cdots+p_kx_k \qquad (24)$$

where y is the output of the system whose value is inferred, $x_1, ..., x_k$ are input variables of the system, $A_1, ..., A_k$ represent fuzzy sets with linear membership functions standing for a fuzzy subspace, in which the rule R can be applied for reasoning.

If the system is described by a set of rules $\{R^i\ /\ i=1,...,n\}$ having the previous form, and the values of input variables $x_1, x_2, ..., x_k$ are $x_1^0, x_2^0,..., x_k^0$, respectively, the output value y is inferred following the next three steps.

Step 1. For each R^i, the value y^i is computed as follows:

$$y^i = p_0{}^i + p_1{}^i x_1{}^0 + \cdots + p_k{}^i x_k{}^0 \tag{25}$$

Step 2. The truth value of the proposition $y = y^i$ is computed as follows:

$$|y = y^i| = |\ x_1{}^0 \text{ is } A_1 \text{ and } \ldots \text{ and } x_k{}^0 \text{ is } A_k\ | \wedge |R^i| = A_1{}^i(x_1{}^0) \wedge \ldots \wedge$$
$$A_k{}^i(x_k{}^0) \wedge |R^i| \tag{26}$$

where $|*|$ means the truth value of the proposition $*$, $\wedge$ stands for the *min* operation, and $A(x) = |x \text{ is } A|$, and it represents the grade of membership of x in A. The value $|R^i|$ is called the *confidence level* in the i-th rule and is usually considered to be 1.

Step 3. The output y is computed as the average of all y^i with the weights $|y = y^i|$,

$$y = \frac{\sum\limits_{i=1}^{n} |y = y^i| \times y^i}{\sum\limits_{i=1}^{n} |y = y^i|} \tag{27}$$

Let us consider the fuzzy model of a system formed by the next two rules:

$$R_1 : IF \ x \text{ is medium\_big THEN } y = 0.2x + 9$$
$$R_2 : IF \ x \text{ is medium\_small THEN } y = 0.6x + 2 \tag{28}$$

Figure 1.10 shows the two linear models corresponding to the two rules and the output of the fuzzy model. The previously described fuzzy inference insures a smooth transition between the two fuzzy subspaces corresponding to the rules R_1 and R_2. It is this property that is appealing when trying to model nonlinear systems.

It is not only the input-output model of a system (Eq. 4) that may be represented in the framework of the Takagi-Sugeno approach, but also the state space model of a system (Eq. 1). For this purpose, Ma *et al.* (1998) use a set of r fuzzy rules having the form

$$IF \ z_1(t) \text{ is } F_{i1} \text{ and } \ldots z_g(t) \text{ is } F_{ig} \quad THEN \quad \begin{cases} \dot{x}(t) = A_i x(t) + B_i u(t) \\ y_i(t) = C_i x(t) \end{cases} \tag{29}$$

where $i = 1, \ldots, r$, F_{ij} ($j = 1, \ldots, g$) are fuzzy sets, $x(t)$ is the state vector, $u(t)$ is the input vector, $y_i(t)$ is the output vector, and $z_1(t), \ldots, z_g(t)$ are some measurable system variables.

In order to perform fault diagnosis of a nonlinear system using its corresponding state space Takagi-Sugeno model, Lopez-Toribio *et al.* (2000) design a fuzzy observer to estimate the system state vector. For the fuzzy observer design, it is assumed that the fuzzy system model is locally observable, i.e., all (A_i, C_i), $i = 1, \ldots, r$, pairs are observable. Each fuzzy rule in the Takagi-Sugeno model has an observer rule associated with itself, with the following general form (Ma *et al.*, 1998):

$$IF \ z_1(t) \text{ is } F_{i1} \text{ and } \ldots z_g(t) \text{ is } F_{ig}$$
$$THEN \quad \begin{cases} \dot{\hat{x}}(t) = A_i \hat{x}(t) + B_i u(t) + G_i\left[y(t) - \hat{y}(t)\right] \\ \hat{y}_i(t) = C_i \hat{x}(t) \end{cases} \tag{30}$$

where G_i, $i = 1, \ldots, r$, are observation error matrices, and $y(t)$ and $\hat{y}(t)$ are the final output of the fuzzy system and the fuzzy observer, respectively.

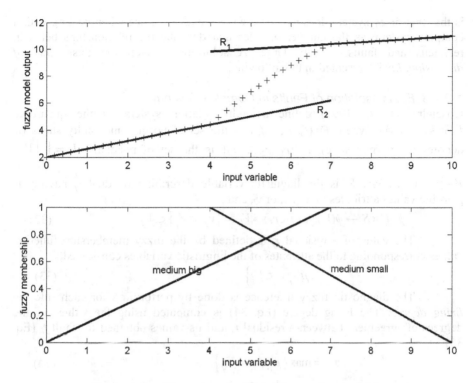

Figure 1.10.   The output of a Takagi-Sugeno fuzzy model.

1.2.2.2. Fuzzy Evaluation of Residuals

Frank (1996) proposes the use of Mamdani-type fuzzy logic for residual evaluation, in order to isolate the faults that occurred. Let $R=\{r_1, r_2, ..., r_m\}$ be the set of residuals. Each residual r_i, $i=1,...,m$, is described by a number of fuzzy sets $\{r_{i1}, r_{i2}, ..., r_{is}\}$, whose membership functions are identified using methods like domain expert knowledge and learning with neural networks. The causal relationships between the residuals and faults are expressed by *if-then* rules having a form similar to Eq. 31.

$$IF\ (effect = r_{ip})\ AND\ (effect = r_{jq})... THEN\ (cause\ is\ the\ k\text{-}th\ fault) \qquad (31)$$

The output of the fuzzy classifier is the faulty vector F. The fuzzy inference process will assign to each component F_i, $i=1,...,m$, a value between 0 and 1 that indicates the degree with which the normal state (the corresponding component is F_0), or the j-th fault, affects the monitored system, $j=1,...,m$. If there is the premise that the system can be affected only by a fault at a time, then the faulty vector contains only one component larger than a preset threshold value, and whose corresponding faulty state represents the actual state of the monitored system. If multiple faults can affect the monitored system, then the components of the classifier output, which are larger than a preset threshold, indicate the faults that occurred in the system.

The advantage of using the previous fuzzy classifier is the fact that fuzzy rules provide details on the mapping of residuals to a faulty state. The disadvantage is that this fuzzy system does not represent a practical choice when dealing with a complex system, as the number of rules that describe the relationships between residuals and faults is very large. A solution to overcome this *curse of dimensionality* is presented in the following.

1.2.2.3. Fuzzy Isolation of Faults in Complex Systems

Koscielny *et al.* (1999) define a fault isolation system as the quadruple $FIS=<F,R,V,\phi>$, where $F=\{f_0, f_1,...,f_K\}$ is the set of normal and faulty states (f_0 denotes the normal state), $R=\{r_1, r_2,..., r_J\}$ is the set of residuals, $V = \bigcup_{r_j \in R} V_j$,

$V_j=\{v_1, v_2,..., v_I\}$, V_j is the linguistic variable describing residual r_j having as possible values attributes $v_1, v_2,...,$ or v_I, and

$$\phi : F \times S \to \phi(V), \quad \phi(f_k,r_j)=V_{kj} = \left\{v_{ji} \in V_j\right\} \subset V_j \tag{32}$$

The value of a residual r_j is defined by the fuzzy membership function values corresponding to the attributes of the linguistic variables considered,

$$\left\{\mu_{ji}/v_i \in V_j\right\} \tag{33}$$

The diagnostic fuzzy inference is done by performing for each rule the *firing degree*. The firing degree (Eq. 34) is computed using the values of the degrees of agreement between a residual r_j and its values obtained for fault f_k (Eq. 35):

$$\sigma_{kj} = \max\left\{\mu_{ji}/v_i \in V_{kj}\right\} \tag{34}$$

$$\delta_k = \frac{\prod\limits_{j=1,...,J} \sigma_{hj}}{\sum\limits_{n=1,...,K} \prod\limits_{j=1,...,J} \sigma_{nj} + \prod\limits_{j=1,...,J} \mu_{jP}} \tag{35}$$

The diagnosis consists of the faults, for which the firing degree is the largest,

$$DGN = \max\left\{f_k/\delta_k = \max \text{ for } k=1,...,K\right\} \tag{36}$$

For diagnosis of complex systems, the dimensions of the sets of faults and residuals are very large and the previous approach does not represent a practical choice. Koscielny *et al.* (1999) simplify the diagnosis procedure noticing that it is not necessary to analyze all residuals. Instead, a subset of residuals R^*, which are useful for fault identification, and a subset of possible faults F^*, need to be dynamically defined.

1.2.3. Neuro-Fuzzy Systems Applications

Palade *et al.* (2002) identify two categories of combinations between neural networks and fuzzy systems. First, there are neuro-fuzzy combinations where each methodology preserves its identity. The system is composed of a set of neural networks and fuzzy systems that work independently but their inputs/outputs are interconnected in order to augment each other's capabilities. These neuro-fuzzy systems belong to the class of *combination hybrid intelligent systems* (Palade *et al.*, 2002). Second, there are neuro-fuzzy systems where one of the two methodologies is fused into the other. The neuro-fuzzy systems in this category belong to the *fusion hybrid intelligent systems* class. Two subcategories can be distinguished. There are systems where the neural networks represent the basic methodology and fuzzy logic the secondary one. In this case, the inputs and/or the outputs and/or the weights of the neural network are fuzzy sets. Also, there are systems where fuzzy logic represents the basic methodology and neural networks the secondary one. These systems feature a set of fuzzy rules put in the form of a neural network in order to make use of the learning, adaptation and parallelism capabilities provided by neural networks.

The neuro-fuzzy systems may be used either for modeling (fault detection) or for classification (fault isolation) purposes. This subsection first presents the neuro-fuzzy systems used for identifying the parameters of Takagi-Sugeno fuzzy models, which may be used for fault detection (Babuska, 2002; Palade *et al.*, 2002; Uppal *et al.*, 2002). Next, a neuro-fuzzy structure used for fault isolation is discussed, more precisely, the neuro-fuzzy hierarchical structure proposed in (Calado *et al.*, 2001). Lastly, the B-spline neural networks (Chen and Patton, 1999; Patton *et al.*, 1999) are shortly presented at the end of this section.

1.2.3.1. Neuro-Fuzzy Systems for Takagi-Sugeno Fuzzy Model Implementation

The most general Takagi-Sugeno model has as consequence of the fuzzy rules ARMA (AutoRegressive Moving Average) models of higher order (Palade *et al.*, 2002), as shown in Eq. 37.

$$R_i : IF \quad x_1 \quad is \quad A_{i1} \quad and \dots \quad x_k \quad is \quad A_{ik}$$

$$THEN \quad y_i(t) = c^i + \sum_{j=1}^{n_1} p_j^i x(t-j) + \sum_{j=1}^{n_2} s_j^i y(t-j) \tag{37}$$

where $i=1,\dots,r$, r is the number of rules, $x=(x_1, x_2, \dots, x_k)$ is the input vector, $p_j^i=(p_{j1}^i, \dots, p_{jk}^i)$, $s_j^i=(s_{j1}^i, \dots, s_{jk}^i)$, and $x(t-j)$, $y(t-j)$, $j=1,\dots,n_1$ or n_2, represent the past values for the inputs and output of the system. If the two sums in the consequent of the rule given in Eq. 37 are missing, we obtain the well-known form of a Takagi-Sugeno model of order zero.

In order to design a Takagi-Sugeno model, the following three sets of parameters need to be identified using the available input-output data measurements (Takagi and Sugeno, 1985):

- The actual input variables $(x_1,\dots,x_k)$ composing the antecedent of the rule.
- $A_{i1},\dots,A_{ik}$ – the membership functions of the fuzzy sets in the rule antecedent.
- c^i, p^i, s^i – the parameters in the consequence of the rule.

The number and the membership functions of the fuzzy sets F_t^s, $t=1,\dots,r_s$, associated with each input variable x_s, $s=1,\dots,k$, must be determined before building the neural network. The space associated with each variable can be empirically partitioned into fuzzy sets by analyzing the way the system operates. This can be a very difficult task when dealing with complex systems. Other techniques that can be employed are clustering and genetic algorithms. The fuzzy sets in the antecedent of the rules for input s, $s=1,\dots,k$, are elements of the set $\{F_t^s \mid t=1,\dots,r_s\}$.

The first set of parameters (actual inputs used in the antecedent) represents a subset of all inputs of the system and it can be determined using the heuristic search algorithm proposed in (Takagi and Sugeno, 1985). The method is concerned with making two choices. The first choice represents the choice of the variables that will appear in the antecedent of the rules. Each variable has associated with itself a fuzzy partition on its space. The second choice represents the number of fuzzy sets in the partition.

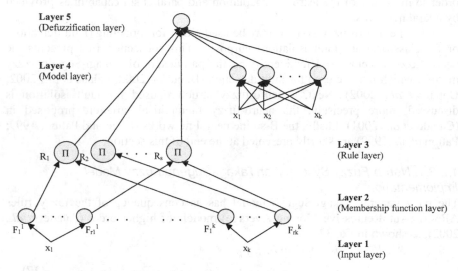

Figure 1.11.   Neuro-fuzzy network for Takagi-Sugeno fuzzy model implementation.

The third set of parameters is identified using training algorithms for neuro-fuzzy systems for Takagi-Sugeno model implementation. These systems put the set of fuzzy rules of the model under the form of a neural network (Palade *et al.*, 2002; Babuska, 2002) (Figure 1.11, Figure 1.12). The parameters are identified during the training of the neuro-fuzzy network. The ARMA model in the consequence of a fuzzy rule is implemented by a subnetwork as shown in Figure 1.12.

For an example of neuro-fuzzy systems for Mamdani-type fuzzy model implementation, and a comparison with the neuro-fuzzy systems for Takagi-Sugeno fuzzy model implementation, see (Palade *et al.*, 2002). The Takagi-Sugeno fuzzy model is preferred for the residual generation phase, when the accuracy of the model represents the main concern. For the residual evaluation phase, neuro-fuzzy classifiers implementing a Mamdani fuzzy model are preferred, because they provide fuzzy rules meaningful to human subjects via the employed linguistic terms in the consequence of the rules.

The disadvantage of the neuro-fuzzy systems is that the architecture of the neuro-fuzzy network can become large for complex systems. This fact poses difficulties for the neuro-fuzzy network training process. The previous fact represents the so-called *curse of dimensionality* and it is inherited from the fuzzy component of the neuro-fuzzy system.

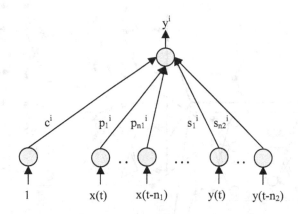

Figure 1.12. The subnetwork corresponding to the i-th neuron in the 4th layer.

1.2.3.2. Neuro-Fuzzy Hierarchical Structures for Fault Isolation

Details on how to use Mamdani-type neuro-fuzzy networks for fault isolation are presented in (Palade *et al.*, 2002). Calado *et al.* (2001) propose a hierarchical architecture of several neuro-fuzzy structures (called by the authors fuzzy-neural networks (FNNs)) for fault isolation purposes. The structure aims to correctly classify input symptoms corresponding to both abrupt and incipient faults (single or multiple), using only abrupt faults symptoms and normal state symptoms during the training phase. The symptoms are generated by selecting from residuals, and their combinations, those signals that provide the best distinction between different operating states of the system.

The hierarchical structure has the three levels shown in Figure 1.13. The first-order differences for all available measurements are used as symptoms. The lower level consists of one FNN that receives as input the considered symptoms. The output of this FNN determines which of the FNNs on the medium level will be activated. That is, if the i-th component of the output has a value close to 1, then the i-th FNN on the medium level will be activated. The number of the FNNs on the medium level is equal to the number of faults considered. Each one of them is also fed with all symptoms considered. The upper level is used to perform an OR operation on the outputs of the activated FNNs on the medium level. The components of the outputs considered for the OR operation must have a value close to 1.

Let us consider the case when the previous methodology is applied to a very complex system. Such a system will usually provide a large number of sensor measurements and, therefore, the number of input symptoms will be very large. Also, such a system will usually feature a large number of faults. In order to increase the number of faults that can be diagnosed, the number of fuzzy sets used must increase too. If the complexity of the rule base is too large, the neuro-fuzzy systems will experience the *curse of dimensionality* too.

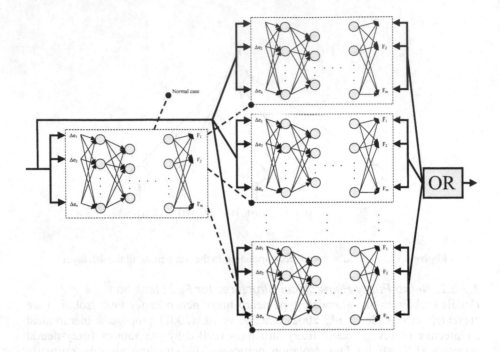

Figure 1.13. A hierarchical structure of neuro-fuzzy networks.

1.2.3.3. B-Spline Neural Networks

The B-spline neural networks are one-layer neural networks with B-spline functions in the hidden layer. A study on the B-spline neural networks and their applications in system modeling is given in Brown and Harris (1995). If the input of the neural network is *n*-dimensional, there is an interval $X^i=[x_{min}{}^i, x_{max}{}^i]$ for the *i*-th dimension, $i=1,...,n$, where all possible input values for the *i*-th dimension lay. Each of these intervals is partitioned into N^i subintervals , $i=1,...,n$. For each subinterval j, $j=1,...,N^i$, the recurrence relationships used to compute a univariate B-spline function of order k are given by Eq. 38.

The univariate B-spline functions previously defined possess the following two properties. First, the functions are defined on a *bounded* support and the output of the function is *positive* on its support (Eq. 39). Second, the sum of the outputs of the functions is always one (Eq. 40).

$$B_{k,i}^j(x) = \left(\frac{x-\lambda_{j-k}}{\lambda_{j-1}-\lambda_{j-k}}\right)B_{k-1}^{j-1}(x) + \left(\frac{\lambda_j - x}{\lambda_j - \lambda_{j-k+1}}\right)B_{k-1}^j(x)$$

(38)

$$B_{1,i}^j(x) = \begin{cases} 1, & \text{if } x \in I_j \\ 0, & \text{otherwise} \end{cases}$$

$$B_{k,i}^j(x) = 0, \ x \notin \left[\lambda_{j-k}, \lambda j\right], \ B_{k,i}^j(x) > 0, \ x \in \left(\lambda_{j-k}, \lambda j\right)$$

(39)

$$\sum_{j=1}^{N^i} B_{k,i}^j(x) = 1, \ x \in \left[x_{min}^i, x_{max}^i\right]$$

(40)

The multivariate B-spline functions are formed by taking the tensor product of n univariate B-spline functions, where one and only one univariate function is defined on each input dimension (Eq. 41). Because the tensor product is used, the properties of the univariate functions are all extended to the multivariate functions.

$$B_k^t(x) = \prod_{i=1}^{n} B_{k_i,i}^t(x_i)$$

(41)

A B-spline neural network with n-dimensional input and p neurons on the hidden layer, standing for as many B-spline univariate ($n=1$) or multivariate functions, is shown in Figure 1.14.

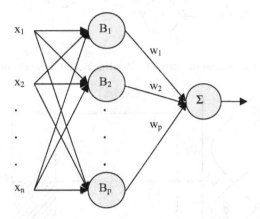

Figure 1.14. The general structure of a B-spline neural network.

The two properties of B-spline functions underlined above show that the output of the neural network, which represents a weighted sum of the p functions in the hidden layer, is always a value in the $[0,1]$ interval. This property is used to perform fault detection on a B-Spline neural network model of the monitored system. Patton *et al.* (1999) and Chen and Patton (1999) use, as input of the neural network, the inputs and the outputs of the system inside a time window. The output of the neural network, the residual $r(t)$, is forced to be 0 when the system operates in normal state, and 1 when a fault occurs in the system.

The fault isolation task can be performed modifying the B-spline neural network model as shown in Figure 1.15 (Patton *et al.*, 1999; Chen and Patton, 1999). The $m+1$ output values of the network correspond to the normal state (F_0) and the faulty states (F_1-F_m) of the system. When the system operates in normal state, the corresponding output value, F_0, is one and all other output values are zero. If the j-th fault occurs, then the value of F_0 moves towards zero and the value of F_j moves towards one.

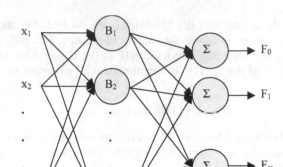

Figure 1.15.   The general structure of a B-spline neural network for fault isolation.

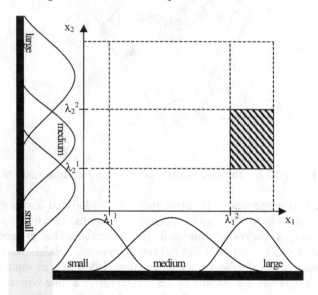

Figure 1.16.   The fuzzy sets corresponding to the univariate B-spline functions.

The structure of a B-spline neural network can be interpreted as a set of fuzzy rules. To each (multivariate) B-spline function, it may be associated a fuzzy rule with the general form

$$IF \ x \ is \ A_i \ THEN \ y \ is \ w_i \tag{42}$$

The fuzzy set A_i represents the fuzzy interpretation of the (multivariate) function B_i. A multivariate function is formed of n univariate functions. Each i-th univariate function can be interpreted as a fuzzy set corresponding to the i-th input (Figure 1.16). The tensor product (Eq. 41) of the univariate functions corresponds to the logical intersection (AND) of their corresponding fuzzy sets, i.e., the hatched area in the figure corresponds to the logical intersection (x_1 is *large*) AND (x_2 is *medium*).

The previous equivalence may be used to insert in the B-spline neural network knowledge from human experts expressed as fuzzy rules (Chen and Patton, 1999; Brown and Harris, 1995). The fact that the (multivariate) B-spline functions can be interpreted linguistically allows the set of fuzzy rules to provide the operator with an explicit description of the causes of the faults. Unfortunately, for a large number of inputs, the set of derived rules becomes too large and the previous advantage is lost (Patton *et al.*, 1999). Also, the B-spline neural networks need a very large learning time even for a modest number of inputs (Patton *et al.*, 1999).

1.2.4. Genetic Algorithms

Genetic algorithms represent the best known and the most commonly used Evolutionary Computing technique. When used for fault diagnosis purposes, in the large majority of cases, genetic algorithms represent a support methodology for other soft computing techniques, especially for parameter tuning tasks. There also are approaches that use genetic algorithms as a stand-alone technique to perform diagnosis.

Genetic algorithms are search procedures based on the mechanisms of natural selection (Goldberg, 1989). Given a population of individuals, natural selection promotes the survival of the fittest individuals from one generation to another. An individual is characterized by a set of *chromosomes*, which represents the encoding of its features. A chromosome is a string of symbols called *genes*. A gene is, in its turn, characterized by its position in the string called *locus*, and a set of possible values called *alleles*. The fitness of an individual is measured via a function called the *objective function*. Any individual from each new generation represents the result of applying natural genetics mechanisms to the individuals from the previous generation. The natural genetics mechanisms combine the strings of two individuals in order to obtain new strings of genes. The use of natural genetics mechanisms insures that, after a number of generations, the population will contain individuals with maximum fitness, i.e., the objective function reaches the maximum value.

Usually the genes of an individual are Boolean variables. In this case, the alleles of every gene are the two Boolean values 0 and 1. One of the advantages of this representation is that, if the features of an individual can be characterized by the numerical values f_i, $i=1,\ldots,p$, then the strings of that individual can binary encode these values. Since an individual is distinguished by the set of its features, which can be numerically characterized, it represents a point ($f_1,\ldots,f_p$) in a p-dimensional space. Another advantage of using the binary representation is that the strings of genes of the individuals can be easily combined to produce new individuals. The large diversity of individuals in this case can be understood as a randomized walk through the p-dimensional space provided by the features of the individuals. This randomized walk can be seen rather as a random search guided by the natural genetics mechanisms towards finding the points (the individuals) with maximum fitness. Genetic algorithms with genes represented as real or integer numbers are also very popular.

If an individual is described using the values of the m features, it means that it will have associated a set of m strings. The strings encode the binary transformation of the m features. As the length of the i-th string must be the same for all individuals in the population, an interval of possible values must be set for each parameter. Setting the right landmarks for each parameter must take into account the fact that the dimensions of these intervals determine the size of the search space.

The number of individuals in the population is usually kept to a constant value n. Each new generation is obtained from the previous one by applying the natural genetics mechanisms. Three largely used such mechanisms are *elitism*, *reproduction* via *crossover*, and *mutation*. The elitism mechanism chooses the most fit e $(e<n)$ individuals from the previous generation and transfers them in the new one. The rest of $n-e$ individuals of the new generation are obtained by applying the reproduction mechanism. This mechanism *selects* two individuals from the population and *combines* their features via crossover and mutation, in order to obtain new individuals.

The selection of the parents of the new individuals is made taking into account the fitness values. More precisely, the percent obtained by dividing the fitness of an individual to the sum of fitness values of all individuals represents the probability with which that individual will be selected to perform reproduction. Therefore, the probability for selecting the most fit individuals for reproduction is larger than the probability of selecting the less fit individuals.

The new individuals are obtained combining the features of selected individuals. The features combination is done by applying the crossover operation for the pairs of strings of genes corresponding to the same feature. The location of the crossing site is selected uniformly random between the first position and the end of the string. During reproduction, the genes of the two new individuals may suffer mutations. That is, a gene having the Boolean value 1 can change its value to 0, and vice versa.

There are two different manners to employ genetic algorithms for fault diagnosis purposes: directly and indirectly. Indirectly, genetic algorithms are used, in a large majority of cases, for tuning the parameters of soft computing-based diagnosis systems, i.e., neural networks (Marcu *et al.*, 2003) or fuzzy logic-based classifiers (Bocaniala *et al.*, 2004; 2005). Metenidis *et al.* (2004) proposed the use of genetic programming (Michalewicz, 1996) for selecting nonlinear systems models to be used for diagnosis purposes. Sun *et al.* (2004) use genetic programming in order to perform feature selection so that the performance of diagnosis achieved via classification reaches a maximum level. In (Spanache *et al.*, 2004), genetic algorithms are used to determine the optimal sensor placement in a plant, in order to achieve the best possible diagnosability. However, genetic algorithms can be used to directly tackle diagnosis problems. Yangping *et al.* (2000) express the diagnosis problem as a function inversion problem, where $S=g(F)$ represents the function to invert, S the available signals from the plant and F the set of faults associated with different parts of the plant. The elements in F represent binary values indicating if the corresponding fault occurred or not. Genetic algorithms are used to simulate g^{-1} in order to estimate which faults occurred.

The main advantage when using genetic algorithms is their capacity to find optimal solutions when searching throughout spaces having unknown and complicated topologies. However, genetic algorithms share the same "black box" feature that neural networks possess. They do not provide information on the behavior of the approached system, as they belong to the class of optimization techniques guided by an objective function. Moreover, in order to construct the function to be optimized, consistent understanding of the behavior of the diagnosed system is required. Besides the two previous facts, another drawback when using genetic algorithms is the usually large computational effort needed to reach a satisfactory optimal solution. It is also important to mention that, when dealing with complex systems, the dimension of the search space is usually very large. This fact has a considerable impact on the amount of resources and the computational time needed by the search process.

1.3. Benchmark Applications

The applications of computational intelligence techniques to fault diagnosis tasks presented in this book have been validated using five benchmarks. The book revolves around two main benchmarks: aero-engines gas path faults (Chapters 2 and 6), and the control valve faults used in the European Commission's FP5 DAMADICS project (Chapters 3, 4, 7 and 10), respectively. Other three chapters are concerned with diagnosis of a power generation plant (Chapter 9), a rolling mill plant (Chapter 8), and electrical engines using vibrations (Chapter 5).

The performance of the gas turbine of an aero-engine can be expressed in terms of a series of performance parameters for the various components of the system. The two main characteristics of the performance of a gas turbine are the efficiency and flow function of compressors and turbines, and the discharge coefficient of nozzles. It is important to mention that these characteristics cannot be directly measured. However, they can be estimated using related measurable parameters, i.e., spool speeds, averaged pressures and temperatures, thrust and air flows. The performance degradation of a component will be reflected by changes in these measurable parameters. The relationship between measurement parameters and performance parameters is highly nonlinear and it can be described using the aerothermodynamics of the gas turbine's components. However, the main difficulty when modelling this nonlinear relationship is the fact that the sensors used to collect the measurement parameters operate in an extremely harsh environment. As a consequence, there is large noise in the measurements and the probability of sensor failure is very high. Therefore, an effective diagnostic method needs to be able to cope with the large noise and measurements uncertainty. This chapter indicates that soft computing methodologies became the preferred tools when dealing with problems of this type. Chapters 2 and 6 employ for diagnosis purposes fuzzy logic and neural networks, respectively. More details on this benchmark problem can be found in these two chapters.

The control valve studied in the European Commission's FP5 DAMADICS project is used as part of the process at sugar factory Cukrownia Lublin S.A., Poland. The valve is used to supply water to the steam generator boiler of an evaporation station. The main technological task of the evaporation station is to thicken the beet juice following the filtering and cleaning processes. It consists of seven evaporators: the first five evaporators work with natural juice circulation, and the last two with juice circulation forced by pumps. The juice condensation process is performed using steam and vapour, which are the same quantities but come from different sources. Steam is produced by a water steam boiler and is delivered mainly to the first evaporator. The vapour is produced in each evaporator and it is used as a heating medium. The evaporation station produces a condensate, which is delivered to the next steam boiler. From this short description, the importance, in economical terms, of monitoring the correct operation of the water supply control valve can be readily assessed. For more information on DAMADICS benchmark, visit the web site, http://www.eng.hull.ac.uk/research/control/ damadics1.htm. The valve was extensively modeled, and a MATLAB/SIMULINK program was developed for simulation purposes (Sá da Costa and Louro, 2003; Bartys *et al.*, 2004). The input to the simulation represents real data, normal behavior and some faulty conditions, collected at the plant. This method provides more realistic conditions for generating the behavior of the system while undergoing a fault. It also makes the FDI task more difficult because the real data input causes the system to feature the same noise conditions as those in the real plant.

1.4. Conclusions

This chapter surveyed the applications of computational intelligence methodologies to fault diagnosis. Throughout the chapter, a special emphasis has been put on the practical limitations of the applicability of these methodologies. Even if computational intelligence methodologies successfully address difficult problems – such as high nonlinearity of the monitored plant, large noise levels in the available sensor measurements, uncertainty – they are able to perform reasonably well only on systems having a reasonable level of complexity. Here, a complex system represents a system whose global behaviour, which emerges from the interactions between its usually large number of basic components, is difficult to accurately describe via an analytical model. The weakness that state-of-the-art computational intelligence methodologies share is their inability to cope with complex systems.

Isermann and Ballé (1997) underline the fact that a single diagnosis method is inadequate for matching all challenges posed by a complex system. Therefore, in the last few years, the fault diagnosis community concentrated its research efforts on distributed fault diagnosis methodologies. The main idea is to partition the monitored system in subsystems having a reasonable complexity level and then to successfully apply state-of-the-art methodologies on each of the subsystems. The global diagnosis of the system is going to be based on all these local diagnosis processes. Implementing the local diagnosis processes using computational intelligence methodologies retains their ability to treat the local nonlinearities, noise and uncertainty. A noteworthy research effort in this direction is the recent European Commission's FP5 MAGIC Project (http://magic.uni-duisburg.de).

It may be concluded that, currently, there are two main trends in the fault diagnosis research field: (i) the earlier trend of finding methodologies suitable for fault diagnosis of systems having a reasonable level of complexity, and (ii) the later trend of finding distributed methodologies able to partition a complex system into small enough subsystems so that the local diagnosis may be performed with state-of-the-art methodologies, and so that the global diagnosis may be obtained in a coherent manner from local diagnosis. The last chapter of the book, Chapter 11, presents a novel distributed fault diagnosis methodology for complex systems, based on the use of causal models.

References

1. Ariton V and Palade V (2005) Human-like fault diagnosis using a neural network implementation of plausibility and relevance. Neural Computing & Applications 14(2):149-165
2. Ayoubi M (1994) Fault diagnosis with dynamic neural structure and application to a turbocharger. In: Proceedings of 1st IFAC Symposium SAFEPROCESS'94, Espoo, Finland, vol. 2, pp. 618-623
3. Babuska R (2002) Neuro-fuzzy methods for modeling and identification. In: Abraham A, Jain LC and Kacprzyk J (eds) Recent Advances in Intelligent Paradigms and Applications, pp. 161-186, Springer-Verlag, Heidelberg
4. Bartys M, Patton RJ, Syfert M, De las Heras S and Quevedo J (2004) Introduction to the DAMADICS Actuator FDI Benchmark Study. Control Engineering Practice, in print (see Articles in Press section of this title on ScienceDirect)
5. Basseville M and Nikiforov IV (1993) Detection of abrupt changes: theory and application. Information and System Science. Prentice Hall, New York
6. Beard R V (1971) Failure accommodation in linear system through self-reorganization (PhD thesis). MIT, Massachusetts, USA
7. Bendtsen JD and Izadi-Zamanabadi R (2002) FDI using neural networks – application to ship benchmark engine gain. In: Preprints of the 15th IFAC World Congress, Barcelona, Spain
8. Bocaniala CD, Sa da Costa J and Palade V (2004) A Novel Fuzzy Classification Solution for Fault Diagnosis. International Journal of Fuzzy and Intelligent Systems 15(3-4):195-206
9. Bocaniala CD, Sa da Costa J and Palade V (2005) Fuzzy-based refinement of the fault diagnosis task in industrial devices. International Journal of Intelligent Manufacturing, 16(6): 599-614
10. Bonnisone PP and Decker KS (1986) Selecting uncertainty calculi and granularity: an experiment in trading off precision and complexity. North-Holland, Amsterdam
11. Breiman L (1996) Bagging predictors. Machine Learning 24(2): 123-140
12. Brown M and Harris C (1995) Neurofuzzy Adaptive Modeling and Control. Prentice Hall International

13. Calado JMG, Korbicz J, Patan K, Patton RJ and Sa da Costa JMG (2001) Soft Computing Approaches to Fault Diagnosis for Dynamic Systems. European Journal of Control 7: 248-286
14. Chen J and Patton RJ (1999) Robust Model-Based Fault Diagnosis for Dynamic Systems. Asian Studies in Computer Science and Information Science. Kluwer Academic Publishers, Boston
15. Chow EY and Willsky AS (1980) Issues in the development of a general algorithm for reliable failure detection. In: Proceedings of the 19th Conference of Decision and Control, Albuquerque, NM, USA
16. Clark RN (1978) Instrument fault detection. IEEE Transactions on Aerospace and Electronic Systems AES-14: 456-465
17. Clark RN, Fosth DC and Walton WM (1975) Detecting instrument malfunctions in control systems. IEEE Transactions on Aerospace and Electronic Systems AES-11: 465-473
18. Cordier MO, Dague P, Dumas M, Levy F, Montmain J, Staroswiecki M and Traves-Massuyes L (2000) AI and automatic control approaches of model-based diagnosis: Links and underlying hypothesis. In: Proceedings of the 4th IFAC Symposium SAFEPROCESS'00, Budapest, Hungary, vol. 1, pp. 274-279
19. Dalmi I, Kovács L, Lóránt I and Terstyánszky G (2000) Diagnosing priori unknown faults by radial basis function neural network. In: Proceedings of the 4th IFAC Symposium SAFEPROCESS'00, Budapest, Hungary, vol. 1, pp. 405-409
20. Ding X and Frank PM (1990) Fault detection via factorization approach. Systems Control Letters 14(5): 431-436
21. Forbus KD (1984) Qualitative process theory. Artificial Intelligence 24: 85-168
22. Frank PM (1987) Fault diagnosis in dynamic system via state estimation – a survey. In: Systems fault diagnostics, reliability and related knowledge-based approaches. D. Reidel Press, Dordrecht, Germany
23. Frank PM (1991) Enhancement of robustness in observer-based fault detection. Preprints of IFAC/IMACS Symposium SAFEPROCESS'91, Baden-Baden, Germany, vol.1, pp. 275-287
24. Frank PM (1996) Analytical and qualitative model-based fault diagnosis – a survey and some new results. European Journal of Control 2: 6-28
25. Frank PM, Ding X and Köppen B (1993) A frequency domain approach for fault detection at the inverted pendulum. In: Proceedings of International Conference on Fault Diagnosis TOOLDIAG'93, Toulouse, France, pp. 987-994
26. Fuente MJ and Saludes S (2000) Fault detection and isolation in a non-linear plant via neural networks. In: Proceedings of the 4th IFAC Symposium SAFEPROCESS'00, Budapest, Hungary, vol. 1, pp. 472-477
27. Gertler J (1991) Analytical redundancy methods in failure detection and isolation. In: Preprints of IFAC/IMACS Symposium SAFEPROCESS'91, Baden-Baden, Germany, vol. 1, pp. 9-21
28. Goldberg DE (1989) Genetic algorithms in search, optimization, and machine learning. Addison-Wesley, Boston, USA
29. Hamscher WC, de Kleer J and Console L (1992) Readings in model-based diagnosis. Morgan Kaufmann, San Mateo, CA, USA

30. Haykin S (1999) Neural networks. A comprehensive foundation. Prentice-Hall
31. Isermann R (1984) Process fault detection based on modeling and estimation methods: A survey. Automatica 20(4): 387-404
32. Isermann R (1991) Fault diagnosis of machine via parameter estimation and knowledge processing – tutorial paper. In: Preprints of IFAC/IMACS Symposium SAFEPROCESS'91, Baden-Baden, Germany, vol. 1, pp. 121-133
33. Isermann R (1997) Supervision, fault-detection and fault-diagnosis methods – an introduction. Control Engineering Practice 5(5): 639-652
34. Isermann R and Ballé P (1997) Trends in the application of model-based fault detection and diagnosis of technical processes. Control Engineering Practice 5(5): 709-719
35. Jones HL (1973) Failure detection in linear systems (PhD thesis). MIT, Massachusetts, USA
36. Kay H (1996) Refining imprecise models and their behaviors (PhD thesis). The University of Texas at Austin, USA
37. de Kleer J and Brown JS (1987) A qualitative physics based on confluences. Artificial Intelligence 24: 7-83
38. de Kleer J and Kurien J (2003) Fundamentals of model-based diagnosis. In: Proceedings of the 5th IFAC Symposium SAFEPROCESS'03, Washington, USA, pp. 25-36
39. de Kleer J and Williams BC (1987) Diagnosing multiple faults. Artificial Intelligence 32: 97-130
40. Koscielny JM, Sedziak D and Zackroczymsky K (1999) Fuzzy-logic fault isolation in large-scale systems. International Journal of Applied Mathematics and Computer Science 9(3): 637-652
41. Krogh A and Vedelsby L (1995) Neural networks ensembles, cross validation, and active learning. In: Advances in neural information processing systems. MIT Press, Cambridge, MA, USA
42. Korbicz, J, Patan K and Obuchowicz A (1999) Dynamic neural networks for process modeling in fault detection and isolation systems. International Journal of Applied Mathematics and Computer Science 9(3): 519-546
43. Kuipers B (1984) Common sense reasoning about causality: deriving behavior from structure. Artificial Intelligence 24: 169:204
44. Kuipers B (1986) Qualitative simulation. Artificial Intelligence 29: 289-338
45. Lopez-Toribio CJ, Patton RJ and Daley S (2000) Takagi-Sugeno Fault-Tolerant Control of an Induction Motor. Neural Computation and Applications 9: 19-28, Springer-Verlag, London, UK
46. Ma XJ,Sun ZQ and He YY (1998) Analysis and design of fuzzy controller and fuzzy observer. IEEE Transactions on Fuzzy Systems 6(1): 41-51
47. Mamdani EH (1976) Advances in the linguistic synthesis of fuzzy controllers. International Journal of Man-Machine Studies 8:669-678
48. Marcu T, Mirea L and Frank PM (1999). Development of dynamic neural networks with application to observer-based fault detection and isolation. International Journal of Applied Mathematics and Computer Science 9(3): 547-570
49. Marcu, T, Köppen-Seliger B, Frank PM and Ding SX (2003) Dynamic functional-link neural networks genetically evolved applied to fault diagnosis.

In: Proceedings of the 7th European Control Conference ECC'03, September 1-4, University of Cambridge, UK

50. Marcu T, Mirea L, Ferariu L and Frank PM (2000) Miscellaneous neural networks applied to fault detection and isolation of an evaporation station. In: Proceedings of the 4th IFAC Symposium SAFEPROCESS'00, Budapest, Hungary, vol. 1, pp. 352-357

51. Mehra RK and Peschon J (1971) An innovations approach to fault detection and diagnosis in dynamic systems. Automatica 7: 637-640

52. Metenidis MF, Witczak M and Korbicz J (2004) A novel genetic programming approach to nonlinear system modelling: application to the DAMADICS benchmark problem. Engineering Applications of Artificial Intelligence 17(4): 363-370

53. Michalewicz Z (1996) Genetic Algorithms + Data Structures = Evolution Programs. Springer, Berlin

54. Mirea L and Marcu T (2002) System identification using functional-link neural networks with dynamic structure. In: Preprints of the 15th IFAC World Congress, Barcelona, Spain

55. Mironovsky LA (1980) Functional diagnosis of linear dynamic systems – a survey. Automation Remote Control 41: 1122-1143

56. Negoita M, Neagu D and Palade V (2005) Computational Intelligence: Engineering of Hybrid Systems. Springer-Verlag

57. Palade V, Patton RJ, Uppal FJ, Quevedo J and Daley S (2002) Fault Diagnosis of An Industrial Gas Turbine Using Neuro-Fuzzy Methods. In: Proceedings of the 15th IFAC World Congress, 21–26 July, Barcelona, pp. 2477–2482

58. Patan K and Parisini T (2002) Stochastic approaches to dynamic neural network training. Actuator fault diagnosis study. In: Preprints of the 15th IFAC World Congress, Barcelona, Spain

59. Patra JC, Pal RN, Chatterji BN and Panda G (1999) Identification of non-linear dynamic systems using functional-link artificial neural networks. IEEE Transactions on Systems, Man and Cybernetics – part B 29(2):254-262

60. Patton RJ (1997) Fault tolerant control: the 1997 situation (survey). In: Proceedings of the IFAC Symposium SAFEPROCESS'97, Pergamon, University of Hull, UK, pp. 1029-1052

61. Patton RJ and Chen J (1991) A review of parity space approaches to fault diagnosis. In: Preprints of IFAC/IMACS Symposium SAFEPROCESS'91, Baden-Baden, Germany, vol.1, pp. 239-255

62. Patton RJ and Chen J (1996) Robust fault detection and isolation (FDI) systems. Dynamics and Control (vol. 74): Techniques in discrete and continuous robust systems. Academic Press

63. Patton RJ and Chen J (1997) Observer-based fault detection and isolation: robustness and applications. Control Engineering Practice 5(5): 671-682

64. Patton RJ and Kangethe SM (1989) Robust fault diagnosis using eigenstructure assignment of observers. In: Fault diagnosis in dynamic systems, theory and application. Control Engineering Series. Prentice Hall, New York

65. Patton RJ, Lopez-Toribio CJ and Uppal FJ (1999) Artificial intelligence approaches to fault diagnosis for dynamic systems. International Journal of Applied Mathematics and Computer Science 9(3): 471-518

66. Patton RJ, Lopez-Toribio CJ and Uppal FJ (2000) Soft computing approaches to fault diagnosis for dynamic systems: a survey. In: Proceedings of the 4th IFAC Symposium SAFEPROCESS'00, Budapest, Hungary, vol. 1, pp. 298-311

67. Puscasu G, Palade V, Stancu A, Buduleanu S and Nastase G (2000) Sisteme de conducere clasice si inteligente a proceselor. MATRIX ROM, Bucharest, Romania

68. Raiman O (1991) Order of magnitude reasoning. Artificial Intelligence 51: 11-38

69. Reiter R (1987) A theory of diagnosis from First Principles. Artificial Intelligence 32: 57-95

70. Roverso D (2000) Neural ensembles for system identification. In: Proceedings of the 4th IFAC Symposium SAFEPROCESS'00, Budapest, Hungary, vol. 1, pp. 478-483

71. Sá da Costa J and Louro R (2003) Modelling and simulation of an industrial actuator valve for fault diagnosis benchmark. In: Proceedings of the Fourth International Symposium on Mathematical Modelling, Vienna, pp. 1212-1221, Agersin-Verlag.

72. Spanache S, Escobet T and Travé-Massuyès L (2004) Sensor Placement Optimisation Using Genetic Algorithms. In: Proceedings of the Fifteenth International Workshop on Principles of Diagnosis DX'04, June 23-25, Carcassonne, France

73. Sun R, Tsung F and Qu L (2004) Combining bootstrap and genetic programming for feature discovery in diesel engine diagnosis. International Journal of Industrial Engineering 11(3): 273-281

74. Takagi T and Sugeno M (1985) Fuzzy identification of systems and its application to modeling and control. IEEE Transactions on Systems, Man and Cybernetics 15(1): 116-132

75. Terstyánszky G and Kovács L (2002) Improving fault diagnosis using proximity and homogeneity measure. In: Preprints of the 15th IFAC World Congress, Barcelona, Spain

76. Tzafestas SG and Watanabe K (1990) Modern approaches to system/sensor fault detection and diagnosis. Journal A 31(4): 42-57

77. Unland R and Ulieru M (2005) Swarm Intelligence and the Holonic Paradigm: A Promising Symbiosis for Medical Diagnostic Systems Design. In: Proceedings of the 9th International Conference on Knowledge-Based and Intelligent Information and Engineering Systems, KES2005, September 14-16, Melbourne, Australia

78. Uppal FJ, Patton RJ and Palade V (2002) Neuro-Fuzzy Based Fault Diagnosis Applied to an Electro-Pneumatic Valve. In: Proceedings of the 15th IFAC World Congress, 21–26 July, Barcelona, Spain, pp. 2483-2488

79. Vidyasagar M (1985) Control systems synthesis: a factorization approach. System and Control Series. North-Holland, MIT Press, Cambridge, MA, USA

80. Viswanadham N, Taylor JH and Luce EC (1987) A frequency-domain approach to failure detection and isolation with application to GE-21 turbine engine control systems. Control-Theory and Advanced Technology 3(1): 45-72

81. Waltz D (1975) Understanding line drawings of scene with drawings. In: The psychology of computer vision. McGraw-Hill, New York
82. Willsky AS and Jones HL (1974) A generalized likelihood approach to state estimation in linear systems subjected to abrupt changes. In: Proceedings of the 1974 IEEE Conference on Control and Decision, Arizona, USA
83. Yangping Z, Bingquan Z and DongXin W (2000) Application of genetic algorithms to fault diagnosis in nuclear power plants. Reliability Engineering and Systems Safety 67: 153-160

2. A Fuzzy Logic Approach to Gas Path Diagnostics in Aero-engines

Luca Marinai and Riti Singh

Engine-related costs contribute a large fraction of the direct operating costs (DOCs) of an aircraft, because the propulsion system requires a significant part of the overall maintenance effort. Thus, to ensure competitive advantage in the aero-engine market, health monitoring systems with gas path diagnostics capability are highly desirable.

In this chapter, an application of fuzzy logic technology to gas path diagnostics for aero-engines performance analysis is presented and the setup procedure for a modern civil turbofan is described, as an example. The objective is to estimate the changes in engine component performance due to the engine degradation over time from the knowledge of only a few measurable parameters, inevitably affected by noise. This is a novel process that achieves effective diagnosis by means of a rule-based pattern-recognition methodology founded on fuzzy algebra, developed to provide an alternative technology versus conventional estimation algorithms.

The inherent capability of fuzzy logic to deal with gas path diagnostics difficulties, thanks to the use of fuzzy set theory and its rule-based nature, is highlighted. First, the problem of noisy measurements is treated at a fuzzy-set level. Second, at the system level the definition of fuzzy rules is used to map input sets of measurements into output faulty classes of performance parameters in a constrained search space; this enables a problem reduction aimed at overcoming the fact that the analytical formulation is undetermined.

The process quantifies the performance parameters' deteriorations through a nonlinear approach, even in the presence of noisy measurements that typically complicate the diagnostic assessment. The diagnostics model's setup as well as its outcome can be attained in a relatively short time, making this technique suitable for on-board use. The accuracy of the technique relative to simulated turbofan data is tested and its advantages and limitations are discussed.

2.1. Introduction

The performance of an aero-engine deteriorates over time as a consequence of its components' degradation. The identification of the exact component(s) responsible for the performance loss facilitates the choice of the recovery action to be undertaken. An engine gas-path diagnostic process calculates changes in the magnitude of the component performance parameters (e.g., efficiency and flow capacity) given a set of measurements (e.g., temperatures, pressures, shaft speed and fuel flow) through the engine. However, accurate assessment is complicated by

(i) only having relatively few measurements available and   (ii) errors in the measurements.

A recent update of gas-path diagnostics (GPD) methodologies is reported in the Von Karman Institute lecture series 2003-01 on gas-turbine condition monitoring and fault diagnosis edited by Mathioudakis and Sieverding (2003). Many pertinent tools have been devised during the last three decades and a critical review of the most used techniques and their applications is provided in (Marinai *et al.*, 2004), highlighting similarities, differences and limitations.

This chapter presents a new gas path diagnostics method. The novelty of this technique lies in the use of fuzzy logic to provide secure isolation and quantification of gas path component faults. Fuzzy logic is introduced because of its inherent capability of dealing with GPD problems due to its rule-based nature and its fuzzy approach. The rule-based architecture is used to perform pattern recognition of measurement fault signatures, while the fuzzy approach is advantageous in dealing with the uncertainties that typically affect the GPD problem, namely, the measurement errors and the undetermined mathematical formulation. These features created a research opportunity; and an application of the method to a modern three-shaft turbofan engine and its encouraging results will show, in this chapter, that the promises of fuzzy logic were not burnt out. A software was devised – see (Marinai, 2004). First, its SFI (single fault isolation) capability was proved – see section 2.5. Then a partial MFI (multiple fault isolation) capability, with up to 2 gas path components considerably faulty simultaneously, was tested – see section 2.6.

2.1.1. A Guide through the Chapter

Section 2.2 is aimed at guiding the reader through the fuzzy logic process step by step from an introduction to the theory to the application to gas-path diagnostics. Section 2.3 introduces the three-spool turbofan configuration involved in the development of the diagnostics methodology and the instrumentation set used. Section 2.4 is then dedicated to the development of the fuzzy diagnostics system for a three-spool engine and to the sensitivity studies carried out for a pertinent setup of the methodology. The graphical user interface (GUI) devised for this purpose is introduced as well. The accuracy of the SFI capability of the system in the presence of noisy measurements and a method used to enhance such a capability is discussed in section 2.5. This section also describes an additional feature of the system whose rules can be tuned over a global deterioration baseline to enhance the SFI role in GPD. A fuzzy diagnostics system able to perform partial MFI and its accuracy are discussed in section 2.6. A second GUI was devised to make use of the fuzzy diagnostics model to compute the diagnoses and plot the results; this is described in section 2.7. The conclusions are presented in section 2.8.

2.2. Fuzzy Logic Systems

2.2.1. Background

Fuzzy logic is a new rule-based approach, founded on the formulation of a novel algebra, typically used in the analysis of complex systems and to enable decision-making processes (Zadeh, 1969).

Fuzzy engineering is the specific research area investigated aimed at modelling engineering processes with fuzzy systems. These are able to provide appropriate approximations of various phenomena if enough rules are defined. The quality of the approximation is strictly related to the quality of the rules. This is not a standard view of fuzzy systems but it is the view taken in this chapter according to the definition of fuzzy engineering given by (Kosko, 1997). A different view is that fuzzy logic is a linguistic theory that models human reasoning with vague rules of thumb and common sense. This holds without any doubt in many applications. Fuzzy systems, as described in the next section, rely on the formulation of fuzzy algebra. This is a generalization of the abstract set theory, based on new definitions concerning fuzzy sets and logical operators (Zadeh, 1969).

Fuzzy logic is used in this research to provide the capability of approximating the relationships between the N-dimensional input space of the gas-path measurements and the P-dimensional output space of the performance parameters by using a number of fuzzy rules. The rules in turn depend on fuzzy sets able to deal with uncertain or vague estimations of the process variables.

Fuzzy logic is all about the relative importance of precision. It is a convenient way to map inputs into outputs (Zadeh, 1969) and the primary mechanism for doing this is a list of if-then statements called fuzzy rules. All the rules are evaluated in parallel and the order of the rules is unimportant. To set up a system that interprets rules, we first have to define all the elements of a fuzzy system (i.e., fuzzy sets, membership functions, logical operators and architecture of the rules) and then the elements of the inference process, namely, the algorithms for implication, aggregation and defuzzification phases. The fuzzy inference process interprets the values in the input vector and, based on a set of fuzzy rules, assigns values to the output vector.

2.2.2. Fuzzy Algebra: Basic Elements of a Fuzzy System Architecture

Engineering science typically deals with uncertain variables and approximations to a fixed number of decimal places that depend on the accuracy capability but also on the necessity and costs of being accurate. When a decision has to be made based on uncertain values of a set of variables, a binary logic based on either-or laws can become a limitation.

A fuzzy system based on multivalue logic can help in modelling a process when a mathematical model of how the system's outputs depend on the inputs is not available or is not accurate, or when it is necessary to deal with the uncertainty present in the inputs. Besides, a fuzzy model is beneficial in order to introduce different sources of information in the decision-making process (data fusion) and when it is advantageous to include expert knowledge or statistical inputs.

Fuzzy logic systems rely on the formulation of a novel abstract set theory and algebra: a generalization of the set theory, based on fuzzy sets as well as logical operators, will be considered below. The four main elements of a fuzzy logic inference process are listed in Figure 2.1 and discussed in the following sections.

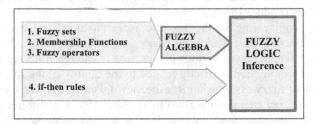

Figure 2.1.   Fuzzy algebra and fuzzy logic inference.

It will be proved that fuzzy set theory, introduced by Zadeh in 1965, is a generalization of abstract set theory. In other words, the former always includes the latter as a special case; definition theorems, and proofs of fuzzy set theory always hold for non-fuzzy sets. Because of this generalization, fuzzy set theory has a wider scope of applicability than traditional set theory in solving engineering problems that involve high degrees of uncertainty and, to some degree, subjective evaluation (Kandel, 1986).

2.2.2.1. Fuzzy Sets

The basic concept behind fuzzy algebra and fuzzy logic systems is the definition of fuzzy sets. A fuzzy set does not have distinctly delineated boundaries and contains elements with a partial degree of membership.

In standard algebra a traditional set includes elements with a Boolean or two-value logic. This means that an element belongs or does not belong to the set. The degree of membership of an element can be only 0 or 1, or 0 or 100%. If we consider the example in Figure 2.2, the numbers $A=51$, $B=60$ and $D=69$ are elements of the set S, while the number $D=71$ is not.

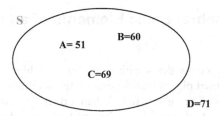

Figure 2.2.   Standard set.

This concept is graphically described in Figure 2.3. The numbers included in the range between 50 and 70 belong to the set of cool air temperature.

On the other hand, a fuzzy set admits elements with a partial degree of membership according to a defined membership function (MF). In the example shown in Figure 2.3 and 2.4, the membership function is triangular; therefore the degree of membership decreases as we approach the margins of the set.

In Figure 2.4 the two overlapping fuzzy sets of cool and right air temperature are considered. A value of temperature such as 68 degrees has distinct values of degree of membership to the two sets and consequently activates the two MFs with two different degrees of activation.

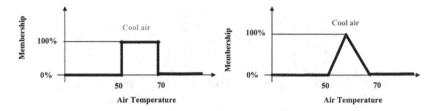

Figure 2.3. Diagrams of a standard set (left) and a fuzzy set (right).

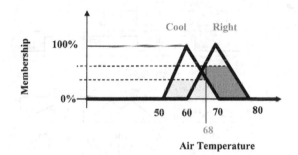

Figure 2.4. Two overlapping fuzzy sets.

Going from the graphical representation to the analytical form, let X denote the space of objects. Then a fuzzy set A in X is a set of ordered pairs

$$A = \{x, \mu_A(x)\}, x \in X \tag{1}$$

where $\mu_A(x)$ is the degree of membership of x in A and the function μ_A is called the membership function (MF). Usually, $\mu_A(x)$ is a number in the interval $[0,1]$, with the grades 1 and 0 representing, respectively, full membership and non-membership in a fuzzy set. It maps each element of the input space X to a membership value. The input space is sometimes referred to as the universe of discourse. The membership function itself can be an arbitrary curve whose shape is defined as a function that suits the problem from the point of view of simplicity, convenience, speed, and efficiency.

Summarizing, the following concepts have been introduced so far:

- Fuzzy set
- Degree of membership
- Membership function (MF)
- Degree of activation (d.o.a.)

The next subsection will consider the logical operators, the third element of the fuzzy inference process – see Figure 2.1.

2.2.2.2. Logical Operators

Fuzzy logic is a generalization of standard Boolean logic. This means that the logical operations, as defined in this section, will hold in standard algebra as well. As far as the logical operators AND, OR, and NOT are concerned, Figure 2.5 shows the truth tables according to traditional logic.

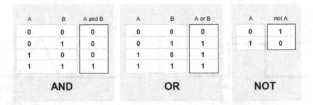

Figure 2.5.   Standard logical operations.

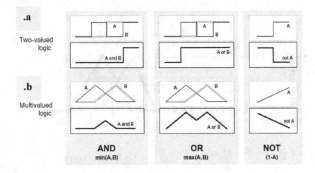

Figure 2.6.   Two-valued and multi-valued logic.

Figure 2.6.a shows a graphical representation of the logical operators in a two-value logic. Many methods are available in the literature for their implementation in a multi-valued logic or fuzzy logic. In this work the following algorithms are considered:

- AND using minimum or product ($a \cdot b$)
- OR using maximum or algebraic sum ($a+b-a \cdot b$)
- NOT using the complement

An example of fuzzy operators using the first options in the list above is shown in Figure 2.6, where we replace A AND B, where A and B are limited to the range (0,1), by using the function $min(A,B)$. Using the same reasoning, we can replace the OR operation with the max function, so that A OR B becomes equivalent to $max(A,B)$. Finally, the operation NOT A becomes equivalent to the operation ($1 - A$). Once the logical operators are defined, any construction using AND, OR, and NOT applied to fuzzy sets can be resolved.

It can be proved that these definitions still hold in traditional algebra, considering Figure 2.7. As an example, considering the AND operator in the table we can see that: $min(0,0)=0$, $min(0,1)=0$, $min(1,0)=0$ and $min(1,1)=1$. Similarly, we can reason for the second options in the list of possible algorithms provided above (e.g., change min with product to implement the AND operator).

A	B	min(A,B)		A	B	max(A,B)		A	1 - A
0	0	0		0	0	0		0	1
0	1	0		0	1	1		1	0
1	0	0		1	0	1			
1	1	1		1	1	1			
AND				**OR**				**NOT**	

Figure 2.7.   Example of logical operators, fuzzy algebra.

In fuzzy algebra AND, OR, and NOT are known as the fuzzy intersection or conjunction (AND), fuzzy union or disjunction (OR), and fuzzy complement (NOT), but as said before their definitions are by no means unique.

2.2.2.3. Fuzzy Rules
Fuzzy rules play a key role in the fuzzy inference process – see Figure 2.1. Fuzzy systems are universal approximators if enough rules are stated. Fuzzy sets and fuzzy operators that constitute the fuzzy algebra are the elements of if-then rule statements. A single fuzzy if-then rule assumes the form "if z is in the fuzzy set A then x is in the fuzzy set B". The if-part of the rule "z is in A" is called the antecedent, while the then-part of the rule "x is in B" is called the consequent.

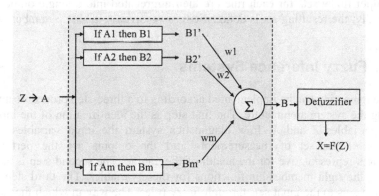

Figure 2.8.   Additive fuzzy system architecture.

With reference to Figure 2.8, an N-dimensional input space (in performance diagnostics, the measurements) is mapped into a P-dimensional output space (performance parameters) by means of m rules. Each input vector partially activates all the rules in parallel, the rule can be associated with different rule-weights w_i, and eventually a defuzzifier calculates the outcome solution based on the activation of the MFs. It can be proved that an additive fuzzy system computes a conditional expectation $E(X|Z)$ and therefore an optimal nonlinear estimation (Kosko, 1997).

Interpreting an if-then rule involves the following phases: (i) evaluating the antecedent (which involves the fuzzification of the input and applying any necessary fuzzy operators) and (ii) applying that result to the consequent (known as implication). In the case of two-valued or binary logic, when the if-part of the rule is true, the then-part is true. In a multi-valued logic the antecedent is a fuzzy statement, so if the antecedent is true to some degree of activation, then the consequent is also true to that same degree.

Therefore, interpreting one if-then rule is a three-part process:
- Fuzzify inputs: resolve all fuzzy statements in the antecedent to a degree of membership between 0 and 1.
- Apply fuzzy operator to multiple part antecedents: If there are multiple parts to the antecedent, apply fuzzy logic operators and resolve the antecedent to a single number between 0 and 1. This is the degree of support for the rule.
- Apply implication method: Use the degree of support for the entire rule to shape the output fuzzy set. The consequent of a fuzzy rule assigns an entire fuzzy set to the output. This fuzzy set is represented by a membership function that is chosen to indicate the qualities of the consequent. If the antecedent is only partially true (i.e., is assigned a value less than 1), then the output fuzzy set is truncated according to the implication method.

In general, one rule by itself does not do much good. What is needed are a number of rules that can play off one another. The output of each rule is a fuzzy set. The output fuzzy sets for each rule are then aggregated into a single output fuzzy set. Finally, the resulting set is defuzzified, or resolved to a single number (Zadeh, 1969).

2.2.3. Fuzzy Inference Systems

Fuzzy engineering can be implemented according to a three-step procedure aimed at defining the system architecture. The first step is the identification of the input and output variables Z and X. In a diagnostics system the input variables are the elements of the set of measurements and the outputs are the performance parameters representative for the health of the engine. The second step is aimed at selecting the right membership functions for these variables. The third step relates the output sets to the input sets through fuzzy rules. The way in which the rules are stated depends on the learning algorithm. Rules in this work are generated running a whole-engine steady-state simulation code (engine model). The choice of the right learning algorithm has a big impact on the accuracy of the fuzzy system.

Once the system architecture is defined, fuzzy inference is the process that computes the outcome provided an input to the system. There are two main types of inference methods known in the literature as Mamdani and Sugeno. A Mamdani-type inference is based on the fact that fuzzy sets are defined for inputs and outputs. Therefore, after the aggregation process there is a fuzzy set for each output variable that needs to be defuzzified.

On the other hand, a Sugeno-type system is based on the definition of the output MFs as single spikes rather than distributed fuzzy sets. The single spike is also known as singleton output membership function and can be considered as a pre-defuzzified fuzzy set. This improves the efficiency of the process simplifying the computation. The outcome is just the weighted average of a few data points. The GPD method developed in this work uses the Mamdani inference strategy.

A typical fuzzy logic system (Figure 2.9) involves fuzzification, rules evaluation and defuzzification phases:

- A fuzzifier turns numeric values (input measurements) into degree of activation of input MFs.
- An inference engine accumulates the effects of each rule on the output MFs; it includes logical operations, implication and aggregation phases.
- A defuzzifier calculates the outcome based on the activation of the output MFs.

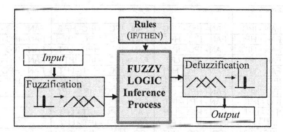

Figure 2.9.   Configuration of a rule-based fuzzy logic system.

2.2.4. Comments on Fuzzy Rules for a Diagnostics System

Among the various gas path diagnostics methods, a distinction can be made (Volponi, 2003) between techniques more suitable for estimating gradual deteriorations and techniques for estimating rapid deteriorations, i.e., where deteriorations represent the faults occurred. We referred to such methods as MFI (multiple-fault isolation) and SFI (single-fault isolation), respectively. The former implies that all the engine components (whose shifts in performance we are estimating) deteriorate slowly whereas the latter implies a rapid trend shift probably due to a single entity (or perhaps two) going awry. AI-based methods such as fuzzy logic systems are more suitable for SFI problems, because they are based on an approximation of all the possible solutions for the limited number of combinations used to train the system. The extension to all possible combinations (even in a limited search-space) is theoretically possible, but extremely burdensome from a computational point of view. In this work, a fuzzy logic diagnostics system was firstly set up to secure an effective SFI capability – see sections 2.4 and 2.5. Then a partial MFI capability was tested considering up to four health parameters (two components) simultaneously deteriorated – see section 2.6.

The number of necessary fuzzy rules grows exponentially with the number of system variables. Any attempt to reduce the number of rules is inevitably associated with less precise approximation capability. In general, we must trade some accuracy for ease of computation.

In this work, a diagnostic system for the three-shaft turbofan was developed – see section 2.4. The six gas path components investigated are: FAN, intermediate pressure compressor (IPC), high pressure compressor (HPC), high pressure turbine (HPT), intermediate pressure turbine (IPT) and low pressure turbine (LPT) – see second column of Table 2.1. When these six components are considered for GPD, the number of possible combinations C of components degraded can be calculated as:

$$C = \frac{n!}{k!(n-k)!} \tag{2}$$

that gives the number of combinations of $n=6$ components taken k at a time. According to Eq. (2, all the possible combinations are listed in Table 2.1.

Table 2.1.   Combinations C of six gas path components taken k at a time

k \\ C	1 at a time	2 at a time	3 at a time	4 at a time	5 at a time	6 at a time
1	FAN	FAN - IPC	FAN - IPC - HPC	FAN - IPC - HPC- HPT	FAN - IPC - HPC- HPT-IPT	FAN-IPC-HPC-HPT-IPT-LPT
2	IPC	FAN - HPC	FAN - IPC - HPT	FAN - IPC - HPC- IPT	FAN - IPC - HPC- HPT-LPT	
3	HPC	FAN - HPT	FAN - IPC - IPT	FAN - IPC - HPC - LPT	FAN - IPC - HPC- IPT-LPT	
4	HPT	FAN - IPT	FAN - IPC - LPT	FAN - IPC - HPT- IPT	FAN - IPC - HPT- IPT-LPT	
5	IPT	FAN - LPT	FAN - HPC- HPT	FAN - IPC - HPT - LPT	FAN - HPC – HPT- IPT-LPT	
6	LPT	IPC - HPC	FAN - HPC - IPT	FAN - IPC - IPT - LPT	IPC - HPC- HPT-IPT-LPT	
7		IPC - HPT	FAN - HPC - LPT	FAN - HPC - HPT - IPT		
8		IPC - IPT	FAN - HPT - IPT	FAN - HPC - HPT- LPT		
9		IPC - LPT	FAN - HPT - LPT	FAN - HPC - IPT - LPT		
10		HPC - HPT	FAN - IPT - LPT	FAN - HPT - IPT - LPT		
11		HPC - IPT	IPC - HPC - HPT	IPC - HPC- HPT - IPT		
12		HPC - LPT	IPC - HPC- IPT	IPC - HPC - HPT - LPT		
13		HPT - IPT	IPC - HPC - LPT	IPC - HPC- IPT - LPT		
14		HPT - LPT	IPC - HPT- IPT	IPC - HPT - IPT - LPT		
15		IPT - LPT	IPC - HPT - LPT	HPC - HPT - IPT - LPT		
16			IPC - IPT - LPT			
17			HPC - HPT - IPT			
18			HPC - HPT - LPT			
19			HPC - IPT - LPT			
20						

Considering that the number of parameters representative of the health of each component is always 2, $2k$ is the number of parameters deteriorated simultaneously in each rule (each run of the engine model) when we simulate k degraded components at a time.

For example, if two degraded components at a time are simulated, four parameters are changed in the generation of each rule.

On the other hand, the equation

$$N = f^g = f^{2k} \tag{3}$$

computes the number of permutations of f (=3 in the example of Table 2.2) fault levels (e.g., 0, 1, 2% change in performance parameters) taken $g=2k$ (=4 in Table 2.2) at a time with repletion. The parameter $g=2k$ represents the number of parameters changed at a time. In the case of Table 2.2 the number of permutations with repetitions are $N=f^{2k}=3^4=81$. As we have six components, we have $C=15$ combinations of 2 components (and 4 parameters) taken at a time: the final number of rules to generate in this example would be the product TotalCombinations = CN = 15·81 = 1215.

Table 2.2. Example of 4 deteriorated parameters at a time

η_i	Γ_i	η_i	Γ_i
0	0	0	0
1	0	0	0
2	0	0	0
0	1	0	0
1	1	0	0
2	1	0	0
..	..	..	..

Summarizing, the number of TotalCombinations for a three-spool engine with six gas path components, and so the number of rules to generate, is given by:

$$TotalCombinations = C \cdot N = f^{2 \cdot k} \cdot \frac{6!}{k!(6-k)!} \qquad (4)$$

where k is the number of degraded components simulated at a time, and f is the number of fault levels, as performance parameters percentage changes from the clean engine.

Given six components and two health parameters per component, we have 12 performance parameters (η and Γ of the components). We define the search space as the 12-dimensional space of the ranges of variability of the 12 parameters in percentage changes from the clean value. The solution of the diagnostic problem will be looked for within the constrained search space.

The learning algorithm devised in this work builds the fuzzy-logic-based diagnostic system with a number of rules equal to *TotalCombinations* as defined above, noting that there is no justification to omit some combinations if the purpose is to approximate the dependency between measurements and performance parameters when the latter vary in a given search space. Nevertheless, the values of the f fault levels can either be chosen as uniformly distributed in the ranges of the search space or not. This work is dedicated to the study of a fuzzy system with uniformly distributed fuzzy rules, so the density of the fuzzy rules is left unchanged through a given search space, though it is varied from system to system to trade accuracy towards computational burden as discussed before.

2.2.4.1. Fuzzy Systems and Neural Networks
A last comment can be made about the strong analogy that exists between fuzzy systems and neural networks. Neural networks, as fuzzy systems, can approximate a function or process that represents a relation of cause and effect and can act as universal approximators. A neural network, instead of stating rules, trains its synapses. The numerical synaptic values change when input data make the neurons fire. This makes a net able to learn to recognise patterns and therefore to map inputs into outputs. The major difference is that, in the case of a neural network, a user has no way to know what the net has learnt or forgotten during the learning process. When the network is trained with new information there is an inevitable tendency to

forget the old ones. On the other hand, fuzzy rules are modular and the user can always put them in or take them out at will.

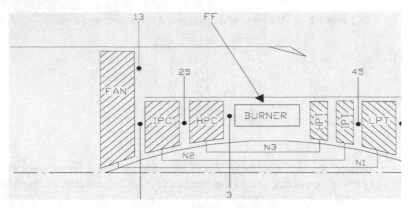

Figure 2.10.   Three-shaft turbofan engine configuration.

Table 2.3.   Measurement set

1	N2 :	IP Shaft Speed
2	N3 :	HP Shaft Speed
3	FF :	Fuel Flow
4	P13 :	FAN tip exit Total Pressure
5	P25 :	HPC entry Total Pressure
6	P3 :	HPC exit Total Pressure
7	T25 :	HPC entry Total Temperature
8	T3 :	HPC exit Total Temperature
9	T45 :	IPT exit Total Temperature
10	T5 :	LPT exit Total Temperature

2.3.   A Three-Spool Engine Configuration and Its Instrumentation

The engine involved with the development of the technique described in this chapter is a three-shaft turbofan and its configuration is shown in Figure 2.10 highlighting the typical sensor locations. The set of measurements available for the diagnostics process within this project is listed in Table 2.3 using the measurements listed in Table 2.4 as power setting and environmental parameters. Sensor noise is assumed to follow a normal distribution whose standard deviation in terms of percentage deviation from the nominal value can be used as a parameter representative of the noise level. Accurate values of standard deviations are provided by the sensor manufacturers but, for the scope of this project, the sensor noise standard deviations listed in Table 2.5 are considered sufficiently accurate and realistic. The performance simulations are undertaken mainly using Turbomatch, a steady-state performance simulation code developed at Cranfield University. The simulations are carried out at a condition of 10000 m of altitude, 0.85 Mach and

0.8% PCN1 (which identifies the percentage of accomplishing the design point condition by low-pressure shaft speed N1).

Table 2.4. Power setting and environmental parameters

1	N1 :	LP Shaft Speed
2	M :	Mach Number
3	Z :	Altitude

Table 2.5. Sensor noise standard deviations in % of the measured value

SENSOR TYPE	STDV$_i$
Temperature	0.4%
Pressure	0.25%
Fuel Flow	0.5%
Shaft Speed	0.05%

2.4. A Fuzzy-Logic-Based Diagnostics System for a Three-Spool Engine

2.4.1. Objectives and Scope

Considering the advantages of fuzzy logic as illustrated in Section 2.2, and according to a thorough literature study reported in (Marinai, 2004; Marinai et al., 2004), the research objectives were precisely to develop a procedure that is:

- Based on a nonlinear model.
- Designed specifically for SFI and/or MFI.
- Capable of detecting with reasonable accuracy significant changes in performance.
- Able to provide a "concentration" capability on the actual fault.
- Competent to make a worthwhile diagnosis using only few measurements (N>M).
- Able to deal with random noise in the measurements.
- Light in computational requirements.
- Fast in undertaking diagnosis for on-wing applications.
- Able to be adapted to similar systems in a reasonably short time: exempt from training and tuning uncertainties, difficulties and dependences for setting-up parameters.
- Free from a lack of comprehensibility due to "black-box" behaviour.

The scope of this section is to illustrate an application of the devised method to a three-spool engine. The most important parameters in the process are identified and optimised through a sensitivity study. Then, the accuracy of the methodology in this specific application is assessed with simulated case studies in section 2.5. Section 2.6 extends the applicability of the method to the MFI problem.

2.4.2. The Methodology and Identification of the Key Parameters

Gas path analysis is formulated here as a problem of recognition of deteriorated measurements patterns by using a rule-based method that has its foundation in fuzzy algebra (Marinai *et al.*, 2003a, 2003b).

The inherent capability of fuzzy systems, previously pointed out in section 2.1, to deal with GPD problems is exploited here in two ways. Firstly, we take into account the uncertainty in the measurements that affects the fault pattern characterization, at a set level. Secondly, at a system level, the learning algorithm devised in this project states fuzzy rules to map input sets of measurements into output sets of performance parameters, in a constrained search space. This enables diagnoses even though the formulation of the diagnostics problem is analytically undetermined.

The diagnostic process, as shown in Figure 2.11, is designed to assess performance parameters percentage changes from a clean engine condition (12 outputs) given the knowledge of the measurement changes (10 inputs) calculated as percentage deviations with respect to a baseline determined by means of an engine model run at a specific power setting and environmental conditions. The fuzzy system $F=R^{10} \rightarrow R^{12}$ uses m rules to map the vector of input delta measurements z to a vector of output delta performance parameters $x=F(z)$. The analysis is undertaken at the operating condition characterised by the following parameters: N1=0.8%, Mach= 0.85, Altitude=10000 m.

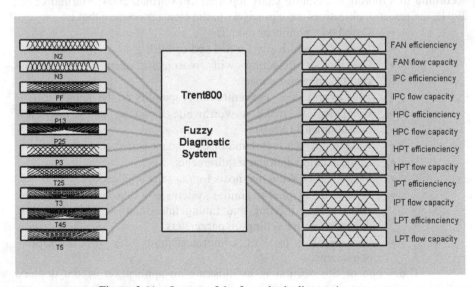

Figure 2.11.   Layout of the fuzzy logic diagnostic system.

Diagnostics is made through a Mandami-type fuzzy inference process. The ranges of variability of the outputs – $\Delta \eta$ and $\Delta \Gamma$ for the six components – define the search space, where the solution is sought. A sensible choice of these ranges for a real-life application would be between -5% and 0 for all the efficiency deltas and for the flow capacity deltas of the compressors, while they can cover positive values for the turbine flow capacity deltas going for example between -5% and +3%. The range of variability of each input variable is evaluated according to the sought output ranges through the engine model.

2.4.2.1. Fault Levels Combinations and If-Then Rules

The learning algorithm proposed in this work states if-then rules that are generated running the engine model and therefore are strictly related to the aero-thermal equations. The use of data obtained from the engine model to generate the rules preserves the linearity of the problem.

The rules have the general form *IF condition-1 AND condition-2 ...THEN statement*. The if-part of the rule refers to the fault signature in the measurements, represented through input MFs, evaluated by running the engine model at a defined deteriorated condition within the search space. The statement in the then-part of the rule refers to this condition characterised with output MFs.

The procedure to state fuzzy rules starts with the definition of the search space for the performance parameters. According to section 2.2.4 the search space includes all the combination of changes in efficiency and flow capacities of the 6 components that the system is meant to deal with. The parameters that characterise the search space are: (i) the number of components that are considered deteriorated simultaneously (1 at a time for SFI), (ii) the maximum and minimum values of the ranges of variability of the performance parameters, and (iii) the increment value that divides each range in a finite number of constant variations (fault levels). For the purpose of illustrating the methodology, we consider the following search space:

- Number of components simultaneously deteriorated = 1 (SFI)
- Maximum variation in compressors' efficiencies = 0%
- Minimum variation in compressors' efficiencies = -3%
- Maximum variation in compressors' flow capacities = 0%
- Minimum variation in compressors' flow capacities = -3%
- Maximum variation in turbines' efficiencies = 0%
- Minimum variation in turbines' efficiencies = -3%
- Maximum variation in turbines' flow capacities = 1%
- Minimum variation in turbines' flow capacities = -3%
- Increment Value= 0.5%

The features of this search space are the followings:

- It defines the 12-dimensional space of the ranges of variability of the 12 parameters in % changes from the clean value.
- It takes into account positive variation of turbines' flow capacity.
- We consider C=6 combinations of one gas path component deteriorated at a time – see section 2.2.4.
- The increment value in the search space is 0.5%. This means that the engine model is run for all the combinations of variations of the performance parameters within the ranges defined above, obtained going from the minima to the maximum in 0.5% steps.

For example, going from 0 to 3% of FAN efficiency the following 7 conditions of deterioration are generated: 0, -0.5, -1, -1.5, -2, -2.5, -3%.

- We note that with 0.5% steps, all the ranges are divided in 7 combinations except for the turbine flow capacity ranges, which are divided into 9 fault levels.
- The number of if-then statements generated is equal to 331.

The solution of the diagnostic problem will be looked for within the constrained search space, so we define a number of fuzzy rules equal to the if-then statements generated running the engine model. Note that the use of a constant increment value implies that the values of the f fault levels are chosen uniformly distributed in the ranges.

2.4.2.2. Input and Output Membership Functions

Fuzzy sets are defined for the inputs and the outputs. Each of the input ranges is spanned with a number M_i of MFs where the index $i=1,...,n$ identifies the i-th measurement. These MFs centred, for each measurement, in the outcome of the engine model run for all the combinations identified in the search space, or in the mean value of a cluster of values grouped according to the procedure. On the other hand, the deviations in performance parameters of the table are always associated with an MF. Similarly, N_j MFs for $j=1,...,p$ are designed for the i-th performance parameter centred in fault level values specified in the search space.

Two types of MFs were considered: triangular, or Gaussian according to equation (5), where m is the midpoint of the function and RMS=σ. The two types of MFs are shown in Figure 2.12.

$$MF(x) = e^{-0.5 \cdot \left(\frac{x-m}{\sigma} \right)^2}$$ (5)

The optimal type of output MFs is not known a priori and therefore a sensitivity study (section 2.4.5) was undertaken to identifying the choice that contributes to an optimal accuracy of the diagnostics system. An example of seven Gaussian MFs spanning the range for FAN $\Delta\eta$ is shown in Figure 2.13.

On the other hand, a preliminary comment can be made here regarding the input MFs. The degree to which the measurement value z belongs to a given MF, in fuzzy algebra, was named $a(z)$. Alternatively, $a(z)$ can be interpreted as the probability that the measurement is the midpoint of the MF given that the measurement value is z. Therefore, we can view the input fuzzy set as a random set of two-point conditional probability densities, where the set degree $a() = $ degree($z \in A$) becomes the local conditional probability $prob\{Z=A \,|\, Z=z\}$. In this sense we can use Gaussian MFs for the input measurements with values of RMS equal to realistic values of sensor noise RMSs. In the opinion of the authors, this choice is an effective and consistent way of designing measurement MFs oriented to tackle the measurement uncertainty problem. However, at this level of the investigation, the possibility of using triangular MFs, generally considered very effective in designing highly dimensional fuzzy systems, is left also for the input variables. This leaves open the opportunity to compare the two input MF types – see section 2.4.5 – to identify the best system layout.

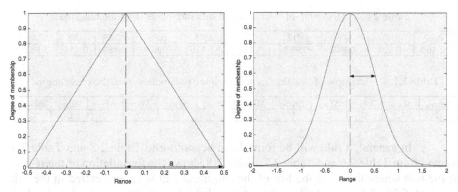

Figure 2.12. Triangular membership function (left) and Gaussian membership function (right).

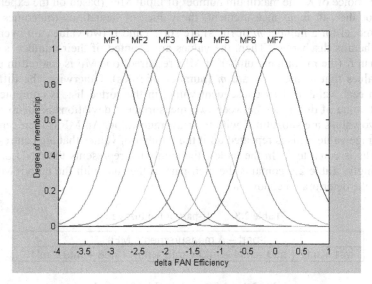

Figure 2.13. Example of 7 Gaussian MFs in a fixed performance parameter range for the output FAN $\Delta\eta$.

2.4.2.3. Fuzzy Rules Generation

Each rule is composed of two parts: (i) the if-part that contains the fault signature in the measurements represented with MFs linked with the AND operator, and (ii) the then-part that contains the MFs of the output performance parameters that characterise the fault condition. Table 2.6 and Table 2.7 contain an example of data necessary to set up a rule generated by running the engine model. The use of data obtained from the engine model to generate the rules preserves the linearity of the problem. A rule states in terms of MFs, what in terms of numerical values can be read as follows: if the pattern in the measurements shows the deviations from a baseline listed in Table 2.6, then the combination of deterioration levels is in Table 2.7.

Table 2.6.   Example of % changes in measurements from the baseline

ΔN2	ΔN3	ΔFF	ΔP13	ΔP25	ΔP3	ΔP5	ΔT25	ΔT3	ΔT45
0.460	-0.008	-0.949	-0.907	-1.117	-1.115	-0.804	0.169	0.111	0.182

Table 2.7.   Example of % deltas in performance parameters from the clean engine

$\Delta\eta_{FAN}$	$\Delta\Gamma_{FAN}$	$\Delta\eta_{IPC}$	$\Delta\Gamma_{IPC}$	$\Delta\eta_{HPC}$	$\Delta\Gamma_{HPC}$	$\Delta\eta_{HPT}$	$\Delta\Gamma_{HPT}$	$\Delta\eta_{IPT}$	$\Delta\Gamma_{IPT}$	$\Delta\eta_{LPT}$	$\Delta\Gamma_{LPT}$
-2	-1.5	0	0	0	0	0	0	0	0	0	0

In general, a rule will be formulated according to Table 2.8 and Table 2.9 created from Table 2.6 and Table 2.7. Table 2.8 shows the formulation of the if-part of the rule where the mf_i is the MF of the i-th input that is either centred in the i-th value of Table 2.6 or centred in the mean value of a cluster of values defined as follows. The algorithm that generates the input MFs for a number m of rules starts with the choice of K, the maximum number of input MFs (based on the experience). Then, for the i-th input measurement, the values of deviations (outcomes of the engine model for a number m of rules) are sorted and if two values are overlapped one of them is discharged. Then, the values are counted; if their number is less or equal than K (the maximum number of MFs required) one MF is centred in each of these values that at the most are m (number of rules). Otherwise, the difference between each value and its consequent value, in the sorted list, is computed. The smallest value of difference between two measurement deviations is identified and these two values are substituted with their average value. An MF is then centred in this average value. This is repeated until the number of values that are centres of the input MFs is equal to K. In the tables, the symbol + represents the AND operator. Accordingly, Table 2.9 contains the then-part of the rule with the output MFs that identify the deteriorated condition.

Table 2.8.   If-part of the fuzzy rule

If-part – Δ measurements MFs
mf1 + mf2 + mf3 + mf4 + mf5 + mf6 + mf7 + mf8 + mf9 + mf10

Table 2.9.   Then-part of the fuzzy rule

Then-part – Δ performance parameters MFs
mf1 , mf2 , mf3 , mf4 , mf5 , mf6 , mf7 , mf8 , mf9 , mf10 , mf11 , mf12

2.4.2.4. Fuzzy Inference: Functional and System Parameters

Fuzzy inference is the process used to perform pattern recognition and therefore to compute mapping between input values and output values.

The inference process consists of feeding an input set of % changes of the 10 measurements that are taken along the gas path (or simulated with the engine model to generate a test case) into the fuzzy logic system that calculates the output performance parameters % changes. The fuzzy inference process includes the following five phases: (i) fuzzification of the input variables, (ii) application of the AND fuzzy operator in the if-part of the rule, (iii) implication from the if-part to the then-part of each rule, (iv) aggregation of the then-parts across the rules, and (v) defuzzification.

The following parameters are referred to as *functional parameters* and can be combined in several ways in designing a fuzzy system:

- AND operator, implemented as: product, minimum.
- Implication method, implemented as: product, minimum.
- Aggregation method, implemented as: summation, maximum
- Defuzzification method, implemented as: centroid, centre of maximum.

The functional parameters were identified as those parameters that characterise the functionality of the inference process. A first sensitivity study is described in section 2.4.5 to identify the combination of parameters most suitable to design a fuzzy-logic-based diagnostic system. There is no reason to think that when the type of engine diagnosed changes this optimal combination of functional parameters should vary. So, the outcome of this first investigation is the choice of the fuzzy functional parameters for a generic diagnostics system.

On the other hand, we define the following *system parameters*:

- Number, type, width of the input MFs. To take into account sensor noise the value of amplitude (s or σ) for the i-th measurement can be expressed as a multiple of its sensor noise RMS_i ($n \cdot RMS_i$).
- Number, type, width of the output MFs. The number of output MFs is always a result of the search space definition. For each of the 12 performance parameters (involved in this application), for a given range of variability, this number depends on the increment value (as defined in section 2.4.2.1) once the search space is defined. This number corresponds to the number f of fault levels that the range is divided into.

Summarizing, for the application described in this chapter, with fixed inputs and outputs, the system parameters to be optimised are six: number, type and width of the input MFs, type and width of output MFs and increment value in the search space.

A second sensitivity study will be carried out in section 2.4.5 aimed at identifying the best values to set up a system for the three-spool engine considered in this work. When implementing a new diagnostic system, a new sensitivity study may be required to identify their optimal values. Nevertheless, the logic and the procedure to choose the parameters remains suitable and the parameters chosen in this work can be used as first attempt values.

2.4.3. Automated Procedure

The procedure to generate fuzzy rules was automated via the graphical user interface (GUI) shown in Figure 2.14. This GUI constitutes the first of two windows of the diagnostics module based on fuzzy logic described in (Marinai, 2004). This first GUI is aimed at setting up fuzzy logic diagnostics models for a given engine. A second interface is aimed at operating the diagnostics models created to estimate the possible faults – see section 2.7.

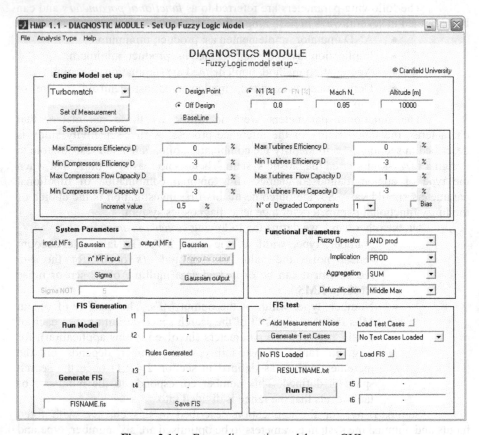

Figure 2.14.   Fuzzy diagnostic model setup GUI.

The first GUI of the diagnostics module, as shown in Figure 2.14, is able to setup a diagnostics model given an engine model (Turbomatch), an operating condition and a search space.

In the GUI the main elements that must be specified are:

- *In the engine model setup frame of the GUI*: engine model used, operating condition, selection of the measurement set (number and type).
- *In the search space definition frame of the GUI*: the ranges of variability of the performance parameters, the number of components simultaneously degraded and the increment value in the ranges.
- *In the system parameters definition frame of the GUI*: number, type and width of the input MFs, type and width of output MFs. (Note that the increment value is defined with the search space.)

- *In the functional parameters definition frame of the GUI*: AND operator, implication, aggregation, and defuzzification algorithms among the techniques listed in section 2.4.2.4.

Once these selections are made, a fuzzy logic inference system (FIS) is generated and saved. An additional frame of the GUI was designed to test FISs by simulating test data with implanted faults as well as measurement noise.

An ulterior feature of this interface is its capability of generating a diagnostics FIS able to diagnose component faults in the presence of systematic errors in the measurements (bias) while identifying the faulty sensor as well. A checkbox in the search space definition frame of the GUI enables the input of an ulterior system parameter called sigma NOT. This feature is discussed in detail in (Marinai, 2004) but not described in this chapter.

2.4.4. Sensitivity Study: Strategy

2.4.4.1. Reasons for the Study. Anticipation of the Results

Section 2.4.5 will present a sensitivity study aimed at identifying our choice of optimal combination of system and functional parameters for an optimal approximation capability of the diagnostics system. The approximation capability is defined as the ability of the method to model and approximate the functional relationship between sets of inputs (fault signature in the measurements) and the right sets of outputs (variations in the performance parameters), without considering, for the moment, the additional complication of measurement errors. Subsequently, in section 2.5, noise is added to the test cases and our optimal selection of the system parameters is modified accordingly, to achieve an enhanced accuracy of the diagnosis.

The sensitivity study (to evaluate the method's approximation capability) includes two sets of tests aimed at carrying out: (i) optimization of the functional parameters, and (ii) optimization of the system parameters. For the benefit of the reader, we anticipate here the results that are justified throughout the next subsection. Our choice of optimal functional parameters is the following:

- AND operator, implemented as: product.
- Implication method, implemented as: product.
- Aggregation method, implemented as: summation.
- Defuzzification method, implemented as: centroid (centre of maximum as second best).

These features identify a fuzzy logic system commonly known as SAM (standard additive model).

On the other hand, the optimal selection of system parameters is:

- Gaussian MFs for input and output.
- Maximum N of MFs fixed to 500. It was found that the more input MFs are defined the better, in fact this value is greater than the number of input MFs that correspond to the combinations in the search space identified for an SFI capability. Nevertheless, in the case of a system with MFI capability, in the opinion of the

authors, a sensible value (e.g., 500) must be given to limit the computational burden.

- Width of MFs equal to 0.15 for the input MFs and equal to 0.5 for the output MFs. Note that the optimal value of the input MFs width to achieve an effective approximation capability is different from the case in which noise is added. In the presence of noise the optimal value for each measurement is different and corresponds to the values of the sensors' noise RMSs assuming that noise is normally distributed, as discussed in section 2.5.
- The number of output MFs is identified by the choice of the increment value in the search space. A smaller increment value is associated with a higher number of rules. Even though it is proved that this is advantageous for the accuracy of the system, it considerably reduces the speed of the calculation.

2.4.4.2. Description of the Case Studies

Test cases were generated, implanting 1771 combinations, deteriorating the six components independently (two parameters at a time) in the ranges of variability defined for the examined search space (see section 2.4.2.1) with an increment value of 0.2.

Table 2.10.   Combinations of functional parameters

case	AND	Implication	Aggregation	Defuzzification
1	Product	Product	Summation	Centroid
2	Minimum	Product	Summation	Centroid
3	Product	Minimum	Summation	Centroid
4	Minimum	Minimum	Summation	Centroid
5	Product	Product	Maximum	Centroid
6	Minimum	Product	Maximum	Centroid
7	Product	Minimum	Maximum	Centroid
8	Minimum	Minimum	Maximum	Centroid
9	Product	Product	Summation	C.O.M
10	Minimum	Product	Summation	C.O.M
11	Product	Minimum	Summation	C.O.M
12	Minimum	Minimum	Summation	C.O.M
13	Product	Product	Maximum	C.O.M
14	Minimum	Product	Maximum	C.O.M
15	Product	Minimum	Maximum	C.O.M
16	Minimum	Minimum	Maximum	C.O.M

In the sensitivity study reported in section 2.4.5, a first series of 16 tests were performed to identify the optimal functional parameters. The test cases were used to assess the approximation capability of 16 different systems whose layouts were designed according to the combinations of functional parameters listed in Table 2.10. For these 16 systems, the system parameters were fixed to the following first-guess values: Gaussian MFs in input and output, maximum N of MFs fixed to 500, width of input MFs equal to 0.25, width of output MFs equal to 0.5, increment value of the search space equal to 0.5%.

Once a best choice of functional parameters was found, it was kept unchanged in the subsequent tests: the second group of tests was undertaken using the same 1771 test cases to evaluate the optimal system parameters among the following possible selections.

- Input MFs type= Gaussian, Triangular.
- Input MFs width= 0.1, 0.15, 0.25, 0.5.
- Output MFs type= Gaussian, Triangular.
- Output MFs width= 0.25, 0.5, 1%.
- Increment value= 0.25, 0.5, 1%.
- Input MFs number= 50, 100, 500.

The strategy used to carry out these tests follows: starting from the first-guess values of system parameters used in the first series of tests (Gaussian MFs in input and output, maximum N of MFs fixed to 500, width of input MFs equal to 0.25, width of output MFs equal to 0.5, increment value of the search space equal to 0.5%), the changes listed in Table 2.11 were made in sequence. For each change in system parameters, the system so generated was tested. The change was carried forward to the successive test only if it outperformed the results from the previous system.

Table 2.11. List of system parameters changes for the sensitivity study

N.	Change to system parameters
1	Input MFs type changed to triangular (from Gaussian)
2	Output MFs changed to triangular
3	Input MFs width increased to 0.5 (from 0.25)
4	Input MFs width reduced to 0.15
5	Input MFs width reduced to 0.1
6	Output MFs width reduced to 0.25 (from 0.5)
7	Output MFs width increased to 1
8	Increment value increased to 1 % (from 0.5%)
9	Increment value reduced to 0.25 %
10	Input MFs number reduced to 100

2.4.4.3. Three Methods to Estimate the System Accuracy

This section introduces three methods that were used to assess the performance parameters' estimation error and therefore the capability of a given diagnostics system to meet the requirements, as discussed below.

For each input set of 10 measurement deviations, the diagnostics process computes 12 deviations in performance parameters. The difference between the implanted deviation in each performance parameter and the corresponding calculated one is computed according to the following equation:

$$\text{Delta} = \text{Implanted} - \text{Calculated} \qquad (6)$$

Method 1. This method computes, for each test case, the max|Delta| (maximum value of |Delta|) calculated for the 12 parameters estimated. Then it assigns to this value different levels of severity according to its amount. Three severity ranges were considered:

- Low severity (LS): max|Delta| < 0.5%
- Medium severity (MS): 0.5%<max|Delta| < 1%
- High severity (HS): max|Delta| > 1%

Therefore for the 1771 test cases created, for each system assessed is calculated: number and % of MS cases and number and % of HS cases (the number and % of LS cases can be obviously deduced).

This method is aimed at evaluating local errors of the system in estimating the performance parameters, pointing out when in each test case the maximum error overcomes fixed thresholds.

Method 2. This technique is used only to assess SFI capability when a fault is implanted in only one component at a time (two parameters simultaneously faulty). The 1771 test cases are divided into six groups characterised by a different faulty component, the number of components being six. This method considers, in each group, only the two parameters affected by deterioration and computes the Deltas for them only. For each parameter in which deterioration is implanted this method computes:

- μ = the mean value of the Deltas across the group of test cases relative to the same component deteriorated.
- σ = the standard deviation of those Deltas.
- $Cl_{95\%}+ = \mu + 1.96\ \sigma$, the corresponding 95% upper confidence limit.
- $Cl_{95\%}- = \mu - 1.96\ \sigma$, the corresponding 95% upper confidence limit.

This approach computes a local error because it considers only the parameters where the deterioration is implanted. It undertakes for these parameters a statistical analysis of the results and therefore it can be used to provide an expected accuracy of the system on them.

Method 3. This method computes, for each test case, the RMS of the Deltas for the N=12 parameters estimated for each calculation, according to the equation

$$RMS = \sqrt{\frac{\sum\limits_{i=i}^{N}(Delta_i)^2}{N}} \tag{7}$$

The average value, $mean$(RMS)=$\underline{RMS}$, of the RMSs calculated for all test cases (1771 in the sensitivity study) is identified as a global parameter to estimate the accuracy of the diagnosis. This method is particularly useful to highlight a smearing tendency (see section 2.2.3) or else the propensity of some of the diagnostics methods to distribute the faults over many engine components even when only a limited number of components are affected by faults.

The three methods are employed in this work in the following cases:

- Methods 1 and 3 are used in the sensitivity study reported in the next section (2.4.5) to provide a quick way of estimating a global accuracy of each system assessed.
- Methods 1, 2 and 3 are then used in section 2.5 to investigate in detail (local and global errors) the approximation capability of the fuzzy diagnostics system and successively its accuracy, in the presence of noisy measurements, for the diagnostics system with the chosen layout.

- Methods 1 and 3 are used in section 2.6 to assess the partial MFI capability of the system.

2.4.5. Sensitivity Study: Results

2.4.5.1. Choice of the Functional Parameters

This section is dedicated to reporting the results of the first part of the sensitivity study to identify the best choice of functional parameters. The 16 different layouts listed in Table 2.10 (section 2.4.4.2) were investigated and the results are summarized in Table 2.12, the number of cases in the two tables being the same. The table contains the results from two techniques to assess the diagnostics system accuracy: Methods 1 and 3 as defined in section 2.4.4.3. In the table, for each system, the results from Method 1 are the number (N) and the percentage (%) of the cases with medium severity (MS) and high severity (HS) errors. Besides, Method 3 provides the average value of the RMS error, for the 1771 test cases.

Table 2.12. Results from Methods 1 and 3 to assist the best choice of functional parameters

case	Method 1		Method 3
	MS cases (N. // %)	HS cases (N. // %)	RMS
1	27 // 0.0152	0 // 0	0.048
2	79 // 0.0446	2 // 0.0011	0.065
3	35 // 0.0198	0 // 0	0.084
4	96 // 0.0542	3 // 0.0017	0.097
5	43 // 0.0243	1 // 0.0005	0.058
6	48 // 0.0271	2 // 0.0011	0.060
7	57 // 0.0322	1 // 0.0005	0.068
8	106 // 0.0599	2 // 0.0011	0.079
9	31 // 0.0175	8 // 0.0045	0.046
10	103 // 0.0582	20 // 0.0113	0.055
11	80 // 0.0452	0 // 0	0.065
12	134 // 0.0757	6 // 0.0034	0.095
13	51 // 0.0288	7 // 0.004	0.074
14	49 // 0.027	8 // 0.0045	0.075
15	50 // 0.028	7 // 0.004	0.076
16	51 // 0.0288	10 // 0.0056	0.075

The outcome of this analysis highlighted two optimal combinations of functional parameters that show a minimum number of MS and HS cases and a minimum average value of RMS. These best layouts are for the cases 1 and 9 that correspond respectively to the following layout:

- **Best choice**: AND=Product, Implication=Product, Aggregation= Summation, Defuzzification=Centroid.
- **Second best choice**: AND=Product, Implication=Product, Aggregation=Summation, Defuzzification=Centre of Maximum.

Case 1 was selected as best choice because it showed: minimum number of MS and zero HS cases. As far as the RMS is concerned, case 1 does not outperform case 9 that is considered to be the second best selection. Nevertheless the difference in RMS for the two systems is negligible. It is worthwhile noticing that the small value of RMS for case 9 indicates a strong concentration capability on the actual fault.

2.4.5.2. Choice of the System Parameters

The procedure to identify the most suitable combination of system parameters was presented in section 2.4.4.2. It consists of a sequence of 10 modifications to the first-guess values. After each change in system parameter, the layout was tested with the 1771 test cases introduced in section 2.4.4.2 and the change was kept in the successive layout only if it outperformed the results from the previous system.

Table 2.13.   Results from Methods 1 and 3 to assist the best choice of system parameters

case	Method 1		Method 3	Set up time	Keep (K) / Reject (R) the change
	MS cases (N. // %)	HS cases (N. // %)	RMS		
1	339 // 0.1914	310 // 0.175	0.282	1 min, 12 sec	R
2	29 // 0.016	0 // 0	0.049	unchanged	R
3	305 // 0.1722	24 // 0.0136	0.112	unchanged	R
4	26 // 0.0147	0 // 0	0.045	unchanged	**K**
5	41 // 0.0232	4 // 0.0023	0.064	unchanged	R
6	26 // 0.0147	2 // 0.0011	0.048	unchanged	R
7	58 // 0.0327	2 // 0.0011	0.237	unchanged	R
8	334 // 0.1942	44 // 0.0248	0.129	23 sec	R
9	10 // 0.0056	0 // 0	0.117	4 min, 8 sec	R
10	28 // 0.0158	2 // 0.0011	0.055	1 min, 12 sec	R

This procedure was applied starting from the best choice of layout identified in section 2.4.5.1. The outcome of this sensitivity study is summarized in Table 2.13. The table case number corresponds to the layout change number of Table 2.11. Table 2.13 presents the results from Methods 1 and 3 (see section 2.4.4.3) and the setup time or else the time to generate a new fuzzy logic inference system, with the new layout, for the search space under investigation. In the last column of the table is reported whether the layout with the change outperforms or not the previous one.

The following change was introduced in the system parameters:

- Input MFs width reduced to 0.15 (case 4), because it reduces the number of MS cases and the <u>RMS</u>.

It is worthwhile noticing that the changes associated with case 9 (increment value reduced to 0.25%) were not introduced. The reasons are that even though the corresponding number of MS cases appreciably drops, the <u>RMS</u> increases indicating a higher tendency to smear the fault in the 12 parameters. Moreover, the setup time increases significantly. It is an ambition of this work to extend the SFI capability of the system to an MFI capability; therefore concerns about the setup time are vital to enable this additional feature in a reasonable time. In fact, the number of rules that needs to be generated increases dramatically in implementing a system able to identify more than two components simultaneously faulty, and so does the setup time accordingly.

Similarly, this procedure was applied starting from the second best layout identified in section 2.4.5.1 to complete the identification of a second optimal layout. The outcome of this second sensitivity study is summarized in Table 2.14. The table case number corresponds to the layout change number of Table 2.11. The following two changes were introduced in the system parameters:

- Input MFs width reduced to 0.15 (case 4).
- Output MFs width increased to 1 (case 7).

Table 2.14. Results from Methods 1 and 2 to assist the best choice of system parameters for the second optimal selection of the functional parameters

case	Keep (K) / Reject (R) the change
1	R
2	R
3	R
4	K
5	R
6	R
7	K
8	R
9	R
10	R

2.5. SFI Accuracy and Tuning

This section is dedicated to a thorough analysis of the SFI accuracy of the fuzzy-logic-based diagnostic system in the following cases:

- To approximate and model the functional relationship between sets of inputs (fault signature in the measurements) and sets of outputs (variations in the performance parameters), without the additional complication of measurements errors. The best layout identified in section 2.4.5.2 is studied in more detail in section 2.5.1.

- To diagnose a fault in one component (SFI) in the presence of noise in the measurements. The accuracy of the system is tested, and how this accuracy can be enhanced changing the input MFs amplitude according to realistic values of sensor noise RMSs is shown in section 2.5.2.
- To diagnose considerable changes in the two health parameters of one component with respect to a previously assessed deteriorated condition. A way of tuning the diagnostics system capable of SFI to estimate such changes and the method's accuracy are reported in section 2.5.3.

2.5.1. Approximation Capability: Accuracy

In section 2.4.5.2 an optimal layout for a fuzzy diagnostics system was identified via a sensitivity study. The system has the following features:

- Functional parameters: AND=Product, Implication=Product, Aggregation=Summation, Defuzzification=Centroid.
- System parameters: Gaussian MFs in input and output, Maximum N of MFs fixed to 500, width of input MFs equal to 0.15, width of output MFs equal to 0.5, increment value of the search space equal to 0.5% (this identifies indirectly the output MFs number – see section 2.4.2.4)

This section presents a more in-depth study of the accuracy of the devised diagnostics process by means of two techniques, introduced in section 2.4.4.3, to assess the system estimation error: Methods 1 and 3. This section is entirely dedicated to the analysis of system's capability of approximating and modelling the functional relationship between inputs and outputs without considering measurement errors.

2.5.1.1. Accuracy Results: Method 2

Figure 2.15 presents Deltas between implanted and calculated performance parameter deteriorations for the 1771 cases.

For each case, efficiency and flow capacity changes were implanted simultaneously for one component: starting from the FAN, on the left of the diagram, to the LPT on the right. Therefore, for each test case shown on the x axis, two values are plotted on the y axis: the corresponding Deltas (errors) in estimating the efficiency and the flow capacity of the component simulated as faulty (the name of the component appears on the top of the diagram for each group of test cases). For each component, a statistical analysis of the result was carried out according to Method 2 and summarized in Table 2.15.

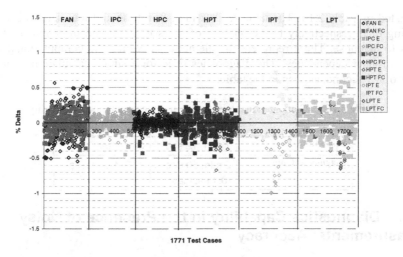

Figure 2.15. SFI capability of the diagnostics system. Results for 1771 test cases.

Table 2.15. Statistics of the diagnostics results, Method 2

	η_{FAN}	Γ_{FAN}	η_{IPC}	Γ_{IPC}	η_{HPC}	Γ_{HPC}	η_{HPT}	Γ_{HPT}	η_{IPT}	Γ_{IPT}	η_{LPT}	Γ_{LPT}
μ	-0.009	-0.003	-0.007	-0.007	-0.009	0.001	0.006	-0.026	-0.040	0.014	-0.032	0.017
σ	0.231	0.136	0.091	0.075	0.089	0.065	0.127	0.131	0.175	0.123	0.165	0.184
$CI_{95\%}+$	0.444	0.264	0.173	0.141	0.166	0.129	0.256	0.230	0.302	0.255	0.292	0.377
$CI_{95\%}-$	-0.461	-0.269	-0.186	-0.154	-0.184	-0.127	-0.243	-0.282	-0.382	-0.227	-0.356	0.344

For each component degraded, the table reports, for each health parameter: the mean value (μ) of the errors between the calculated and the implanted performance parameter changes, over the test cases relative to that specific component, the standard deviation (σ) of such an error, and the derived 95% confidence intervals ($CI_{95\%}$). For each parameter it can be concluded that, with 95% confidence, the error is contained between $CI_{95\%}+$ and $CI_{95\%}-$.

2.5.1.2. Accuracy Results: Method 3
A second performance parameters' estimation error is introduced by computing, for each test case, the RMS of the Deltas for the 12 parameters at each calculation, according to the procedure previously described in Method 3. This analysis reveals that the fuzzy logic system has a good accuracy on the parameters not affected by the implanted faults, or else it has a good "concentration" capability on the actual fault. The average value of the RMS error, for the 1771 test cases, was 0.045, which is a considerably low value.

2.5.1.3. Computational Time Required
One of the most favourable aspects of using fuzzy logic to implement a system capable of SFI, is its speed: once an automated setup procedure is designed (see GUI section 2.4.3) such a system is quick and easy to setup and equally fast when operated to diagnose a fault. The computational time obviously depends on the computer used but sensible figures for a current average computational capability

are listed in Table 2.16. The table reports the setup time and the diagnostics time relating them respectively to the number of rules to setup and the number of test cases to diagnose. These represent the elements on which the computational time has a stronger dependency. The diagnostics time for a single calculation is on the order of 0.1 second, as seen in the table.

Table 2.16.   Computational time with current computational capability

Processing	Time	Dependency
Setup time	1 min, 12 sec	331 rules
Diagnostic Time	2 min, 50 sec (0.1 sec/case)	1771 test cases

2.5.2. Diagnostics Capability in the Presence of Noisy Measurements: Accuracy

The sensitivity study illustrated in section 2.4.5 provided us with two best choices of layout for a fuzzy diagnostics system that required approximating and modelling the input–output functional relationship as defined in section 2.4.2. This section studies how these two systems perform when they are demanded to diagnose a fault given a set of measurements affected by noise. Moreover a way to enhance the accuracy changing the input MFs amplitude according to sensor noise RMSs is discussed. The systems have the following features:

- System 1 (best choice):
  - Functional parameters: AND=Product, Implication= Product, Aggregation=Summation, Defuzzification= Centroid.
  - System parameters: Gaussian MFs in input and output, maximum N of MFs fixed to 500, width of input MFs equal to 0.15, width of output MFs equal to 0.5, increment value of the search space equal to 0.5% (this identifies indirectly the output MFs number – see section 2.4.2.4).
- System 2 (second best choice):
  - Functional parameters: AND=Product, Implication= Product, Aggregation=Summation, Defuzzification= Centre of Maximum.
  - System parameters: Gaussian MFs in input and output, maximum N of MFs fixed to 500, width of input MFs equal to 0.15, width of output MFs equal to 1, increment value of the search space equal to 0.5%.

As far as the functional parameters are concerned, System 1 belongs to the category of SAM systems. On the other hand, System 2 is a quasi-SAM system: the main difference lies in the defuzzification algorithm, implemented as center of maximum (COM) function. The 1771 test cases were modified adding to the i-th element of the measurement set a random number that represents a realistic noise level according to the type of sensor required. The random number is generated as follows. Table 2.17 lists, for different types of sensors, realistic values of sensor noise standard deviations $SDTV_i$ as a percentage of the measured value, the noise being assumed to follow a Gaussian distribution. For each measurement of the 1771 test cases, a random number is generated from a normal distribution with mean zero, and standard deviation $SDTV_i$, according to the value in the table. This random number represents the % deviation the corresponding measurement must be varied to simulate the noise.

Table 2.17. Sensor noise standard deviations in % of the measured value

Sensor type	$STDV_i$
Temperature	0.4%
Pressure	0.25%
Fuel Flow	0.5%
Shaft Speed	0.05%

Once the random component is added to the measurements of the 1771 test cases to simulate the presence of noise, they are used to test Systems 1 and 2.

Figure 2.16 represents the Deltas between implanted and calculated performance parameter deteriorations for the 1771 cases.

Table 2.18. Statistics of the diagnostics results for System 1, Method 2

	η_{FAN}	Γ_{FAN}	η_{IPC}	Γ_{IPC}	η_{HPC}	Γ_{HPC}	η_{HPT}	Γ_{HPT}	η_{IPT}	Γ_{IPT}	η_{LPT}	Γ_{LPT}
μ	-0.08	-0.03	-0.04	-0.05	-0.14	-0.09	-0.12	0.02	-0.08	0.04	-0.04	-0.01
σ	0.64	0.30	0.39	0.35	0.58	0.34	0.41	0.37	0.41	0.30	0.33	0.29
$CI_{95\%}+$	1.16	0.56	0.72	0.64	1.01	0.57	0.68	0.75	0.73	0.62	0.61	0.56
$CI_{95\%}-$	-1.33	-0.62	-0.81	-0.74	-1.28	-0.75	-0.92	-0.70	-0.89	-0.54	-0.70	-0.58

The test cases are divided into six groups characterised by a different faulty component. Figure 2.16 considers, in each group, only the two parameters affected by deterioration and shows the Deltas only for them. Moreover, for each parameter in which deterioration is implanted, Table 2.18 reports the statistical results according to Method 2. It can be seen in Figure 2.16 how the values of Deltas are much higher compared to the case without noise. This can also be observed in Table 2.18 where high values of σ are reported. The RMS increased as well up to 0.147 (Method 3) and the results showed 483 cases (27%) with MS errors and 105 cases (5.9%) with HS errors (Method 1) – see Table 2.19.

Table 2.19. Summary of accuracy results for System 1 via Methods 1 and 3 over 1771 cases

case	Method 1		Method 3
	MS cases (N. // %)	HS cases (N. // %)	RMS
1	483 // 0.27	105 // 0.059	0.147

Table 2.20.   Statistics of the diagnostics results for System 1 with enhanced capability of dealing with noisy data, Method 2

	η_{FAN}	Γ_{FAN}	η_{IPC}	Γ_{IPC}	η_{HPC}	Γ_{HPC}	η_{HPT}	Γ_{HPT}	η_{IPT}	Γ_{IPT}	η_{LPT}	Γ_{LPT}
μ	-0.07	-0.02	-0.03	-0.02	-0.12	-0.03	-0.09	0.02	-0.07	0.04	-0.02	-0.01
σ	0.42	0.24	0.26	0.17	0.40	0.17	0.25	0.31	0.24	0.20	0.26	0.20
$CI_{95\%}+$	0.75	0.46	0.48	0.30	0.67	0.29	0.41	0.64	0.40	0.44	0.49	0.39
$CI_{95\%}-$	-0.89	-0.49	-0.54	-0.35	-0.90	-0.36	-0.58	-0.59	-0.55	-0.36	-0.53	-0.40

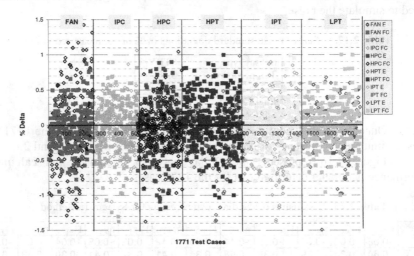

Figure 2.16.   SFI capability of System 1. Results for 1771 test cases.

To improve the system accuracy that is dramatically affected when noisy data are analysed, the input MFs amplitudes were modified. It was proved to be advantageous to differentiate them: different values of amplitude were used for different input. The most suitable choice was found to be to use as input MFs amplitude for the different measurement types exactly the values of sensor noise standard deviation listed in Table 2.17.

The improved results obtained with System 1 with enhanced capability of dealing with noisy data are shown in Figure 2.17. The deltas are considerably more localised within | 0.5 | %, and considering that this is also the order of magnitude of the noise introduced in some of the measurements, it is in the opinion of the authors a positive outcome. The improvement can also be appreciated in Table 2.20, noticing the considerable reduction of the values of σ. The RMS obtained with the enhanced system was reduced to 0.08 (Method 3) and the results showed 201 cases (11%) with MS errors and 33 cases (1.8%) with HS errors (Method 1) – see Table 2.21.

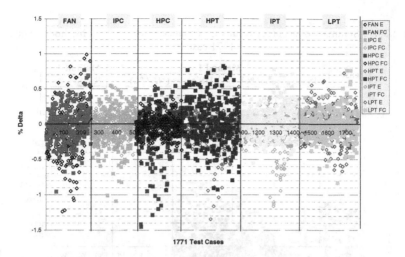

Figure 2.17. SFI capability of System 1 with enhanced capability of dealing with noisy data. Results for 1771 test cases.

Table 2.21. Summary of accuracy results for enhanced System 1 via Methods 1 and 3 over 1771 cases

case	Method 1		Method 3
	MS cases (N. // %)	HS cases (N. // %)	RMS
1	201 // 0.11	33 // 0.018	0.08

Due to the fact that Systems 1 and 2, as defined at the beginning of this section, provided similar type of outcomes, it was considered here worthwhile to also study the behaviour of System 2 in the presence of noise in the measurements. In the same way that System 1 was adapted to deal with noisy data, also for System 2 it was necessary to change the amplitudes of the input MFs according to the noise level implanted. Figure 2.18 shows the results obtained with the enhanced System 2. The outcome as expected is similar to the one previously reported for the enhanced System 1. The values of σ detailed in Table 2.22 (Method 2) are comparable in magnitude to the values of Table 2.20 for the enhanced System 1 even though slightly worse. The RMS obtained with the enhanced System 2 calculated for the 1771 cases was equal to 0.09 (Method 3) but the results showed 183 cases (10%) with MS errors and 30 cases (1.6%) with HS errors outperforming the enhanced System 1 when evaluating the system accuracy with Method 1 – see Table 2.23.

Table 2.22. Statistics of the diagnostics results for System 2 with enhanced capability of dealing with noisy data, Method 2

	η_{FAN}	Γ_{FAN}	η_{IPC}	Γ_{IPC}	η_{HPC}	Γ_{HPC}	η_{HPT}	Γ_{HPT}	η_{IPT}	Γ_{IPT}	η_{LPT}	Γ_{LPT}
μ	-0.06	-0.02	-0.03	-0.02	-0.10	-0.04	-0.08	0.02	-0.08	0.04	-0.02	0.00
σ	0.44	0.25	0.28	0.17	0.43	0.17	0.27	0.32	0.26	0.21	0.27	0.21
$CI_{95\%}+$	0.81	0.47	0.51	0.31	0.74	0.31	0.44	0.65	0.43	0.45	0.51	0.40
$CI_{95\%}-$	-0.92	-0.51	-0.58	-0.35	-0.95	-0.38	-0.61	-0.60	-0.58	-0.37	-0.56	-0.41

Table 2.23.   Summary of accuracy results for enhanced System 2 via Methods 1 and 3 over 1771 cases

| case | Method 1 | | Method 3 |
	MS cases (N. // %)	HS cases (N. // %)	RMS
1	183 // 0.10	30 // 0.016	0.09

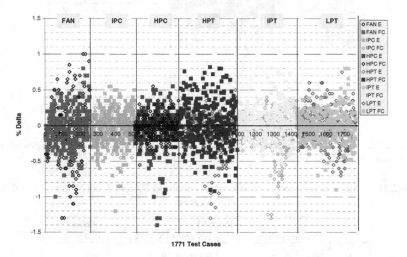

Figure 2.18.   SFI capability of System 2 with enhanced capability of dealing with noisy data. Results for 1771 test cases.

2.5.2.1. Remarks

It may be concluded that in this section an important milestone in this project was proved. Two fuzzy system layouts were identified as capable of performing SFI capability in the presence of noisy measurements and their accuracy was evaluated with the three different methods introduced in section 2.4.4.3. The enhanced System 1 outperformed the enhanced System 2 in the accuracy tests provided by Methods 2 and 3, but underperformed when the accuracy was estimated with Method 1.

2.5.3. Tuning Capability to Enhance the SFI Role in GPD

An SFI system is used to evaluate considerable changes in only two performance parameters of one component. The application of an SFI approach in a real-life case becomes useful under the assumption that only one component can be faulty. This assumption becomes more realistic if the changes are estimated in a short space of time, or else the diagnosis is made to assess only changes in the performance parameters from a very recent known condition. In fact, if on the contrary the time scale increases, it is more likely that two or more gas path components are degraded.

These considerations create a new opportunity of using SFI systems coupled with MFI systems (e.g., linear estimation methods). MFI approaches are limited when estimating considerable changes (i.e., > 1%) but are advantageous when calculating small deteriorations that inevitably affect all the parameters simultaneously over the engine operating time. The procedure represented in Figure 2.19 is an attempt at suggesting how this coupling could be implemented. The procedure described relies on the idea that SFI and MFI systems compute a solution in parallel for every flight mission of the engine. The two systems at flight n calculate deltas in measurements from a baseline not of a clean engine but of the global deterioration level estimated at flight n-1. Therefore the two systems do not calculate the absolute changes in performance parameters, with respect to a clean engine, but the relative changes with respect to the deteriorated condition evaluated at the previous flight. The relative changes computed at flight n are then added to the global deterioration level to obtain the absolute changes with respect to the clean condition.

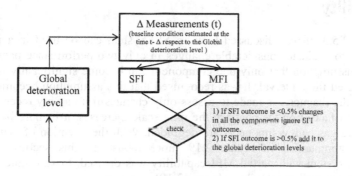

Figure 2.19. MFI and SFI coupling.

Let us assume that at flight number one the engine is clean and no deterioration is detected. At a given point in time (flight n) the MFI system detects small deteriorations in all performance parameters, no considerable changes (<0.5) are detected by the SFI and therefore it is ignored. At flight n+1 instead something happens and one component gets severely damaged. The SFI estimates changes > 0.5% (in a real application the value 0.5% should be replaced with a more correct value obtained in validating the suggested procedure), therefore the SFI outcome is used to update the global deterioration level instead of the MFI result.

In the light of this proposed framework, in this work an automated procedure (see GUI from section 2.4.3) was devised to tune the rules of the fuzzy diagnostics system on top of a known deterioration level for all the 12 performance parameters (baseline). This baseline is assumed to be calculated at the previous flight with an MFI method and represents the global deterioration level in Figure 2.19. Let us assume, for example, that the values listed in Table 2.24 represent the baseline of deterioration. The SFI is now required to assess whether there are considerable changes from this already existing level of deterioration.

The results shown in Figure 2.20 were obtained using the enhanced System 1 as defined in the previous section that was tuned to the baseline of Table

2.24. A new set of 1771 test cases were generated with fault implanted in the ranges defined by the search space identified in section 2.4.2.1 but superimposed on the global deteriorations of Table 2.24; the measurements calculated running the engine model were disturbed adding a random component according to the same procedure described in the previous section. It is important to observe that these results cannot precisely (i.e., case by case) be compared to the results from the previous set of test cases because, having added a random component, the two sets could have slightly different severity of noise level. But a comparison can be made looking at the statistical figures. Table 2.25 presents analogous results to Table 2.22 (Method 2). The RMS obtained with the tuned diagnostics system calculated for the 1771 cases was equal to 0.089 (Method 3) and the results showed 172 cases (9%) with MS errors and 22 cases (1.2%) with HS errors (Method 1) – see Table 2.26.

2.6.   A Fuzzy Diagnostics System with Partial MFI Capability

In section 2.5.3, it was discussed how an SFI system can be used in a real-life application to evaluate considerable changes in only two performance parameters, under the assumption that only one component can become significantly faulty in the considered time interval. It was recognised that this assumption becomes more realistic if the diagnosis is made to assess only changes from a very recent known condition. In fact, if on the contrary the time scale increases, it is more likely that two or more gas path components are degraded. With the intention of making the procedure summarized in Figure 2.19 more robust, in this section a fuzzy diagnostics system with partial MFI capability was devised, to substitute the SFI process in the coupling procedure (Figure 2.19).

Table 2.24.   Global deterioration level, baseline

$\Delta\eta_{FAN}$	$\Delta\Gamma_{FAN}$	$\Delta\eta_{IPC}$	$\Delta\Gamma_{IPC}$	$\Delta\eta_{HPC}$	$\Delta\Gamma_{HPC}$	$\Delta\eta_{HPT}$	$\Delta\Gamma_{HPT}$	$\Delta\eta_{IPT}$	$\Delta\Gamma_{IPT}$	$\Delta\eta_{LPT}$	$\Delta\Gamma_{LPT}$
-0.5	-0.4	-0.2	-0.5	-0.3	-0.2	-0.3	0.5	-0.4	0.3	-0.6	0.5

Table 2.25.   Statistics of the diagnostics results for tuned enhanced System 1, Method 2

	η_{FAN}	Γ_{FAN}	η_{IPC}	Γ_{IPC}	η_{HPC}	Γ_{HPC}	η_{HPT}	Γ_{HPT}	η_{IPT}	Γ_{IPT}	η_{LPT}	Γ_{LPT}
μ	-0.07	-0.02	-0.03	-0.02	-0.07	-0.01	-0.09	0.00	-0.06	0.02	-0.04	-0.02
σ	0.36	0.22	0.28	0.18	0.32	0.16	0.27	0.30	0.20	0.19	0.23	0.19
$CI_{95\%}+$	0.64	0.40	0.52	0.32	0.56	0.30	0.44	0.58	0.34	0.39	0.41	0.35
$CI_{95\%}-$	-0.78	-0.45	-0.58	-0.37	-0.70	-0.32	-0.62	-0.58	-0.46	-0.34	-0.50	-0.38

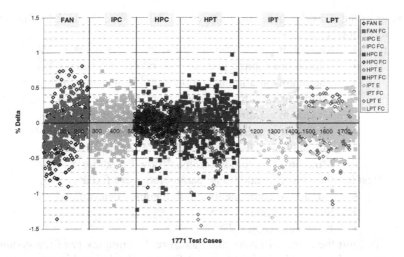

Figure 2.20. SFI capability of the tuned enhanced System 1. Results for 1771 test cases.

Table 2.26. Summary of accuracy results for tuned enhanced System 1 via Methods 1 and 3 over 1771 cases

case	Method 1		Method 3
	MS cases (N. // %)	HS cases (N. // %)	RMS
1	172 // 0.09	22 // 0.012	0.089

The process with partial MFI capability is in principle similar to the SFI systems described so far. It is able to quantify considerable deviation in performance parameters and it uses the nonlinear approach based on fuzzy logic. Moreover it is able to quantify changes in more than two parameters simultaneously: in this work the system was tested with up to two components degraded at a time, four parameters simultaneously deteriorated. In the context of section 2.5.3, this allows relaxing the previously stated assumption requiring that no more than two components can become considerably degraded in one mission.

2.6.1. System Layout

A fuzzy diagnostics system with partial MFI capability was devised in this work for a three-shaft turbofan engine. The inputs and outputs of the diagnostic process are the same shown in Figure 2.11 (section 2.4.2). The system is designed to assess performance parameters percentage changes from a clean engine condition (12 outputs) given the knowledge of the measurement changes (10 inputs) calculated as percentage deviations with respect to a baseline determined by means of an engine model run at the specific power setting and environmental conditions (defined in section 2.4.2).

This section describes a system able to quantify considerable changes in up to two components degraded simultaneously (four performance parameters)

according to the considerations made in section 2.2.4 – see Table 2.1. The search space was defined as follows:

- Maximum variation in compressors' efficiencies = –1%
- Minimum variation in compressors' efficiencies = –3%
- Maximum variation in compressors' flow capacities = –1%
- Minimum variation in compressors' flow capacities = –3%
- Maximum variation in turbines' efficiencies = –1%
- Minimum variation in turbines' efficiencies = –3%
- Maximum variation in turbines' flow capacities = –1%
- Minimum variation in turbines' flow capacities = –3%

Besides, the following additional parameters were fixed:

- Number of components simultaneously deteriorated = 2
- Step of increment = 0.5%
- Number of rules = 19440

To limit the number of rules and therefore the complexity of the system no rules were stated to provide the input–output functional relationship corresponding to fault levels between 0% and –1%. Note that even though the ranges in the search space are defined between –1% and –3%, the 0% fault levels are always included in the search space. Therefore, the above definition of search space only excludes the -0.5% fault level compared to the search space defined in section 2.4.2. This choice slightly affects the accuracy at low deterioration levels (around 0.5%) but it was recognised that a higher accuracy is required when assessing higher changes in the performance parameters (e.g., 3%). Besides, in this work a strong commitment was devoted to meeting the requirement of devising a fast system for on-wing applications, and therefore a reduction in the number of rules (excluding the –0.5% fault level) was driven by time-related concerns.

2.6.2. Partial MFI Capability: Results

2.6.2.1. Test Cases
A series of 1201 test cases resulting from the combinations of three fault levels (0, -1.2, -2.7) taken 4 at a time (4 parameters deteriorated at a time) was generated. A random component was added to the measurements of the test cases to simulate the presence of noise, according to the procedure described in section 2.5.2.

2.6.2.2. Results: Accuracy and Computational Time
Method 1 and 3 introduced in section 2.4.4.3 were used here to assess the system accuracy in performing partial MFI capability. The RMS obtained considering only the 12 outputs relative to the performance parameters, for the 1201 cases, was equal to 0.1123 (Method 3) and the results showed 201 cases (16.7%) with MS errors and 70 cases (5.8%) with HS errors (Method 1) – see Table 2.27.

A typical result, in addition to the 1201 cases, is presented in Table 2.28 and Table 2.29. Table 2.28 lists the implanted faults in the FAN and HPC. The 12 outputs of the diagnostics system are shown in Table 2.29. A remarkable concentration capability of the fuzzy diagnostics system can be noted.

As far as the computational time is concerned, Table 2.30 reports the setup time and diagnostics time together with the number of rules stated and the number of test cases diagnosed, representing the elements on which the computational time has a stronger dependency. A system with partial MFI capability requires a considerably increased number of rules (19440 in this example) that inevitably affects the computational time. The diagnostics time for a single calculation is approximately 12 seconds, about 100 times the time required by the corresponding system with SFI.

Table 2.27. Summary of accuracy results for System 1 via Methods 1 and 3 over 1201 cases

case	Method 1		Method 3
	MS cases (N. // %)	HS cases (N. // %)	RMS
1	201 // **0.1674**	70 // **0.0583**	0.1123

Table 2.28. Implanted deterioration (partial MFI)

$\Delta\eta_{FAN}$	$\Delta\Gamma_{FAN}$	$\Delta\eta_{IPC}$	$\Delta\Gamma_{IPC}$	$\Delta\eta_{HPC}$	$\Delta\Gamma_{HPC}$	$\Delta\eta_{HPT}$	$\Delta\Gamma_{HPT}$	$\Delta\eta_{IPT}$	$\Delta\Gamma_{IPT}$	$\Delta\eta_{LPT}$	$\Delta\Gamma_{LPT}$
-1.8	-2.2	0	0	-2.3	-2.7	0	0	0	0	0	0

Table 2.29. Estimated deterioration (partial MFI), typical result

$\Delta\eta_{FAN}$	$\Delta\Gamma_{FAN}$	$\Delta\eta_{IPC}$	$\Delta\Gamma_{IPC}$	$\Delta\eta_{HPC}$	$\Delta\Gamma_{HPC}$	$\Delta\eta_{HPT}$	$\Delta\Gamma_{HPT}$	$\Delta\eta_{IPT}$	$\Delta\Gamma_{IPT}$	$\Delta\eta_{LPT}$	$\Delta\Gamma_{LPT}$
-1.51	-2.43	-0.01	0.00	-2.38	-2.54	0.00	0.02	0.00	-0.00	0.01	0.03

Table 2.30. Computational time with current computational capability

Processing	Time	Dependency
Set-up time	18 min, 35 sec	19440 rules
Diagnostics Time	240 min (12 sec/case)	1201 test cases

2.7. Operating the Diagnostics Model through the GUI

The diagnostics software developed within this work is constituted by two GUIs. The first one, presented in Figure 2.14 of section 2.4.3, was devised to automatically set up a fuzzy diagnostics model. Figure 2.21 shows the second graphical user interface that operates the fuzzy diagnostic model previously set-up and assesses the changes in the 12 performance parameters. Once the engine and its simulation model are selected, the readings from the engine can be input and the diagnosis made by means of the diagnostic system previously generated and saved. Alternatively, a fault can be implanted simulating the corresponding measurements deviations using the engine model. These are used to test a new generated fuzzy diagnostics system with simulated data. This interface can be used to operate models either with or without capability of dealing with biases (Marinai, 2004), as mentioned in section 2.4.3, but this is not covered in this chapter. The results can be eventually plotted.

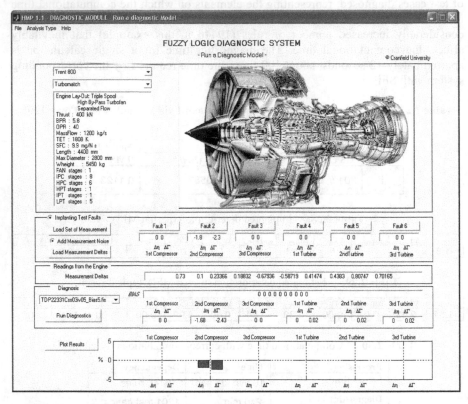

Figure 2.21.   GUI that operates the fuzzy diagnostic models.

2.8. Conclusions

Fuzzy logic is introduced in this work because of its inherent capability of dealing with GPD problems due to its rule-based nature and its fuzzy approach. This created a research opportunity, and a novel diagnostics procedure was devised; an application of the method to a three-shaft turbofan engine and its promising results were discussed in this chapter.

In the light of the technical requirements identified for advanced gas path diagnostics (see section 2.4.1), it can be concluded that fuzzy logic showed significant advantages and inherent features well suited to GPD problems, as discussed below.

> • Volponi (2003) pointed out the necessity to develop different algorithms to address the problem of estimating gradual and rapid deteriorations, namely, MFI (multiple fault isolation), generally based on linear approaches, and SFI (single fault isolation)

methods necessarily based on nonlinear approaches, respectively. The fuzzy diagnostics system described above was proved to preserve the nonlinearity present in the aero-thermal relationships between the performance parameters and the gas path measurements.

- Fuzzy diagnostics, as conceived in this chapter, in order to be effective, relies on the statement of an exhaustive number of rules defined within a performance parameters search space. This becomes cumbersome when the number of parameters that are considered simultaneously and that are changing increases (tests were performed with one gas path component degraded at a time – SFI, and with up to two components and so four performance parameters deteriorated at a time – partial MFI).

- Fuzzy diagnostics system with SFI or partial MFI capability can operate coupled with a linear MFI algorithm as long as a global deterioration level is updated every flight. The rules must be tuned over the calculated global deterioration level estimated at the previous flight; this is enabled by the significantly rapid set-up phase devised for the fuzzy diagnostics system presented above.

- Fuzzy diagnostics systems do not show a tendency to smear the results over all the performance parameters (that for example affects Kalman filter-based diagnostics methods), demonstrating on the contrary good concentration capability.

- Fuzzy diagnostics systems do not require completely observable systems with the same number of inputs and outputs. (A system $Z=h(X)$ is said to be completely observable if every state X (vector) can be determined from the observation of Z (vector) – Marinai, 2004.)

- A considerable enhancement of the diagnostics accuracy in the presence of noisy data can be obtained choosing the input measurement MFs amplitudes according to the different values of sensor noise standard deviations available for different sensors. Marinai (2004) formulates a statistical interpretation of the fuzzy systems. An analogous fuzzy diagnostics system was described in Marinai (2004) that was able to diagnose component faults in the presence of systematic errors in the measurements (bias) while identifying the faulty sensor as well. This result was achieved by means of a procedure that introduces the NOT operator in the statement of the rules.

- As far as the computational time is concerned, fuzzy diagnostics systems show:
  - Considerably fast setup phase (e.g., approximately 1 minute for an SFI system), especially when compared with the very long training period required by a neural network with comparable diagnostics features. This enables the setup of a

new system for a new operating condition or over a calculated deterioration baseline in a short period of time.
  – Fast diagnostics time suitable for on-line applications.
- The computational time depends on the number of rules stated and, therefore, on the number of parameters simultaneously deteriorated at a time.
- Fuzzy logic diagnostics models are advantageous when different sources of information (e.g., oil analysis, oil debris analysis, vibration analysis, expert knowledge, statistical inputs, etc.) need to be combined in the decision-making process (data fusion). Such a feature can also be used to combine results computed with different GPD techniques gaining in accuracy and reliability of the results. Once the diagnosis is performed, a prognostics algorithm (Marinai *et al.*, 2003b) can be introduced to assess and predict into the future health condition of the engine or one of its components for a fixed time horizon or predict the time to failure.
- The modular nature of the fuzzy rules stated to devise a diagnostics system enables the user with a high level of system comprehensibility.
- The adaptation of a fuzzy diagnostics system to different gas turbines is expected to be simple according to the procedures described above. However, a sensitivity study to optimise the fuzzy system parameters is strongly advisable.

References

1. Kandel A (1986) Fuzzy mathematical techniques with applications. Addison-Welsey, USA.
2. Kosko B (1997) Fuzzy engineering. Prentice Hall, New Jersey.
3. Marinai L, Ogaji S, Sampath S and Singh R (2003a) Engine Diagnostics - Fuzzy Logic Approach. In: Proceedings of the Seventh International Conference on Knowledge-Based Intelligent Information & Engineering Systems – KES'03, Oxford, 3-5 September.
4. Marinai L, Singh R and Curnock B (2003b) Fuzzy-logic-based diagnostic process for turbofan engines. In: Proceedings of ISABE 2003, XVI International Symposium on Air Breathing Engines, Cleveland, Ohio, 31 August - 5 September.
5. Marinai L, Singh R, Curnock B and Probert D (2003c) Detection and prediction of the performance deterioration of a turbofan engine. In: Proceedings of the International Gas Turbine Congress 2003, Tokyo, 2-7 November.
6. Marinai L (2004) Gas path diagnostics and prognostics for aero-engines using fuzzy logic and time series analysis (PhD Thesis). School of Engineering, Cranfield University.

7. Marinai L , Probert D and Singh R (2004) Prospects for aero gas-turbine diagnostics: a review. Applied Energy.
8. Mathioudakis K and Sieverding CH (2003) Gas Turbine Condition Monitoring & Fault Diagnosis. In: Von Karman Institute Lecture Series 2003-01, Brussels, Belgium, 13-17 January.
9. Volponi A (2003) Extending gas-path analysis coverage for other fault conditions. In: Von Karman Institute Lecture Series 2003-01, Gas Turbine Condition Monitoring & Fault Diagnosis, Brussels, Belgium, 13-17 January.
10. Zadeh LA (1969) Toward a theory of fuzzy systems. NASA CR-1432, Washington, DC.
11. Fuzzy Logic Toolbox User's Guide. The MathWorks Inc., Natick, MA.

3. Fault Detection and Isolation of Industrial Processes Using Optimized Fuzzy Models

Luis Mendonça, João Sousa and José Sá da Costa

Model-based fault detection and isolation represents an approach that has received increasing attention in the academic and industrial fields, due to economical and safety-related matters. This approach has a large variety of methods in the literature considering mathematical models and modern control theory. However, in practice it is very difficult to achieve accurate models for complex nonlinear plants. If the plant structure is not completely known, the diagnosis has to be based primarily on data or heuristic information. The inherent characteristics of fuzzy logic theory make it suitable for fault detection and isolation (FDI). Fault detection can benefit from nonlinear fuzzy modelling and its fast and robust implementation, its capacity to embed apriori knowledge and its ability of generalization. Consequently fault diagnosis can profit from a transparent reasoning system, which can embed operator experience, but also learn from experimental and/or simulation data. Thus, fuzzy logic-based diagnostic is advantageous since it allows the incorporation of apriori knowledge and lets the user understand the inference of the system. This chapter proposes the application of optimised fuzzy models to FDI systems, using a regularity criterion to select the relevant model inputs and a real-coded genetic algorithm to optimise the fuzzy models. An industrial valve simulator is used to obtain abrupt and incipient faults in the system. The optimised fuzzy models used in the FDI system were able to detect and isolate the twelve abrupt and incipient faults considered.

3.1. Introduction

A system that includes the capacity of detecting, isolating and identifying faults is called a fault diagnosis and isolation system (FDI) (Chen and Patton, 1999). Fault detection and isolation methods are used to detect any discrepancy between the system outputs and model outputs. It is assumed that these discrepancy signals are related to a fault. However, the same difference signals respond to model plant mismatches or noise in real measurements, which are erroneously detected as a fault. For a simple fault that can be detected by a single measurement, a conventional threshold check may be appropriated. However, since in complex industrial systems it is usually very difficult to directly measure the state of the process, more sophisticated solutions are needed. In this case a model-based approach will be more suitable. This requires process modelling, which proves to be a very demanding task, especially when dealing with a nonlinear process.

The idea of model-based fault detection is to compare output signals of the model with the real measurements available in the process, thereby generating the residuals, which are fault indicators giving information about the location and timing of a fault. There is an increasing demand for man-made dynamical systems to become safer and more reliable. These requirements extend to process industrial plants, which are basically controlled by servo-actuated flow control valves. Taking into consideration that malfunction of a valve in many hazardous applications can cause serious consequences, the fault diagnosis of industrial servo-actuated valves is a very important task. When the malfunction is detected and isolated, a quick response might prevent the monitored system from expensive damages and loss of efficiency and productivity.

The developments of model-based fault diagnosis began at various places in the early 1970s. This approach to fault diagnosis in dynamic systems has been receiving more and more attention over the last two decades. The availability of a good model of the monitored system can significantly improve the performance of diagnostic tools, minimizing the probability of false alarms. The inconsistency between the data from the system measurements and the corresponding signals of the model is called a *residual*. The *residual generation* is then identified as an essential problem in model-based FDI, since if it is not performed correctly, some fault information could be lost. Therefore, the model-based FDI approach requires precise mathematical relationships relating the model to the process, to allow detection of small abrupt and incipient faults quickly and reliably.

Different analytical estimation methods are available, such as Kalman filters (Eide and Maybeck, 1996) and Luenberger observers (Clark, 1979), among others (Chen and Patton, 1999). However, the requirements for precise and accurate analytical models imply that any resulting modelling error will affect the performance of the resulting FDI system. This is particularly true for dynamically nonlinear and uncertain systems, which represent the majority of real processes. Therefore, the main assumption made when using the model-based FDI approach is that a precise mathematical model of the plant is required. This makes quantitative model-based approaches very difficult to use in real systems, since any non-modelled dynamics can affect the performance of the FDI scheme. A way to overcome this problem is to design robust algorithms, where the effects of disturbances on the residual are minimized, and the sensitivity to faults is maximized. Many approaches have been developed including unknown input observers (Duan and Patton, 2001; Frank, 1990) and eigenstructure assignment observers (Shen *et al.*, 1998), as well as frequency domain techniques for robust FDI filters (Gertler, 1998), such as minimization of multiobjective functions that did not prove to be successful for nonlinear cases.

Recently, soft computing methods like neural networks, expert systems, fuzzy systems and neuro-fuzzy systems have been used with relative success (Calado *et al.*, 2001). Fuzzy techniques have received special attention due to their fast and robust implementation, their capacity to embed apriori knowledge, their performance in reproducing nonlinear mappings, and their ability of generalization. The description of some nonlinear systems can be very difficult to achieve by means of analytical equations. The use of fuzzy systems theory is a natural tool to handle nonlinear and uncertain conditions. The use of fuzzy models increases the capability of FDI to work with systems characterized by incomplete information and noise. Thus, fuzzy logic techniques are now being investigated in the FDI research community as a powerful modelling and decision-making tool (Borner and Isermann, 2003), along with neural networks (Schwarte *et al.*, 2003) and other more traditional techniques such as nonlinear and robust observers (Chen and Patton, 1999), parity space methods (Gertler, 1998; Kinnaert, 2003), and hypothesis-testing theory (Laengst *et al.*, 2003). The key advantage of fuzzy logic is that it enables the system behaviour to be described by "if-then" relations. The main trend in developing fuzzy FDI systems has been to generate residuals using either parameter estimation or observers, and allocate the decision-making to a fuzzy-logic inference engine. By doing so, it has been possible to combine symbolic knowledge with quantitative information and, thereby, minimize the false alarm rate. Indeed, the key benefit of fuzzy logic is that it lets the operator describe the system behaviour or the fault–symptom relationship with simple "if-then" rules (Koscielny and Syfert, 2003).

In this chapter, a model-based fuzzy FDI approach is presented. The symptoms are generated using fuzzy observers and plant measurements. The underlying idea is to predict the system outputs from the available inputs and outputs of the process, thus identifying a fuzzy model directly from data. The residual is then a weighted difference between the predicted and the actual outputs. In our approach, fuzzy observers are built for normal and faulty operations allowing the detection and isolation of the considered faults. The structure of the fuzzy models for FDI is determined using the regularity criterion (RC) to find, automatically, the relations between input and output variables, as presented in (Sugeno and Yasukawa, 1993). The obtained model is optimised by using a real-coded genetic algorithm (GA) introduced in (Setnes and Roubos, 2000). This chapter proposes the use of RC and GA for identifying fuzzy models of an industrial valve, to be used for detection and isolation of abrupt and incipient faults.

The chapter is organized as follows. Section 3.2 presents a brief overview of methods for fault detection and isolation. In this section, classical and fuzzy methods for FDI are presented. Further, a fuzzy model-based architecture for FDI is proposed. Fuzzy modelling is briefly presented in Section 3.3, where the regularity criterion is described. The GA for optimal parameter estimation is described in Section 3.4. The case study and the obtained results are presented in Section 3.5. Finally, the conclusions are drawn in Section 3.6.

3.2. Fault Detection and Isolation

Different approaches have been developed in FDI. One of the first ones was the *failure detection filter*, which is applied to linear systems (Beard, 1971). After that, different methods and approaches were developed such as the application of identification methods to fault detection of jet engines (Rault *et al.*, 1971) and the correlation methods applied to leak detection (Siebert and Isermann, 1976). Some years later, Isermann (1984) presented a survey on process fault detection methods based on modelling parameters and state estimations. Model-based methods for fault detection and diagnosis applied to chemical processes are presented in

(Himmelblau, 1978), the first book about this approach. In the frequency domain, FDI is applied using the frequency spectra as criterion to isolate the faults (Ding and Frank, 2000). Other FDI approaches are based on residual generators. These generators are based on approaches like physical or hardware redundancy methods, or analytical or functional redundancy methods (Chen and Patton, 1999).

   Physical or hardware redundancy methods are a traditional approach to fault diagnosis, which use multiple sensors, actuators and components to measure and control a particular variable. The major problems encountered with these methods are the extra equipment and maintenance cost, as well as the additional space required to accommodate this equipment (Isermann and Ballé, 1997). These disadvantages increase the necessity of using other methods, easier to use and with small costs. Therefore, *analytical or functional redundancy methods* can be used instead. These methods use redundant analytical relationships among various measured variables of the monitored system (Chen and Patton, 1999).

3.2.1. Analytical Redundancy Methods

In the analytical redundancy scheme, the resulting difference generated from the comparison of different variables is called the *residual* or *symptom signal*. These variables are measured signals with estimated values, generated by a mathematical model of the considered system. When the system is in normal operation the residual should be close to zero, and when the fault occurs the residual should be larger than zero. This property of residuals is used to determine whether or not faults have occurred. Some examples of residual generators based on the analytical redundancy scheme are the Kalman filter, Luenberger observers, state and output observers and parity relations, among others (Chen and Patton, 1999).

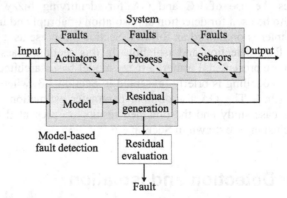

Figure 3.1.   Diagram of model-based fault detection.

   The model-based FDI method can be defined as the *detection* and *isolation* of faults in a system by means of methods that extract features from residual signals. Setting fixed or variable thresholds on residual signals generated from differences between actual measurements and their estimates obtained by using the process model thus detect faults. A number of residuals can be designed, where each one of them must be sensitive to individual faults occurring in different locations of the system. The analysis of each residual, once the threshold is exceeded, leads to the fault isolation. The general principle of model-based FDI is presented in Figure 3.1, where the two main stages are: *residual generation* and *residual evaluation*, which can be described as follows:

(1) **Residual generation** – generates residual signals using available inputs and outputs from the monitored system.

(2) **Residual evaluation** – examines residuals for the likelihood of faults and the decision rule is then applied to determine if a fault occurred.

The accuracy of the model describing the behaviour of the monitored system is crucial in model-based fault detection. However, the impossibility of obtaining complete knowledge and understanding of the monitored process increases the uncertainty in the model. Therefore, methods to reduce sensitivity to modelling uncertainty are used in FDI. However, sensitivity reduction sometimes does not solve the problem, since the sensitivity reduction may be associated with a reduction of the sensitivity to faults (Chen and Patton, 1999; Gertler, 1998). Thus, the main reliability problem of FDI is modelling uncertainty, which is unavoidable in real industrial systems. The design of an effective and reliable FDI scheme for residual generation should take into account modelling uncertainty with respect to sensitivity to faults. The problems introduced by model uncertainties, disturbances and noises in model-based FDI have been considered in (Gertler, 1998).

The generation of symptoms is therefore the main issue in model-based fault diagnosis. When the systems are in faulty state, the symptoms present the fault behaviour. Considering two different types of behaviour, the faults used in this chapter are either *abrupt* or *incipient*

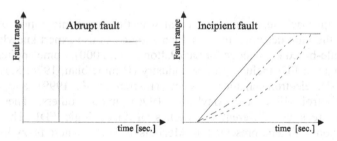

Figure 3.2.   Abrupt and incipient faults behaviour.

Abrupt faults are faults modelled as stepwise function and incipient faults are faults modelled by using smooth functions, i.e., functions that vary slowly with time. Figure 3.2 presents the behavior of abrupt and incipient faults. Considering the problems concerning modelling of industrial processes, the diagnosis of *incipient faults* using model-based FDI is sometimes very difficult. This situation is the consequence of a small visibility in the first moments of residuals when an incipient fault occurs, because they can be hidden by the uncertainty. The increasing interest in incipient fault detection demands finding new approaches. The developed FDI techniques present different properties with respect to diagnosis of different faults. This development achieved a reliable FDI technique because it includes the advantages of integrating different methods. In (Isermann and Ballé,

1997) some basic FDI methods are evaluated, and the trends in the application of model-based FDI to technical processes are presented.

When information about relations between symptoms and faults is available in the form of diagnostic models, various methods of reasoning can be applied. Typical approximate reasoning methods are:

- Probabilistic reasoning;
- Possibilistic reasoning with fuzzy logic;
- Reasoning with artificial neural networks.

Methods like neural networks, expert systems, fuzzy systems and neuro-fuzzy systems have been used with success in model-based FDI (Calado *et al.*, 2001). From the several described possibilities, fuzzy logic is a natural tool to handle complicated and uncertain conditions, considering that the characteristics of the systems are not precisely known. Sometimes, noise contamination and uncertainty effects affect the residuals in fault-free conditions. The consequence of this influence is the residual variation around the zero. This situation is very dangerous because it hides faulty effects. The capability to describe vague and imprecise facts and work with systems when complete information is not available makes fuzzy logic a powerful tool in this case. The fuzzy approach in FDI is used to generate symptoms, i.e., fuzzy descriptions, to detect and to isolate the fault (Dexter and Benouarets, 1997; Isermann, 1998). Takagi-Sugeno fuzzy models can be used to describe nonlinear dynamics of a plant where faults can occur, see e.g. (Hellendoorn *et al.*, 2001; Mendonca *et al.*, 2003).

3.2.2. Fuzzy Methods in FDI

The fuzzy approach supports in a natural way the direct integration of a human operator in the fault detection process. Fuzzy logic can use expert knowledge in the form of a rule-based knowledge format (Patton *et al.*, 2000). Some application areas of fuzzy logic in FDI include process industry (Himmelblau, 1978; Koscielny and Syfert, 2003), electromechanical systems (Insfran *et al.*, 1999), and traffic and avionics control (Eide and Maybeck, 1996) among others. These possible application areas use different approaches of fuzzy logic FDI. The frequency spectrum is one of them, presented in (Mechefske, 1998), where fuzzy logic is used to classify the frequency spectra of various rolling element bearing with faults.

The use of model-based FDI is another approach, as presented in (Lu *et al.*, 1998), where diagnostic models containing a fast fuzzy rule generation algorithm and a rule-based inference engine are used. The use of fuzzy reference models is proposed in (Dexter and Benouarets, 1997). In this approach, fuzzy models describe faulty and normal operation, and a classifier based on fuzzy matching performs diagnosis. In (Lopez-Toribio *et al.*, 2000), an approach is proposed where identification of local linear models using the TS fuzzy modelling strategy is solved using a convex optimisation technique involving linear matrix inequalities in order to find the optimum set of fuzzy models. The approach presented in this chapter is also based on fuzzy models. The fuzzy models to be used in FDI are obtained using the automatic approach proposed in (Vieira *et al.*, 2004, 2005).The next section presents the proposed architecture for FDI used in this chapter, as introduced in (Mendonca *et al.*, 2003).

3.2.3. Proposed Architecture for FDI

This chapter uses a straightforward architecture to detect, isolate and identify faults. The FDI system is based on fuzzy models identified directly from data and optimised using genetic algorithms. The model-based technique uses an optimised fuzzy model for the process running in normal operation, and one optimised model for each of the faults to be detected. Suppose that a process is running, and n possible faults can be detected. The fault detection and isolation system proposed for these n faults is depicted in Figure 3.3.

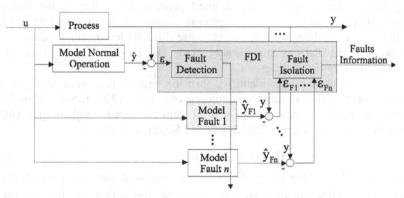

Figure 3.3.   Fault detection and identification scheme.

The multidimensional input of the system, **u**, enters both the process and an optimised model (observer) in normal operation. The vector of residuals ε is defined as

$$\varepsilon = \mathbf{y} - \hat{\mathbf{y}},\qquad(1)$$

where **y** is the output of the system and $\hat{\mathbf{y}}$ is the output of the optimised model in normal operation. When any component of ε is larger than a certain threshold δ, the system indicates a fault occurrence, i.e., a fault is detected. In this case, n optimised models, one for each fault, are activated, and n vectors of residuals are computed. Each residual i, with $i=1,...,n$, is computed as

$$\varepsilon_{F_i} = \mathbf{y} - \hat{\mathbf{y}}_{F_i},\qquad(2)$$

where $\hat{\mathbf{y}}_{F_i}$ is the output of the observer for fault i. The residuals $\varepsilon_{F_i},...,\varepsilon_{F_n}$ are evaluated, and the fault or faults isolated are the outputs of the FDI system. In this chapter, all models, i.e., the model for normal operation and the models for the n faults, are fuzzy models reproducing the dynamic behaviour of the process, for each considered situation, i.e., normal operation and system operating while any of the n faults occurred. This technique proved to be adequate to identify models extracted from real data, as in the example described in this chapter, which is an industrial servo-actuated pneumatic valve with six abrupt faults and six incipient faults.

Considering that this chapter proposes a fuzzy model-based FDI technique, the next section presents briefly fuzzy modelling.

3.3.   Fuzzy Modelling

Fuzzy modelling often follows the approach of encoding expert knowledge expressed in a verbal form in a collection of if-then rules, creating a model structure. Parameters in this structure can be adapted using input–output data. When no prior knowledge about the system is available, a fuzzy model can be constructed entirely on the basis of system measurements. In the following, we consider data-driven modelling based on fuzzy clustering. This approach avoids the well-known bottleneck of knowledge acquisition (Babuska, 1998; Sousa and Kaymak, 2002). Fuzzy models are acquired from sampled process data, utilizing the functional approximation capabilities of fuzzy systems. Assume that data from an unknown system $y = F(\mathbf{x})$ is observed. The aim is to use this data to construct a deterministic function $y = f(\mathbf{x})$ that can approximate $F(\mathbf{x})$. The function f is represented as a collection of fuzzy if-then rules.

The system to be identified can be represented as a multiple-input multiple-output (MIMO) nonlinear autoregressive (NARX) model. This MIMO system can be decomposed into several multiple-input single-output (MISO) models, without loss of generality (Sousa and Kaymak, 2002)

$$\hat{y}(k+1) = f(x(k)), \qquad (3)$$

where $x(k) \subset \mathbf{R}^n$ is the state of the system, and contains previous inputs and outputs. Only MISO models are considered in the following, for the sake of simplicity. We consider rule-based models of the Takagi-Sugeno (TS) type (Takagi and Sugeno, 1985). The representation of (3) as an affine TS model is given by

$$R_i : \textbf{If } x_1 \textbf{ is } A_{i1} \textbf{ and } ... \textbf{ and } x_n \textbf{ is } A_{in}$$
$$\textbf{then } y_i = a_{i1}x_1 + \cdots + a_{in}x_n + a_{i(n+1)} \qquad (4)$$

with $i = 1,2,\ldots,K$, where K is the number of fuzzy rules. Here, R_i is the i-th rule, A_{i1}, ..., A_{in} are fuzzy sets defined in the antecedent space, $\mathbf{x} = [x_1, \ldots, x_n]^T$ is the antecedent vector, and y_i is the rule output variable. The aggregated output of the model, $\hat{y}$, is calculated by taking the weighted average of the rule consequents:

$$\hat{y} = \frac{\sum_{i=1}^{K} \beta_i y_i}{\sum_{i=1}^{K} \beta_i}, \qquad (5)$$

where β_i is the degree of activation of the i-th rule:

$$\beta_i = \prod_{j=1}^{n} \mu_{A_{ij}}(x_j), \quad i = 1,2,\ldots,K \qquad (6)$$

and $\mu_{A_{ij}}(x_j) : \mathbf{R} \to [0,1]$ is the membership function of the fuzzy set A_{ij} in the antecedent of R_i. The nonlinear identification problem is solved in two steps: structure identification and parameter estimation.

3.3.1.   Structure Identification

In this step, the designer must choose first the order of the model and the significant state variables x of the model. To identify the model (4), the regression matrix $\mathbf{X}^T = [x_1, \ldots, x_N]$ and an output vector $\mathbf{y}^T = [y_1, \ldots, y_N]$ are constructed from the available data. Here $N \gg n$ is the number of samples used for identification. The objective of identification is to construct the unknown nonlinear function $\mathbf{y} = f(\mathbf{x})$ from the data, where f is the TS fuzzy model in (3).

Considering complex processes with a large number of controlled variables, the use of an automatic approach to obtain the structure identification of fuzzy models is an interesting approach, because it is difficult to find the relations between input and output variables. As the relations between the process variables are not well known, an automatic criterion is used to determine which input variables influence each output. In this chapter, a *regularity criterion* (*RC*) is used to choose the fuzzy model structure (Sugeno and Yasukawa, 1993). To apply this criterion, the identification data must be divided into two groups, A and B. The regularity criterion is used e.g. for group method of data handling, and it is defined as follows:

$$RC = \left[\sum_{i=1}^{k_A} (y_i^A - y_i^{AB})^2 / k_A + \sum_{i=1}^{k_B} (y_i^B - y_i^{BA})^2 / k_B \right] / 2 \tag{7}$$

where k_A and k_B are the number of data points of groups A and B, respectively, y_i^A and y_i^B are the output data of groups A and B, respectively, y^{AB} is the model output for group A estimated using the data from group B, and y^{BA} is the model output for group B estimated using the data from group A.

Thus, using two groups of data, A and B, two fuzzy models are built for each group, starting with only one input. The RC is computed for each model, and the one that minimizes RC is selected as the best one. In the next step, the input already selected is fixed, i.e., it belongs to the system's structure, and different input candidates are added to the previous fuzzy model from the remaining ones. When this second step finishes, the fuzzy model has two inputs. This second input is chosen as the one that minimizes the value of RC, as before. This procedure repeats until the value of RC increases. This method implies that a fuzzy model must be created each iteration. The number of fuzzy rules (or clusters) that best suits the data must be determined for that identification. The criterion to determine the number of clusters is based on the evaluation of the cost function $S(c)$ proposed in (Sugeno and Yasukawa, 1993):

$$S(c) = \sum_{k=1}^{N} \sum_{i=1}^{c} (\mu_{ik})^m \left(\|x_k - v_i\|^2 - \|v_i - \bar{x}\|^2 \right) \tag{8}$$

where N is the number of data to be clustered, c is the number of clusters ($c \geq 2$), x_k is the kth data point, $\bar{x}$ is the mean value for the inputs, v_i is the center of the ith cluster, μ_{ik} is the grade of the kth data point belonging to the ith cluster and m is an adjustable weight. The number of clusters c is increased from 2 up to the number that gives the minimum value for $S(c)$. Note that this minimum can be local. However, this procedure diminishes the number of rules and consequently the complexity of the fuzzy model. The parameter m has a great importance in this criterion. The bigger the m is the bigger the optimum number of clusters. This value is adjustable and is usually between 1.5 and 2, see (Sugeno and Yasukawa, 1993).

Having the inputs selected by the RC algorithm and the number of clusters from Eq. (8), a fuzzy model using the Gustafson-Kessel (GK) fuzzy clustering algorithm (Gustafson and Kessel, 1979) is built. Using this algorithm it is possible to exclude variables with poor performance. Summarizing, the structure of fuzzy models is obtained using the following algorithm:

1. *Cluster the data using fuzzy c-means with 2 initial clusters and compute (8);*
2. *Increase the number of clusters until (8) reaches its minimum;*
3. *Divide the data set into two groups A and B;*
4. *REPEAT for each state in the state vector that does not belong to the inputs of the model;*
5. *Build two models, one using data group A and other using data group B;*
6. *Compute (7);*
7. *Select the input with the lowest RC as a new input of the model;*
8. *UNTIL RC increases or the end of the state vector is reached;*
9. *Select the final inputs;*
10. *Using the number of clusters given from (8) and the inputs selected by (7), build a fuzzy model using GK clustering algorithm.*

3.3.2. Parameter Estimation

The number of rules, K, the antecedent fuzzy sets, A_{ij}, and the consequent parameters, $\mathbf{a}_i = [a_{i1}, \ldots, a_{in}, a_{i(n+1)}]$ are determined in this step, by means of fuzzy clustering in the product space of $X \times Y$. Given $\mathbf{Z}^T = [\mathbf{X}, \mathbf{y}]$ to be clustered and an estimated number of clusters K, the GK clustering algorithm proposed in (Gustafson and Kessel, 1979) is applied to compute the fuzzy partition matrix $\mathbf{U}$. Unlike the popular fuzzy c-means algorithm (Bezdek, 1981), the Gustafson-Kessel algorithm applies an adaptive distance measure.

The fuzzy sets in the antecedent of the rules are obtained from the partition matrix $\mathbf{U}$, whose ikth element $\mu_{ik} \in [0,1]$ is the membership degree of the data object $\mathbf{z}_k$ in cluster i. One-dimensional fuzzy sets A_{ij} are obtained from the multidimensional fuzzy sets defined pointwise in the ith row of the partition matrix by projections onto the space of the input variables x_j:

$$\mu_{A_{ij}}(x_{jk}) = \text{proj}_j(\mu_{ik}), \qquad (9)$$

where proj is the pointwise projection operator (Kruse *et al.*, 1994). The pointwise defined fuzzy sets A_{ij} are approximated by suitable parametric functions in order to compute $\mu_{A_{ij}}(x_j)$ for any value of x_j. The consequent parameters for each rule are obtained using a common weighted least-square estimation. Let $\mathbf{X}_e$ denote the matrix $[\mathbf{X};\mathbf{1}]$ and let $\mathbf{W}_i$ denote a diagonal matrix in $\mathbf{R}^{NxN}$ having the degree of activation, $\beta_i(\mathbf{x}_k)$, as its kth diagonal element as defined in (6). Assuming that the columns of $\mathbf{X}_e$ are linearly independent and $\beta_i(\mathbf{x}_k) > 0$ for $1 \le k \le N$, the weighted least-squares solution of $\mathbf{y} = \mathbf{X}_e \mathbf{a}_i + \varepsilon$ becomes

$$\mathbf{a}_i = \left[\mathbf{X}_e^T \mathbf{W}_i \mathbf{X}_e \right]^{-1} \mathbf{X}_e^T \mathbf{W}_i \mathbf{y}. \qquad (10)$$

3.4. Optimal Parameter Estimation Using Genetic Algorithms

Fuzzy models obtained using the identification method presented in the previous section are usually not optimal. This section presents the optimisation method for fuzzy models that uses a real-coded genetic algorithm proposed in (Setnes and Roubos, 2000).

Among the techniques especially suitable for constrained, nonlinear optimisation problems are the *evolutionary computation* techniques, which include evolutionary strategies (Rault *et al.*, 1971), evolutionary programming (Fogel, 1991) and *genetic algorithms* (GA). In the following, we concentrate on GA since they are the most studied and described methodology (Michalewicz, 1999).

Genetic algorithms can be used for a variety of purposes, their most important application being in the field of optimisation because of their ability to search efficiently in large search spaces, which makes them more robust with respect to the complexity of the optimisation problem compared to the more-conventional optimisation techniques (Michalewicz, 1999). Since Holland (1971) first proposed the idea of genetic algorithms, many researchers have suggested extensions and variations to the basic genetic algorithm. With the advent of artificial intelligence techniques, many applications of the genetic algorithms have been reported, especially in combination with other artificial intelligence techniques such as neural networks and fuzzy systems. Gradually, genetic algorithms are becoming an important part of hybrid intelligent systems.

GA are inspired by the biological process of natural selection, performing selection, crossover and mutation over a population, in order to achieve a global optimum. Instead of searching from general-to-specific hypotheses or from simple-to-complex, genetic algorithms generate successor hypotheses by repeatedly mutating and recombining parts of the best currently known hypotheses. GA are applied to an existing population of individuals, the chromosomes. At each iteration of the genetic process, an evolution is obtained by replacing elements of the population by offspring of the most fitted elements of that same population. In this way, the best fit individuals have a higher probability of having their offspring (that represent variations of itself) included in the next generation. GA evaluates the individuals in the population by using a *fitness function*. This function indicates how good a candidate solution is. It can be compared with an objective function in classical optimisation. Inspired by the "survival of the fittest" idea, the genetic algorithms maximise the fitness value, in contrast with classical optimisation, where one usually minimises the objective function. It has been observed that genetic algorithms are valuable optimisation tools, especially for nonconvex optimisation in the presence of constraints (Michalewicz, 1999).

The fitness of the individuals within the population is assessed, and new individuals are generated for the next generation. The following genetic operators are available for this purpose:

- **Selection** – chooses chromosomes according to their fitness for mating, i.e., for producing offspring. Fitter individuals get a higher probability to mate, and their genetic material is exploited.

- **Crossover** – exchanges genetic material in the form of short allele strings (a part of a chromosome) between the parent chromosomes. This reordering or recombination includes the effects of both exploration and exploitation.
- **Mutation** – introduces new genetic material by random changes to explore the search space.

The chromosome representation determines the GA structure. With a population size equal to L, the parameters of each fuzzy model are encoded in a chromosome S_l, with $l = 1, \ldots, L$ as a sequence of elements describing the fuzzy sets in the rule antecedents followed by the parameters of the rule consequents. Considering a model with M fuzzy rules, an n-dimensional premise and $n + 1$ parameters in each consequent function, a chromosome is encoded as:

$$s_l = \left(ant_1, \ldots, ant_M, \mathbf{a}_1, \ldots, \mathbf{a}_M \right), \tag{11}$$

where $\mathbf{a}_i$ contains the consequent parameters of rule R_i, and ant_i contains the parameters of the antecedent fuzzy sets A_{ij}, $j = 1, \ldots, n$. In the initial population $S^0 = \left\{ s_1^0, \ldots, s_L^0 \right\}$, s_1^0 is the initial model, and $s_2^0, \ldots, s_L^0$ are created by random variation (uniform distribution) around s_l^0 within the defined constraints (Setnes and Roubos, 2000).

The evolutionary process presented in this chapter is supported by a roulette wheel elitist selection method. This means that the chromosomes which yield a better fitness have a higher chance to survive and generate offspring and that the best fit chromosome in a certain generation always survives and evolves to the following generation. In order to establish a relation between the fitness of the chromosomes and the probability of their selection for operation (manipulation by a genetic operator) or deletion the following formula is used:

$$P_i = \frac{\min_j (J_j)}{J_i}, i, j = 1, \ldots, L, \tag{12}$$

where J_i is the performance of an individual measured in terms of the *mean squared error* (MSE):

$$J_i = \frac{1}{N} \sum_{k=1}^{N} (y_k - \hat{y}_k)^2, \tag{13}$$

where y_k is the real output of the system, and $\hat{y}_k$ is the output estimated by the fuzzy model. When a chromosome is selected for an operation, the chance of its manipulation by a crossover operator is 95% and the probability of a mutation occuring is 5%.

To promote the evolution of the population towards a better fitness in the concerned domain, two major types of genetic operators are used: crossover and mutation. In this chapter, when a chromosome is selected for a genetic operation, each of the two operators has equal chance of being applied.

Let $t = 0,1,\ldots,N_g$ be the generation number, s_u and s_v be chromosomes selected for operation, $k \in \{1,\ldots,L\}$ is the position of an element in the chromosome and $u_k^{\min} = 0$ and $u_k^{\max} = 1$ are the lower and upper bounds on the parameter encoded by element k. Real-coded GA is used because binary-coded or classical

GAs (Goldberg, 1989) are less efficient when applied to multidimensional or high precision problems. The bit strings can become very long and the search space blows up (Michalewicz, 1999). In this chapter, three different types of crossover operations are considered:

- Simple arithmetic crossover, where s_u^t and s_v^t are crossed over at the ℓ th position (ℓ being chosen randomly), thus creating two offsprings:

$$s_u^{t+1} = \left(u_1,...,u_\ell,v_{\ell+1},...,v_g \right) \tag{14}$$

and

$$s_v^{t+1} = \left(v_1,...,v_\ell,u_{\ell+1},...,u_g \right). \tag{15}$$

- Whole arithmetic crossover, where $r \in [0,1]$ is a random number with uniform distribution, and a linear combination of s_u^t and s_v^t results in:

$$s_u^{t+1} = r(s_u^t)+(1-r)s_v^t \tag{16}$$

and

$$s_v^{t+1} = r(s_v^t)+(1-r)s_u^t. \tag{17}$$

- Heuristic crossover, where s_u^t and s_v^t are combined creating two offsprings:

$$s_u^{t+1} = s_u^t +r(s_v^t - s_u^t) \tag{18}$$

and

$$s_v^{t+1} = s_v^t +r(s_u^t - s_v^t). \tag{19}$$

These operators revealed to be the most appropriate for the current optimisation. Three mutation operators have been considered, which are the following:

- Uniform mutation, where a random selected element v_ℓ is replaced by v_ℓ' which is a number in the range $\left[u_\ell^{\min},u_\ell^{\max} \right]$.
- Multiple uniform mutation, which is a uniform mutation of ℓ randomly selected elements.
- Gaussian mutation, where all elements of a chromosome are mutated such that

$$s_u^{t+1} = (u_1',...,u_k',...,u_g'), \tag{20}$$

where $u_\ell' = u_\ell + f_\ell$, with $\ell = 1,...,g$, and f_ℓ is a random number drawn from a Gaussian distribution.

The genetic algorithm for fuzzy model optimisation, as used in this chapter, is summarized as follows (Setnes and Roubos, 2000):

Given the data matrix Z and the structure of the fuzzy rule base derived using the RC in (7), select the number of generations N_g and the population size L.

1. *Create the initial population based on the derived fuzzy model structure.*

2. *Repeat genetic optimisation for t = 1, ...,N_g:*
    a) *Select the chromosomes for operation and deletion.*
    b) *Create the next generation: operate on the chromosomes selected for operation and substitute the chromosomes selected for deletion by the resulting offspring.*
    c) *Evaluate the next generation by computing the fitness for each individual.*
3. *Select the best individual (solution) from the final generation.*

The next section presents the application of fuzzy models, which use the inputs selected with the RC criterion, are identified using GK fuzzy clustering and are optimised by real-coded GA, to a servo-actuated industrial valve.

3.5.   Case Study

A pneumatic servo-actuated industrial control valve is used as test bed for the fault detection and diagnosis approach proposed in this chapter. This valve is situated on the outlet of thick juice from the fifth section of the evaporation station of the Lublin Sugar Factory in Poland that is associated with the DAMADICS project (http://www.eng.hull.ac.uk/research/control/damadics1.htm).

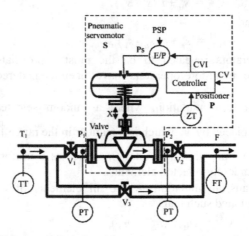

Figure 3.4.   Diagram of the industrial servo-actuated pneumatic valve considered.

3.5.1. Description of the System

The actuator-valve used in this chapter is depicted in Figure 3.4. The actuator consists of three main parts: body of the valve, actuator (e.g., spring-and-diaphragm pneumatic servomotor) and positioner controller. Furthermore, each of the three main parts contains the components shown in Figure 3.4, which are the following: positioner supply air pressure, PSP; air pressure transmitter, PT; volume flow rate transmitter, FT; temperature transmitter, TT; rod position transmitter, ZT; electro-pneumatic converter, E/P; cut-off valves, V_1 and V_2; by-pass valve, V_3; pneumatic servomotor chamber pressure, Ps; and controller output, CVI.

The valve body is the component that determines the flow through the valve. A change of the restricted area in the valve regulates the flow. There are many types of valve bodies, and the differences between them relate to the form by which the restricted flow area changes. This chapter addresses the globe valve case, but the FDI method can easily be applied to other types of valve bodies. Modelling of the flow through the valve body is not an easy task since most of the underlying physical phenomena are not fully understood (Sa da Costa and Louro, 2003). The most common approach to determine the flow through a valve is to use dimensional analysis (White, 1994) based on the model of the flow through a sharp-edged orifice.

There are many types of actuators: electrical motors, hydraulic cylinders, spring-and-diaphragm pneumatic servomotor, etc. The most common type of actuator is the spring-and-diaphragm pneumatic servomotor due to its low cost. This actuator consists of a rod that has, at one end, the valve plug, and at the other end the plate. The plate is placed inside an airtight chamber and connects to the walls of this chamber by means of a flexible diaphragm.

The positioner controller, shown in Figure 3.5, determines the flow of air into the chamber. The positioner is the control element that performs the position control of the rod. It receives a control reference signal from a computer controlling the process, passes it through a second order filter, prior to the PID control action that leads the rod's displacement to that reference signal. The positioner comprises, as well, a position sensor and a electrical-pneumatic (E/P) transducer. The first determines the actual displacement of the rod so that the error between the actual and desired position (reference signal) can be obtained. The E/P transducer receives a signal from the PID controller transforming it in a pneumatic valve-opening signal that adds or removes air from the pneumatic chamber. This transducer is also connected to a pneumatic circuit and to the atmosphere. If the controller indicates that the rod should be lowered, the chamber is connected to the pneumatic circuit. If, on the other hand, the rod should be raised, the connection is established with the atmosphere, thus allowing the chamber to be emptied.

3.5.2. Valve Modelling

The valve simulator presented in (Sa da Costa and Louro, 2003) is used to obtain the data for each of the abrupt and incipient faults tested in this chapter. Table 3.1 presents the faults considered in this chapter and their description. Each of the presented faults is used considering their abrupt and incipient behaviours.

From a complete analysis of the variables described in subsection 3.5.1, it can be concluded that for FDI purposes the most relevant variables are the flow process value, PV, and the servomotor rod displacement, X. Therefore, these variables have been considered as outputs of the fuzzy model. Moreover, the variables found to be relevant for this model are the following: pressure inlet valve, P_1; pressure outlet valve, P_2; temperature at the inlet, T_1; and control value for the inlet valve, CV. The mean squared error is used as the performance index to measure the residuals of fuzzy models:

$$\text{MSE}_i = \frac{1}{N}\sum_{k=1}^{N}\left(y-\hat{y}_{F_i}\right)^2,\qquad(21)$$

where **y** is a system output and $\hat{y}_{F_i}$ is the correspondent fault model i output.

The variance accounted for (VAF) is a widely used measure to test the validity of a model, and it is defined as

$$\text{VAF} = \frac{1 - \text{cov}(y_i - \hat{y}_i)}{\text{cov}(y_i)} \times 100\%.\qquad(22)$$

Let the real output be y_i, the predicted output by the model be $\hat{y}_i$, and cov be the covariance of the respective vector. When VAF = 100%, the model explains all the variability in the real outputs.

The set of identification data used to build the valve model in normal operation contains 2000 samples. Figures 3.6 and 3.7 present both outputs of the process under normal operation.

Two fuzzy models have been identified using the fuzzy modelling approach described in this chapter for flow and rod displacement. The MSE obtained from (21) is 0.09 for flow and 0.03 for rod displacement when the system is without faults. The obtained VAF values are 81.2% and 57.6% for flow and rod displacement, respectively.

Using the fuzzy modelling approach described in this chapter, fuzzy models have been identified for each fault considered. The performance of the obtained models for each output in terms of VAF is shown in Table 3.2 for abrupt faults and for incipient faults. This table shows that it was possible to obtain accurate models for each fault. Moreover, the RC was able to select properly the most relevant inputs for the fuzzy models.

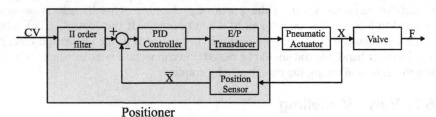

Positioner

Figure 3.5.   Positioner controller.

Table 3.1.   Faults description

Faults	Description
*F*1	Valve clogging
*F*5	External leakage
*F*7	Medium evaporation or critical flow
*F*17	Unexpected pressure change across the valve
*F*18	Fully or partly opened bypass valves
*F*19	Flow rate sensor fault

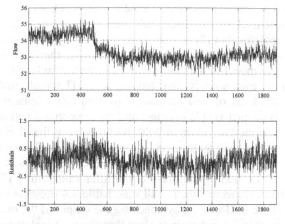

Figure 3.6. Top: Flow output. Bottom: Flow residuals.

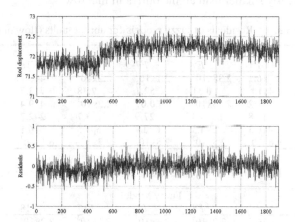

Figure 3.7. Top: Rod displacement output. Bottom: Rod displacement residuals.

Table 3.2. VAF of the fuzzy models for abrupt (left) and incipient (right) faults models of the servo-actuated valve

Faults	RC		GA		Faults	RC		GA	
	flow	disp.	flow	disp.		flow	disp.	flow	disp.
F1	74.0	74.9	75.2	75.3	F1	99.9	98.0	99.9	98.3
F5	74.1	57.6	74.8	58.3	F5	94.6	62.7	95.4	63.6
F7	97.3	99.9	97.8	99.9	F7	97.4	96.4	98.3	96.9
F17	79.8	62.1	80.5	62.7	F17	95.9	84.9	96.5	85.6
F18	73.1	59.3	74.3	60.6	F18	98.4	60.7	99.4	62.3
F19	75.4	60.9	76.0	61.4	F19	99.9	84.3	99.9	85.6

3.5.3. FDI Results

The FDI scheme proposed in this chapter, which is presented in Figure 3.3, has been applied to the industrial valve to detect and isolate the abrupt and incipient faults $F1$, $F5$, $F7$, $F17$, $F18$ and $F19$.

Tables 3.3 and 3.4 present the MSE of residuals, for flow and rod displacement, as defined in (21) when each abrupt fault occurs in the system. The faulty residuals, as defined in (2), are obtained after the fault detection. Each row in the tables corresponds to the fault that occurs during the simulation, and each column indicates the model of the fault used to isolate the fault. The residual for the fault considered in each row is depicted in bold. The fault isolation is made considering the residuals of two outputs: flow and rod displacement. The FDI system used in this chapter is able to detect and isolate correctly all six abrupt faults considered. By checking the values in bold, it can be seen that they are most often the smallest in the respective row. In some cases the isolation needs the two outputs. As an example, row 5 in Table 3.4 indicates that fault $F18$ has been simulated, and the isolation system has very similar values for $F17$, $F18$ and $F19$ (0.03, 0.04 and 0.03, respectively). Recall that Table 3.4 presents the MSE for the rod displacement output. However, by checking the output of the other variable, the flow, in row 5 of Table 3.3, it becomes clear that the fault isolated is $F18$, because its residual is clearly smaller than all the others in that row.

Table 3.3.   Residuals of fuzzy models for abrupt faults (flow output)

Faults	$F1$	$F5$	Fuzzy Model $F7$	$F17$	$F18$	$F19$
$F1$	**16.2**	2.38×10^3	2.1×10^3	2.2×10^3	440.1	9.6×10^3
$F5$	2.4×10^3	**0.31**	52.1	7.38	713.7	2.2×10^3
$F7$	17.2	2.15×10^3	**0.07**	2.2×10^3	439.4	9.6×10^3
$F17$	12.8	3.3	27.9	**3.7**	242.7	12.8
$F18$	416.3	794.3	672.9	687.5	**6.1**	5.9×10^3
$F19$	9.6×10^3	2.5×10^3	2.8×10^3	2.7×10^3	6.1×10^3	**24.8**

Table 3.4.   Residuals of fuzzy models for abrupt faults (rod displacement output)

Faults	$F1$	$F5$	Fuzzy Model $F7$	$F17$	$F18$	$F19$
$F1$	**16.3**	2.2×10^3	2.8×10^3	2.2×10^3	2.2×10^3	2.2×10^3
$F5$	2.1×10^3	**0.13**	0.65	0.24	0.16	0.14
$F7$	661.1	5.1×10^3	**2.72**	5.1×10^3	5.1×10^3	5.1×10^3
$F17$	1.2	1.23	1.12	**0.34**	51.8	0.34
$F18$	2.1×10^3	0.037	0.15	0.03	**0.04**	0.03
$F19$	2.1×10^3	0.037	0.15	0.03	0.03	**0.02**

Figure 3.8 (left) shows the output data collected from the simulator of industrial servo-actuated valve when the abrupt fault $F1$ occurs. The sampling time is equal to 1s. The residuals obtained using the fuzzy models in normal operation when valve clogging (fault $F1$) occurs are shown in Figure 3.8 (right). The occurred fault is detected; in the figure it can be seen that both residuals and, for flow and rod displacement respectively, present one zone with large values. When the block Fault Detection in Figure 3.3 detects faults, the faulty models, in our case the fuzzy observers for $F1$, $F5$, $F7$, $F17$, $F18$ and $F19$, are activated. The simulated residuals obtained for abrupt fault $F1$ are depicted in Figure 3.9 (left). These residuals are very close to zero, and thus the abrupt fault $F1$ is isolated using the fuzzy observer. Figure 3.9 (right) presents the residuals of the model for another fault, $F5$, when the

same abrupt fault $F1$ occurs. In this case, the fault is not isolated because the obtained residuals present large values for each of the output variables, as expected. Large residual values are also obtained for the other models of faults considered.

Besides abrupt faults, six incipient faults have also been simulated. Tables 3.5 and 3.6 present the results obtained when each incipient fault occurs in the system. These tables, as in the abrupt faults case, present the MSE of the fuzzy models for the residuals. The values in bold contain the residual for the fault considered. The six incipient faults proposed in this chapter are isolated correctly with the proposed FDI scheme.

The output of the system when incipient fault $F1$ occurs is shown in Figure 3.10 (left). The detection of incipient fault $F1$, when this fault occurs after 500 s, is presented in Figure 3.10 (right). In this case, both residuals present large values, which confirm that the system is faulty. The residuals obtained when the incipient fault $F1$ occurs are depicted in Figure 3.11 (left). Both residuals are very close to zero, and thus incipient fault $F1$ is correctly isolated.

Further, the residuals of another fault model, when the incipient fault $F1$ occurred in the system, are depicted in Figure 3.11 (right). In this case, the fault is not isolated because the obtained residuals present large values for both output variables. As for the abrupt faults, some faults can only be isolated when both outputs are considered. Thus, using only one output is not enough to isolate incipient faults correctly.

Table 3.5. Residuals of fuzzy models for incipient faults (flow output)

Faults	Fuzzy Model					
	$F1$	$F5$	$F7$	$F17$	$F18$	$F19$
$F1$	**0.05**	1.7×10^3	1.5×10^3	1.4×10^3	481.7	1.2×10^3
$F5$	3	**0.12**	13.5	0.39	266.6	0.22
$F7$	2.7×10^3	2.2×10^3	**0.17**	2.2×10^3	2.2×10^3	2.8×10^3
$F17$	3.5	1.02	8.3	**0.43**	38.6	2.3
$F18$	0.79	584.5	475.3	390.7	**3.35**	3.5×10^3
$F19$	35.8	1.5×10^3	1.9×10^3	1.5×10^3	3.1×10^3	**0.08**

Table 3.6. Residuals of fuzzy models for incipient faults (rod displacement output)

Faults	Fuzzy Model					
	$F1$	$F5$	$F7$	$F17$	$F18$	$F19$
$F1$	**5.8**	1.7×10^3	1.7×10^3	1.75×10^3	1.74×10^3	1.75×10^3
$F5$	352.9	**0.03**	1.22	0.04	0.03	0.043
$F7$	4.9×10^3	4.9×10^3	**5.5**	5.1×10^3	5×10^3	5×10^3
$F17$	0.5	0.2	4.22	**0.09**	12.3	602.2
$F18$	1.6×10^3	0.04	1.7	0.046	**0.03**	0.046
$F19$	2.6×10^3	0.15	3.3	0.03	0.14	**0.03**

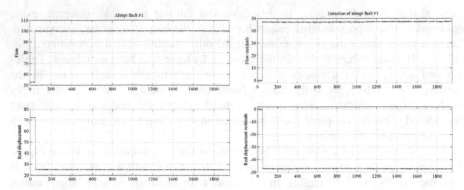

Figure 3.8.   Left: Flow and rod displacement output data (abrupt fault $F1$). Right: Detection of abrupt fault $F1$.

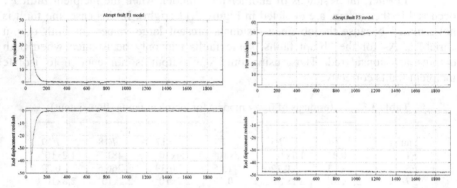

Figure 3.9.   Left: Isolation of abrupt fault $F1$. Right: Model of abrupt fault $F5$ residuals when abrupt fault $F1$ occurs.

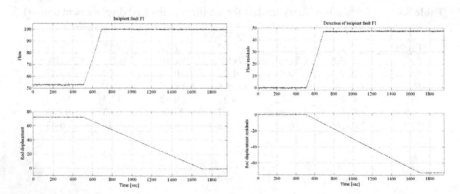

Figure 3.10.   Left: Flow and rod displacement output data (incipient fault $F1$). Right: Detection of incipient fault $F1$.

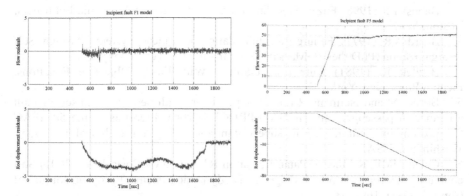

Figure 3.11. Left: Isolation of incipient fault $F1$. Right: Model of incipient fault $F5$ residuals when incipient fault $F1$ occurs.

3.6. Conclusions

This chapter proposed an FDI scheme based on fuzzy models. In this approach, fuzzy models (observers) are used both for normal operation and for each faulty operation. The fuzzy observers are obtained from simulated data driven by real data. The inputs of the fuzzy models are selected using the RC algorithm, and the parameters of the fuzzy models are optimised using a real-coded genetic algorithm. The FDI scheme uses these fuzzy observers to compute the residuals. The application of this approach to a pneumatic servomotor actuated industrial valve has shown its ability to detect and isolate six abrupt and six incipient faults. Note that the data contains noise, which increases the difficulty to detect and isolate the faults.

Future research will consider the extension of the proposed FDI scheme to a larger number of faults, and the inclusion of intermittent faults to be detected and isolated.

Acknowledgements

This work is supported by the "Programa do FSE-UE, PRODEP III, acção 5.3, no âmbito do III Quadro Comunitário de apoio".

References

1.   Hellendoorn J, Ichtev A and Babuška R (2001) Fault detection and isolation using multiple Takagi-Sugeno fuzzy models. In: Proceedings of IEEE International Fuzzy Systems Conference, vol. 3(2-5), pp. 1498-1502.

2.   Babuška R (1998) Fuzzy Modeling for Control. Kluwer Academic Publishers, Boston, MA.
3.   Beard VR (1971) Failure Accommodation in Linear System Through Self Reorganization (PhD thesis). Massachusetts Institute of Technology, USA.
4.   Bezdek JC (1981) Pattern Recognition With Fuzzy Objective Functions. Plenum Press, New York.
5.   Borner M and Isermann R (2003) Supervision, fault detection and sensor fault tolerance of passenger cars. In: SAFEPROCESS'2003, Preprints of the 5th IFAC Symposium on fault detection, supervision and safety for technical processes, Washington, USA.
6.   Calado JMF, Korbicz J, Patan K, Patton RJ and Sa da Costa JMG (2001) Soft computing approaches to fault diagnosis for dynamic systems. European Journal of Control 7(2-3): 169-208.
7.   Chen J and Patton R (1999) Robust Model-Based Fault Diagnosis for Dynamic Systems. Kluwer Academic Publishers, Boston, MA.
8.   Clark RN (1979) The dedicated observer approach to instrument failure detection. In: Proceedings of the 18th IEEE Conference on Decision Control, Fort Lauderdale, Florida, pp. 237-241.
9.   Sa da Costa JMG and Louro R (2003) Modelling and simulation of an industrial actuator valve for fault diagnosis benchmark. In: Proceedings of the Fourth International Symposium on Mathematical Modelling, Vienna, 5-7 February.
10.   Dexter AL and Benouarets M (1997) Model-based fault diagnosis using fuzzy matching. IEEE Transactions on Systems, Man, and Cybernetics. Part A 27(5): 673-682.
11.   Ding X and Frank PM (2000) Fault detection via factorization approach. Systems Control Letters 14(5): 431-436.
12.   Duan GR and Patton RJ (2001) Robust fault detection using Luenberger-type unknown input observers: a parametric approach. International Journal of Systems Science 32(4): 533-540.
13.   Eide P and Maybeck B (1996) An MMAE failure-detection system for the F-16. IEEE Transactions on Aerospace and Electronic Systems 32(3): 1125-1136.
14.   Fogel D (1991) System Identification Through Simulated Evolution: A Machine Learning Approach to Modeling. Ginn Press.
15.   European Community's FP5. Research training network DAMADICS project, http://www.eng.hull.ac.uk/research/control/damadics1.htm.
16.   Frank PM (1990) Fault diagnosis in dynamic systems using analytical knowledge based redundancy: A survey of some new results. Automatica 26(3): 459-474.
17.   Gertler J (1998) Fault Detection and Diagnosis in Engineering Systems. Marcel Dekker, New York.
18.   Goldberg DE (1989) Genetic Algorithms in Search, Optimization, and Machine Learning. Addison-Wesley, New York.
19.   Gustafson DE and Kessel WC (1979) Fuzzy clustering with a fuzzy covariance matrix. In: Proceedings of the 18th IEEE Conference on Decision and Control, pp. 761-766, San Diego, CA, USA.

20. Himmelblau DM (1978) Fault Detection and Diagnosis in Chemical and Petrochemical Processes. Elsevier, Amsterdam.
21. Holland JH (1971) Adaptation in Natural and Artificial Systems. The University of Michigan Press.
22. Insfran AHF, da Silva APA and Lambert Torres G (1999) Fault diagnosis using fuzzy sets. Engineering Intelligent Systems for Electrical Engineering and Communications 7(4): 177-182.
23. Isermann R (1984) Process fault detection based on modelling and estimation methods: A survey. Automatica 20(4): 387-404.
24. Isermann R (1998) On fuzzy logic applications for automatic control, supervision and fault diagnosis. IEEE Transactions on Systems, Man, and Cybernetics Part A 28(2): 221-235.
25. Isermann R and Ballé P (1997) Trends in the application of model-based fault detection and diagnosis of technical processes. Control Engineering Practice 5(5): 709-719.
26. Kinnaert M (2003) Fault diagnosis based on analytical models for linear and nonlinear systems - a tutorial. In: SAFEPROCESS'2003, Preprints of the 5th IFAC Symposium on fault detection, supervision and safety for technical processes, Washington, USA.
27. Koscielny JM and Syfert M (2003) Fuzzy logic applications to diagnostics of industrial processes. In: SAFEPROCESS'2003, Preprints of the 5th IFAC Symposium on fault detection, supervision and safety for technical processes, Washington, USA, pp. 771-776.
28. Kruse R, Gebhardt J and Klawonn F (1994) Foundations of Fuzzy Systems. John Wiley and Sons, Chichester, UK.
29. Laengst W, Lapp A, Stuebbe K, Schirmer J, Kraft D and Kiencke U (2003) Automated risk estimation based on fault trees and fuzzy probabilities. In: SAFEPROCESS'2003, Preprints of the 5th IFAC Symposium on fault detection, supervision and safety for technical processes, Washington, USA.
30. Lopez-Toribio CJ, Patton RJ and Daley S (2000) Takagi-Sugeno fuzzy fault-tolerant control of an induction motor. Neural Computing and Applications 9(1): 19-28.
31. Lu Y, Chen TQ and Hamilton B (1998) A fuzzy diagnostic model and its application in automotive engineering diagnosis. Applied Intelligence 9(3): 231-243.
32. Mechefske CK (1998) Objective machinery fault diagnosis using fuzzy logic. Mechanical Systems and Signal Processing 12(6): 855-862.
33. Mendonca LF, Sa da Costa JMG and Sousa JM (2003) Fault detection and diagnosis using fuzzy models. In: Proceedings of European Control Conference, ECC'2003, pp. 1-6, Session Fault Diagnosis 2, Cambridge, UK.
34. Michalewicz Z (1999) Genetic Algorithms + Data Structures = Evolution Programs. Springer, Berlin, 3rd edition.
35. Patton RJ, Frank PM and Clark RN (2000) Issues of Fault Diagnosis for Dynamic Systems. Springer-Verlag, London.
36. Rault A, Richalet A, Barbot A and Sergenton JP (1971) Identification and modelling of a jet engine. In: DISCOP'91, IFAC Symposium on Digital Simulation of Continuous Processes.

37. Schefel HP (1995) Evolution and Optimum Seeking. Wiley.
38. Schwarte A, Kimmich F and Isermann R (2003) Model-based fault detection of a diesel engine with turbo charger – a case study. In: SAFEPROCESS'2003, Preprints of the 5th IFAC Symposium on fault detection, supervision and safety for technical processes, Washington, USA.
39. Setnes M and Roubos JA (2000) GA-fuzzy modeling and classification: complexity and performance. IEEE Transactions on Fuzzy Systems 8(5): 509-522.
40. Shen LC, Chang SK and Hsu PL (1998) Robust fault detection and isolation with unstructured uncertainty using eigenstructure assignment. Journal of Guidance, Control & Dynamics 21(1): 50-57.
41. Siebert H and Isermann R (1976) Fault diagnosis via on-line correlation analysis. Technical Report 25-3, VDI-VDE, Darmstadt, Germany.
42. Sousa JM and Kaymak U (2002) Fuzzy Decision Making in Modeling and Control. World Scientific, Singapore.
43. Sugeno M and Yasukawa T (1993) A fuzzy-logic-based approach to qualitative modeling. IEEE Transactions on Fuzzy Systems 1(1): 7-31.
44. Takagi T and Sugeno M (1985) Fuzzy identification of systems and its applications to modelling and control. IEEE Transactions on Systems, Man, and Cybernetics 15(1): 116-132.
45. Vieira S, Sousa JMC and Durão F (2004) Combination of fuzzy identification algorithms applied to a column flotation process. In: Proceedings of IEEE International Conference on Fuzzy Systems FUZZ-IEEE'2004, pp. 421-426, Budapest, Hungary.
46. Vieira S, Sousa JMC and Durão F (2005) Fuzzy modeling of a column flotation process. Minerals Engineering. (in print)
47. White F (1994) Fluid Mechanics. McGraw-Hill.

4.   A Fuzzy Classification Technique Applied to Fault Diagnosis

Cosmin Danut Bocaniala and José Sá da Costa

This chapter describes a novel fuzzy classification methodology for fault diagnosis. There are three main directions of applying fuzzy classifiers to fault diagnosis: neuro-fuzzy classifiers, classifiers based on collections of fuzzy rules, and classifiers based on collections of fuzzy subsets. The contributed fuzzy classification methodology described in this chapter follows the last direction. The main advantages of the developed fuzzy classifier are the high accuracy with which it delimits the areas corresponding to different system states, i.e., the normal state and the different faulty states, and the fine precision of discrimination inside overlapping areas. In addition, the classifier needs to tune only a small numbers of parameters, i.e., the number of parameters equals the number of system states considered. The methodology is validated by application with very good results to fault diagnosis of a control flow valve from an industrial device.

4.1. Introduction

The goal of fault diagnosis research is improving the security, efficiency, maintainability and reliability of industrial plants. There are two main types of systems that are addressed: safety-critical systems such as nuclear plants and aircraft, and lower safety-critical systems such as process and manufacturing plants. A fault diagnosis system is a monitoring system that is used to detect faults and diagnose their location and significance in a system (Chen and Patton, 1999). The diagnosis system performs mainly the following tasks: fault detection – to indicate if a fault occurred or not in the system, and fault isolation – to determine the location of the fault.

According to Duda and Hart (1973), classification represents "the assignment of a physical object or event to one of several prespecified categories." Fault diagnosis represents a suitable application field for classification methods, as its main purpose is to achieve an optimal mapping of the current state of the monitored systems into a prespecified set of system states. The set of system states includes the normal state and the faulty states (Ariton and Palade, 2005). A general framework for applying classification methods to fault diagnosis problems is given in (Leonhardt and Ayoubi, 1997). Fault diagnosis is described as "a sequential process involving two steps: the symptoms extraction and the actual diagnostic task." The symptoms are extracted on the basis of the measurements provided by the actuators and sensors in the monitored system. The actual diagnostic task is to map the points in the symptoms space into the set of considered faults. For this reason, the use of classification techniques represents a natural choice when designing a fault diagnosis system.

There are three main ways for applying fuzzy classifiers to fault diagnosis that can be found in the literature. Fault diagnosis may be performed using collections of fuzzy rules (Frank, 1996; Koscielny *et al.*, 1999). Let $R=\{r_1, r_2,...,r_m\}$ be the set of residuals. Each residual r_i, $i=1,...,m$, is described by a number of fuzzy sets $\{r_{i1}, r_{i2},...,r_{is}\}$. The causal relationships between the residuals and faults are expressed by if-then rules having a form similar to

$$IF\ (effect = r_{ip})\ AND\ (effect = r_{jq})...THEN\ (cause\ is\ the\ k - th\ fault) \qquad (1)$$

The output of the fuzzy classifier is the faulty vector F. The fuzzy inference process will assign to each component F_i, $i=0, 1,...,n$, where n is the number of faults – a value between 0 and 1 that indicates the degree with which the normal state (the corresponding component is F_0) or the j-th fault affects the monitored system, $j=1,...,m$. If there is the premise that the system can be affected only by a fault at a time, then the faulty vector contains only one component larger than a preset threshold value, and whose corresponding faulty state represents the actual state of the monitored system. If multiple faults can affect the monitored system, then the components of the classifier output, which are larger than a preset threshold, indicate the faults that occurred in the system. The main advantage of using sets of fuzzy rules is that they make transparent the relationships between symptoms and faults via the use of linguistic terms. However, notice that if the number of fuzzy sets used is increasing, the number of linguistic terms used to label them also increases. It follows that the linguistic informational burden of the operator may increase too beyond reasonable limits.

Combinations between fuzzy logic and neural networks, i.e., neuro-fuzzy systems, are used to create diagnosis systems robust to uncertainties and noise (Palade *et al.*, 2002; Uppal *et al.*, 2002). Calado *et al.* (2001) propose a hierarchical structure of several fuzzy-neural networks (FNN) for fault isolation purposes. The hierarchical structure has three levels. The first order differences for all available measurements are used as symptoms. The lower level consists of one FNN that receives as input the considered symptoms. The output of this FNN determines which of the FNNs on the medium level will be activated. That is, if the i-th component of the output has a value close to 1, then the i-th FNN on the medium level will be activated. The number of the FNNs on the medium level is equal to the number of faults considered. Each one of them is also fed with all symptoms considered. The upper level is used to perform an OR operation on the outputs of the activated FNNs on the medium level. The components of the outputs considered for the OR operation must have a value close to 1. The main advantage of the neuro-fuzzy systems is that the learning, adaptation and parallelism capabilities provided by neural networks may be used to tune the fuzzy rules parameters. The main drawback of the neuro-fuzzy classifiers, like the one presented before, is represented by a possible too large number of parameters to be tuned, i.e., fuzzy membership functions and neural network weights.

A third direction is to represent the normal state and each faulty state of the system as a fuzzy subset of the symptoms space (Boudaoud and Masson, 2000). The quality of this last direction is given by its capabilities to learn the topological structure of the space. Boudaoud and Masson (2000) propose two main steps for the design of such a pattern recognition diagnosis system: analysis and exploitation. The analysis phase is performed off-line and it transforms the available measurements, labelled with the corresponding operating state of the system, into a collection of fuzzy subsets standing for regions in the measurements space describing the operating states into the measurements space. The exploitation phase corresponds to the on-line diagnosis process using classification into the regions found before.

The fuzzy subsets defining the normal state and the faulty states of the system represent hyperboxes B defined by a minimum point m and a maximum point M in the symptoms space (Boudaoud and Masson, 1996). Figure 4.1 shows a hyperbox in R^3. This type of fuzzy subsets has been used with the fuzzy min-max clustering algorithm proposed by Simpson (1993). The maximal size of each hyperbox is tuned so that the misclassification rate is minimal. The particularities of the fuzzy subsets defined by hyperboxes, i.e., full membership inside hyperboxes and partial membership around hyperboxes boundaries, allow diagnosis to consist of three possible cases: (i) the system state is stationary, (ii) the system is in transition between two possible states, and (iii) the system is stabilizing in a new state. It is important to mention that the hyperboxes used during the diagnosis process are not allowed to overlap (Simpson, 1993). This does not mean that the areas in the symptoms space corresponding to different states do not overlap, but that the hyperboxes delimit the sub areas where points have full membership. Diagnosing the partial membership areas as transitions between two states compensates the loss of diagnosis information due to this approach.

Notice that the dimension of each hyperbox depends on only three constraints: its minimum point, its maximum point, and a parameter that controls the decreasing rate of membership to B value when the distance between a test point u and B increases. Thus, the main advantage of the third direction compared to the previous two directions is the smaller number of parameters to be tuned, i.e., three times the number of system states considered, which leads to a smaller designing time for the classifier. However, the transparency of relationships between symptoms and faults given by the use of linguistic terms is lost.

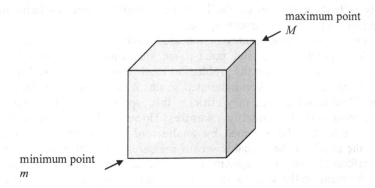

Figure 4.1.   A hyperbox in R^3 defined by minimum and maximum points.

The classification methodology described in this chapter follows the last direction mentioned. The methodology is described in detail in our previous papers (Bocaniala *et al.*, 2004; 2005). The main property of this methodology is the large accuracy with which it learns the topological structure of the symptoms space. The fuzzy subsets built by the classifier approximate with a very small error the areas in the symptoms space corresponding to different system states. Its accuracy also manifests through handling with fine precision the discrimination inside overlapping areas.

The fuzzy subsets defined by this methodology express better the topological properties of the symptoms space than hyperboxes used in (Boudaoud and Masson, 1996). Details are given further in the chapter. Also, similar to the methodology proposed in (Boudaoud and Masson, 1996), the methodology in this chapter also needs to tune only a small numbers of parameters, i.e., the number of parameters equals the number of system states considered. Details are given further in the chapter as well.

The chapter is organized as follows. Section 4.2 presents the theoretical aspects of the described fuzzy classification methodology. The case study, DAMADICS benchmark (http://www.eng.hull.ac.uk/research/control/damadics1.htm), is concerned with fault diagnosis of a valve intended to supply water to a steam generator boiler. Section 4.3 provides a detailed analysis of the faults studied by the benchmark. Section 4.4 presents the detection and isolation of the valve faults using the contributed fuzzy classifier. Section 4.5 summarizes the original contributions of this chapter and mentions possible directions for future work.

4.2. Theoretical Aspects of the Contributed Fuzzy Classification Methodology

The fuzzy subsets used by the classification methodology described in this chapter are induced (built) on the basis of a point-to-set similarity measure between a point and a set of points in the measurements space (Baker, 1978). The point-to-set similarity is built at its turn on the basis of a point-to-point similarity measure between points in the measurements space.

One of the particularities of the methodology is the fact that one may choose those point-to-point and point-to-set similarities that provide the best classification performance for the problem at hand. Thus, the methodology may be seen as a template that may be instantiated so that it fits the specific characteristics of the problem to solve. One may criticize this aspect as it implies searching by trials the most suitable similarity measures. However, hints on what measures should be used may be obtained by analysis of the measurements used. For instance, the trends in the available sensor measurements may reflect in the same way the effects of a fault on a system. Therefore, the use of a measure of similarity between the trends in the sensor signals over a time window may prove to be a good choice.

In order to facilitate the understanding of the theoretical concepts presented in the following, a simple problem shown in Figure 4.2 is used. The figure shows the points corresponding to two categories characterized by two measurements.

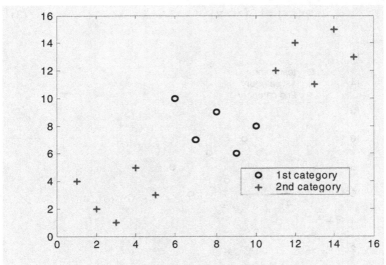

Figure 4.2.   The simple problem used to illustrate the theoretical aspects.

4.2.1. Point-to-Point Similarity Measure Based on Distance Functions

The similarity between two points u and v, $s(u,v)$, may be expressed using a complementary function, $d(u,v)$, expressing dissimilarity. Baker (1978) expresses dissimilarity by using the distance function in Eq. 2. Notice that, in this case, the functions s and d are complementary with regard to unit value, $s(u,v)=1-d(u,v)$. The β parameter plays the role of a threshold value for the similarity measure. For a data point u, all points v residing at a distance $\delta(u,v)$ smaller than β will bear some similarity with u. As for the points residing at distances larger than or equal to β, the similarity $s(u,v)$ is null. The contour plot of the point-to-point similarity function when Eq. 2 is used is shown in Figure 4.3. The distance measure used is the Euclidean measure.

$$h^{\beta}\left(\delta\left(u,v\right)\right) = \begin{cases} \delta\left(u,v\right)/\beta, & \text{for } \delta\left(u,v\right) \le \beta \\ 1, & \text{otherwise} \end{cases} \tag{2}$$

4.2.2. Point-to-Point Similarity Measure Based on Pearson Correlation

The Pearson correlation (Weisstein, 1999) measures the similarity in the trends of two signals. Let us suppose that s and t represent the measurements of two signals over the same time window. The formula used to compute the correlation between the vectors s and t is given in Eq. 3. The terms zs and zt represent the z-scores of s

and t, respectively. The z-score of a vector is obtained by first subtracting the mean value and then dividing by its standard deviation. The product between zs and zt is the dot product and n represents the length of the time window.

$$p(s,t) = 1 - (zs \cdot zt)/n \tag{3}$$

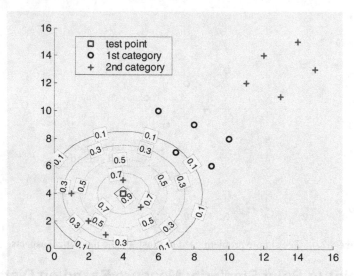

Figure 4.3.   The point-to-point similarity measure for $\beta=5$ in Eq. 2.

The values of this correlation measure fall in [0,2] interval, where 0 stands for perfect correlation and 2 stands for perfect anticorrelation. Figure 4.4 shows two pairs of shapes corresponding to these two cases. There is a parallel between the terms "correlation"/"anticorrelation" and the terms "similarity"/"dissimilarity." Indeed, the function p may play the same role as the dissimilarity function d in the previous subsection. In this case, the maximum value for $d(s,t)$, which is equal to $p(s,t)$, is 2. The functions s and d are complementary with regard to this value; thus, $s(u,v)=2-d(u,v)$.

4.2.3. Point-to-Set Similarity Measure

The similarity measure between two data points may be extended to a similarity measure between a point and a set of points (Baker, 1978). In this chapter, if the point-to-point similarity is given by Eq. 2, the similarity between a given point u and a set of points S is computed as the mean value of the point-to-point similarity values between u and each v in S (Eq. 4, where n denotes the number of elements in S). Notice that the value of $r(u,S)$ stays inside [0,1] interval, as $s(u,v)$ also stays inside [0,1] interval and the cardinal of S is n.

$$r(u,S) = \frac{\sum\limits_{v \in S} s(u,v)}{n} \tag{4}$$

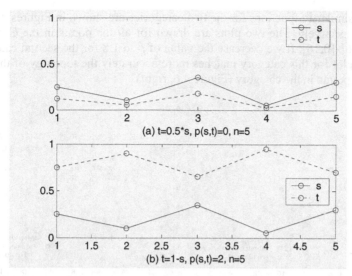

Figure 4.4. Perfect Pearson correlation (a) and perfect Pearson anticorrelation (b).

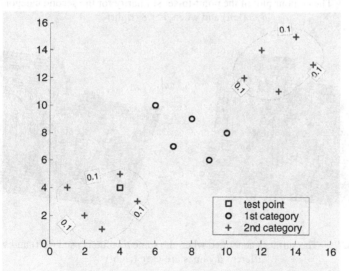

Figure 4.5. The contour plot of the point-to-set similarity for the first category ($\beta=3$).

The effect of using the β parameter is that only those data points from S, whose distance to u is larger than β, contribute to the point-to-set similarity value. The explanation is that only these points have a nonzero similarity with u. It follows that the similarity value between u and S is decided within the neighborhood defined by β.

It has been observed in practice that, if different (dedicated) β parameters are used for different categories to express the point-to-point similarity (Eq. 2), the performance of the classifier increases substantially. Let us consider that the value of the β parameter is 3 for both categories in the problem. The contour plots of the point-to-set similarity functions for the two categories are shown in Figures 4.5 and 4.6 (left), respectively. The two plots are drawn for all the points in the Cartesian product [0,16]x[0,16]. If we decrease the value of β to 1.8 for the second category, the contour plot for this category matches more accurately the topology of the area occupied by points in the category (Figure 4.6, right).

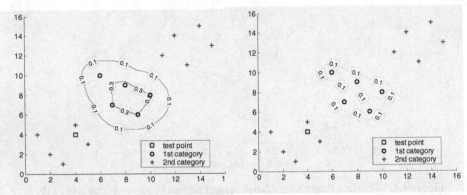

Figure 4.6.   The contour plot of the point-to-set similarity for the second category when β=3 (left) and when β=1.8 (right)

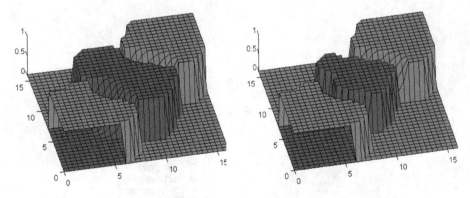

Figure 4.7.   The surfaces generated when the same β value is used (left) and when different β values are used (right)

4.2.4. Fuzzy Subsets Induced by Single Point-to-Set Similarity Measures

Let $C=\{C_i\}_{i=1,...,m}$ be the set of all points in the measurements space, associated with the problem to solve, where C_i, $i=1,...,m$, represents the set of all points corresponding to the i-th considered category. The membership function of the fuzzy subset $Fuzz_i$ induced by C_i, computed on the basis of a given point-to-set similarity measure, is given in Eq. 5. The n value represents the cardinal of C, and the n_i value represents the cardinal of C_i.

$$\mu_i\left(u\right) = \frac{r(u, C_i)}{r(u, C)} \tag{5}$$

If the values of the β parameters considered are the same: 3 for both categories, the obtained fuzzy subsets (surfaces) corresponding to the two categories are shown in Figure 4.7 (left). If different values for the β parameters are used: 3 for the first one and 1.8 for the second one, the surface corresponding to the second category shrinks to match better the topology of the area occupied by the points in that category (Figure 4.7, right).

A point u presented at the input of the classifier is assigned to the category C_z whose corresponding degree of assignment $\mu_z(u)$ is the largest (Eq. 6). In case of ties, the assignment to a category cannot be decided and the point is rejected.

$$u \in z\text{-th category} \Leftrightarrow \mu_z\left(u\right) = \max_{i=1,\dots,m} \mu_i\left(u\right) \tag{6}$$

4.2.5. Fuzzy Subsets Induced by Multiple Point-to-Set Similarity Measures

The practice showed that there are problems for which classifiers designed by using only one point-to-set similarity measure does not provide satisfactory results (Bocaniala et al., 2004). When situations like these are met, the advantages brought by two or more similarity measures may be combined in order to improve the performance of the classifier (Bocaniala e. al., 2004), i.e., a hybrid approach is used. This aspect has also been noticed by Baker (1978).

In the following, a few possible approaches, when trying to combine the use of two or more similarity measures, are suggested:

- similarity measures: the β parameter may be applied only to one of the similarity measures used; if more than one similarity measure is used, then there is a β parameter for each one of them.
- cluster affinity measures: there may be only one cluster affinity measure resulting from the combination of all similarities used; or, there may be one cluster affinity measure for each similarity used.
- fuzzy membership functions: the fuzzy membership functions represent combinations of cluster affinity measures if more than one such measure exists.

If the β parameter is applied to only one of the similarity measures used, then all other cluster affinity measures will be computed for the neighbourhood defined by this β parameter.

In this chapter, a hybrid approach based on Euclidean distance and Pearson correlation is used. For details see the case study in Section 4.3.

4.2.6. Designing and Testing the Classifier

Let m be the number of the categories considered for the problem to be solved. The proposed methodology first groups the set of all available data C into clusters according to the category they belong to, C_i, $i=1,\dots,m$. In order to design and test the classifier, each subgroup C_i is split in three representative and distinct subsets, C_i^{ref}, C_i^{param}, and C_i^{test}. On the basis of these subsets three sets unions, REF, PARAM and TEST, are defined (Eq. 7). They are called the *reference patterns* set, the *parameters tuning* set, and the *test* set, respectively. A subset is considered representative for a given set if it covers that set in a satisfactory manner. In the following, the semantic for the expression *satisfactory covering subset* adopted in this thesis is explained. Then, the role of each one of the three unions is detailed. It is to be noticed that the union of subsets having the satisfactory covering property for a set represents also a satisfactory covering subset of that set.

$$REF = \bigcup_{i=1}^{m} C_i^{ref}$$

$$PARAM = \bigcup_{i=1}^{m} C_i^{param} \qquad (7)$$

$$TEST = \bigcup_{i=1}^{m} C_i^{test}$$

4.2.6.1. Satisfactory Covering Subsets

For the work presented in this thesis, a *satisfactory covering subset* represents a subset of data that preserves (with a given order of magnitude) the distribution of the data associated with the problem. Selecting the elements that compose a satisfactory covering subset for a given data set can be costly. Therefore, it is more convenient to use selection methods that provide convenient approximations for satisfactory covering subsets. Such a method is proposed in the following.

Let us consider a given finite data set A that contains r points in a multidimensional space. First, the maximum distance, *max*, between two elements is computed. During this computation a pair of elements, (a,b), with maximum distance between them is memorized. Then, one of the elements, let it be a, is considered as the centre of s hyperspheres, S_i, $i=1,...,s$. The user must provide the s value. Each one of the S_i hyperspheres has a radius equal to

$$r_i = i \frac{max}{s}, \quad i = 1,...,s \qquad (8)$$

The next step is to consider the partition induced by the next subsets,

$$P_0 = \{a \in A / a \; inside \; S_1\}$$
$$P_j = \{a \in A / a \; inside \; S_{j+1} - S_j\}, \quad j = 1,...,s-1 \qquad (9)$$

The cardinal of the subset that approximates the satisfactory covering subset is set to a previous given percent t of elements from A. The distribution of elements from A in the partition elements P_0, ..., P_{s-1} is not equal. This distribution is taken into account when distributing the percent t among the partition members. Each partition member P_j, $j=1$, ..., $s-1$, will be allocated a number of p_j elements. The approximation subset is composed by randomly selecting p_j elements from the P_j subset, $j=1$, ..., $s-1$.

4.2.6.2. Reference Patterns Set (REF)

The point-to-set similarity measures are defined for the representative subsets C_i^{ref}, $i=1,...,m$. Therefore, when using a single point-to-set similarity measure, the fuzzy membership functions are computed as

$$\mu_i(u) = \frac{r(u, C_i^{ref})}{r(u, C)} \qquad (10)$$

4.2.6.3. Parameters Tuning Set (PARAM)

The shape of the membership functions μ_i, associated to the fuzzy sets $Fuzz_i$, depends not only on the representative subset C_i^{ref}, but also on the value of the β_i parameter, $i=1,...,m$. The algorithm for tuning the parameters β_i, $i=1,...,m$, of the classifier represents a search process in an m-dimensional space for the parameter vector $(\beta_1, \beta_2,..., \beta_m)$ that meets, for each category, the maximal correct classification criterion and the minimal misclassification criterion. In order to perform this search, different methodologies may be used, i.e. genetic algorithms (Bocaniala et al., 2003), hill-climbing (Bocaniala and Sa da Costa, 2004a) and particle swarm optimisation (PSO) (Bocaniala and Sa da Costa, 2004b). In practice, the PSO methodology proved to be the fastest.

The search for optimal parameters when using genetic algorithms and hill-climbing may be accelerated by using an *optimised initial population* (Sa da Costa et al., 2003). An optimised initial population can be obtained by performing an iterative search that starts with an individual whose parameters have very small values. Then, at each next step, the values of the parameters will be increased/decreased so that the fitness of the obtained individual, i.e., the classifier performance, increases.

4.2.6.4. Testing Set (TEST)

The performance of the classifier is measured according to its generalization capabilities when applied on the *TEST* set. It is to be noticed that the *TEST* set contains data that were not presented before at the input of the classifier and that is representative for the whole data set *C*. The practice showed that the performance of the classifier may improve if the testing is performed after adding the data in the *PARAM* set to the *REF* set.

4.3.   Detailed Analysis of Faults in the Case Study

The DAMADICS benchmark (http://www.eng.hull.ac.uk/research/control/dama dics1.htm) is concerned with fault diagnosis of a valve intended to supply water to a steam generator boiler. The valve is used as part of the process at sugar factory Cukrownia Lublin S.A., Poland. It is made up of three parts: a valve body, a spring-and-diaphragm pneumatic actuator and a positioner (Figure 4.8). The valve body is the equipment that sets the flow through the pipe system. The flow is proportional to the minimum flow area inside the valve (2), which, in turn, is proportional to the position of a rod (5). The spring-and-diaphragm actuator determines the position of this rod. The spring-and-diaphragm actuator is composed of a rod, which at one end is connected to the valve body and the other end has a plate, which is placed inside a pneumatic chamber (8). The plate is connected to the walls of the chamber by a flexible diaphragm. This assembly is supported by a spring. The position of the rod is proportional to the pressure inside the chamber, which is determined by the positioner. The positioner is basically a control element. It receives three signals: a measurement of the position of the rod (x), a reference signal for the position of the rod (CV) and a pneumatic signal from a compressed air circuit in the plant. The positioner returns an airflow signal, which is determined by a classic feedback control loop of the rod position. The airflow signal changes the pressure inside the chamber.

There are several sensors included in the system that measure the variables that influence the system, namely, the upstream and downstream water pressures, the water temperature, the position of the rod (x) and the flow through the valve (F). These measurements are intended for controlling the process but they can also be used for FDI purposes. This means that the implementation of this sort of system will not imply additional hardware. The first three measurements, as well as the control value (CV), may be seen as the inputs to the system whilst the latter two may be seen as its outputs. The two output values, the sensor for measuring the position of the rod (x) and the sensor for measuring the water flow through the valve (F), provide variables that contain information relative to the faulty behaviours.

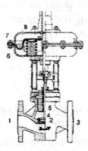

Figure 4.8.   The valve studied by DAMADICS benchmark.

The sensor measurements corresponding to some faults cannot be obtained directly from the real process as the occurrence of these faults may have disastrous consequences on the system. Therefore, the valve needed to be extensively modelled using the physical laws that govern its behaviour (Louro, 2003; Sa da Costa and Louro, 2003). The MATLAB/SIMULINK model obtained may be used to simulate any faulty behaviour.

The faults in the benchmark have been simulated for 20 different values of fault strength, uniformly distributed between 5% and 100%, and different input values for the reference signal. The previous set of fault strengths represents a good approximation of all possible faulty situations involving the faults in the benchmark. All faults have been simulated two times for all their fault strengths. The simulation lasted for 70 seconds the first time and for 20 seconds the second time. The fault has been introduced at the 50th second the first time and at the 10th the second time. The data obtained during the first simulation have been used to design the classifier, i.e., 50% for the *REF* set and 50% for the *PARAM* set. The data obtained during the second simulation have been used as the *TEST* set. For the second round of simulation a shorter time has been chosen, i.e., the fault is introduced in the system for only 10 seconds, as good fault diagnosis methodologies need to have very short time intervals for detection and isolation of abrupt faults.

The input to the simulation is taken from real data collected at the plant. This method provides more realistic conditions for generating the behaviour of the system while undergoing a fault. It also makes the FDI task more difficult because the real data input causes the system to feature the same noise conditions as those in the real plant.

The valve is affected by a total of 19 faults that may have abrupt and/or incipient behaviour (Table 4.1). In this chapter only the abrupt manifestation of the faults has been considered. The large majority of faults, 14 out of 19, manifest an abrupt behaviour.

Table 4.1.   The set of faults considered in DAMADICS benchmark

Fault	Description	Abrupt behavior			Incipient
		small	medium	big	behaviour
F1	Valve clogging	x	x	x	
F2	Valve plug or valve seat sedimentation			x	x
F3	Valve plug or valve seat erosion				x
F4	Increase of valve or bushing friction				x
F5	External leakage (leaky bushing, covers, terminals)				x
F6	Internal leakage (valve tightness)				x
F7	Medium evaporation or critical flow	x	x	x	
F8	Twisted servo-motor's piston rod	x	x	x	
F9	Servomotor's housing or terminals tightness				x
F10	Servomotor's diaphragm perforation	x	x	x	
F11	Servomotor's spring fault			x	x
F12	Electro-pneumatic transducer fault	x	x	x	
F13	Rod displacement sensor fault	x	x	x	x
F14	Pressure sensor fault	x	x	x	
F15	Positioner feedback fault			x	
F16	Positioner supply pressure drop	x	x	x	
F17	Unexpected pressure change across the valve			x	x
F18	Fully or partly opened bypass valve	x	x	x	x
F19	Flow rate sensor fault	x	x	x	

As mentioned in the introduction of this chapter, the sensor that measures the rod position (x) and the sensor that measures the flow (F) provide variables that contain information relative to the faults. The difference dP between the upstream pressure measurement (P_1) and the downstream pressure measurement (P_2) is also considered (besides x and F) as it permits to differentiate *F17* from the other faults. For the rest of the faults, the previous difference always has negligible values (close to zero).

The effects of three out of the 14 abrupt faults on these three sensor measurements are not distinguishable from the normal behaviour (*N*), {*F8*, *F12*,

F14}. Therefore, in the following, these cases are not studied. They can be dealt with if further sensors are added to the system. There can be distinguished three groups of faults, {*F2, F19*}, {*F7, F10*}, and {*F11, F15, F16*}, for which exists a strong similarity between their effects on the measurements, i.e., large overlapping. There is also noncritical overlapping between the groups of faults {*F1, F7*} and {*F13, F18*}.

4.4.   Results of Fault Diagnosis Using the Fuzzy Classifier

The previous section indicated the three sensor measurements, x, F and dP, that provide the best distinction among the faults. In order to provide the classifier with information on the dynamics of the system, the state of the system is described using the aggregate of these values over a time window of 5 time-steps. More precisely, the state of the system represents a point in a 15-dimensional space, $(x_{t-4}, ..., x_t, F_{t-4}, ..., F_t, dP_{t-4}, ..., dP_t)$, where t is the time instance when the system state is recorded. The classifier performs detection and isolation in one single step. If the classifier outputs the same fault label for two consecutive states then the system is diagnosed as being affected by that fault.

The classifier employed in this chapter is built using a hybrid approach based on Euclidean distance and Pearson correlation. Pearson correlation allows the trends in the x and F signals to provide supplementary separation between different faults. As mentioned before, a point in a 15-dimensional space describes the system state, i.e. the record over 5 consecutive time-steps for dP, x and F values. Therefore, the point has associated two vectors that represent the trend for x and F signals over the 5 time-step window. Three point-to-set similarity measures are used, based on the three similarity measures induced by the Euclidean distance (r_E), Pearson correlation for x (r_{P_x}), and Pearson correlation for F (r_{P_F}), respectively. The β parameters are applied only to the point-to-point similarity measure based on the Euclidean distance. If the β parameters are applied only to one of the point-to-point similarity measures used, then all other point-to-set similarity measures will be computed for the neighbourhood defined by these β parameters. The point-to-set similarity measures corresponding to each of the two Pearson correlations are given by Eq. 11, where p_x and p_F stand for the point-to-point similarities based on Pearson correlation for x and F, respectively. Finally, the fuzzy membership functions represent a combination of the three point-to-set similarity measures (Eq. 12). The terms σ, τ and ξ weight the contribution of each point-to-set similarity measure to the overall value. The search process for the optimal β parameters may be extended to also tune the values of these terms.

$$r_{P\_x}(u, C_i) = \sum_{\substack{\text{all } v \text{ in the} \\ \text{neighbourhood} \\ \text{defined by } \beta_i}} \left(2 - p_x(u, v)\right)$$

$$r_{P\_F}(u, C_i) = \sum_{\substack{\text{all } v \text{ in the} \\ \text{neighbourhood} \\ \text{defined by } \beta_i}} \left(2 - p_F(u, v)\right) \tag{11}$$

$$\mu_i(u) = \frac{\sigma * \dfrac{r_E(u,C_i)}{r_E(u,C)} + \tau * \dfrac{r_{P\_x}(u,C_i)}{r_{P\_x}(u,C)} + \xi * \dfrac{r_{P\_F}(u,C_i)}{r_{P\_F}(u,C)}}{\sigma + \tau + \xi} \qquad (12)$$

The process of fault detection and isolation will follow the next two steps. First, only one category per fault is considered, containing all the points associated with all possible fault strengths. Second, more than one category for one fault is considered. These categories are formed by allowing for single fault strengths or groups of fault strengths to form distinct categories (Bocaniala et al., 2004). The second step is taken in order to increase even more (if possible) the isolation capabilities of the classifier until distinguishing between different fault strengths.

For the first step, one category per fault is considered and a classifier is built for this particular set of categories. The isolation matrix obtained is shown in Table 4.2. The normal state (N) is separable/well-classified from the faulty states in proportion of 99.60%. The comment *"not visible"* stands for situations when the effects of the corresponding fault strengths are not visible. Analysing the content of Table 4.2 the following facts may be deduced. The classifier correctly recognizes the five groups of overlapping faults mentioned in Section 4.3. Notice that the large overlapping between F11, F15 and F16 is almost completely solved. Notice also that in the case of faults F1, F10, F18 and F19, the effects of the small fault strengths are not distinguishable from the normal state. The previous analysis proves the high accuracy with which the classifier is able to delimit the areas corresponding to different categories, and the fine precision of discrimination inside overlapping areas. However, the content of Table 4.2 raises questions like the next one: if the classifier outputs the label F15, then is this fault in the system really F15 (and if it is which fault strength does it have), or is it fault strength 95% of F11, or is it fault strength 75% of F16? The second step of the process of detection and isolation investigates the answers to questions like the previous one, i.e., tries to improve the isolation.

For the second step, more than one category per fault is considered. These categories are formed by allowing for single fault strengths or groups of fault strengths to a distinct category (Bocaniala et al., 2004). As will be seen, this refinement increases the isolation between different faults and between different fault strengths of the same fault. The effects of the refinement are studied considering the faults grouped according to the overlapping between them, i.e., {F1, F7}, {F2, F19}, {F7, F10}, {F11, F15, F16}, {F13, F18} and {F17}. For each group of faults the next analysis is performed. First, for each fault, the clustering into groups of fault strengths is found by considering the fault strengths as separate categories and building the corresponding classifier. For each fault, the identified groups of fault strengths represent the new set of categories per fault. Second, using the previous sets of categories per fault, another classifier is built in order to check the isolation properties. The result of these analyses is presented in Tables 4.3 to 4.7. The notation used is FiFSj, where i and j respectively stand for the fault label and fault strength (given as a number between 0 and 100). The labelling convention for the clusters formed by more than one fault strength is to use the label corresponding to the smallest fault strength in the group, i.e., the two clusters for F2 are labelled F2FS70 and respectively F2FS80.

Table 4.2. The isolation matrix for the case when only one category per fault is considered

	1 (5%)	2 (10%)	3 (15%)	4 (20%)	5 (25%)	6 (30%)	7 (35%)	8 (40%)	9 (45%)	10 (50%)	11 (55%)	12 (60%)	13 (65%)	14 (70%)	15 (75%)	16 (80%)	17 (85%)	18 (90%)	19 (95%)	20 (100%)
F1	[	-	-	-	N	-	]	[	-	-	-	-	-	F1	-	-	-	-	]	F7
F2	[	-	-	-	not considered in the benchmark				-	-	-	-	]	F2	F2	F19	F2	F2	F19	F2
F7	[	-	-	-	-	-	-	-	-	F7	-	-	-	-	-	-	-	-	-	]
F10	[	-	-	-	N	-	-	]	F10	F10	(not visible)	F10	F10	F10	F10	[	-	F7	-	]
F11	[	-	-	-	not considered in the benchmark				-	-	-	-	]	(not visible)	F11	F11	F11	F15	F11	F11
F13	F18	F18	F13	F18	[	-	-	-	-	-	-	-	F13	-	-	-	-	-	-	]
F15	[	-	-	-	not considered in the benchmark				-	-	-	-	]	F15	F15	F15	(not visible)	F15	F16	F15
F16	[	-	-	-	-	-	N	-	-	-	-	-	]	F15	[	-	F16	-	]	
F17	[	-	-	-	not considered in the benchmark				-	-	-	-	]	[	-	-	F17	-	-	]
F18	N	[	-	-	F13	-	]	[	-	-	-	-	-	F18	-	-	-	-	-	]
F19	N	N	[	-	F19	]	F2	[	-	-	-	-	-	F19	-	-	-	-	-	]

Table 4.3. The isolation matrix for the group of faults {*F1, F7*} in case when more than one category per fault is considered

	1 (5%)	2 (10%)	3 (15%)	4 (20%)	5 (25%)	6 (30%)	7 (35%)	8 (40%)	9 (45%)	10 (50%)	11 (55%)	12 (60%)	13 (65%)	14 (70%)	15 (75%)	16 (80%)	17 (85%)	18 (90%)	19 (95%)	20 (100%)
F1	[	-	-	-	N	-	-	]	F1FS45	F1FS50	F1FS55	F1FS60	F1FS65	F1FS70	F1FS75	F1FS80	F1FS85	F1FS90	F1FS95	F7
F7	[	-	-	-	-	-	-	-	-	-	F7	-	-	-	-	-	-	-	-	]

Table 4.4. The isolation matrix for the group of faults {*F2, F19*} in case when more than one category per fault is considered

	1 (5%)	2 (10%)	3 (15%)	4 (20%)	5 (25%)	6 (30%)	7 (35%)	8 (40%)	9 (45%)	10 (50%)	11 (55%)	12 (60%)	13 (65%)	14 (70%)	15 (75%)	16 (80%)	17 (85%)	18 (90%)	19 (95%)	20 (100%)
F2	[	-	-	-	not considered in the benchmark			-	-	-	-	-	]	F19FS15	F2FS75	F19FS30	F2FS80	F2FS70	F19FS30	F2FS80
F19	N	N	[	-	F19FS15	]	F19FS30	[	-	-	-	F19FS35	-	-	]	F19FS80	[	-	F19FS35	]

Table 4.5. The isolation matrix for the group of faults {*F7, F10*} in case when more than one category per fault is considered

	1 (5%)	2 (10%)	3 (15%)	4 (20%)	5 (25%)	6 (30%)	7 (35%)	8 (40%)	9 (45%)	10 (50%)	11 (55%)	12 (60%)	13 (65%)	14 (70%)	15 (75%)	16 (80%)	17 (85%)	18 (90%)	19 (95%)	20 (100%)
F7	[	-	-	-	-	-	-	-	-	-	F7	-	-	-	-	-	-	-	-	]
F10	[	-	-	-	N	-	-	]	F10FS45	F10FS45	(not visible)	F10FS45	F10FS45	F10FS70	F10FS70	[	-	F7	-	]

Table 4.6. The isolation matrix for the group of faults {*F13, F18*} in case when more than one category per fault is considered

	1 (5%)	2 (10%)	3 (15%)	4 (20%)	5 (25%)	6 (30%)	7 (35%)	8 (40%)	9 (45%)	10 (50%)	11 (55%)	12 (60%)	13 (65%)	14 (70%)	15 (75%)	16 (80%)	17 (85%)	18 (90%)	19 (95%)	20 (100%)
F13	F13FS5	F18FS10	F13FS5	F18FS10	F13FS5	[	-	-	-	-	-	-	-	F13FS40	-	-	-	-	-	]
F18	N	F18FS10	F13FS5	[	-	F18FS10	]	[	-	-	-	-	-	F18FS40	-	-	-	-	-	]

Table 4.7. The isolation matrix for the group of faults {*F11, F15, F16*} in case when more than one category per fault is considered

	1 (5%)	2 (10%)	3 (15%)	4 (20%)	5 (25%)	6 (30%)	7 (35%)	8 (40%)	9 (45%)	10 (50%)	11 (55%)	12 (60%)	13 (65%)	14 (70%)	15 (75%)	16 (80%)	17 (85%)	18 (90%)	19 (95%)	20 (100%)
F11	[	-	-	-	not considered in the benchmark			-	-	-	-	]	(not visible)	F11	F11	F11	F11	F11	F11	
F15	[	-	-	-	not considered in the benchmark			-	-	-	-	]	F15FS70	F15FS75	F15FS80	(not visible)	F15FS70	F15FS80	F15FS70	
F16	[	-	-	-	-	-	N	-	-	-	-	]	F15FS75	[	-	F16FS85	-	]		

Notice that the isolation results have improved radically. For instance, the medium and large fault strengths of *F19*, 40-100%, are separated from the small ones, 5-35%; while misclassification of *F19* with *F2* occurs only for the small strengths of *F19*. The overlapping between faults *F13* and *F18* occurs now only between small fault strengths, i.e., between 5% and 30% for *F13* and 10% and 35%

for *F18*. The medium and large strengths of both faults are now perfectly separated from each other.

4.5. Conclusions

This chapter presented a novel fuzzy classification methodology applied to fault diagnosis. There are three main directions of applying fuzzy classifiers to fault diagnosis: neuro-fuzzy classifiers, classifiers based on collections of fuzzy rules, and classifiers based on collections of fuzzy subsets. The fuzzy classification methodology described in this chapter follows the last direction. The main property of this methodology is the large accuracy with which it learns the topological structure of the symptoms space. The fuzzy subsets built by the classifier approximate with a very small error the areas in the symptoms space corresponding to different categories. Its accuracy also manifests through handling with fine precision the discrimination inside overlapping areas.

The technique of building fuzzy subsets used with the contributed methodology is based on the work of Baker (1978). The original contributions are (i) the use of different (dedicated) β parameters for different categories to express the point-to-point similarity in order to increase the performance of the classifier, (ii) developing the idea acknowledged by Baker (1978) that the use of fuzzy subsets induced by multiple point-to-set similarity measures may increase the performance of the classifier, (iii) for the case study, the use of a 5 time-step time window that allows information on the system dynamics to be used with the classifier, and (iv) also for the case study, the improvement in the isolation capability by allowing single fault strengths or groups of fault strengths to form distinct categories used with the classifier.

Future research on the fuzzy classification methodology needs to concentrate on obtaining a computational complexity of both design and test phase that is small enough to make the classifier suitable for application to fault diagnosis of real systems. The computational complexity of the design phase has already been significantly reduced by using the particle swarm optimisation technique (Bocaniala and Sa da Costa, 2004a; 2004b). Also, it has been observed in practice that the classifier generalises reasonably well even for small dimensions of the *REF* and *PARAM* sets (Bocaniala, 2003). Or, the computational complexity of both the design and test phase depends heavily on the sizes of these two sets. This leads to the conclusion that a technique might be found so that the sizes of these two sets drop substantially and so that the performance of the classifier stays at least the same. An answer might be found by studying the kernel methods (Shawe-Taylor and Cristianni, 2004).

Acknowledgements

This work was partially supported by the European Commission's FP5 Research Training Network Program – Project "DAMADICS – Development and

Application of Methods for Actuator Diagnosis in Industrial Control Systems," and by Fundação para a Ciência e a Tecnologia, Minister of Science, Innovation and Technology, Portugal, grant number SFRH/BD/18651/2004

References

1.   Ariton V and Palade V (2005) Human-like fault diagnosis using a neural network implementation of plausibility and relevance. Neural Computing & Applications 14(2):149-165.
2.   Baker E (1978) Cluster analysis by optimal decomposition of induced fuzzy sets (PhD thesis). Delftse Universitaire Pres, Delft, Holland.
3.   Bocaniala CD (2003) Tehnici de inteligenţă artificială aplicate în diagnoza defectelor: Aplicaţii ale tehnicilor de clasificare (Technical Research Report within doctoral training). University "Dunarea de Jos" of Galati, Romania, 2003. (available in English for download at www.gcar.dem.ist.utl.pt/pessoal/cosmin/index.htm)
4.   Bocaniala CD and Sa da Costa J (2004a) Tuning the Parameters of a Fuzzy Classifier for Fault Diagnosis. Hill-Climbing vs. Genetic Algorithms. In: Proceedings of the Sixth Portuguese Conference on Automatic Control (CONTROLO 2004), 7-9 June, Faro, Portugal, pp. 349-354.
5.   Bocaniala CD and Sa da Costa J (2004b) Tuning the Parameters of a Fuzzy Classifier for Fault Diagnosis. Particle Swarm Optimization vs. Genetic Algorithms. In: Proceedings of the 1st International Conference on Informatics in Control, Automation and Robotics ICINCO 2004, 25-28 August, Setubal, Portugal, vol. 1, pp. 157-162.
6.   Bocaniala CD, Sa da Costa J and Louro R (2003) A Fuzzy Classification Solution for Fault Diagnosis of Valve Actuators. In: Proceedings of 7th International Conference on Knowledge-Based Intelligent Information & Engineering Systems, Oxford, UK, September 3-5, Part I, pp. 741-747, LNAI Series, Springer-Verlag, Heidelberg, Germany.
7.   Bocaniala CD, Sa da Costa J and Palade V (2004) A Novel Fuzzy Classification Solution for Fault Diagnosis. International Journal of Fuzzy and Intelligent Systems 15(3-4): 195-206.
8.   Bocaniala CD, Sa da Costa J and Palade V (2005) Fuzzy-based refinement of the fault diagnosis task in industrial devices. International Journal of Intelligent Manufacturing 16(6): 599-614.
9.   Boudaoud N and Masson M (1996) The diagnosis of technological system: on-line fuzzy clustering using gradual confirmation of prototypes. In: Proceedings of CESA'96, France.
10.   Boudaoud N and Masson M (2000) Diagnosis of transient states using pattern recognition approach. JESA – European Journal of Automation 3: 689-708.
11.   Calado JMG, Korbicz J, Patan K, Patton RJ and Sa da Costa JMG (2001) Soft Computing Approaches to Fault Diagnosis for Dynamic Systems. European Journal of Control 7: 248-286.

12. Chen J and Patton RJ (1999) Robust Model-Based Fault Diagnosis for Dynamic Systems. Asian Studies in Computer Science and Information Science, Kluwer Academic Publishers, Boston.
13. Duda RO and Hart PE (1973) Pattern classification and scene analysis. John Wiley & Sons, New York.
14. European Community's FP5, Research Training Network DAMADICS Project, http://www.eng. hull.ac.uk/research/control/damadics1.htm.
15. Frank PM (1996) Analytical and qualitative model-based fault diagnosis – a survey and some new results. European Journal of Control 2: 6-28.
16. Koscielny JM, Sedziak D and Zackroczymsky K (1999) Fuzzy-logic fault isolation in large-scale systems. International Journal of Applied Mathematics and Computer Science 9(3): 637-652.
17. Leonhardt S and Ayoubi M (1997) Methods of fault diagnosis. Control Engineering Practice 5(5): 683-692.
18. Louro R (2003) Fault Diagnosis of an Industrial Actuator Valve (MSc dissertation). Instituto Superior Técnico, Lisbon, Portugal.
19. Palade V, Patton RJ, Uppal FJ, Quevedo J and Daley S (2002) Fault Diagnosis of An Industrial Gas Turbine Using Neuro-Fuzzy Methods. In: Proceedings of the 15th IFAC World Congress, 21–26 July, Barcelona, pp. 2477–2482.
20. Sa da Costa J, Bocaniala CD and Louro R (2003) A Fuzzy Classifier for Fault Diagnosis of Valve Actuators. In: Proceedings of IEEE Conference on Control Applications CCA 2003, Istanbul, Turkey.
21. Sa da Costa J and Louro R (2003) Modelling and simulation of an industrial actuator valve for fault diagnosis benchmark. In: Proceedings of the Fourth International Symposium on Mathematical Modelling, Vienna, pp. 1212-1221, Agersin-Verlag.
22. Shawe-Taylor J and Cristianini N (2004) Kernel methods for pattern analysis. Cambridge University Press.
23. Simpson PK (1993) Fuzzy min-max neural networks – Part 2: Clustering. IEEE Transactions on Fuzzy Systems 1(1): 32-45.
24. Uppal FJ, Patton RJ and Palade V (2002) Neuro-Fuzzy Based Fault Diagnosis Applied to an Electro-Pneumatic Valve. In: Proceedings of the 15th IFAC World Congress, 21–26 July, Barcelona, Spain, pp. 2483-2488.
25. Weisstein EW (1999) Correlation Coefficient. From MathWorld--A Wolfram Web Resource, http://mathworld.wolfram.com/CorrelationCoefficient.html.

5. Fuzzy-Statistical Reasoning in Fault Diagnosis

Dan Stefanoiu and Florin Ionescu

When searching for faults threatening a system, the human expert is sometimes performing an amazingly accurate analysis of available information, frequently by using only elementary statistics. Such reasoning is referred to as "fuzzy reasoning," in the sense that the expert is able to extract and analyse the essential information of interest from a data set strongly affected by uncertainty. Automating the reasoning mechanisms that represent the foundation of such an analysis is, in general, a difficult attempt, but also a possible one, in some cases. The chapter introduces a nonconventional method of fault diagnosis, based upon some statistical and fuzzy concepts applied to vibrations, which intends to automate a part of human reasoning when performing the detection and classification of defects.

5.1. Introduction

Nowadays, the classical fault tolerant design paradigm is enriched by new methods and techniques (Wilsky, 1976; Reiter, 1987; Isermann, 1993; 1997). The trade-off between costs involved by ignoring fault prevention and costs of hyper-safety of systems is improved. The effort in designing satisfactory modules aptly to prevent failures is decreased, due to important technological advances. In a complete structure of fault detection and diagnosis, a module concerned with monitoring of system symptoms and anticipation for possible failures is included. In general, the symptoms are detected by using two kinds of methods: *analytical* and *heuristic*.

The *analytical methods* are involved with systems for which the characteristic parameters are measurable (or quantifiable). These parameters are determined by analysing either some signals or the system itself. For instance, the basic parameters of monitored signals are: the amplitude, the variance, the auto-correlation, the power spectral density, etc. Basically, the system analysis is founded on an identification model, in general parametric (Söderström and Stoica, 1989). Various models are used, such as: (auto)regressive, state representation, described by some parity equations, etc. The model parameters are deduced from measured input-output data by system identification techniques. In both cases, a quantitative expertise has to be performed. This consists mostly of comparisons between the measured values and a set of *tolerated* values assigned to normal behaviour of the system. The malfunction symptoms appear when the parameters start to systematically provide values beyond tolerances. Moreover, a classification of symptoms can be realized, depending on the difference between the measured and tolerated values.

Sometimes, the analytical approach is not sufficient or cannot be performed (especially because the characteristic parameters are not quantifiable). Moreover, the symptoms meaning is important for interpretation of associated faults. Often, this relies on the qualitative assessment of a human operator as expert. The expert experience plays an important role in symptoms investigation. For this reason, one says that the detection of symptoms is performed by using *heuristic methods* (from *heuriskein* (Greek) – to search, to investigate). The nonquantifiable information observed from the system could be reflected for example by: colours, smells, noise tones, etc. However, some quantifiable parameters, but with "fuzzy" values, represented by linguistic terms like: "small," "medium," "large," "about null," etc., belong to this category as well. The human operator integrates this information in a quasi-empirical history of system functioning. Qualitative comparisons are performed between the observed information and the information specified by the history. The history includes not only information about the normal functioning states, but also about the maintenance process, repairs, fault types, lifetime, fatigue, etc. The decision concerning the symptoms and faults is based on operator's skills, experience or flair and is affected by uncertainty. However, the experience about the system can be improved through a learning mechanism.

Like in medicine, fault prevention remains a demanding task that requires both *self-anticipation* from the system and *intelligent approach* from the user. Usually, a self-anticipatory system transmits information about its behaviour through some *anticipating signals*. For example, human or animal muscles have different electrochemical activity just before they are damaged, due to high intensity and long effort (von Tscharner, 2000). Another example is issued from mechanical systems, for which the vibrations are anticipating signals (Angelo, 1987; Bedford and Drumheller, 1994; McConnell, 1995; Wowvk, 1995). Their intimate structure changes some time before a failure occurs (Braun, 1986). But this change is so fast and sometimes so difficult to distinguish that, without special detection and decoding techniques, it could be ignored. These techniques focus on the extraction of vibration main characteristics (features), in order to classify the possible faults. In general, the strategy adopted within a fault detection method starting from vibrations consists of the following stages: signal acquisition, signal analysis (in order to extract features), features grouping, faults classification (eventually adaptively, through a continuously learning mechanism), fault identification (if present).

Vibration acquired from mechanical systems is interesting mainly for its capacity to encode information about the defects or faults threatening them. Several distinct efforts in detection of machinery defects can be noticed, but only in the last few decades has vibration become crucial for automating this process. The earliest method, which dates back to the first days of machinery (and which is still in use today), is founded on a trained observer or listener referred to as (*expert*) *analyst*. A person with a great deal of experience in working with a particular machine or engine can detect flaws in operating machinery, by simply "watching" or "listening" to it. Very often, the resulting diagnosis, based on empirical observations and deductions, is amazingly accurate, but difficult to model. Other subsequent attempts became more systematic and used some parameters, such as: the lubricant temperature (which, unfortunately, provides too late a diagnosis, after the defects are already severe), the oil cleanness (which requires an exhaustive and often inefficient analysis), the noise level of acoustic emission (which is often enabled only by already fatigued elements), etc.

The most efficient methods in early detection of defects are using signal processing (SP) techniques (Oppenheim and Schafer, 1985; Proakis and Manolakis, 1996). These methods differ from many typical SP applications where the noise attenuation is a fundamental requirement. When using vibrations, exactly the noise is the most concerned part in the analysis. This is due to the fact that not only the natural oscillations of machinery could encode the defective behaviour, but also the noise corrupting them. Moreover, the applications revealed that the signal-to-noise ratio (SNR) is extremely small for vibrations encoding information about defects. Therefore, the models of vibration used in fault detection and diagnosis (fdd) are, in fact, models of their noisy parts, encoding all the information about defect types and their severity degrees.

One of the most interesting applications in fdd is concerned with bearings, due to their simple structure and large integration within mechanical systems (Howard, 1994; FAG OEM and Handel AG, 1996; 1997). By inspecting the spectrum of vibration acquired from bearings, some researchers believed that its irregular shape is mainly due to the environmental noise and correlation between different components. Hence, they introduced techniques to "remove" the white noise and decorrelate the data, based on SP concepts such as: *autocorrelation*, *backstrum*, or *cepstrum*, but the irregularities are only slightly smoothed and the defect severity is difficult to derive. Perhaps the most popular method to extract information about defects in bearings (and geared coupling) is the (spectral) envelope analysis (EA). Some of these techniques (especially EA) are described in (Stefanoiu and Ionescu, 2002). They are poorly modelling the humanlike diagnosis, which probably requires nonconventional approaches. Actually, one can notice that experienced analysts perform a kind of fault classification, by simply inspecting the spectrum. Moreover, they are able to improve the accuracy of classification for every new case they analyse. It is by far not completely known what kind of reasoning lies behind their diagnosis, but one has assumed that the brain performs a qualitative statistical assessment inputting some pattern recognition mechanisms towards this goal. A very interesting approach combining statistics and pattern recognition has been introduced in (Xi et al., 2000). This is in fact an attempt of automating human reasoning, which resulted in a quite efficient and simple fdd algorithm, though with unavoidable limitations.

In this research, one started from the largely accepted idea that *human reasoning is also fuzzy*. This means that a solution to a problem could be issued even from unclear, vague or ambiguous information, i.e., from information strongly affected by uncertainty. Usually, the analyst considers the solution the most "plausible" one, according to the available data. When an fdd or/and classification has to be performed from vibrations, the analyst's experience is crucial for the accuracy of subsequent analysis. Unfortunately, the analyst has to cope not only with external perturbations affecting the data, but also with his/her own subjectivism when performing such an analysis. Usually, this analysis is based on some simple statistical assessments aiming to increase its objectivity. Therefore, the reasoning hidden behind data analysis could be automated by performing a combination between *spectral statistics* and *fuzzy clustering* (in entropy sense (Klir and Folger, 1988)), which should decrease both the subjectivism and the perturbations influence. Moreover, comparisons between the tested vibration and a *standard* (defect free) vibration could be performed, without specifying from the beginning the number of classes and/or their meaning, which has to be discovered later. In fact, this approach combines analytic and heuristic points of view, in order to build a model of human reasoning when performing fdd.

The chapter is structured as follows. The fuzzy-statistical reasoning method is presented in depth in the next section, which has two main parts: the first one is devoted to vibration acquisition and preprocessing, whereas within the second one, the fuzzy-statistical model is described. The resulting algorithm is practically listed in Section 5.2 as well, simultaneously with the method description. The simulation results and their interpretations are given in Section 5.3. The graphical simulations are presented in the Appendix. Some concluding remarks complete the chapter.

5.2.   The Fuzzy-Statistical Reasoning Method

One (but probably not unique) way to overcome some fdd limitations when using spectral or envelope analysis is to combine the spectral representation with statistics and subsequently to use a fuzzy model aiming to minimize the diagnosis uncertainty. This approach is described next.

5.2.1. Method Overview

When measuring vibrations of a mechanical system, several signals are combined together within the resulting data, such as: natural oscillations, interference signals (due to interactions between its different parts); defect encoding noise, indicating that something is wrong with one or more of its parts and environmental noise. The *crude mechanical vibration* is converted into an *electrical vibration* signal (v) by means of a sensor connected to a transducer (which could induce slight distortions). For example, in the case of a bearing, if data v are rich enough (few thousands of rotations), the vibration spectrum $|V|$ looks like that in Figure 5.1. Two cases could be discussed here.

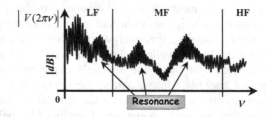

Figure 5.1.   Overall vibration spectrum in case of defects.

When the bearing is defect free, the spectral energy is mainly concentrated inside the *low-frequency* band (LF) encoding information about oscillations and their natural frequencies (derived from bearing geometry, depending on shaft rotation speed). Few multiples of natural frequencies are replicated within the spectrum, but their power has an exponential decay (due to damping). In the case of defective bearing, the idea that the defect noise is basically generated by visible or microscopic quasi-random shocks has been largely accepted today. Shocks are modelled by trains of impulses and they put the sensor into resonance state. Usually, sensor resonance appears at (very) high frequency, but, by convolution with a train of impulses, it is replicated towards low frequency as well. In Figure 5.1, this is suggested by the energy concentration around some peaks located in *middle-frequency* band (MF). Usually, a resonance peak is mixed with basic LF spectrum as well, such that it could hardly be distinguished. The *high-frequency* band (HF) rather encodes information about resonance corrupted by environmental noises. The spectrum could change (even dramatically), depending on the applied load, sensor locations, shaft speed, bearing mounting, etc.

The EA principle is easy to explain now: select one of the resonance peaks, apply a bandpass filter on the vibration around the selected resonance, take the *envelope* of the resulting signal and zoom the LF part of the spectral envelope. If isolated, the defect appears now as distinctive peaks at locations depending again on natural frequencies. The higher the peaks are, the more severe the defect.

But the analyst just looks at the spectrum and provides the diagnosis by observing the changing parts relatively to the standard spectrum, though the latter has no constant shape. This means he/she is focusing on some spectral subbands that reveal significant shape and energy differences from the standard. Moreover, the similar differences are grouped in classes and each class points to a certain defect or combination of defects (with some confidence degree).

Therefore, when automating this kind of reasoning, the following operations could be involved: define a set of statistical parameters (sp) that quantify the information about shape and energy of a signal; split the spectrum into a number of subbands; compare the tested and standard subbands in terms of sp; group the results in similarity classes, by using a global fuzzy relation between them; select the best fault class, according to an entropy-based criterion aiming to minimize the information uncertainty. This constitutes the kernel of the method described hereafter. The presentation covers two main parts. The first one is concerned with vibration acquisition and preprocessing. The second one is devoted to the fuzzy-statistical model.

5.2.2. Vibration Data Acquisition and Pre-processing

Let us denote the raw vibration data by v. In practice, v is a finite length, finite bandwidth and discrete time signal encoding the information about defects that could exist within the tested component. In this case, the signal is acquired from bearings. The acquisition and preprocessing procedure encompasses several steps that are described next.

<u>Step 1</u>: **Set the acquisition parameters.**

The first parameter employed in data acquisition is the sampling rate, denoted by v_s. The selection of v_s is extremely important for the next analysis. On the one hand, v_s should be large enough, in order to avoid aliasing (Oppenheim and Schafer, 1985; Proakis and Manolakis, 1996). On the other hand, large v_s values involve expensive devices. Therefore, a suitable value should be selected, such that the resulting signal encode most part of the desired information about defects and the acquisition costs be affordable.

The sensor characteristic usually extends beyond 140–150 kHz. If defects exist, the sensor resonance is replicated towards LF and MF bands within the vibration spectrum (see Figure 5.1). At least 3 or 4 resonance peaks are located in the 0–20 kHz band and at least 2 of them lie inside the 0–10 kHz subband. In fact, the analyst focuses on this LF subband. Usually, the vibration spectrum extends beyond the limit of 20 kHz, but the band of interest remains 0–10 kHz (the SNR decreases rapidly beyond 10–12 kHz, because of HF noises that dominate the other fast decaying vibration components). All these arguments lead to the following trade-off in vibration acquisition:

   a. Prefilter the sensor signal by using a *low-pass analogic anti-aliasing filter* (Proakis and Manolakis, 1996) that removes the HF components beyond 150 kHz;
   b. Use the *sigma-delta modulation technique* (Proakis and Manolakis, 1996), in order to restrict the signal in the range 0–12 kHz, to attenuate the quantization noise and to avoid aliasing (a new low-pass analogic filter is applied in the end);
   c. Sample the resulting analogic signal by setting a rate of at least 20–24 kHz (i.e., $v_s \geq 20$ kHz), according to Shannon-Nyquist Sampling Theorem (Oppenheim and Schafer, 1985; Proakis and Manolakis, 1996).

A standard sampling rate that has been employed for example in (Maness and Boerhout, 2001) is $v_s = 25.6$ kHz, which yields accurate vibration spectra in the range 0–12.8 kHz. Observe the powers of 2 hidden behind these values: $25600 = 2^8 \times 100$ and $12800 = 2^7 \times 100$, which avoids some computational errors due to division by multiples of 2.

Another parameter of interest is the vibration length, denoted by N. Normally, this is set according to the main rotation frequency v_r and sampling rate v_s. The vibration data should include a minimum number of complete rotations, n_r (usually, $n_r \geq 2000$). Then, obviously:

$$N = \lfloor n_r v_s / v_r \rfloor \qquad (1)$$

For example, if $n_r = 2000$, $v_r = 50$ Hz (3000 rpm) and $v_s = 25.6$ kHz, the number of vibration data is: $N = 2^{10} \times 10^3 = 1,024,000$ samples, which takes 40 s. Usually, N is also set as a power of 2 multiple and this is the reason, in Eq. 1, v_s is sometimes set with the same property. This setting is very useful in evaluation of spectrum, when using a fast fourier transform (FFT) algorithm (Oppenheim and Schafer, 1985; Proakis and Manolakis, 1996).

Usually, the apparatus performing the vibration acquisition (connected to the sensor) could be tuned by only specifying these two parameters: v_s and N or the duration of acquisition. The corresponding operations necessary to store the data in a memory are transparent for the user.

Step 2: Construct the raw vibration.
The sensor capacity of perception is determined by its bearing position. Different data could be obtained for different locations on the same bearing. When the bearing is under load, this variability is even more accentuated. This gives rise to the problem of appropriate sensor location, which is uncertain. The uncertainty could be attenuated if several sensors are located in different positions (instead of a single one). Unfortunately, in this case, other problems occur. For example, the acquired signals have to be mixed in a unique raw vibration, by synchronizing them appropriately. Another problem is that the number of sensors could increase the cost of acquisition solution. Sensors should be as light as possible, in order to introduce insignificant distortions into the genuine vibration. But, the lighter the sensor, the more expensive. Also, in general, sensors have slightly different characteristics. The bigger the sensor number, the more difficult to denoise the data. Hence, a suitable number of sensors should be employed, such that the acquired signals be easy to synchronize and the cost of acquisition be affordable.

An interesting and efficient solution is introduced in (Maness and Boerhout, 2001), as illustrated in Figure 5.2. Two sensors are employed to acquire the horizontal and the vertical vibrations, denoted by v_x and, v_y, respectively.

These are, in fact, two quadrature signals easy to synchronize, by considering them the real and the imaginary part of raw vibration:

$$v \equiv v_x + jv_y \tag{2}$$

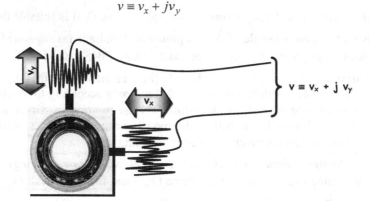

Figure 5.2.   Construction of raw vibration from two quadrature signals.

The resulting signal is complex valued, but its sensitivity to sensors location is attenuated. In the absence of load, there are no significant differences between quadrature signals in terms of magnitude. If a load is applied, these differences become important and should be accounted. In this case, Eq. 2 should be replaced by:

$$v \equiv av_x + jbv_y \tag{3}$$

where $a > 0$ and $b > 0$ are two constants selected such that av_x and bv_y have approximately the same range of variation. For example, in the case of vertical load, a could be set to 1 (no horizontal load), whereas b should be set inside $(0,1)$ interval, since the load amplifies the defect noise of vibration.

Step 3: **Vibration segmentation and windowing.**

The vibration data set $\{v[n]\}_{n \in \overline{0,N-1}}$ is quite large. If the Fourier transform (FT) were to be applied on this set, the evaluation could be very slow. Moreover, the resulting spectrum is practically useless since the vibration signals are also *non-stationary* (Cohen, 1995). In other words, the spectrum is time varying. This involves the overall spectrum reflecting the intimate behaviour of vibration only on average, whereas, on the contrary, the spectrum variations are important for learning as much as possible about how the bearing runs. Therefore, the vibration segmentation becomes a necessity. In this context, one operates with two concepts: (vibration) *frames* and (vibration) *segments*.

A *frame* is a subset of successive samples that could not be further segmented. Frames could or could not be overlapped. In this approach, the frames are *nonoverlapping*, but the overlapping effect is hidden behind the concept of *segment*. One can denote by v_m the m-th frame of vibration (where $m \in \overline{0,M}$) and by $N_f \leq N$ the frame length (constant for all frames). Obviously, the number of nonoverlapped frames is:

$$M + 1 = \lceil N / N_f \rceil \tag{4}$$

where $\lceil a \rceil$ is the smallest integer superior or equal to $a \in \varnothing$. It is suitable that N_f be a divisor of N. For example, if N is a power of 2 multiple (as suggested within the previous step), then N_f could be 512, 1024, 2048, etc. For the model constructed next, one requires that $M \geq 2$ (i.e., at least 3 frames should be available). The frame length should be selected not only according to N, but also to the minimum resolution of frame spectrum (at least 400 rays for vibration in the range 0–10 kHz). The statistical part of the model constructed later is sensitive to N_f, since it determines the precision of corresponding sp.

A vibration *segment* includes three successive (nonoverlapping) frames: the *previous* frame (v_{m-1}), the *current* frame (v_m) and the *next* frame (v_{m+1}), for $m \in \overline{1,M-1}$. Thus, the vibration data could generate up to $M-1$ segments of length $3N_f$ each. Unlike frames, segments are overlapping (two of the three frames in a segment are identical within the next segment), in order to prevent marginal effects when filtering. Actually, the characteristic frame of a segment is the current one, located in the middle. Its left and right neighbours are only playing the role of background signals, which avoids zero-padding and performs a smooth passage from a frame to another, when filtering.

The samples of neighbour signals could or could not be as important as the samples of current frame in a segment. This feature is controlled through *windowing*. The windowing technique is very simple, in fact. Let w be a $3N_f$-length window that slides along the vibration data with a step of N_f samples. Then the current segment is extracted from raw vibration by simply multiplying v and w in a certain position $(0, \ N_f, \ 2N_f, \ ..., \ (M-2)N_f)$. The sliding effect is suggested in Figure 5.3, where the window support is given by three successive frames (a segment, in fact). The window symmetry axis should be centred on the current frame middle point.

Several windows are usually employed in SP (Proakis and Manolakis, 1996). Some of them are weighting not only the neighbour frames but also some samples of central frame (like the window in Figure 5.3). The most utilized windows are the following nine, expressed next only for their N_w-length support $n \in \overline{0, N_w - 1}$, with $N_w \geq 2$.

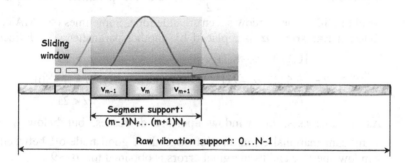

Figure 5.3.   Windowing the raw vibration.

1.   Rectangular (Oppenheim and Schafer, 1985; Proakis and Manolakis, 1996): $w[n] = 1$.

2.   Bartlett (or triangular) (Oppenheim and Schafer, 1985; Proakis and Manolakis, 1996): $w[n] = 1 - \dfrac{2\left|n - \dfrac{N_w - 1}{2}\right|}{N_w - 1}$.

3.   Blackman (Oppenheim and Schafer, 1985; Proakis and Manolakis, 1996): $w[n] = 0.42 - 0.5\cos\dfrac{2n\pi}{N_w - 1} + 0.8\cos\dfrac{4n\pi}{N_w - 1}$.

4.   Chebyshev: recursive algorithm (see MATLAB function **chebwin**). Besides the support length (N_w), a second parameter is necessary: $r_w > 0$, which stands for the attenuation in decibels (dB) of the window spectrum side lobe with respect to the main lobe. As r_w increases, the window aperture decreases, but below 70 dB, significant marginal errors are

introduced. A good trade-off between the window aperture and its marginal errors is obtained for $r_w \in [80,100]$ dB.

5.   Hamming (Oppenheim and Schafer, 1985; Proakis and Manolakis, 1996): $w[n] = 0.54 - 0.46\cos\dfrac{2n\pi}{N_w - 1}$.

6.   Hanning (Oppenheim and Schafer, 1985; Proakis and Manolakis, 1996): $w[n] = \dfrac{1}{2}\left(1 - \cos\dfrac{2n\pi}{N_w - 1}\right)$.

7.   Kaiser   (Kaiser,   1974;   Proakis   and   Manolakis,   1996):

$$w[n] = \frac{\sinh\left[\alpha\sqrt{\left(\dfrac{N_w - 1}{2}\right)^2 - \left(n - \dfrac{N_w - 1}{2}\right)^2}\right]}{\sinh\left[\alpha\dfrac{N_w - 1}{2}\right]},$$ where sinh stands for the

hyperbolic sine ($\sinh x \overset{def}{=} \dfrac{e^x - e^{-x}}{2}$) and the parameter $\alpha > 0$ is the height in dB of the window spectrum side lobe. Sometimes (see MATLAB function **kaiser**), α is replaced by another parameter, β, defined as follows: $\beta = \begin{cases} 0.1102(\alpha - 8.7), & \alpha > 50 \\ 0.5842(\alpha - 21)^{0.4} + 0.07886(\alpha - 21), & \alpha \in [21,50] \\ 0, & \alpha < 21 \end{cases}$

As β increases, the window aperture decreases, but below $\beta = 6$, significant marginal errors are introduced. A good trade-off between the window aperture and its marginal errors is obtained for $\beta = 9$.

8.   Lanczos (Proakis and Manolakis, 1996):

$$w[n] = \left[\frac{\sin 2\pi\left(\dfrac{2n - N_w + 1}{2(N_w - 1)}\right)}{2\pi\left(\dfrac{2n - N_w + 1}{2(N_w - 1)}\right)}\right]^L,$$ where the exponent $L > 0$ controls the

window aperture. As L increases, the window aperture decreases, but below the unit value ($L < 1$), significant marginal errors are introduced. A good trade-off between the window aperture and its marginal errors is obtained for $L = 1$.

9.   Tukey (Proakis and Manolakis, 1996):

$$w[n]=\begin{cases}1, & \left|n-\dfrac{N_w-1}{2}\right|\leq\alpha\dfrac{N_w-1}{2}\\[2em]\dfrac{1}{2}\left[1+\cos\left(\dfrac{n-(1+\alpha)\dfrac{N_w-1}{2}}{(1+\alpha)\dfrac{N_w-1}{2}}\pi\right)\right], & \alpha\dfrac{N_w-1}{2}<\left|n-\dfrac{N_w-1}{2}\right|\leq\dfrac{N_w-1}{2}\end{cases}$$

where the parameter $\alpha\in(0,1)$ controls the percentage of rectangular window centred inside. For the vibration segment, a good choice is $\alpha=1/3$, since the central frame takes only one third of the whole segment.

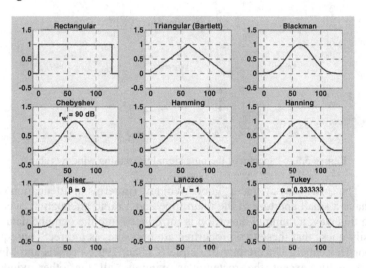

Figure 5.4. Nine of the most utilized signal processing windows.

All windows above are symmetric, as shown in Figure 5.4, where, beside the window shape, the parameter values are also depicted for Chebyshev, Kaiser, Lanczos and Tukey windows. But not all windows of this collection have the same performances when using them in SP applications. Their efficiency depends on the specific criteria that have to be matched. Although some windows seem to have the same shape, they are actually quite different. The differences are better emphasized by their spectra, as drawn in Figure 5.5. The graphics are plotted by using the spectral power expressed in dB and on all horizontal axes normalized frequencies are represented. *The main lobe* lies in LF subband, whereas the *side lobes* extend to MF and HF subbands. The main lobe is best emphasized for windows like Blackman, Chebyshev or Kaiser. (For the last two, the main lobe height relative to the first side lobe can be controlled.) One of the most employed criterions in selection of the appropriate window is the *attenuation performed by the side lobes*. Since the window multiplies the data, their corresponding FT are convoluted (according to the Inverse Convolution Theorem (Oppenheim and Schafer, 1985; Proakis and Manolakis, 1996)). Hence, the genuine data spectrum is distorted by the window spectrum. Ideally, the window spectrum is not distorting the genuine one only if it is identical to the unit (or Dirac) impulse. In another words, only the main lobe should be present (not the side lobes) and its aperture should be null in spectral images below. But, as one can see from the windows' spectra, none of them verify this (ideal) property.

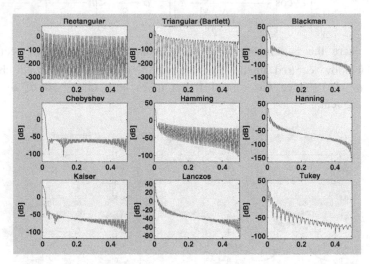

Figure 5.5.   Spectra of the nine signal processing windows above.

Thus, one can say that a "good" window (in terms of attenuation criterion) should have a small aperture of the main lobe and a rapid attenuation over the side lobes. In this way, a minimal distortion is introduced into the genuine data. But one may easily guess that these two properties are opposite, as a direct consequence of the Gabor-Heisenberg Uncertainty Principle (Cohen, 1995; Proakis and Manolakis, 1996). Actually, except the rectangular window, all the other windows are performing a trade-off between the main lobe aperture and the side lobes attenuation.

The rectangular window, which anyone is tempted to select for its simplicity, is, in fact, the worst one in terms of side lobes attenuation, but probably one of the best in terms of main lobe aperture. The triangular window improves in some respect this trade-off, but not essentially. Among the other windows, Blackman, Hanning and Kaiser prove very good performances. (the Hanning window is actually employed in many filter design methods.)

But, for the purpose of our model, the Tukey window is very likely the most appropriate. As one can see, its shape in the time domain (Figure 5.4) is very well adapted to the manner in which the vibration segments are constructed: one important central frame and two lateral auxiliary frames (that should gradually be weighted). In frequency, a good trade-off between main lobe aperture and side lobes attenuation is realized (see again Figure 5.5). Therefore, the vibration segments are built by windowing the data with a Tukey window (for $\alpha = 1/3$). Note that all the other eight windows have been tested by simulation, but none of them could overtake the Tukey window in terms of final defect classifications properties. But, actually, the method presented here is not very sensitive to the employed window, which constitutes an advantage.

Denote by s_m (for $m \in \overline{1, M-1}$) the current segment resulting after windowing the data by w. Then the windowing effect could be described by:

$$s_m \equiv [v_{m-1} \ v_m \ v_{m+1}] \cdot w \tag{5}$$

Step 4: Digital filtering of vibration data.

The vibration segments s_m are utilized next in a filtering procedure aiming to remove the LF oscillatory part and, eventually, some HF noise. The filters are digital. Unlike many approaches regarding vibrations filtering, here, one takes benefits from the modern and powerful finite impulse response (FIR) filters design procedures described, for example in (Proakis and Manolakis, 1996).

Two types of digital FIR filters could be employed: high-pass and band-pass. The first one just removes most of the harmonic natural oscillations. The second one could moreover remove the HF noise inherited by vibration data especially from environmental sources. For these filters, some parameters should be set, in order to perform the design: the filter length (N_h), the left cutoff frequency (v_{lc}) and the right cutoff frequency (v_{rc}, in case of high-pass filters).

The filter length should be large enough to yield good filters characteristics, but it should not overtake the segment length. A suitable choice is $N_h \in \{N_f, N_f + 1\}$, provided that the frame length is sufficiently large. (According to FIR procedure design, in the case of high-pass filters, the length must be odd. If N_f is even, then N_h should be set to $N_f + 1$.)

The left cutoff frequency v_{lc} has to be set such that the decaying natural harmonics in raw vibration are strongly attenuated or removed. Thus, on the one hand, $v_{lc} \geq v_{lc,min}$, where the inferior limit $v_{lc,min}$ is set to 7-10 times the maximum natural frequency of oscillation. On the other hand, increasing the left cutoff frequency beyond a limit of 2 kHz may result in a loss of information about possible defects. Thus, v_{in} should be set in the range $[v_{lc,min}, 2000]$ [Hz].

Unlike within the EA method, here, the right cutoff frequency v_{rc} should ensure a sufficiently wide pass band, in order to extract all information encoding defects. If the anti-aliasing analogic filters do not remove some HP noises, then v_{rc} should be selected such that they are attenuated in subband $[v_{rc}, v_s / 2]$. Normally, the width of this subband should not be larger than v_{lc}, but this is not a requirement. Sometimes, the right cutoff is imposed by a central symmetry frequency, usually selected according to a resonance peak in vibration spectrum.

In Figure 5.6, the characteristics of two filters have been depicted: a high-pass one (to the left) and a band-pass one (to the right). For both filters, $N_f = 2048$, but the high-pass one must have an odd number of coefficients.

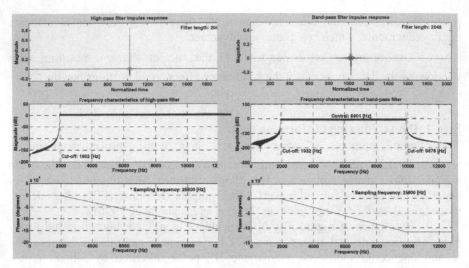

Figure 5.6.   High-pass (left) and band-pass (right) filter characteristics.

The time domain characteristics (the impulse responses) are less suggestive than the frequency domain characteristics (magnitude and phase of frequency responses). "Good" filters should have an abrupt change at the cut-off frequency, a strong attenuation in stop band(s), no ripples on the main lobe and linear phase. In this figure, the left and right cutoff frequencies have been set to $v_{lc} = 1932$ Hz and $v_{rc} = 9876$ Hz, whereas the sampling frequency is $v_s = 25.6$ kHz. Actually, the band-pass filter was centred on 5.9 kHz. The attenuation in stop bands is quite strong, thanks to the large filter lengths.

Segments are one by one filtered. If h is the impulse response of the selected filter, then any filtered segment is simply obtained by convolution: $s_m * h$. Since $N_h \in \{N_f, N_f + 1\}$, its length is $3N_f$ as well. This involves $s_m * h$ could also be split into three frames with same length (N_f):

$$s_m * h \equiv [v_{h,m-1} \; v_{h,m} \; v_{h,m+1}] \tag{6}$$

The reason the filtered segment is split again into three frames in Eq. 6 is very simple. The filter was not actually applied to all frames in s_m but to its main frame, the central one. The lateral frames are only context signals that tell to the filter there are nonnull signal values before and after the main frame. Since filters are shift invariant linear systems (Oppenheim and Schafer, 1985; Proakis and Manolakis, 1996), the main frame in Eq. 6 is also the central one. Therefore, from the filtered segment, only one frame is extracted for the next step: $v_{h,m}$. Note that, in general, $v_{h,m}$ is different from $v_m * h$ and it is closer to the real behaviour of filtered vibration, due to the lateral frames. Also, the first and the last raw vibration frames (v_0 and v_M) are only involved as context signals aiming to avoid marginal errors. They are not furthermore transmitted.

The resulting filtered frames could be considered as nonoverlapping, since the main frame of the segment becomes the context (auxiliary) frame for the next segment. There are $M-1$ filtered frames $\{v_{h,m}\}_{m\in\overline{1,M-1}}$. These are inputs for the fuzzy-statistical model described next. Note that a set of standard (defect free) vibration preprocessed data $\{v_{h,m}^0\}_{m\in\overline{1,M-1}}$ is also provided by the same technique.

5.2.3. The Fuzzy-Statistical Model

The steps aiming to construct the fuzzy-statistical model are grouped into two categories: construction of the spectral statistic information about the filtered frames $\{v_{h,m}\}_{m\in\overline{1,M-1}}$ and utilization of this information in a fuzzy approach.

Step 1: Spectrum evaluation and segmentation.
The spectrum of each frame $v_{h,m}$ (or $v_{h,m}^0$) is evaluated by using one of the powerful existing FFT algorithms (Oppenheim and Schafer, 1985; Proakis and Manolakis, 1996). Denote by $V_{h,m}$ (respectively by $V_{h,m}^0$) the spectrum of current (filtered) frame ($m\in\overline{1,M-1}$), i.e., the magnitude of its FT. Since the spectrum is symmetric for real valued data sequences, it follows that only the first $N_f/2$ rays could be accounted, which corresponds to a bandwidth of $v_s/2$.

The main difference between spectra encoding information about defects $V_{h,m}$ and defect-free spectra $V_{h,m}^0$ is that the former have a bigger variability among frames, whereas the later vary within some minimum and maximum bounds, close to each other. The variability could be expressed in various ways, but, for this model, sp are employed to quantify the spectral behaviour.

By convention, let $V_{h,m}^*$ stand for any of two spectra above ($V_{h,m}$ or $V_{h,m}^0$). The full frequency band of each spectrum $V_{h,m}^*$ is uniformly segmented next into $K\geq 1$ subbands, in order to evaluate a set of local sp. Such a frequency segment (subband) should include between 5 and 10 rotations of main shaft, in order to construct a consistent set of sp. Thus, the segment bandwidth should be set between $5v_r$ and $10v_r$ (i.e., K should vary in the range $[1/10,1/20]v_s/v_r$). The minimum bound yields a good *frequency resolution* (i.e., narrow subbands), but a smaller sp accuracy than the maximum bound, where, however, the resolution is worst. Obviously, the sp consistency (accuracy) depends on the number of accounted data. In this case, the consistency depends on the number of rays included in a segment, that is, on the segment bandwidth. The bigger the bandwidth, the more consistent the sp, but the less focused on local spectral variation. A good compromise is realized for $8v_r$:

$$K = \lceil v_s/16v_r \rceil \tag{7}$$

The number of rays within each frequency subband (except possibly the one located at the highest frequency) is:

$$N_K = \lfloor N_f / 2K \rfloor \tag{8}$$

For example, $N_f = 2048$, $v_r = 50$ Hz (3000 rpm), and $v_s = 25.6$ kHz lead to: $K = 32$ subbands (of 400 Hz bandwidth each) and $N_K = 32$ rays/sub-band, according to Eqs. 7 and 8.

By convention, sub-bands are indexed from 0 to $K-1$.

Splitting the spectrum in a number of equally spaced subbands may not be the best solution to focus on spectral power local variation. However, the trade-off between frequency resolution (or K) and sp accuracy (or N_K) determines the minimum bandwidth for carrying out the statistical analysis. Nonuniform segmentations could be realized by compacting together two or more adjacent subbands with minimum bandwidth. But the fdd method described here is independent on the type of frequency segmentation. Therefore, for the sake of simplicity, the segmentation is kept uniform hereafter.

To conclude this step, a final remark should be noted. Filtering the vibration segments involves a separation of frequency stop subbands and pass subbands. The statistical parameters might not be similarly employed for any of these 2 subband types, because the information encoded inside the stop subbands is probably extremely poor and noisy compared to the information inside the pass subbands. Since the whole band was practically quantified by K values, separation lines between stop and pass subbands have to be defined. Obviously, the cut-off frequencies v_{lc} and v_{rc} belong to some subbands as follows:

$$v_{lc} \in [K_{lc}, K_{lc}+1)\frac{v_s}{2K} \quad \text{and} \quad v_{rc} \in (K_{rc}-1, K_{rc}]\frac{v_s}{2K} \tag{9}$$

where

$$K_{lc} = \lfloor 2K v_{lc} / v_s \rfloor \quad \text{and} \quad K_{rc} = \lceil 2K v_{rc} / v_s \rceil \tag{10}$$

For example, if, like previously, $v_{lc} = 1932$ Hz and $v_{rc} = 9876$ Hz, whereas $v_s = 25.6$ kHz and $K = 32$, then: $K_{lc} = 4$ and $K_{rc} = 25$.

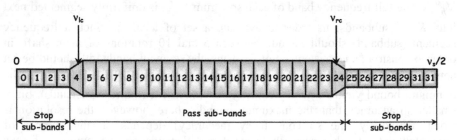

Figure 5.7.   An example of frequency segmentation.

Normally, the transition subbands (i.e., including the cutoff frequencies) should be pass type, in order to avoid removing useful side information. Therefore, the stop subbands are: {0, 1, ..., $K_{lc}-1$, K_{rc}, ..., $K-1$}. Consequently, the pass subbands are: { K_{lc}, ..., $K_{rc}-1$ }. For the previous example, the stop and pass subbands are: $\{0, 1, 2, 3, 25, 26, ..., 31\}$, respectively $\{4, 5, ..., 23, 24\}$, as depicted in Figure 5.7.

Step 2: Definition of sp and construction of relative statistical vectors.
Using statistics to extract information about defects from raw vibration is not a new idea. Many analysts perform diagnosis with the help of some parameters such as the *root mean square* (RMS) or the *peak value* evaluated either from vibration data or their spectrum.

A quasi-complete statistical set of parameters includes the following 12 parameters: *peak (to valley)* (Δv); *average* ($\bar{v}$); *absolute average* ($\overline{|v|}$); *energy* (E_v); *normalized energy* (E_v^N); *root mean square* (RMS_v); *peak to average ratio* (PAR_v); *crest factor* (CF_v); *impulse factor* (IF_v); *shape factor* (SF_v); *clearance factor* (CLF_v); *Kurtosis* (K_v). Their definitions are listed in Eq. 11, for any N-length data series, $\{v[n]\}_{n \in \overline{0,N-1}}$ (such as vibrations or their spectra):

$$\Delta v \overset{def}{=} \frac{1}{2}\left[\max_{n \in 0,N-1}\{v[n]\} - \min_{n \in 0,N-1}\{v[n]\} \right]; \quad \bar{v} \overset{def}{=} \frac{1}{N}\sum_{n=0}^{N-1} v[n]; \quad \overline{|v|} \overset{def}{=} \frac{1}{N}\sum_{n=0}^{N-1}|v[n]|;$$

$$E_v \overset{def}{=} \sum_{n=0}^{N-1}|v[n]|^2; \quad E_v^N \overset{def}{=} \frac{1}{N}\sum_{n=0}^{N-1}|v[n]|^2; \quad RMS_v \overset{def}{=} \sqrt{\frac{1}{N}\sum_{n=0}^{N-1}(v[n]-\bar{v})^2};$$

$$PAR_v \overset{def}{=} \frac{1}{|v|}\max_{n \in 0,N-1}\{|v[n]|\}; \quad CF_v \overset{def}{=} \frac{\Delta v}{RMS_v}, \quad IF_v \overset{def}{=} \frac{\Delta v}{\overline{|v|}}; \tag{11}$$

$$SF_v \overset{def}{=} \frac{RMS_v}{\overline{|v|}}; \quad CLF_v \overset{def}{=} \frac{\Delta v}{\frac{1}{N}\left(\sum_{n=0}^{N-1}\sqrt{|v[n]|}\right)^2}; \quad K_v \overset{def}{=} \frac{\frac{1}{N}\sum_{n=0}^{N-1}(v[n]-\bar{v})^4}{RMS_v^4}$$

The first six parameters are concerned with energetic characteristics, whereas the other six quantify different shape properties. Obviously, the number of data, N, is a measure of sp accuracy. (The accuracy increases with N.)

Usually, the values of parameters defined in Eq. 11 are compared to standard values corresponding to defect-free systems. Their biases could indicate the desired information about defects (including estimations of severity degree). Though the number of parameters to account for is large enough, no one is able to extract all the necessary information about defects.

Once the frequency segmentation has been realized, some sp should be evaluated within every subband. Note that the set of 12 sp above is redundant. For example, in (Xi *et al.*, 2000), one states that peak-to-valley is similar to RMS, to energy and to absolute average; impulse factor is similar to shape factor; kurtosis is similar to crest factor. These similarities are not realized in sense of similarity measure from physics, but in terms of some features ad hoc defined in the context of that research. Therefore, a safe approach is to take into consideration as much sp as possible. An obvious remark is that, for nonnegative data (like spectral powers), the absolute average is identical to the average. Also, it is better to evaluate the normalized energy instead of pure energy, especially in the case of nonuniform frequency segmentation (when subbands have different numbers of rays and, thus, their energy becomes noncomparable). Thus, only 10 sp are retained in this context. They are denoted according to time and frequency segmentations performed so far:

peak (to valley) ($\Delta V_{h,m}^{*}$); *average* ($V_{h,m}^{*}$); *normalized energy* ($E_{h,m}^{N,*}$); *root mean square* ($RMS_{h,m}^{*}$); *peak to average ratio* ($PAR_{h,m}^{*}$); *crest factor* ($CF_{h,m}^{*}$); *impulse factor* ($IF_{h,m}^{*}$); *shape factor* ($SF_{h,m}^{*}$); *clearance factor* ($CLF_{h,m}^{*}$); *kurtosis* ($K_{h,m}^{*}$).

As usual, the $*$ employed in notations points to any of 2 vibration data types: acquired from the tested bearing ($*$ vanishes) or from the standard (defect free) bearing ($*$ is replaced by 0).

Any of the sp above takes K values for every frame $m \in \overline{1, M-1}$ (one value for each subband). The number of rays per subband determines their consistency, N_K. For example, $RMS_{h,m}^{*}$ could be evaluated as follows:

$$RMS_{h,m}^{*}[k] \overset{def}{=} \sqrt{\frac{1}{N_K} \sum_{n=0}^{N_K-1} \left(V_{h,m}^{*}[kN_K + n] - \overline{V_{h,m}^{*}[k]} \right)^2}, \ \forall k \in \overline{0, K-1} \qquad (12)$$

where the local average is:

$$\overline{V_{h,m}^{*}[k]} \overset{def}{=} \frac{1}{N_K} \sum_{n=0}^{N_K-1} V_{h,m}^{*}[kN_K + n], \ \forall k \in \overline{0, K-1} \qquad (13)$$

A $10 \times K$ statistical matrix $S_{h,m}^{*}$ could be constructed for every spectral frame $V_{h,m}^{*}$, by stacking the sp values in successive row vectors, as enumerated above. Thus, for example, the RMS value in Eq. 13 is the element $[4, k+1]$ of matrix $S_{h,m}^{*}$, i.e., $S_{h,m}^{*}[4, k+1] = RMS_{h,m}^{*}[k]$, whereas the fourth row of the matrix packs all RMS values among subbands. The generic element of matrix $S_{h,m}^{*}$ is $S_{h,m}^{*}[i, j]$, where $i \in \overline{1,10}$, $j = k+1 \in \overline{1, K}$ and $m \in \overline{1, M-1}$.

When the tested bearing is defect-free (standard), the statistical values of matrices $S_{h,m}^{0}$ vary within some acceptable tolerances among frames. Thus, in this case, the values of every sp are located inside a min-max domain, whose bounds depend on the evaluation subband. More specifically, let P_i^{*} be the i-th sp in the list above (for $i \in \overline{1,10}$). (For example, $P_2^{*} \equiv V^{*}$, $P_4^{*} \equiv RMS^{*}$, etc.) Then its value for the m-th frame and the k-th sub-band is $P_i^{*}[m,k]$. For the standard vibration, $P_i^{0}[\bullet, k]$ could vary in the range $\left[P_i^{\min}[k], P_i^{\max}[k] \right]$ among frames, but within the same subband (k). A natural manner to evaluate the min-max bounds is to account for all frames:

$$P_i{}^{\min}[k] = \min_{m \in \overline{1, M-1}} \left\{ P_i{}^0[m,k] \right\}, \ P_i{}^{\max}[k] = \max_{m \in \overline{1, M-1}} \left\{ P_i{}^0[m,k] \right\}, \ \forall k \in \overline{0, K-1} \quad (14)$$

This involves that two remarkable matrices could be constructed, by gathering together all minimum or maximum values evaluated in Eq. 14:

$$\boldsymbol{S}^{\min}[i,j] = P_i{}^{\min}[j-1], \ \boldsymbol{S}^{\max}[i,j] = P_i{}^{\max}[j-1], \ \forall i \in \overline{1,10}, \ \forall j \in \overline{1,K} \quad (15)$$

The same result is obtained if the min and max operators are applied elementwise on matrices $\left\{ \boldsymbol{S}^0_{h,m} \right\}_{m \in \overline{1, M-1}}$. In practice, the min and max values are furthermore *corrected* by multiplication with constants $\sigma^{\min} < 1$ and $\sigma^{\max} > 1$, respectively, , in order to avoid diagnosing as defective the defect-free bearings. For example, $\sigma^{\min} = 0.6$ and $\sigma^{\max} = 1.1$. The lower bound is, however, less important than the upper bound and this is the reason the constant $\sigma^{\min}$ is not 0.9 (the symmetrical value of $\sigma^{\max} = 1.1$), but 0.6. By convention, hereafter, one preserves the same notations $P_i{}^{\min}[k]$ and $P_i{}^{\max}[k]$ for corrected bounds as well.

Defective bearings provide vibrations that exceed some or all the (corrected) bounds in matrices defined by Eq. 15. The biases of sp P_i outside the standard range could indicate the desired information about defects, including estimations of severity degree. Note that defects could be detected not only when maximum bound is overtaken, but also if the minimum bound is undertaken. The second effect is especially induced by lubrication defects, excessive wear or multiple-point defects (when the phases of FT could lead to energy attenuation inside some subbands). In order to quantify the severity degree of defects, the sp are replaced by the relative statistical parameters (rsp), defined as explained next.

There are two types of assessments when performing the comparison between sp and their bounds: by accounting for both min and max limits or by considering only the max limit. Both limits should be accounted for pass subbands, whereas only the max limit is sufficient for the stop bands. In the first case, for each sp P_i ($i \in \overline{1,10}$) one defines a corresponding rsp R_i as follows:

$$R_i[m,k] \overset{def}{=} \frac{1}{\sqrt{10}} \begin{cases} P_i[m,k]/P_i^{\max}[k], & \text{if } P_i[m,k] > P_i^{\max}[k] \\ 1, & \text{if } P_i[m,k] \in \left[P_i^{\min}[k], P_i^{\max}[k] \right], \\ P_i^{\min}[k]/P_i[m,k], & \text{if } 0 < P_i[m,k] < P_i^{\min}[k] \end{cases} \quad (16)$$

$$\forall m \in \overline{1, M-1}, \ \forall k \in \overline{0, K-1}$$

Similarly, in the second case, the definition of rsp can be expressed as:

$$R_i[m,k] \overset{def}{=} \frac{1}{\sqrt{10}} \begin{cases} P_i[m,k]/P_i^{\max}[k], & \text{if } P_i[m,k] > P_i^{\max}[k] \\ 1, & \text{if } P_i[m,k] \leq P_i^{\max}[k] \end{cases}, \quad (17)$$

$$\forall m \in \overline{1, M-1}, \ \forall k \in \overline{0, K-1}$$

The same philosophy was employed in both definitions of Eqs. 16 and 17: if the maximum bound is exceeded, evaluate how many times the parameter overtakes the bound; if the minimum bound is exceeded, evaluate how many times the bound overtakes the parameter; set by 1 the rsp when the parameter stays within the tolerance limits.

Note that, independently of the sp type, the values of different rsp could now be compared, thanks to their relative nature. Thus, for example, although RMS (P_4) is not comparable with kurtosis (P_{10}), the relative RMS (R_4) has values varying in a similar range to the relative kurtosis (R_{10}). Therefore, the rsp values of the same frame within the same subband could be packed in a 10-length column vector $R = [R_1, R_2, ..., R_{10}]^T$. The purpose of the $1/\sqrt{10}$ factor employed in both definitions above is to normalize the vector R in the following sense:

$$\|R[m,k]\| \geq 1, \quad \forall m \in \overline{1, M-1}, \quad \forall k \in \overline{0, K-1} \tag{18}$$

and $\|R[m,k]\| = 1$ if the spectrum of the m-th frame behaves normally within the k-th subband (as for the defect-free bearing). Starting with the next step, Euclidean norms $\|R[m,k]\|$ are actually employed. For a more general approach, other norms could be considered as well. For example, one can consider that not all sp have the same weight and thus a weighting matrix $Q \in \mathcal{Q}^{10\times10}$ (eventually diagonal) has to multiply left the rsp vector R . The norm of the resulting vector QR is in fact a generalized Euclidean Q-norm.

Returning to Eqs. 16 and 17, a special case remains to be considered: the null parameter values, when both bounds have to be accounted. If one recalls the sp definitions in Eq. 11, it is easy to see that not all parameters could be null, even when the input data consists of a finite length null signal. This property is proven by those parameters quantifying the signal shape, since a part of the shape information is the signal length (denoted by N in Eq. 11). In fact, simple algebraic manipulations lead to the following interesting limits when the signal v tends to the null signal:

$$\lim_{v\to0} \Delta v = \frac{0}{2} = 0 \ ; \ \lim_{v\to0} \bar{v} = \frac{0}{N} = 0 \ ; \ \lim_{v\to0} |\bar{v}| = \frac{0}{N} = 0 \ ;$$

$$\lim_{v\to0} E_v = 0^2 = 0 \ ; \ \lim_{v\to0} E_v^N = \frac{0^2}{N} = 0 \ ; \ \lim_{v\to0} RMS_v = \frac{\sqrt{N-1}}{N} 0 = 0 ;$$

$$\lim_{v\to0} PAR_v = N \ ; \ \lim_{v\to0} CF_v = \frac{N}{2\sqrt{N-1}} \ ; \ \lim_{v\to0} IF_v = \frac{N}{2} \ ; \tag{19}$$

$$\lim_{v\to0} SF_v = \sqrt{N-1} \ ; \ \lim_{v\to0} CLF_v = \frac{N}{2} \ ; \ \lim_{v\to0} K_v = \frac{N^2 - 3N + 3}{N-1}$$

Thus, the shape parameters are null if and only if the signal is empty. Practically, in context of spectral frames, they are always nonnull. But the energetic parameters could be null inside some subbands, if and only if all corresponding rays are null. Usually, if in a pass subband all rays are null, either a severe defect is announcing or there are some important errors within the available data. The second hypothesis could be confirmed when the spectrum is null for many pass subbands. But, if only few isolated pass subbands provide null data, then the first hypothesis is more plausible. In this case, the rsp should be set to a value equal to or more than $10P_i^{\max}[k]$, for all subbands where $P_i[m,k]=0$. The reason for this setting will become obvious in the next step.

An average set of norms $\{\|R[i,k]\|\}_{i\in\overline{1,m}}$ is also evaluated for each sub-band, after every $m\in\overline{1,M-1}$ processed frames:

$$\overline{\|R\|}[m,k] \stackrel{def}{=} \frac{1}{m}\sum_{i=1}^{m}\|R[i,k]\|, \ \forall k\in\overline{0,K-1} \tag{20}$$

This entity is extremely useful for initialising the fuzzy model. In fact, one can consider that the processing starts from a *virtual frame* that provides the average information about rsp norms at any moment. Set the index of virtual frame by $m=0$ and change notation $\overline{\|R\|}[m,k]$ by $\|R[0,k]\|$. In the new notation, the current number of frames was omitted, in order to unify all notations regarding the rsp norms. But, hereafter, one can consider by convention that the set of rsp norms $\{\|R[i,k]\|\}_{i\in\overline{0,m}}$ always starts with the average of currently processed frames $\{\|R[i,k]\|\}_{i\in\overline{1,m}}$ in the first position. This average could recursively be upgraded, from a frame to another, according to the equation below:

$$\overline{\|R\|}[m+1,k] = \frac{m\overline{\|R\|}[m,k]+\|R[m+1,k]\|}{m+1}, \ \forall k\in\overline{0,K-1} \tag{21}$$

After processing the first frame, the average is identical to $\|R[1,k]\|$, but starting from the second processed frame, the average and the other rsp norms are, in general, different. Therefore, within the next steps, one shall assume that the average starts to be evaluated after at least two frames have been processed.

Step 3: Definition and construction of a *statistical network*.

Let $\|R[m,k]\|_{dB}$ be the value of $\|R[m,k]\|$ expressed in dB (for $m\in\overline{0,M-1}$, i.e., including the average (Eq. 20). Then the severity degree of defect could be expressed in terms of a grid, in dB as well. Usually, there are 4 severity types: *normal* (when no defect seems to be detected), *incipient, medium* and *severe*. The separation values between severity types could be set as follows: 1, $[2]_{dB}\approx 6\,dB$ and $[10]_{dB}=20\,dB$. Thus, if $\|R[m,k]\|$ varies in the range $[1,1.22)$, no defect is present; for range $[1.22,2)$, the defect is incipient; inside the range $[2,10)$, the defect is medium and if $\|R[m,k]\|$ is more than 10, the defect is severe. The grid could refine the severity levels for every type as follows: 0, 1, $[\sqrt2]_{dB}\approx 3$, $[2]_{dB}\approx 6$, $[3]_{dB}$, $[4]_{dB}$, ..., $[9]_{dB}$, $[10]_{dB}=20$ [dB] ($L=12$ levels). Let $\Lambda=[\lambda_l]_{l\in\overline{0,L-1}}\in\mathbb{Q}_+^L$ be the L-length vector of all severity levels expressed in dB and set $\lambda_L=\infty$.

All settings above aimed to build a map like the one depicted in Figure 5.8 and referred to as the *statistical network* (sn). Thus, for each subband, a box cell is assigned to every severity degree. Each value $\|R\,[m,k]\|_{dB}$ is uniquely located inside such a box, as suggested by the diamonds in figure. In this example, the location of rsp norms of a frame is depicted. The maximum rsp norm is reached inside subband #5, where an incipient-medium defect is announced. Its severity degree is $\cong 5.89$ dB (at least one sp is about 1.97 times out of standard min-max range). Note that the box cells corresponding to severe defects are *open*, in the sense that their height varies depending on maximum pointed severity degree (if applicable). On the contrary, the other box cells have fixed heights (but differ from one severity degree to another).

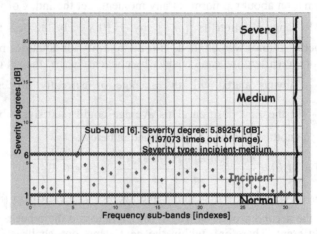

Figure 5.8.   A statistical network example.

The sn provides in fact a *statistical map* of possible defects, simpler than the spectrum image. And yet, it is difficult to perform a good fdd by only inspecting this map. Therefore, a technique of grouping network cells in similarity classes could make this task easier.

Step 4: Covering the statistical network with clusters.
The previous steps prepared the fuzzy model construction. Starting from this step, a fuzzy approach is combined with statistics in order to provide defect classifications expressed as partitions of sn above. This approach is based on concepts of *fuzzy relations* and *fuzzy entropy* (Klir and Folger, 1988) and its kernel has already been integrated into another (but very different) method concerned with identification of main structures inside Multi-Agent Systems (Ulieru *et al.*, 2000).

In context of vibrations, the fuzzy model relies on the fact that every frame encodes the same information about existing defects (if the frame length is large enough to induce a good accuracy of sp). Consequently, the statistical maps resulting from every frame reveal about the same correlation between those box cells that actually encode the defect, whereas the remaining cells are less correlated. More specifically, the rsp norms from different frames "fall" more often into the same boxes for those subbands that seem to be directly affected by the defect. One can say that rsp norms *occur* more often inside box cells that apparently encode the systematic spectrum biases caused by a specific defect.

Therefore, the basic idea is first to construct a similarity fuzzy relation between box cells within sn and then to unpack the result as different classifications comprising similarity classes. A *similarity class* is actually a group of box cells that seem to point to the same fault or group of faults (with some confidence degree).

In construction of a fuzzy relation between box cells, the first action is to specify how the sn could be covered by collections of box cells for every spectral frame. Any collection of box cells is referred to in this context as a *cluster*. Denote by $B_{l,k}$ the generic box-cell of sn, where $l \in \overline{0, L-1}$ is the severity level and $k \in \overline{0, K-1}$ is the frequency subband. A natural way to construct clusters is to consider two types of sn covers as follows:

  a. a horizontal one, $\mathscr{H}$, with L clusters, each of which includes only constant severity level box cells: $C_l = \left\{ B_{l,k} \right\}_{k \in \overline{0, K-1}}$

  $(l \in \overline{0, L-1})$;

  b. a vertical one, $\mathscr{G}$, with K clusters, each of which includes only box cells corresponding to the same frequency subband:
  $D_k = \left\{ B_{l,k} \right\}_{l \in \overline{0, L-1}}$ $(k \in \overline{0, K-1})$.

Thus:

$$\mathscr{H} = \bigcup_{l=0}^{L-1} C_l \text{ and } \mathscr{G} = \bigcup_{k=0}^{K-1} D_k \qquad (22)$$

Note that the covers in Eq. 22 are independent of frame index (they preserve the same structure for all frames), since, at this stage, one focuses only on the structural information about how the sn could be roughly organized. The information about defects encoded by rsp norms will be accounted for in a future stage.

An example of horizontal and vertical clusters is displayed in Figure 5.9.

Other structures of sn covering could be considered as well, for example, the one consisting of cross-clusters obtained by taking the union between horizontal and vertical clusters (also illustrated in Figure 5.9). But the main advantage of coverings above is that they lead to one of the simplest fuzzy relation construction algorithms.

The box cells that belong to the same cluster are in fact entities verifying the same elementary crisp (binary) relation. Two crisp relations could thus be stated: (a) two box cells are in the same relationship if they reveal the same severity level; (b) two box cells are in the same relationship if they point to the same frequency subband. The characteristic (index) functions describing these crisp relations are $KL \times KL$ binary matrices, where the element (i, j) is unitary only if the box cells i and j are in relation to each other (otherwise, the element (i, j) is null). These matrices could be expressed only after linearization of sn indices. Thus, the box cell $B_{l,k}$ located in plane by the indices (l, k) is equivalently located on a lineal by the index $i_{l,k}$. There are two possibilities to derive the expression of index $i_{l,k}$: by enumerating all columns or by enumerating all rows of sn. In this approach, one selects to enumerate the sn rows, starting from bottom to top (see Figure 5.10). Thus, the first group of box cells is associated with normal behaviour. The incipient, medium and severe defect box cells follow (in this order).

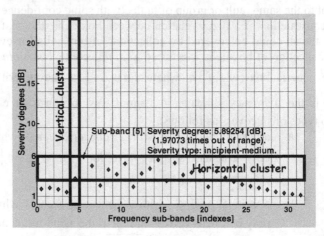

Figure 5.9.   Horizontal and vertical clusters inside the statistical network.

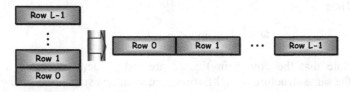

Figure 5.10.   Linear enumeration of box cells in a statistical network.

The index $i_{l,k}$ is then: $i_{l,k} = lK + k$, $\forall l \in \overline{0,L-1}$, $\forall k \in \overline{0,K-1}$. Conversely: $l = \lfloor i_{l,k} / K \rfloor$ and $k = i_{l,k}\%K$, $\forall i_{l,k} \in \overline{0,LK-1}$, where $\lfloor a \rfloor$ is the integer part of $a \in \varnothing$ and $n\%N$ is the rest of division between integers n and N.

Since any of the two sn covers provided by a frame is a union of its (disjoint) clusters, the associated global binary crisp relation is also a union of elementary crisp relations. Hence, the global characteristic matrix is obtained by summing together all corresponding elementary matrices. The specific form of the selected covers leads to the global characteristic matrices given in Eq. 23.

As a toy example, set $L = 2$ and $K = 3$. The corresponding sn looks as in Figure 5.11 and its covers are:

    a.   Horizontal: $\mathcal{H} = \{B_{00}, B_{01}, B_{02}\} \cup \{B_{10}, B_{11}, B_{12}\}$

    b.   Vertical: $\mathcal{G} = \{B_{00}, B_{10}\} \cup \{B_{01}, B_{11}\} \cup \{B_{02}, B_{12}\}$

Horizontal cover   Vertical cover

$$H = \begin{bmatrix} U_{K \times K} & O_{K \times K} & \cdots & O_{K \times K} \\ O_{K \times K} & U_{K \times K} & \cdots & O_{K \times K} \\ \vdots & \vdots & \ddots & \vdots \\ O_{K \times K} & O_{K \times K} & \cdots & U_{K \times K} \end{bmatrix}_{\substack{L \times L \\ \text{blocks}}} \qquad G = \begin{bmatrix} I_{K \times K} & I_{K \times K} & \cdots & I_{K \times K} \\ I_{K \times K} & I_{K \times K} & \cdots & I_{K \times K} \\ \vdots & \vdots & \ddots & \vdots \\ I_{K \times K} & I_{K \times K} & \cdots & I_{K \times K} \end{bmatrix}_{\substack{L \times L \\ \text{blocks}}} \qquad (23)$$

where $U_{K \times K}$, $O_{K \times K}$ and $I_{K \times K}$ are the $K \times K$ all unit, all zero and identity matrices, respectively, expressed as:

$$U_{K \times K} = \begin{bmatrix} 1 & 1 & \cdots & 1 \\ 1 & 1 & \cdots & 1 \\ \vdots & \vdots & \ddots & \vdots \\ 1 & 1 & \cdots & 1 \end{bmatrix}_{K \times K}, O_{K \times K} = \begin{bmatrix} 0 & 0 & \cdots & 0 \\ 0 & 0 & \cdots & 0 \\ \vdots & \vdots & \ddots & \vdots \\ 0 & 0 & \cdots & 0 \end{bmatrix}_{K \times K}$$

$$(24)$$

$$I_{K \times K} = \begin{bmatrix} 1 & 0 & \cdots & 0 \\ 0 & 1 & \cdots & 0 \\ \vdots & \vdots & \ddots & \vdots \\ 0 & 0 & \cdots & 1 \end{bmatrix}_{K \times K}$$

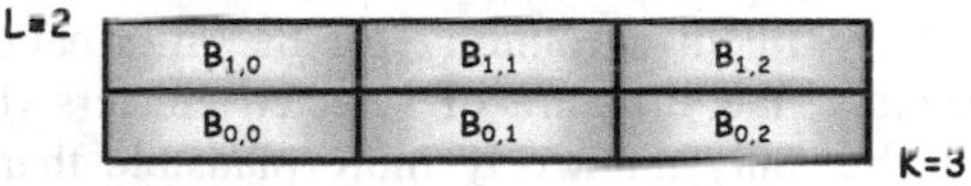

Figure 5.11. A toy statistical network.

Then Eqs. 23 and 24 imply:

$$U_{3 \times 3} = \begin{bmatrix} 1 & 1 & 1 \\ 1 & 1 & 1 \\ 1 & 1 & 1 \end{bmatrix}, O_{3 \times 3} = \begin{bmatrix} 0 & 0 & 0 \\ 0 & 0 & 0 \\ 0 & 0 & 0 \end{bmatrix}, I_{3 \times 3} = \begin{bmatrix} 1 & 0 & 0 \\ 0 & 1 & 0 \\ 0 & 0 & 1 \end{bmatrix}$$

Horizontal cover   Vertical cover

$$H = \begin{bmatrix} U_{3 \times 3} & O_{3 \times 3} \\ O_{3 \times 3} & U_{3 \times 3} \end{bmatrix} = \begin{bmatrix} 1 & 1 & 1 & 0 & 0 & 0 \\ 1 & 1 & 1 & 0 & 0 & 0 \\ 1 & 1 & 1 & 0 & 0 & 0 \\ 0 & 0 & 0 & 1 & 1 & 1 \\ 0 & 0 & 0 & 1 & 1 & 1 \\ 0 & 0 & 0 & 1 & 1 & 1 \end{bmatrix} \quad G = \begin{bmatrix} I_{3 \times 3} & I_{3 \times 3} \\ I_{3 \times 3} & I_{3 \times 3} \end{bmatrix} = \begin{bmatrix} 1 & 0 & 0 & 1 & 0 & 0 \\ 0 & 1 & 0 & 0 & 1 & 0 \\ 0 & 0 & 1 & 0 & 0 & 1 \\ 1 & 0 & 0 & 1 & 0 & 0 \\ 0 & 1 & 0 & 0 & 1 & 0 \\ 0 & 0 & 1 & 0 & 0 & 1 \end{bmatrix} \quad (25)$$

The matrices in Eq. 23 (or Eq. 25) are actually binary maps of the two crisp relations that every frame provides. The position of every unit value shows which couple of box cells are in relation to each other. These relations are in fact rough approximations of the following relation directly related to defects: *two box cells are in relation to each other if they point to the same fault.* Of course, at this time, we don't know exactly which box cells verify this property and this is the reason one operated with two approximations. Any horizontal or vertical cluster could include abnormal box cells pointing to the subband affected by a specific defect or, respectively, to the severity degree proved by a specific defect. The approximations are refined next by using the rsp norms, until specific defect classes are obtained.

Step 5: Evaluating the occurrence degrees.

The covers constructed above do not partake in the fuzzy relation that one intends to construct, but their clusters do. Recall that, unlike within crisp relations, two entities are in a fuzzy relation to each other only if they belong to a crisp relation with some membership degree (Klir and Folger, 1988). The membership values express the uncertainty regarding the specific relationship between entities. Within the crisp approach, this relationship is either certainly existing or certainly not existing. There are no other possibilities. Within the fuzzy approach, two entities could be in a relationship, but this assertion has a degree of uncertainty varying from 0 (certainly not) to 1 (certainly yes).

The relationships between sn box cells should also be fuzzy, for two main reasons. Firstly, the horizontal and vertical clusters could not be totally reliable since, in general, they gather together boxes inside of which some rsp norms fall and boxes that are untouched by these norms, even for long strings of vibration data. These act in fact as different entities inside the sn. They were only roughly gathered together, according to structural criteria of same severity level or frequency subband, but without accounting for the information provided by the vibration itself. Secondly, the structure of selected clusters (horizontal, vertical) could not be certain, but only intuitively more plausible than another structure. Fortunately, the final fuzzy relation is not that sensitive to the initial clustering of box cells and refines these approximations.

The horizontal and vertical clusters encode no information about defects unless they are put into correspondence with the rsp norms. In reality, after processing $m+1 \in \overline{1,M}$ frames (including the virtual one naturally associated with the average information about rsp norms – see Eq. 20), inside every box cell $B_{l,k}$ a number of rsp norms could occur. Refer to this number as (*occurrences*) *counter* and denote it by $N_m[l,k]$. Obviously, since for each subband $k \in \overline{0,K-1}$ a unique severity level λ_l ($l \in \overline{0,L-1}$)exists such that:

$$\lambda_l \le \|\mathsf{R}\,[m,k]\|_{\mathrm{dB}} < \lambda_{l+1} \qquad (26)$$

it follows that:

$$0 \le N_m[l,k] \le m+1,\ \forall m \in \overline{0,M-1},\ \forall l \in \overline{0,L-1},\ \forall k \in \overline{0,K-1} \qquad (27)$$

Null counter values are associated with those box cells for which no rsp norms occurred so far. Furthermore, another obvious property holds:

$$\sum_{l=0}^{L-1}\sum_{k=0}^{K-1} N_m[l,k] = K(m+1),\ \forall m \in \overline{0,M-1} \qquad (28)$$

i.e., the total amount of counters equals the number of subbands touched by all currently processed frames, including the virtual one.

After processing a new frame, the counters are upgraded following a rule given by Eq. 27:

$$N_{m+1}[l,k] = \begin{cases} N_m[l,k]+1, & \text{if } \lambda_l \leq \|\mathbf{R}[m+1,k]\|_{\text{dB}} < \lambda_{l+1} \\ N_m[l,k], & \text{otherwise} \end{cases}, \quad \begin{bmatrix} \forall m \in \overline{0,M-2} \\ \forall l \in \overline{0,L-1} \\ \forall k \in \overline{0,K-1} \end{bmatrix} \quad (29)$$

which means: increment by 1 only those counters corresponding to box cells where the rsp norms occurred. However, this rule is not that simple. The virtual frame gives the initial values of these counters and, thus, they could change depending on the number of currently processed frames, $m+1 \in \overline{1,M}$. So, Eq. 29 must be understood as a recursive recipe where the initial values are also dependent on the current step of upgrading. Consequently, a counter could even be incremented by 2 and not by 1, or decreased by 1, when the average moves its position.

A consistent set of *occurrence degrees* is constructed and one-by-one associated with the collection of sn box cells, by using counters. Denote by $v_m[l,k]$ the occurrence degree uniquely associated with box cell $B_{l,k}$, after processing $m+1 \in \overline{1,M}$ frames (starting from the virtual one). Two possible definitions could be used to set $v_m[l,k]$, according to Eqs. 27 and 28:

$$v_m[l,k] \stackrel{def}{=} \frac{N_m[l,k]}{m+1} \quad \text{or} \quad v_m[l,k] \stackrel{def}{=} \frac{N_m[l,k]}{K(m+1)} \quad (30)$$

In both cases $v_m[l,k] \in [0,1]$, but for the first one:

$$\sum_{l=0}^{L-1} v_m[l,k] = 1 \text{ and } \sum_{l=0}^{L-1}\sum_{k=0}^{K-1} v_m[l,k] = K \quad (31)$$

whereas for the second one:

$$\sum_{l=0}^{L-1} v_m[l,k] = \frac{1}{K} \text{ and } \sum_{l=0}^{L-1}\sum_{k=0}^{K-1} v_m[l,k] = 1 \quad (32)$$

From a probabilistic point of view, Eqs. 31 and 32 show that only the second definition in Eq. 30 could be associated to the occurrence frequency of rsp norms inside box cells. But, in the context of fuzzy logic theory, requirements like the last one in Eq. 32 are often not necessary (Klir and Folger, 1988). The only requirement is to include the occurrence degree variation in range [0,1]. One of the main drawbacks of the second definition is the rapid decay towards null values of all occurrence degrees, due to product $K(m+1)$. No occurrence degree could increase. Even if a counter is upgraded, its value is only increased by maximum 2, whereas the corresponding occurrence degree is decreased about K times. In contrast, the first definition keeps the occurrence degrees more balanced and, furthermore, the occurrence degrees could increase. The last remark is due to a very simple algebraic property:

$$\frac{n}{m} > \frac{n}{m+1} > \frac{n-1}{m+1}, \ \forall n,m > 0, \text{ but } \frac{n}{m} \leq \frac{n+1}{m+1} < \frac{n+2}{m+1}, \text{ if } 0 < n \leq m \quad (33)$$

Since the first definition provides occurrence degrees that are more sensitive to counters upgrading than the second one, it will be selected for the next steps. In fact, the occurrence degree is only raw information about rsp norms distribution over the statistical map. More processing operations are necessary in order to derive the uncertainty degrees associated with the elementary crisp relations previously constructed.

An example of the two-dimension occurrence degrees distribution is displayed in Figure 5.12. The distribution is improved after every new processed frame.

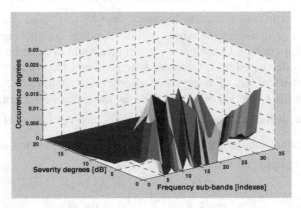

Figure 5.12.   An occurrence distribution over the statistical network.

At this point, one can say that box cells supporting the biggest occurrence degrees are very likely directly associated to the defect type. But it is not that simple to build a group of such box-cells, based only on a set of occurrence degrees, because the attempt is rather empirical and affected by uncertainty. A systematic method to construct similarity classes by using statistical information is then necessary. Also, as already mentioned, it is desirable that every class be associated with some confidence degree.

The occurrence degrees are in fact values of some membership functions that change the nature of clusters from crisp to fuzzy. More specifically, consider the generic horizontal and vertical clusters, C_l and D_k, respectively. Then their associated membership functions are: $\mu_{m,l}(B_{l,k}) = v_m[l,k]$ for any box cell $B_{l,k} \in C_l$ and $\eta_{m,k}(B_{l,k}) = v_m[l,k]$ for any box cell $B_{l,k} \in D_k$.

Thus, $(C_l, \mu_{m,l})$ and $(D_k, \eta_{m,k})$ are now fuzzy sets. The new definitions are superior to the former ones, since the rsp norms have been accounted. Now, if the box cell $B_{l,k}$ that belongs to a crisp cluster C_l has a null occurrence degree, it cannot belong to the fuzzy cluster $(C_l, \mu_{m,l})$. For simplicity, denote the values of membership functions by $\mu_{m,l}[k]$ and $\eta_{m,k}[l]$, respectively (i.e., $\mu_{m,l}$ and $\eta_{m,k}$ could also be treated as vectors from $[0,1]^K$ and $[0,1]^L$, respectively).

Note that the membership functions change from a frame to another, though the crisp clusters are independent of frames. Hence, the fuzzy clusters have variable structure depending on the number of processed frames, which is closer to the real behaviour of sn (variable) structure.

Step 6: **Associating certainty degrees with elementary crisp relations.**
A unique *certainty degree* should be associated with every cluster C_l or B_k. This is a number that expresses, on the one hand, the certainty in considering the corresponding cluster and, on the other hand, the degree of box cells affiliation with the elementary fuzzy relation the cluster naturally generates. The membership matrix of elementary fuzzy relation is simply derived by multiplication between the cluster certainty degree and its characteristic matrix. This idea is developed next, but, first, the certainty degrees have to be evaluated.

The evaluation of certainty degrees is based on the concepts of *fuzzy* and *uncertainty measures* (Klir and Folger, 1988). Obviously, certainty is opposite to uncertainty. An interesting fuzzy/uncertainty measure is the Shannon Fuzzy Entropy (SFE). Its definition relies on the *multidimensional Shannon function* below:

$$S(x) = -\sum_{n=1}^{N}\left[x_n \log_2 x_n + (1-x_n)\log_2(1-x_n)\right], \ \forall x = [x_1 \ ... \ x_n]^T \in [0,1]^N \qquad (34)$$

The Shannon function originated from the concept of *entropy*, first utilized in physics. Thus, if one restricts the sum in Eq. 34 to the first half, replaces "$\log_2$" by "$\ln$" (John Nepper's natural logarithm) and sets $x \in [0,1]^N$ as a discrete probability density (i.e., verifying $\sum_{n=1}^{N} x_n = 1$), then the entropy is obtained:

$$H(x) = -\sum_{n=1}^{N} x_n \ln x_n \qquad (35)$$

When $N=1$, the entropy from Eq. 35 is associated with the event for which the probability was considered. The opposite event is described by the opposite probability: $1-x$. Hence, the second half of the sum in Eq. 34 becomes the entropy of the opposite event. The Shannon function thus expresses the total entropy of an entity, by accounting for not only its classical entropy, but also the entropy of its opposite. Note that, in Eq. 34, no restriction (like the one verified by probability densities) is imposed. The Shannon function is an instrument utilized in many domains, but was defined in the context of information theory, as a concept quantifying the information encoded or transported by an entity. Its unit is the bit. This is the reason the natural logarithm was replaced by $\log_2$ in the original definition of entropy.

Several interesting properties of the Shannon function could be noted. For this approach, the following two are of the most concern. Firstly, the function is bounded and reaches several null minima, but only one maximum. No other minima are possible, but the null ones are reached on the border of definition domain (the hypercube $[0,1]^N$). Secondly, the maximum value is exactly the dimension of input argument, i.e., N. It is reached for the middle point argument, the function being symmetrical. For example, in Figure 5.13, the graphics of the only two Shannon functions that could be viewed are drawn.

When the argument in Eq. 34 is provided by values of the membership function describing a fuzzy set, the SFE is obtained. In this case, SFE has several interpretations. As a general fuzzy measure, SFE quantifies how close to the crisp state is the fuzzy set (or its *fuzziness*). The bigger the SFE value is, the less crisp the set (i.e., the fuzzier). But SFE could also play the role of *uncertainty measure*. Uncertainty has two major facets: *vagueness* and *ambiguity* (Klir and Folger, 1988; Ulieru *et al.*, 2000).

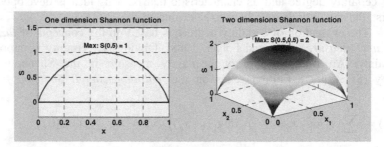

Figure 5.13.   One- and two-dimension Shannon functions

The SFE is a *vagueness measure*. The bigger the SFE value is, the more vague the fuzzy set description, i.e., the more uncertain (or unreliable) the information about that set. Thus, maximum entropy means maximum uncertainty and fuzziness. The smaller the SFE values, the better.

Let us now get back into the context of previous steps. The certainty degree of a cluster should be opposite to its entropy (uncertain (vague) clusters should have small certainty degrees). Also, another property should be verified: the bigger the occurrence degrees of its box cells, the smaller its entropy. Since SFE has one maximum and several null minima (pointing to the lack of uncertainty), the values of membership functions $\mu_{m,l}$ and $\eta_{m,k}$ must be translated from [0,1] to [0.5,1] by a simple affine transformation, before using them subsequently:

$$v_m[l,k] \leftarrow \frac{v_m[l,k]+1}{2} \qquad (36)$$

(By convention, one preserves the same notation for the translated values.)

Denote by $\alpha_{m,l}$ the certainty degree of horizontal cluster C_l, after processing $m+1$ frames (where $l \in \overline{0,L-1}$ and $m \in \overline{0,M-1}$). Similarly, $\beta_{m,l}$ stands for the certainty degree of vertical cluster D_k, after processing $m+1$ frames (where $k \in \overline{0,K-1}$ and $m \in \overline{0,M-1}$). The values of $\alpha_{m,l}$ and $\beta_{m,l}$ are then evaluated in three steps (by accounting for all previous remarks): compute the SFE of fuzzy clusters $(C_l, \mu_{m,l})$ and $(D_k, \eta_{m,k})$; normalize the SFE by K and, respectively, by L; subtract the result from 1. This is summarized in Eqs. 37 and 38.

The normalization applied in Eqs. 37 and 38 is necessary because the certainty degrees have to vary only in the range [0,1], as well. This restriction is imposed by another meaning of a certainty degree, regarding the covers: any cluster belongs to an sn fuzzy cover with some membership degree. Actually, the crisp covers $\mathcal{H}$ and $\mathcal{G}$ are transformed into fuzzy covers, by a similar mechanism employed to transform crisp clusters into fuzzy clusters. Their membership functions are the following: $\mu_m(C_l) = \alpha_{m,l}$ for any cluster $C_l \in \mathcal{H}$ and $\eta_m(D_k) = \beta_{m,k}$ for any cluster $D_k \in \mathcal{G}$. Thus, $(\mathcal{H}, \mu_m)$ and $(\mathcal{G}, \eta_m)$ are now fuzzy sets, but their elements are other fuzzy sets (the fuzzy clusters, in fact). Like for fuzzy clusters, covers membership functions depend on the number of processed frames ($m+1$) (where $m \in \overline{0, M-1}$).

$$\begin{cases} \alpha_{m,l} = 1 - \dfrac{S(\mu_{m,l})}{K} \\ S(\mu_{m,l}) = -\sum_{k=0}^{K-1} \left[\mu_{m,l}[k] \log_2 \mu_{m,l}[k] + (1-\mu_{m,l}[k]) \log_2 (1-\mu_{m,l}[k]) \right] \end{cases} \quad (37)$$

$$\begin{cases} \beta_{m,k} = 1 - \dfrac{S(\eta_{m,k})}{L} \\ S(\eta_{m,k}) = -\sum_{l=0}^{L-1} \left[\eta_{m,k}[l] \log_2 \eta_{m,k}[l] + (1-\eta_{m,k}[l]) \log_2 (1-\eta_{m,k}[l]) \right] \end{cases} \quad (38)$$

Step 7: Constructing the α-sharp cuts of fuzzy relation.
Every fuzzy cluster generates, in association with its certainty degree, an elementary fuzzy relation between the box cells it includes. The membership matrix describing this relation is simply obtained by multiplication between the characteristic matrix of crisp cluster and the corresponding certainty degree. More specifically, if C_l and D_k are the generic horizontal and vertical clusters (as usual), then, after processing $m+1$ frames, their corresponding certainty degrees are $\alpha_{m,l}$ and $\beta_{m,k}$, respectively. One can denote by H_l and G_k the characteristic matrices of C_l and D_k, respectively. Then, obviously:

Horizontal cluster   Vertical cluster

$$H_l = \begin{bmatrix} O_{K \times K} & \cdots & O_{K \times K} & \cdots & O_{K \times K} \\ \vdots & \ddots & \vdots & \cdots & \vdots \\ O_{K \times K} & \cdots & U_{K \times K} & \cdots & O_{K \times K} \\ \vdots & \cdots & \vdots & \ddots & \vdots \\ O_{K \times K} & \cdots & O_{K \times K} & \cdots & O_{K \times K} \end{bmatrix}_{\substack{L \times L \\ \text{blocks}}} \qquad G_k = \begin{bmatrix} I_{K \times K}^k & I_{K \times K}^k & \cdots & I_{K \times K}^k \\ I_{K \times K}^k & I_{K \times K}^k & \cdots & I_{K \times K}^k \\ \vdots & \vdots & \ddots & \vdots \\ I_{K \times K}^k & I_{K \times K}^k & \cdots & I_{K \times K}^k \end{bmatrix}_{\substack{L \times L \\ \text{blocks}}} \quad (39)$$

where the block $U_{K \times K}$ is located on the main diagonal in position (l,l) of matrix H_l, whereas the block $I_{K \times K}^k$ consists of one unit value on the main diagonal in position (k,k) of matrix G_k (all remaining values being null).

The elementary fuzzy relations are described by the following membership matrices: $\alpha_{m,l}H_l$ (horizontal) and $\beta_{m,k}G_k$ (vertical). The corresponding relations are α-sharp cuts of fuzzy relation after processing $m+1$ frames (where $m \in \overline{0, M-1}$). (See the definition of α-sharp cut in (Ulieru *et al.*, 2000.) In fact, this definition is similar to the definition of α-cut (Klir and Folger, 1988), but the inequality sign was replaced by the equality one.)

For example, recall the toy sn in Figure 5.11. For that structure, two horizontal and three vertical elementary fuzzy relations are available after every processed frame:

$$
\alpha_{m,0}H_0 = \begin{bmatrix}
\alpha_{m,0} & \alpha_{m,0} & \alpha_{m,0} & 0 & 0 & 0 \\
\alpha_{m,0} & \alpha_{m,0} & \alpha_{m,0} & 0 & 0 & 0 \\
\alpha_{m,0} & \alpha_{m,0} & \alpha_{m,0} & 0 & 0 & 0 \\
0 & 0 & 0 & 0 & 0 & 0 \\
0 & 0 & 0 & 0 & 0 & 0 \\
0 & 0 & 0 & 0 & 0 & 0
\end{bmatrix}
\quad
\alpha_{m,1}H_1 = \begin{bmatrix}
0 & 0 & 0 & 0 & 0 & 0 \\
0 & 0 & 0 & 0 & 0 & 0 \\
0 & 0 & 0 & 0 & 0 & 0 \\
0 & 0 & 0 & \alpha_{m,1} & \alpha_{m,1} & \alpha_{m,1} \\
0 & 0 & 0 & \alpha_{m,1} & \alpha_{m,1} & \alpha_{m,1} \\
0 & 0 & 0 & \alpha_{m,1} & \alpha_{m,1} & \alpha_{m,1}
\end{bmatrix}
$$

$$
\beta_{m,0}G_0 = \begin{bmatrix}
\beta_{m,0} & 0 & 0 & \beta_{m,0} & 0 & 0 \\
0 & 0 & 0 & 0 & 0 & 0 \\
0 & 0 & 0 & 0 & 0 & 0 \\
\beta_{m,0} & 0 & 0 & \beta_{m,0} & 0 & 0 \\
0 & 0 & 0 & 0 & 0 & 0 \\
0 & 0 & 0 & 0 & 0 & 0
\end{bmatrix}
\quad
\beta_{m,1}G_1 = \begin{bmatrix}
0 & 0 & 0 & 0 & 0 & 0 \\
0 & \beta_{m,1} & 0 & 0 & \beta_{m,1} & 0 \\
0 & 0 & 0 & 0 & 0 & 0 \\
0 & 0 & 0 & 0 & 0 & 0 \\
0 & \beta_{m,1} & 0 & 0 & \beta_{m,1} & 0 \\
0 & 0 & 0 & 0 & 0 & 0
\end{bmatrix} \quad (40)
$$

$$
\beta_{m,2}G_2 = \begin{bmatrix}
0 & 0 & 0 & 0 & 0 & 0 \\
0 & 0 & 0 & 0 & 0 & 0 \\
0 & 0 & \beta_{m,2} & 0 & 0 & \beta_{m,2} \\
0 & 0 & 0 & 0 & 0 & 0 \\
0 & 0 & 0 & 0 & 0 & 0 \\
0 & 0 & \beta_{m,2} & 0 & 0 & \beta_{m,2}
\end{bmatrix}
$$

Equation 40 reveals another interesting property: the box cells that are very far from each other could not be in the same relation, even in the case of fuzzy relations. This is the case, for example, of box cells located at different severity levels and opposite subbands, such as $B_{0,0}$ and $B_{1,2}$ or $B_{1,0}$ and $B_{0,2}$. Practically, it is very unlikely that these box cells could associate together to reveal the same defect. But this property could be cancelled for the global fuzzy relation providing defect classifications, since such limitations are only intuitive.

Step 8: Constructing the fuzzy relation.

Two operations are applied in order to build the final fuzzy relation between sn box cells: aggregation of the (elementary) α-sharp cuts and evaluation of the transitive cover. The aggregation is simply performed through the max fuzzy union (Klir and Folger, 1988):

$$\mathcal{R}_m = \left[\bigcup_{l=0}^{L-1} \alpha_{m,l} H_l\right] \cup \left[\bigcup_{k=0}^{K-1} \beta_{m,k} G_k\right] \tag{41}$$

Thus, the membership matrix describing the crude fuzzy relation $\mathcal{R}_m$ is constructed by means of the elementwise max operator ("max•") applied on all matrices corresponding to fuzzy relation of the right term in Eq. 41:

$$\mathcal{M}_m = \max\bullet\left\{\max_{l\in 0,L-1}\bullet\{\alpha_{m,l}H_l\}, \max_{k\in 0,K-1}\bullet\{\beta_{m,k}G_k\}\right\} \tag{42}$$

Note that the same max operations like in Eq. 42 have been applied to obtain the characteristic matrices in Eq. 23, but by using unit certainty grades (since the relations were crisp). Obviously, the dimension of matrix $\mathcal{M}_m$ is $KL \times KL$.

For the toy example above, the membership matrix $\mathcal{M}_m$ is:

$$\mathcal{M}_m = \begin{bmatrix} \max\{\alpha_{m,0},\beta_{m,0}\} & \alpha_{m,0} & \alpha_{m,0} & \beta_{m,0} & 0 & 0 \\ \alpha_{m,0} & \max\{\alpha_{m,0},\beta_{m,1}\} & \alpha_{m,0} & 0 & \beta_{m,1} & 0 \\ \alpha_{m,0} & \alpha_{m,0} & \max\{\alpha_{m,0},\beta_{m,2}\} & 0 & 0 & \beta_{m,2} \\ \beta_{m,0} & 0 & 0 & \max\{\alpha_{m,1},\beta_{m,0}\} & \alpha_{m,1} & \alpha_{m,1} \\ 0 & \beta_{m,1} & 0 & \alpha_{m,1} & \max\{\alpha_{m,1},\beta_{m,1}\} & \alpha_{m,1} \\ 0 & 0 & \beta_{m,2} & \alpha_{m,1} & \alpha_{m,1} & \max\{\alpha_{m,1},\beta_{m,2}\} \end{bmatrix}$$

As one can see, some box cells are (co)related with various (un)certainty degrees, but between some other box cells no relationship seems to exist. The null values inside matrix $\mathcal{M}_m$ are always the same, independently of how many frames are processed (because of the horizontal and vertical crisp clusters), whereas the nonnull values vary from a frame to another (because of the occurrence degrees). Denote the generic element of $\mathcal{M}_m$ (i.e., the membership degree) by $\mathcal{M}_m[i,j]$ (where $i,j \in \overline{1,KL}$).

The resulting matrix $\mathcal{M}_m$ is *symmetric* and *reflexive* (since the elementary matrices H_l and G_k verify these two properties). Thus $\mathcal{R}_m$ is a *proximity* relation, but it is not necessarily *fuzzy transitive*. (See (Klir and Folger, 1988) for definitions.) Even though all elementary matrices H_l and G_k would describe (crisp) equivalence relations (i.e., all of them would be transitive as well), it is possible that $\mathcal{R}_m$ is nontransitive. This means, in general, $\mathcal{R}_m$ is not a *similarity* (fuzzy) relation. However, the similarity is a very important property, because the defect classes should also be (nonoverlapped) similarity classes. The direct involvement of similarity property in the construction of defect classes is revealed at the next step. Let us focus now on the transitivity property.

Actually, the transitivity property is the most difficult to insure in the case of fuzzy relations, because it is expressed (for example) as follows, differently from the crisp case (Klir and Folger, 1988; Ulieru et al., 2000):

$$\mathcal{M}_m[i,j] \geq \max_{n\in 1,KL} \min\{\mathcal{M}_m[i,n],\mathcal{M}_m[n,j]\}, \forall i,j \in \overline{1,KL} \tag{43}$$

This is the *max-min (fuzzy) transitivity*. An equivalent matrix form of Eq. 43 can straightforwardly be derived:

$$\mathcal{M}_m \geq \bullet \left(\mathcal{M}_m \circ \mathcal{M}_m \right) \tag{44}$$

where "$\circ$" points to *fuzzy multiplication* (*product*) between matrices with compatible dimensions (involving the composition of the corresponding fuzzy relations). This multiplication is expressed starting from classical matrix multiplication, where max operator is used instead of summation and min operator is used instead of product. Also, "$\geq \bullet$"in Eq. 44 means that the ordering relation focuses on matrix elements and not globally, on matrices.

The lack of transitivity can be corrected by generating the *transitive closure* of $\mathcal{R}_m$, which is defined as the smallest transitive fuzzy relation including $\mathcal{R}_m$ (according to fuzzy inclusion) (Klir and Folger, 1988). A simple procedure allows us to compute this closure for any fuzzy relation $\mathcal{R}$:

Step 1.   Compute the following fuzzy relation: $\overline{\mathcal{R}} = \mathcal{R} \cup (\mathcal{R} \circ \mathcal{R})$.

Step 2.   If $\overline{\mathcal{R}} \neq \mathcal{R}$, replace $\mathcal{R}$ by $\overline{\mathcal{R}}$, i.e., $\mathcal{R} \leftarrow \overline{\mathcal{R}}$ and go to Step 3. Otherwise, $\overline{\mathcal{R}} = \mathcal{R}$ is the transitive closure of the initial $\mathcal{R}$.

It is not so difficult to prove that this procedure preserves the reflexivity and symmetry of $\mathcal{R}_m$ (Ulieru *et al.*, 2000), so that the transitive closure $\overline{\mathcal{R}}_m$ is a similarity relation. Also, in terms of membership matrices, $\mathcal{M}_m$ is replaced by $\overline{\mathcal{M}}_m$, derived according to the procedure above (but with max instead of union operator and with (max-min) fuzzy multiplication instead of composition operator).

The procedure is very efficient. The only limitation in terms of network granularity is here the dimension of $\mathcal{M}_m$ (i.e., $KL \times KL$), which could be very large. But, nowadays, the existing computing performances could yield reasonable running time for matrices with more than one million elements.

The main difference between $\mathcal{R}_m$ and $\overline{\mathcal{R}}_m$ is that $\overline{\mathcal{R}}_m$ is defined by means of a smaller number of membership degrees than $\mathcal{R}_m$. In general, small grades vanish. This is very suitable, since, probably, small membership degrees are mostly due to various noises still affecting the vibration data, even after filtering. In other words, by computing the transitive closure, *the statistical data have been denoised*. Another difference between the two fuzzy relations is that box cells previously unrelated (according to $\mathcal{R}_m$) could now be related (according to $\overline{\mathcal{R}}_m$). This means the nonnull values in $\mathcal{M}_m$ could overwrite the null ones. In general, inside the matrix $\overline{\mathcal{M}}_m$, null values could seldom appear. This effect is correcting the initial rough assumption that some box cells could never be related to each other.

Step 9: Generating the defect classifications.

The values in $\overline{\mathcal{M}}_m$ are referred to as (*fuzzy*) *confidence degrees*. The number of distinctive confidence degrees is $P_m \leq KL(KL+1)/2$, for each $m \in \overline{1, M-1}$ (due to symmetry). They could decreasingly be sorted: $\gamma_{m,0} > \gamma_{m,1} > \cdots > \gamma_{m,P_m-1}$ (by using natural new notations instead of $\mathcal{M}_m[i,j]$). For each confidence degree $\gamma_{m,p}$

($p \in \overline{0, P_m - 1}$), a partition of statistical network is generated, by evaluating the corresponding α -*cut* of fuzzy relation $\overline{\mathcal{R}}_m$ (Klir and Folger, 1988). Every α -cut plays the role of *defect classification* and is actually a partition of sn. Any class in such a partition gathers the cells with similar statistical properties and, therefore, is a *similarity class*. Obviously, all box cells with null occurrence degrees (see, for example, some high severity box cells in Figure 5.8) are grouped in an *inactive cluster* and do not actually partake in the classification. The inactive cluster is the same for any classification, if the number of processed frames, $m + 1$, is constant, but its topology could change as m varies.

Let $C_{m,p} = \left\{ F_{m,p,q} \right\}_{q \in \overline{0, Q_{m,p} - 1}}$ be the defect classification corresponding to confidence degree $\gamma_{m,p}$ ($p \in \overline{0, P_m - 1}$). Inside, there are $Q_{m,p}$ defect classes generically denoted by $F_{m,p,q}$. Usually, the classifications are listed in decreasing order of their confidence degrees. Moreover, it is well known that such an arrangement reveals a *holonic* behaviour (Ulieru *et al.*, 2000). That is, the confidence is also a measure of classifications granularity: as confidence decreases, a larger number of classes group more and more together. For maximum confidence, every cell is also a class, which means maximum of granularity as well ($Q_{m,0}$ equals the number of box cells with nonnull occurrence degrees). For minimum confidence, all cells are grouped in a single class, the granularity being also minimum ($Q_{m, P_m - 1} = 1$). Thus the trend of finite string $\left\{ Q_{m,p} \right\}_{p \in \overline{0, P_m - 1}}$ is decreasing when the confidence degree is decreasing. Only one classification shall be selected from this collection, as described in the next step.

Some examples of defect classes together with their confidence degrees are described in the section devoted to simulation results.

Step 10: Selecting the optimum classification.
Besides the confidence degree, the SFE of every class could also be evaluated. Actually, like in case of covers $\mathcal{H}$ and $\mathcal{G}$, every classification (an sn partition, in fact) is a fuzzy set with fuzzy sets (the defect classes) as elements. The membership functions associated with defect classifications are denoted by $\rho_{m,p}$ (where $m \in \overline{1, M - 1}$ and $p \in \overline{0, P_m - 1}$). Thus, $\left(C_{m,p}, \rho_{m,p} \right)$ is a fuzzy set and the membership function $\rho_{m,p}$ could be derived by means of a similar argument like in Step 6. There is, however, an important difference here. The entropy of a fuzzy set comprising fuzzy sets as elements should depend on the entropy of every element. If all elements would have small/large entropy values, then the set should also have small/large entropy. Consequently, the membership function $\rho_{m,p}$ has to reflect the normalized entropy of each defect class:

$$\begin{bmatrix} \rho_{m,p} & : & C_{m,p} & \rightarrow & [0,1] \\ & & F_{m,p,q} & \mapsto & \rho_{m,p}\left(F_{m,p,q}\right) \stackrel{def}{=} \rho_{m,p,q} = \frac{1}{2}s_N\left(F_{m,p,q}\right) \end{bmatrix} \tag{45}$$

In Eq. 45, $s_N\left(F_{m,p,q}\right)$ is the normalized entropy of defect class $F_{m,p,q}$ (where $q \in \overline{0, Q_{m,p} - 1}$). To evaluate $s_N\left(F_{m,p,q}\right)$, first identify all the box cells that belong to $F_{m,p,q}$ (together with their translated occurrence degrees – see Eq. 36), then use the definition in Eq. 34 and finally divide the result by the number of box cells. For example, consider that the following classification has been obtained inside the toy sn in Figure 5.11: $C_{m,p} = \left\{F_{m,p,q}\right\}_{q \in \overline{0,1}}$, where the defect classes are $F_{m,p,0} = \left\{B_{0,0}, B_{1,1}\right\}$ and $F_{m,p,1} = \left\{B_{0,1}, B_{0,2}, B_{1,2}\right\}$. (The box cell $B_{1,0}$ belongs to the inactive cluster.) Then:

$$s_N\left(F_{m,p,0}\right) = -\frac{1}{2}\left[v_m[0,0]\log_2 v_m[0,0] + \left(1 - v_m[0,0]\right)\log_2\left(1 - v_m[0,0]\right)\right. \tag{46}$$
$$\left. + v_m[1,1]\log_2 v_m[1,1] + \left(1 - v_m[1,1]\right)\log_2\left(1 - v_m[1,1]\right)\right];$$

$$s_N\left(F_{m,p,1}\right) = -\frac{1}{3}\left[v_m[0,1]\log_2 v_m[0,1] + \left(1 - v_m[0,1]\right)\log_2\left(1 - v_m[0,1]\right)\right. \tag{47}$$
$$+ v_m[0,2]\log_2 v_m[0,2] + \left(1 - v_m[0,2]\right)\log_2\left(1 - v_m[0,2]\right)$$
$$\left. + v_m[1,2]\log_2 v_m[1,2] + \left(1 - v_m[1,2]\right)\log_2\left(1 - v_m[1,2]\right)\right]$$

The division by 2 in Eq. 45 is required because SFE is nonmonotonic (recall Figure 5.13). The values of $s_N\left(F_{m,p,q}\right)$ varying in the range [0,1] are now restricted to the range [0,1/2], which involves the final entropy increases when the (translated) occurrence degrees decrease.

After the membership function $\rho_{m,p}$ has been evaluated, the entropy of classification $C_{m,p}$ is computed by using again the definition stated in Eq. 34:

$$s(\rho_{m,p}) = -\sum_{q=0}^{Q_{m,p}-1}\left[\rho_{m,p,q}\log_2\rho_{m,p,q} + (1 - \rho_{m,p,q})\log_2(1 - \rho_{m,p,q})\right] \tag{48}$$

Note that the normalization is meaningless in Eq. 48, since the entropy also encodes information about the number of defect classes (clusters). Therefore, in general, the entropy values $\left\{s(\rho_{m,p})\right\}_{p \in \overline{0, P_m - 1}}$ prove a decreasing trend, since the number of defect classes (i.e., the maximum of entropy) decreases when the confidence degree decreases. This involves the entropy values $\left\{s(\rho_{m,p})\right\}_{p \in \overline{0, P_m - 1}}$ and the confidence degrees $\left\{\gamma_{m,p}\right\}_{p \in \overline{0, P_m - 1}}$ are opposite.

A "good" classification should have high confidence degree and low entropy. This could be selected by means of a cost function that encodes the opposite behaviour of entropy and confidence degree. In order to define such a function, it is first necessary to transform the entropy and the confidence degrees into maps comparable to each other. Before this operation, the comparison between them is impossible, because they vary in different ranges. The transformation is affine:

$$
\gamma_{m,p}^{01} \overset{def}{=} \frac{\gamma_{m,p} - \min\limits_{p \in 0, P_m - 1} \left\{ \gamma_{m,p} \right\}}{\max\limits_{p \in 0, P_m - 1} \left\{ \gamma_{m,p} \right\} - \min\limits_{p \in 0, P_m - 1} \left\{ \gamma_{m,p} \right\}}
\tag{49}
$$

$$
s^{01}(\rho_{m,p}) \overset{def}{=} \frac{s(\rho_{m,p}) - \min\limits_{p \in 0, P_m - 1} \left\{ s(\rho_{m,p}) \right\}}{\max\limits_{p \in 0, P_m - 1} \left\{ s(\rho_{m,p}) \right\} - \min\limits_{p \in 0, P_m - 1} \left\{ s(\rho_{m,p}) \right\}}
\tag{50}
$$

Obviously, both normalized maps $\gamma_{m,p}^{01}$ and $s^{01}(\rho_{m,p})$ vary in the range $[0,1]$ and, moreover, they are reaching the extreme values 0 and 1.

Define the cost function S_m as the geometric mean between the values of the map defined by Eq. 49 and the opposite values of the map defined by Eq. 50, over the classification indexes set:

$$
\begin{bmatrix}
S_m : & \overline{0, P_m - 1} & \rightarrow & [0,1] \\
& p & \mapsto & S_m[p] \overset{def}{=} \sqrt{\gamma_{m,p}^{01} \left[1 - s^{01}(\rho_{m,p}) \right]}
\end{bmatrix}
\tag{51}
$$

In this context, S_m expresses the opposite entropy weighted by confidence degrees. Other cost functions could also be employed in this aim (such as the arithmetic mean or another algebraic combination between $\gamma_{m,p}^{01}$ and $s^{01}(\rho_{m,p})$). But, in any case, this function could only have a finite number of maxima (or minima) that realize the trade-off between entropy and confidence degree. In the case of cost function S_m, the best compromise is reached for its global maximum. Thus, the best classification $C_m^{opt} = C_{m, p_m^{opt}}$ is selected by solving the following simple optimisation problem:

$$
p_m^{opt} = \arg \max_{p \in 0, P_m - 1} S_m[p]
\tag{52}
$$

An example of how the optimum classification is selected by solving the problem stated by Eqs. 51 and 52 is displayed in Figure 5.14, where only 51 frames have been processed (including the virtual one). The opposite variation between the confidence degree and the (opposite) entropy, as well as the shape of their geometric mean are clearly drawn. In this example, 32 classifications are available and the optimum resulting index is $p_m^{opt} = 14$, which points to the 15th classification as being the optimum one. Note that the 19th classification is a sub-optimal one, though its entropy–confidence compromise is also maximum, but locally (and close to the global maximum). The number of classes inside the optimum classification is 82 (most of them being singletons). As one shall see in the section devoted to simulation results, the optimum classification constitutes an image map about the specific fault(s) distorting the standard spectrum. Also, the classification confidence is $\gamma_{50,14} \cong 0.7$ and its entropy is $S(\rho_{50,14}) \cong 81.06$. The entropy is quite high (close to its maximum, 82), since the number of processed frames is modest (only 51) and thus the occurrence degrees are inaccurate. As the number of processed frames increases, the entropy goes down, farther from its maximum.

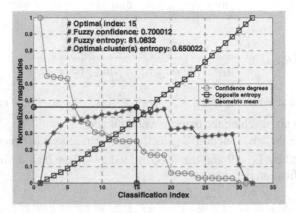

Figure 5.14.   Selecting the optimum defect classification.

The most difficult part of the fuzzy model is the classification map interpretation (or analysis). This means that specific defects should be put into direct correspondence with map topologies. The subsequent analysis is more rigorous and simpler to perform than by inspecting the vibration spectrum, since a part of analyst reasoning has already been automated. Accounting for all classes in a map is sometimes sufficient to perform an accurate diagnosis. But, sometimes, this attempt leads to a rather complicated analysis. Therefore, some specific class (or a reduced number of classes) should be emphasized as representing the defect(s). One option is to consider the biggest class as revealing all subbands affected by the defect(s). A different option is to extract the minimum entropy class, which, in general, is smaller than the biggest class and, therefore, more focused on few subbands. These are very likely the most affected by defect(s). (Recall that minimum entropy means maximum occurrence degree of rsp norms.) Other representing classes could also be selected.

In order to complete the method, it is perhaps useful to show how an optimum cluster (or group of clusters) could be selected inside the best classification C_m^{opt} by using the normalized SFE as cost function. Thus, the index of optimum defect class(es) is (are) evaluated by solving the following optimisation problem:

$$q_m^{opt} = \underset{q \in 0, Q_{m, p_m^{opt}} - 1}{\arg \min} S_N \left(\mathsf{F}_{m, p_m^{opt}, q} \right) \tag{53}$$

For the example in Figure 5.14, the minimum (normalized) entropy of the optimum defect class inside the best classification is about 0.65. All the other classes have entropy values at least as large as this value. Therefore, the corresponding cluster is representing in the best manner a specific defect.

But selecting an optimum defect class is less important than selecting the optimum classification. As already mentioned, sometimes, the classification configuration is itself a good image about defects, provided that its interpretation is not too difficult to perform. A very desirable property of such an interpretation is to reveal multiple defects by simple combinations of single defect maps. In general, this property is difficult to achieve. But the interpretation principle could be the same, independently of single or multiple-point defects generating the maps.

Note that, in this approach, the number of processed frames was considered variable. Though the notations are more complicated (the index m is omnipresent), one can clearly see how the concepts utilized inside are varying depending on this variable. The main reason the method was presented in terms of processed frames number is to show that its implementation could be performed by following either an on-line or an off-line strategy. For the on-line implementation the best classification should be provided after every processed frame (or group of frames). Step 8 is the critical one, since the evaluation of transitive cover could be time consuming when the product KL is too big (over 1500, with the actual computing performances). In this case, the best solution is to perform the defect classification only after several frames have been processed. This means the strategy is quasi-off-line (or even off-line). In general, the number of processed frames improves the method accuracy, since the estimation of occurrence degrees is more and more precise.

5.3. Simulation Results and Discussion

The two algorithms previously described constitute the kernel of a simulator designed to test the fuzzy-statistical reasoning method. The testing platform and the simulation results are described next.

5.3.1. The Testing Platform

The vibration data are acquired from bearings through a platform designed on purpose. Three main systems are connected, as illustrated by the pictures in Figure 5.15: a mechanical stand, a vibration data acquisition and pre-processing apparatus and a personal computer (PC).

The mechanical stand consists of the following elements:
1.   A three-phase electrical engine, Siemens type, with maximum rotation speed of 2740 rot/min (about 45.67 Hz), working at 380 V and with a power of 370 W.
2.   A couple of bearings mounted into mechanical seats, appropriately designed to fit to their geometry. The seats are easy to dismount in order to change the bearings, when necessary. The bearing near the engine is a standard high-quality one, without defects. The other bearing could also be standard (identical to the first one, in order to acquire the standard

vibration data) or a tested one, with possible defects (for raw vibration acquisition). All bearings are provided by Romanian and German industries. (See their geometry in Figure 5.16.).

3.   A couple of metallic discs mounted between bearings, on the same axis, which play a double role. On the one hand, they produce a load of about 200 N applied in a radial-axial manner on bearings. This leads to a contact angle of 40° inside the bearings. On the other hand, they are creating an inertial momentum that rejects some external perturbations and keeps the rotation speed constant.

4.   An elastic coupling between engine axis and load axis, aiming to attenuate the engine self-sustained vibrations or shaft wobbling that could corrupt the data.

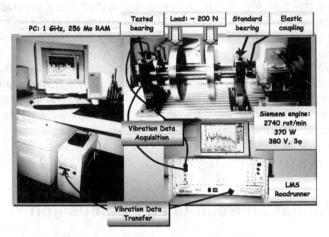

Figure 5.15.   The bearings testing platform.

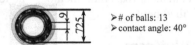

➢ # of balls: 13
➢ contact angle: 40°

Figure 5.16.   Geometrical characteristics of tested bearings.

The geometrical characteristics of tested bearings (illustrated in Figure 5.16) lead in fact to a very small variation of natural frequencies, depending on contact angle. Thus, even the contact angle is not accurately set, and its influence over the natural frequencies is not decisive. The biggest natural frequency is about 325 Hz.

The vibration is acquired by using two light accelerometers. The definition in Eq. 2 is adopted to provide the complex valued vibration data, because both sensors are far enough from the direction of applied load. A very powerful apparatus has been employed to acquire vibration data: an *LMS Roadrunner* (LMS International, 1999). Its capabilities extend far beyond the minimal ones required by this method: accurate prefiltering of data, simultaneous acquisition on at least two channels and selectable recording format. The Roadrunner integrates a microcomputer with a user-friendly interface that allows the user to work as comfortably as with any PC. It is also endowed with at least four channels (their number could be extended), compatible with a large number of sensors. The maximum allowed sampling frequency is 100 kHz. In this application, the sampling frequency has been set to $v_s = 25.6$ kHz. Data are saved in ASCII format, with 22 digits of representation. From Roadrunner, data are transferred to a PC, via floppy discs. The PC has the following main characteristics: 1 GHz (frequency), 256 Mb RAM (memory), 40 Gb (hard disk capacity). They rate the PC at the average of actual (public) technological level (years 2001, 2002). A laptop could also be successfully employed to implement the method.

5.3.2. Initial Simulation Parameters

In the description of the platform above, the shaft rotation speed and the sampling frequency were given: $v_r \cong 45.67$ Hz and $v_s = 25\,600$ Hz. Thus, a complete rotation takes about 21.9 ms, encoded by 560 vibration data samples. The vibration data length is set to $N = 2^{22} = 4,194,304$ samples, which takes 163.84 s in 7482 full rotations (see Eq. 1).

The vibration frame length is set to $N_f = 2^{13} = 8192$ samples (320 ms, ~15 full rotations). The number of nonoverlapped frames is then 512 (see Eq. 4), whereas every data segment includes three successive frames, as explained in the previous section. The frame length involves a frequency resolution of 3.125 Hz.

The window selected to smooth the overlapping between segments is Tuckey type, with 33.33% rectangular shape (see Figures 5.4 and 5.5). A high-pass filter will be applied to windowed segments. The LF cutoff frequency is set 7 times the largest natural frequency: $v_{lc} = 7 \times 325 = 2275$ Hz.

The vibration spectrum is segmented into $K = 32$ subbands. Every subband includes 128 rays for a bandwidth of 400 Hz. This setting realizes a good compromise between sp accuracy (each one is computed by using 128 spectral values) and bandwidth. The severity levels are set as already explained ($L = 12$ levels).

5.3.3. Comparative Discussion on Simulation Results

The experiments have been organized according to the following scenario:
1.   Collect raw vibration data from four tested bearings: a standard (defect free) one (labelled **S720913**, according to its geometry); one with a chop on the inner race (**I720913**); one with a spall on the outer race (**O720913**); one with chops on both inner and outer races (**M720913**).
2.   Apply EA to detect the severity degree of defects and to check if multiple defects on bearing **M720913** are visible or not. The following settings are performed in this aim: consider vibration segments of more than 1 s length; operate with 1/3-octave filters appropriately designed (as described in (Barkov *et al.*,1995a,b)); take full rectified envelope; focus on

the LF sub-band of envelope spectrum, for a bandwidth at least equal to 2 kHz.

3.   Apply the fuzzy reasoning method.

A. Envelope analysis results

A standard horizontal vibration data segment of about 1.3 s (32,768 samples, 4 frames) and a zoom on the portion between 0.2 s and 0.25s are represented Figure 5.17a. The shape is almost harmonic, as expected. In Figure 5.17b, the corresponding spectrum is represented in dB, with a resolution of 0.78125 Hz (16,384 rays on half band 0-12.8 kHz). The energy of vibration is practically concentrated in LF-MF subband 0-5 kHz. The sensor resonance is insignificant. The peaks into the LF band are due to bearing natural frequencies. The envelope of standard signal, as well as a similar zoom as before, is drawn in Figure 5.18a. Signals appear very close to the white noise. Actually, the LF part of the envelope spectrum in Figure 5.18b reveals a quasi-constant variation on all frequencies around the spectral acceleration of 102.7 cm/s^2 (the spectrum average).

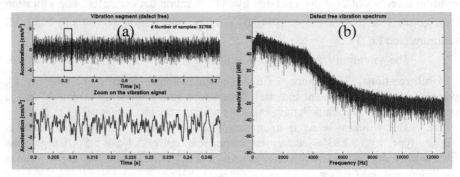

Figure 5.17.   Standard vibration (a) and its spectrum (b) (bearing **S720913**).

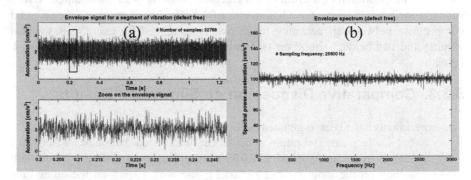

Figure 5.18.   Standard envelope vibration (a) and its spectrum (b) (bearing **S720913**).

For the next three cases, the length of vibration data segments is identical to the standard set above. The vibration segments are represented in Figures 5.19a, 5.20a and 5.21a, while their corresponding spectra are found in Figures 5.19b, 5.20b and 5.21b (see Appendix). The time variations appear to be more irregular than previously. The harmonic behaviour is distorted by a noise encoding the defect type. The effect of modulation could be seen in the zoomed portions of these signals, especially for the outer race defect. The sensors are forced to resonate and this effect is replicated towards LF and MF bands in all spectra. A significant resonance peak is located in band 6-10 kHz for all defective bearings, while it is missing for standard bearing. Also, peaks are more emphasized within the LF spectral zone for defective bearings than for standard.

The 1/3-octave filter (specific to EA) has been designed such that its central frequency is located somewhere in the median spectral valley between 4 and 6 kHz. Actually, it is selected as the minimum point of the spectral median in subband 4-6 kHz. This corresponds to the selection performed in (Barkov *et al.*,1995a,b) where the central frequency is located in a subband corresponding to the flattest zone of spectrum. In this specific case, the bandwidth is determined by the resonance peak flanking the valley to the right (in subband 6-10 kHz). The bandwidth is set as 3/2 times the difference between the location of this peak and the central frequency. The filter length is set to 2048 coefficients, in order to preserve high accuracy of filtering.

Figures 5.19, 5.20 and 5.21 are also concerned with the envelope signals (c) and the corresponding (envelope) spectra (d). In the case of single-point defects (Figures 5.19c and 5.20c), the abnormal behaviour is illustrated by the spectral envelope prominent peaks located around the multiples of natural frequency corresponding to the defective part: $BPFI = 325.061$ Hz (*Ball Pass Frequency on the Inner race*) or $BPFO = 268.606$ Hz (*Ball Pass Frequency on the Outer race*). The peaks decay exponentially, such that starting from the 9th multiple, they are practically sunk into the noisy part of spectrum. The severity degree is quite easy to estimate from these graphics, if the height of the largest peak is compared to the average standard envelope spectrum: about 3.5 (i.e., 10.88 dB) for inner race defect and about 4.5 (i.e., 13.06 dB) for outer race defect. This rates the defects as medium ones. Note, however, that the estimation could not be extremely accurate, since the vibration segments lengths are small (only 1.3 s, i.e., about 59 full rotations). An accurate estimation requires at least 100 rotations, but this increases the noisy part in all spectra, such that spectral estimation techniques should be employed (Oppenheim and Schafer, 1985; Proakis and Manolakis, 1996), in order to provide readable spectra.

Refer now to the multiple-point defect (Figure 5.21c). The envelope spectrum is so noisy that, practically, it is impossible to isolate some characteristics related to the defect type, though the spectrum in Figure 5.21b does not look very different from the spectra in Figures 5.19b and 5.20b. The energy increase revealed by the envelope spectrum is mainly due to the vibration signal itself (see Figure 5.21a), which has a larger energy level than in the case of single-point defects (Figures 5.19a and 5.20a). But the general level of noise is also increased. The EA failure in this case could have some plausible explanations. Besides the 1/3-octave filter selection (note that EA is very sensitive to this filter), perhaps the vibration model considered here cannot match the interpretation principle that worked well in the case of single-point defects (i.e., associate the natural frequencies directly to defect nature and location).

B. Fuzzy-statistical reasoning results

The three vibration signals have been entered into two MATLAB programs implementing the method described in the previous section. Thus, after collecting all information about rsp norms occurrences in box cells of sn, three occurrence degrees distributions have been obtained. For single point defects, there are two main rsp norms concentrations: one for MF and one for HF zones, but the most rsp norms seem to occur in the MF zone. On the contrary, for multiple defects, they occur rather in the HF zone. Thus, a first criterion for discriminating between single- and multiple-point defects is revealed.

After constructing the fuzzy model, a number of faults classifications resulted, for each tested bearing: 30 for **I720913**, 32 for **O720913** and 27 for **M720913**. The selection of an optimum faults classification is automatically performed (as described). The trade-off between the confidence degree (Eq. 49) and the classification entropy (Eq. 50) is quantified by means of geometric mean criterion (Eq. 51) that points to the optimal classification index. The variation of confidence degree and entropy among classifications as well as the shape of the geometric mean are illustrated in Figures 5.22, 5.25 and 5.28, for each bearing. The optimum classification indexes are: #20 for **I720913**, #20 for **O720913** and #17 for **M720913**. The corresponding optimum classification maps are pictured in Figure 5.23 (inner race defect), Figure 5.26 (outer race defect) and Figure 5.29 (multiple defects). For each classification, the representation is illustrated by using the grey levels scale to the right. One recognizes the sn by looking at the grid of each map. Thus, box cells that belong to the same class (cluster) have the same colour. Moreover, inside every box, the index of class the box belongs to is written, except the boxes that do not partake in the classification and belong to the inactive cluster. Besides the numerical parameters describing the classification minimum entropy (optimal) cluster, the average of rsp norms is represented as a curve passing through the map. Obviously, clusters are more or less grouped around this curve for all classifications.

As already mentioned, the most difficult part of the fuzzy model is the interpretation (or analysis) of classification maps. This means specific defects should be put into direct correspondence with map topologies. Such an analysis is more rigorous and simpler to perform than by inspecting the vibration spectrum, since a part of analyst reasoning has already been automated.

The shape of inactive cluster or of the rsp norms average could already constitute an image of defect types. For the three optimum classifications described above, the inactive clusters are all different, though their shapes are closer to each other for single-point defects. But this effect is noticed in EA as well: Figures 5.19d and 5.20d are not very different, since the values of the two corresponding natural frequencies are close to each other (BPFI=325.061 Hz and BPFO=268.606 Hz). The inactive cluster for multiple defects seems to be quite different, but the same interpretation principle or rules as for single-point defects could be used. In the case of EA, the interpretation rule that worked very well for single-point defects is useless in the case of multiple-defect spectrum (Figure 5.21d).

Another entry yielding map interpretation is to focus not on the inactive cluster, but rather on the active ones. Of course, one could consider all classes in a map (optimal or suboptimal). But this involves a complicated analysis. Therefore, some specific class (or a reduced number of classes) should be emphasized as representing the defect(s). An option is to consider the biggest class as revealing all subbands affected by the defect(s). A different option is to extract the minimum entropy class (optimal cluster), which, in general, is smaller than the biggest class and, therefore, more focused on a few subbands. These are very likely the most affected by defect(s). (Recall that minimum entropy means maximum occurrence degree of rsp norms.) Other representing classes could also be selected.

The optimal detected clusters are the following:

  a. for bearing **I720913** (inner race defect): cluster #13, with normalized entropy 0.516168, focusing on subband 5200-5600 Hz (MF);

  b. for bearing **O720913** (outer race defect): cluster #20, with normalized entropy 0.711234, focusing on subband 4800-5200 Hz (MF);

  c. for bearing **M720913** (inner and outer race defects): cluster #27, with normalized entropy 0.709225, focusing on subband 12.4-12.8 kHz (very HF).

That the optimal clusters #13 and #20 are located in adjacent box cells is not coincidental, but is due to the fact that the corresponding natural frequencies have values close to each other. The extreme HF subband pointed by the multiple defects is somehow surprising. A better interpretation could be given by considering other sub-optimal classifications (see the next discussion). But, in any case, a good insight concerning the "full optimality" (optimal clusters into optimal classifications) is the following: single-point defects are indicated by optimal clusters around the LF or MF peaks of rsp norms average (and there is a correlation between natural frequencies and focused subbands), while the optimal clusters of multiple-point defects seem to be located around the HF peak of average. A more refined frequency segmentation, with a larger number of subbands than here ($K \geq 64$) could probably help the user to make a sharper distinction between focused subbands in the case of single-point defects. Practically, the EA results are obtained by the fuzzy reasoning method as well. Concerning the multiple-point defects, it is possible that a frequency interpretation in terms of natural frequencies cannot be performed, but increasing K should lead to the same effect: the distinction between different defects should be easier to achieve. Unfortunately, the number of subbands (K) can only be increased at the expense of running time, especially due to the procedure evaluating the fuzzy transitive closure, which is the most time-consuming part of the algorithm (exponential type).

The severity degree estimated here is located on the 4th level (between 6 and 9.54 dB) – the first medium severity one – for single-point defects and on the 5th level (between 9.54 and 12.04 dB) for multiple defects. The first location is close to the severity degree estimated by EA for inner race defect (10.88 dB), but quite different from the outer race defect estimated severity (13.06 dB). For multiple defects, EA offers no severity degree estimation, but in this case the location of multiple defects optimal cluster is closer to the outer race severity (13.06 dB). Both estimations here are below the estimations proposed by EA. Since the severity degrees are conventionally set and in both methods the raw vibrations have been affected by filtering, the comparison in terms of severity degree is probably irrelevant. One could only note that, for the fuzzy-statistical method, the estimated severity degree for multiple defects seems to be plausible, because the general level of vibration noise has been increased. This effect is proven by Figures 5.17a, 5.19a, 5.20a and 5.21a, where the amplitude of corresponding raw vibrations is about 3 cm/s^2 for standard and inner race defect, 2 cm/s^2 for outer race defect, but 5 cm/s^2 for multiple defects.

In order to extract more insights concerning classification map interpretation, several classifications should be depicted around the optimal ones. Their confidence and granularity are decreasing with classification index (according to the holonic phenomenon). In this context, some suboptimal classifications have been represented in Figure 5.24 (inner race defect), Figure 5.27 (outer race defect) and Figure 5.30 (multiple defects). They are selected according to the geometric mean values of Figures 5.22, 5.25 and 5.28. Thus, the suboptimal classifications have the best geometric mean values under the maximum one in every case. Sometimes, this requirement is fulfilled by local maxima, as in the case of bearings **O720913** and **M720913**. One could notice how box cells are more and more grouped together as the classification index increases.

An interesting observation could be noted with regard to all these maps: the optimal cluster (indicated by the optimal classification) is also optimum (with minimum entropy) for a large number of suboptimal classifications surrounding the optimal one, in the case of single-point defects. Though its index is changing (due to holonic phenomenon), its location is identical. The optimal cluster persistence among faults classifications is another good insight about the single-point defect nature, because, for multiple defects, the optimum cluster changes among classifications. However, in the case of multiple defects, it seems that another optimal cluster could also be considered, but extracted from suboptimal configurations. This is in fact the cluster #11 in classification #16 (as well as in classifications #13, #14, and #15, although not shown here). If one revisits Figure 5.27, one could notice that all these classifications, though suboptimal, prove a good compromise between confidence and entropy (they are only slightly below the optimal classification). Their unique optimum cluster focuses on the subband 7200-7600 Hz (still on the HF peak), but points to a lower severity degree (on level 3-6 dB, incipient).

One can infer from this analysis that selecting the cluster detected as optimal for the maximum number of classifications could be a good hint about the defect nature. But a reliable diagnosis requires a whole set of inference rules (and not isolated ones), in order to associate classification maps with specific defects and their severity degrees. A good achievement is that, by fuzzy-statistical reasoning, defects could be classified regardless of their nature as single- or multiple-point ones.

5.4.   Concluding Remarks

Although with some obvious limitations, the method presented above aims to automate a part of human reasoning when detecting and classifying defects and to improve the multiple defect diagnosis. The main advantage of this method is that the defect classification maps could allow the user to perform a reliable detection and diagnosis of defects, independently of their nature. Another advantage is its generality. On the one hand, the natural oscillation frequencies of the tested component play only a secondary role. On the other hand, gears, belt transmissions, or other vibration sources could replace bearings, provided that at least a good description of possible defects is a priori known in each case. Note that prefiltering is not mandatory: the fuzzy model could work with the whole raw vibration as well as with prefiltered data. The method's main drawbacks are the complexity (slightly bigger than EA complexity) and the difficulties in finding appropriate interpretations for classification maps.

Approaching the human reasoning in fault diagnosis is a demanding task. Not only because human reasoning is a complex mechanism (far to be completely understood nowadays), but also because such an attempt is mostly concerned with the inexplicable part of reasoning.

5.5. Appendix. Graphical Simulation Results

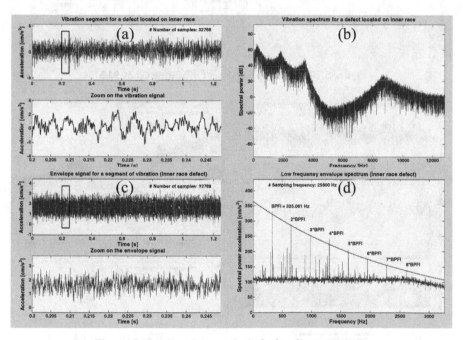

Figure 5.19.   Envelope analysis for bearing I720913.

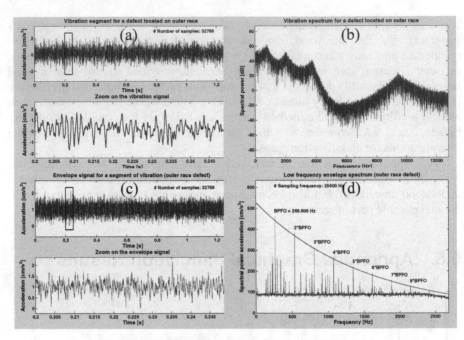

Figure 5.20.   Envelope analysis for bearing O720913.

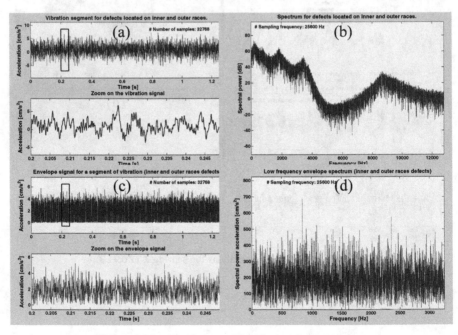

Figure 5.21.   Envelope analysis for bearing M720913.

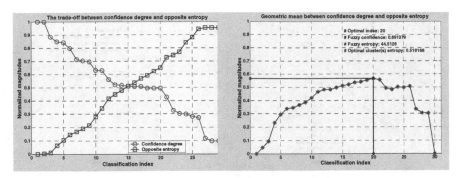

Figure 5.22. Selecting the optimum defect classification for bearing **I720913**.

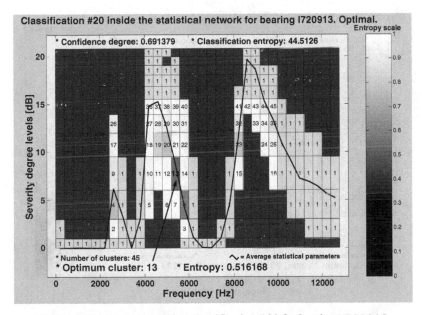

Figure 5.23. Optimum defect classification # 20 for bearing **I720913**.

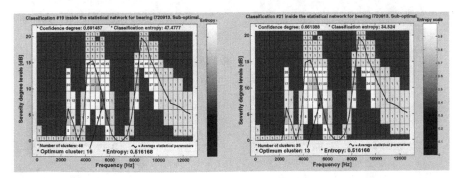

Figure 5.24. Suboptimal defect classifications #19 and #21 for bearing **I720913**.

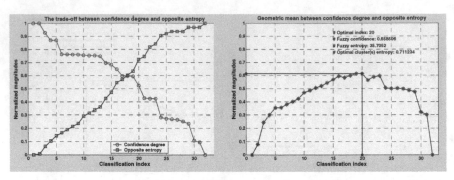

Figure 5.25.   Selecting the optimum defect classification for bearing O720913.

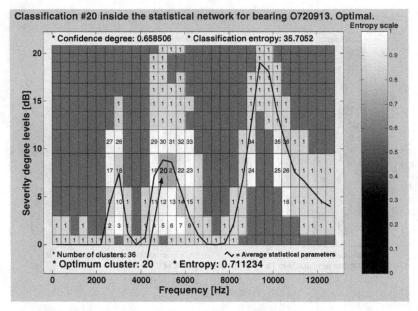

Figure 5.26.   Optimum defect classification # 20 for bearing O720913.

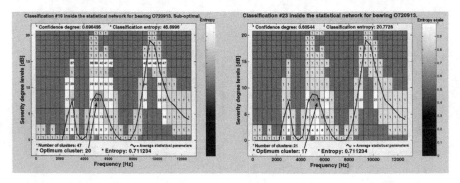

Figure 5.27.   Suboptimal defect classifications #19 and #23 for bearing O720913.

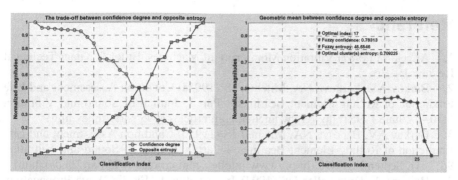

Figure 5.28.   Selecting the optimum defect classification for bearing M720913.

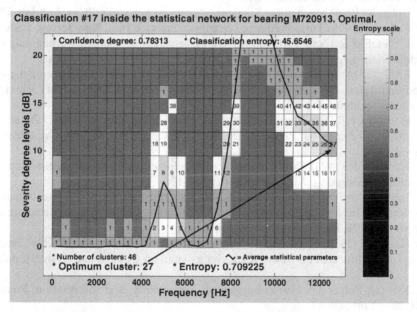

Figure 5.29.   Optimum defect classification # 17 for bearing M720913.

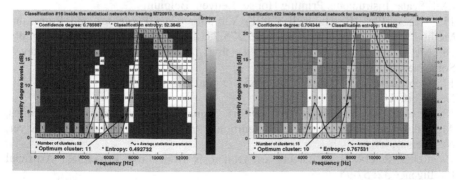

Figure 5.30.   Suboptimal defect classifications #16 and #22 for bearing M720913.

References

1.   Angelo M (1987) Vibration Monitoring of Machines. Bruel & Kjiaer Technical Review 1:1–36
2.   Barkov AV, Barkova NA, Mitchell JS (1995a) Condition Assessment and Life Prediction of Rolling Element Bearings – Part 1. Journal of Sound and Vibration 6:10–17, June 1995 (http://www.inteltek.com/articles/sv95/part1/index.htm)
3.   Barkov AV, Barkova NA, Mitchell JS (1995b) Condition Assessment and Life Prediction of Rolling Element Bearings – Part 2. Journal of Sound and Vibration 9:27–31, September 1995 (http://www.inteltek.com/articles/sv95/part2/index.htm)
4.   Bedford A, Drumheller DS (1994) Introduction to Elastic Wave Propagation. John Wiley & Sons, Chichester, UK
5.   Braun S (1986) Mechanical Signature Analysis. Academic Press, London, UK
6.   Cohen L (1995) Time-Frequency Analysis. Prentice Hall, New Jersey, USA
7.   FAG OEM & Handel AG (1996) Wälzlagerschäden – Schadenserkennung und Begutachtung gelaufener Wälzlager. Technical Report WL 82 102/2 DA
8.   FAG OEM & Handel AG (1997) Rolling Bearings – State-of-the-Art, Condition-Related Monitoring of Plants and Machines with Digital FAG Vibration Monitors. Technical Report WL 80-65 E
9.   Howard I (1994) A Review of Rolling Element Bearing Vibration: Detection, Diagnosis and Prognosis. Report of Defense Science and Technology Organization, Australia
10. Isermann R (1993) Fault Diagnosis of Machines via Parameter Estimation and Knowledge Processing. Automatica 29(4):161-170
11. Isermann R (1997) Knowledge-Based Structures for Fault Diagnosis and its Applications. In: Proceedings of the 4th IFAC Conference on System, Structure and Control, SSC'97, Bucharest, Romania, pp.15-32
12. Kaiser JF (1974) Nonrecursive Digital Filter Design Using the I_0–sinh Window Function. In: Proceedings of the IEEE Symposium on Circuits and Systems, pp.20-23
13. Klir GJ, Folger TA (1988) Fuzzy sets, Uncertainty, and Information. Prentice Hall, New York, USA
14. LMS International (1999) LMS Scalar Instruments Roadrunner. User Guide. LMS Scalar Instruments Printing House, Leuven, Belgium
15. Maness PhL, Boerhout JI (2001) Vibration Data Processor and Processing Method. United States Patent No. US 6,275,781 B1 (http://www.uspto.gov/go/ptdl/)
16. McConnell KG (1995) Vibration Testing. Theory and Practice. John Wiley & Sons, New York, USA
17. Oppenheim AV, Schafer R (1985) Digital Signal Processing. Prentice Hall, New York, USA
18. Proakis JG, Manolakis DG (1996) Digital Signal Processing. Principles, Algorithms and Applications (third edition). Prentice Hall, Upper Saddle River, New Jersey, USA
19. Reiter R (1987) A Theory of Diagnosis from First Principles. Artificial Intelligence 32: 57-95
20. Söderström T, Stoica P (1989) System Identification. Prentice Hall, London, UK

21. Stefanoiu D, Ionescu F (2002) Mathematical Models of Defect Encoding Vibrations. A Tutorial. Journal of the American-Romanian Academy (ARA), Montréal, Canada, Vol. 2001-2002
22. von Tscharner V (2000) Intensity Analysis in Time-Frequency Space of Modelled Surface Myoelectric Signals by Wavelets of Specified Resolution, preprint
23. Ulieru M, Stefanoiu D, Norrie D (2000) Identifying Holonic Structures in Multi-Agent Systems by Fuzzy Modeling. In: Kusiak A & Wang J (eds) Art for Computational Intelligence in Manufacturing, CRC Press, Boca Raton, Florida, USA
24. Willsky AS (1976) A Survey of Design Methods for Failure Detection Systems. Automatica 12:601-61
25. Wowk V (1995) Machinery Vibration. Balancing. McGraw-Hill, Upper Saddle River, New York, USA
26. Xi F, Sun Q, Krishnappa G (2000) Bearing Diagnostics Based on Pattern Recognition of Statistical Parameters. Journal of Vibration and Control 6:375–392

6. Artificial Neural Networks in Fault Diagnosis: A Gas Turbine Scenario

Stephen Ogaji and Riti Singh

Gas turbines are used for aero and marine propulsion, power generation and as mechanical drives for a wide range of industrial applications. Often, they are affected by gas path faults, which have hitherto been diagnosed by techniques such as fault matrixes, fault trees and gas path analysis. In this chapter, an artificial neural network approach to fault diagnosis is presented. The networks involved are trained to detect, isolate and assess faults in some of the components of a single spool gas turbine. The hierarchical diagnostic methodology adopted involves a number of decentralised networks trained to handle specific tasks. All sets of networks were tested with data not used for the training process. The results, when compared with available diagnostic tools, show that significant benefits can be derived from the actual application of this technique.

6.1. Gas Turbine Faults

Gas turbines (GT) are mechanical devices operating on a thermodynamic cycle with air as the working fluid. The air is compressed in a compressor, mixed with fuel and burnt in a combustor, with the gas expanded in a turbine to generate power used in driving the compressor and external loads (thrust or shaftpower) depending on requirements.

The main gas path components of the GT, which are compressor, combustor and turbines, are usually very reliable, but could result in low availability of the whole unit if a forced unexpected outage is encountered, as it can take some considerable time to repair them. This is made worse if the breakdown occurred when the maintenance crew was unprepared for it. Improving availability and reducing life cycle costs of the GT require maintenance schemes, such as condition-based maintenance (CBM), which advocates maintenance only when it is necessary and at the appropriate time rather than after a fixed number of operating hours or cycles. For the operational health of the engine to be regularly monitored for gas path faults, such measurable parameters as shaft speed, pressures, temperatures, fuel flow and shaftpower/thrust are required.

The gas path of a gas turbine is affected by a number of faults, which degrades its performance. The following succinctly presents the most common faults that affect the gas path.

      a.   **Fouling:** This is one of the most common causes of engine performance deterioration facing users of gas turbines and it can account for more than 70% of all engine performance loss accumulated during operation (Diakunchak, 1992). Fouling is the accumulation of deposits on the blade surfaces causing an increase in surface roughness, changes in shape of airfoil/airfoil inlet angle and reduction in airfoil throat opening (Diakunchak, 1992; Zaita *et al.*, 1998). Fouling primarily results in mass flow and compressor delivery pressure (CDP) reduction, and ultimately in power reduction and increased heat rate (Diakunchak, 1992; Aker and Saravanamuttoo, 1989; Lakshminarasimha *et al.*, 1994), with a slight change in compressor efficiency (Agrawal *et al.*, 1978).

b.   **Tip Clearance:** Tip clearance has the effect of reducing both efficiency and flow capacity in a compressor. There is a much greater response of efficiency drop to tip clearance than fouling.

c.   **Erosion:** Materials exposed to particle impacts are eroded and subjected to deterioration of their surface quality, changes in airfoil profile and throat openings, with increases in blade and seal clearances. With the gas turbine, the result of this on the gas path component is a decrease in performance. In the compressor, the eroded blade leads to loss of compressor delivery pressure and mass flow rate while on turbine nozzles/blades erosion has the effect of increasing turbine flow function and reducing efficiency, and hence output power.

d.   **Corrosion:** When loss of materials from flow path components is caused by the chemical reaction between the components and contaminants that enter the gas turbine with the inlet air, fuel or injected water/steam, the process is called corrosion. Corrosion is experienced more at the hot end with the presence of elements such as vanadium, sodium and lead enhancing high-temperature corrosion of turbine airfoils. The effect is a reduction of engine performance.

e.   **Object Damage:** This is the result of an object striking the gas path components of the gas turbine engine. The origin of such particles could be via the inlet section with the working fluid (foreign object damage (FOD)) or particles from the engine itself breaking off and being carried downstream (domestic object damage (DOD)). Here, again, the effect is a deterioration of the engine's performance. The fault signature with respect to its effect on performance is sometimes identical to that of fouling.

6.2. Engine Reliability, Availability and Diagnostic Techniques

Operation and maintenance costs of a gas turbine contribute a major portion of the annual maintenance budget of a company. In view of the changes in world economy towards globalisation and openness of the market, any efforts that can reduce the total cost of ownership and life cycle cost of the equipment will be added advantages.

The primary objectives of all maintenance strategies are to reduce equipment downtime, increase reliability and availability of the equipment, which at the same time optimise the life cycle costs of the equipment. Normally, costs associated with the design and manufacture of the engine are fixed and rarely influenced by the users. Therefore, in order to increase the overall profit and be competitive in the open market, the users are left to manage the life cycle costs of the engine during its operation and maintenance.

Reliability is generally described in terms of the failure rate or mean time between failures (MTBF), while availability is normally associated with total downtime. In general, current technology has ensured that the gas turbines for industrial application, especially for base load power plant operation, have high levels of reliability. However, when the turbines are removed from operation due to forced outages, the downtime incurred depends on the time required to complete the necessary repair or maintenance action, hence affecting its availability (Singh, 2001).

Figure 6.1 illustrates the comparison of forced outage rate and total downtime for major components of a typical gas turbine. Overall outage rate of a gas turbine is normally affected by unreliability of "soft components" such as instrumentation and control systems. However, their downtime can be managed to acceptable levels, as they are either easily replaceable or generally designed with redundancy. On the other hand, gas path components such as compressor and turbine reliability are high. However, when a forced outage is caused by these components, the maintenance downtime can be excessive. This is because these components are normally not held in spares, either by the users or manufacturers, due to their high costs but low demand. The long time for maintenance action results in low availability of the engine for usage, when required. As shown in Figure 6.2, if the time between maintenance actions is 10,000 hours, but the engine downtime is 3 months due to unavailability of spare parts, then the engine overall availability achieved would be only 80%. If, however, an appropriate technique to predict the failure of these components is used, the parts can be preordered some months ahead. The new maintenance downtime is then only due to actual repair time. If the downtime were reduced to 3 days, then the availability would be 99.5%. This improvement clearly provides significant impact to plant overall economics (Singh, 2001) and can only be brought about if better knowledge of plant performance is available. Enhanced knowledge of the gas path components of the gas turbine would help to optimally schedule maintenance and, in fact, is a key feature of an engine health monitoring (EHM) scheme.

Gas path fault diagnostic techniques can be grouped into two categories: qualitative and quantitative approaches.

Qualitative techniques: This includes all approaches that try to ascertain the presence of a fault without placing a value on the level of fault. Examples of this technique include fault matrix and fault trees (Singh, 1999). The procedure here is to take measurements from the engine and try to match them against predetermined patterns of known faults. A major limitation of this technique is that only one fault can be identified at a time and, because of the nature of results obtained, the extent of deterioration may not be known.

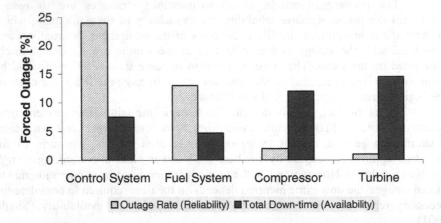

Figure 6.1.   Gas turbine major components' outage rates and total downtimes.

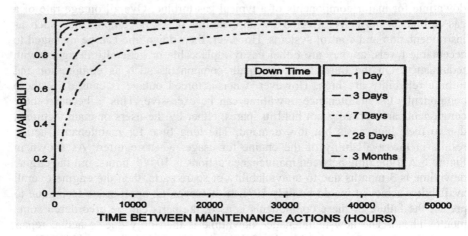

Figure 6.2.   Availability vs. downtime.

Quantitative techniques: with the inherent limitations of the qualitative techniques, there was a need for quantitative methods. The work of Urban (Urban, 1972) gave rise to what is now commonly known as gas path analysis (GPA). The theory behind this is simple. The analytical performance of gas turbine engine is based upon component characteristics and aerothermo relationships. For a well-defined characteristic, an aerothermo model can provide the engine performance in terms of dependent or measurable parameters such as pressures, temperatures, spool speed, etc. and independent nonmeasurable parameters such as efficiencies and flow capacities. During the operation of an engine, the performance deteriorates because of gas path degradation and faults. Each of these faults affects the independent parameters and because they cannot be directly measured, the faults need to be detected, isolated and quantified by using the relationship between the dependent and independent parameters (Figure 6.3). Artificial neural networks (ANN) and genetic algorithms (GA) are other quantitative techniques being explored for engine diagnostics.

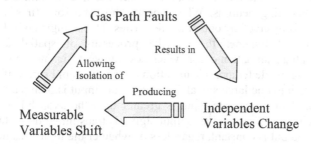

Figure 6.3. Principles underlying gas path analysis.

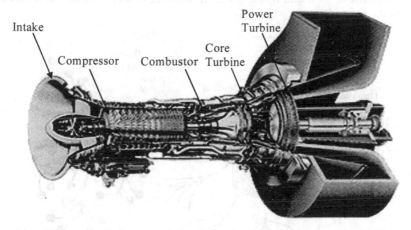

Figure 6.4. Typical two-shaft aeroderivative gas turbine with power turbine.

In the following sections, we review the need for engine diagnostics and maintenance, introduce ANNs, present some aspects of the ANNs application to diagnostic problems, highlight some features of ANNs that make them amenable to GT diagnostics, as well as their limitations, and finally discuss their application to gas path fault diagnosis of a developed case study. The engine used for this analysis is a two-shaft aeroderivative gas turbine, thermodynamically similar to the Rolls Royce Avon. A sectioned picture of this engine's configuration is shown in Figure 6.4 with some of the gas path components indicated.

6.3. Artificial Neural Networks

Eustace and Merrington. (1995) described a neural network as a diagrammatic representation of a mathematical equation that receives values (inputs) and gives out results (outputs). Neurobiology estimates the human brain to consist of one hundred billion nerve cells or neurons. These communicate via electrical signals that are short-lived impulses or "spikes" in the voltage of the cell wall membrane. Biological neurons (Figure 6.5) have three principal components: the dendrites, the cell body (soma) and the axon. A neuron's dendritic tree is connected to about a thousand neighbouring neurons. When one of those neurons fires, a positive or negative charge is received by one of the dendrites. The strengths of all the received charges are added together through the processes of spatial and temporal summation. Spatial summation occurs when several weak signals are converted into a single large one, while temporal summation converts a rapid series of weak pulses from one source into one large signal. The aggregate input is then passed to the cell body or soma. If the aggregate input is greater than the axon hillock's threshold value, then the neuron *fires*, and an output signal is transmitted down the axon. The strength of the output is constant, regardless of whether the input was just above the threshold, or a hundred times as great. The output strength is unaffected by the many divisions in the axon; it reaches each terminal button with the same intensity it had at the axon hillock.

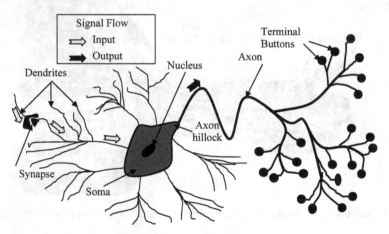

Figure 6.5.   A typical biological neuron.

Although ANNs have been around since the late 1950s, it was not until mid-1980 that algorithms became sophisticated enough for general applications. Also referred to as connectionist architectures, parallel-distributed processing systems, an ANN is an information-processing paradigm inspired by the way the densely interconnected, parallel structure of the mammalian brain processes information. ANNs are collections of mathematical models that emulate some of the observed properties of biological nervous systems and draw on the analogies of adaptive biological learning. The key element of the ANN paradigm is the novel structure of the information processing system. It is composed of a large number of highly interconnected processing elements that are analogous to neurons and are tied together with weighted connections that are analogous to synapses. A typical neuronal model is thus comprised of weighted connectors, an adder and a transfer function (Figure 6.6).

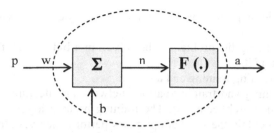

Figure 6.6.   A single mathematical neuronal model.

The basic relationship here is:

$$n = wp + b \tag{1}$$
$$a = F(wp + b) \tag{2}$$

where

a = network output signal
w – weight of input signal
p = input signal
b = neuron specific bias
F = transfer/activation function
n = induced local field or activation potential

Learning in biological systems involves adjustments to the synaptic connections that exist between the neurons. This is true for ANNs as well. Learning typically occurs by example through training, or exposure to a truthed set of input/output data where the training algorithm iteratively adjusts the connection weights (synapses). These connection weights store the knowledge necessary to solve specific problems. From Eqs. 1 and 2, it can be seen that a simple neuron performs the linear sum of the product of the synaptic weight and input with the bias, which value is then passed through an activation or transfer function that limits the amplitude of the output of a neuron. Activation functions can take various forms ranging from hard limit, through pure linear to sigmoid and the choice of which to use depends on the desired output from the network and the characteristics of the system being modelled.

Typical and practical networks are normally multi-input and probably multilayered and in such cases, the variables in Eqs. 1 and 2 now take a different format with **w** being the matrix of weights and **a**, **p** and **b** representing vectors of their respective definitions.

Two key similarities between biological and artificial networks (Haykin, 1999) are:

1.   Their building blocks are highly interconnected computational devices though the artificial neurons are much inferior to their biological counterparts.

2.   The function of the network is determined by the nature of connection between the neurons.

The inherent nonlinearity in GT performance and diagnostic relationships and the obvious limitations of the analytical model-based technique otherwise known as GPA, make the need for consideration of alternative techniques such as ANNs inevitable.

The basic steps involved in obtaining a typical supervised feedforward ANN include:

1.   Assessing the problem to be solved in a bid to seek the possibility of discretising it.
2.   Generating training and test data.
3.   Defining and training various network architectures in order to seek the optimal architecture(s). The training process joggles the weights and biases to obtain the set that optimises performance via reduced errors and good generalisation. The weight adjustment for the case of a back propagation network that operates on the gradient descent technique is done via the relation:

$$\Delta w_{ij} = \eta \left(-\frac{\partial E(n)}{\partial w_{ij}} \right) + \alpha \Delta w_{ij} (n-1) \tag{3}$$

where E is the difference between the outputs and the targets for the nth input otherwise called the "error" to be minimised, η and α are the learning rate and momentum constants, respectively.

4.   Testing the ANNs with enough data to ascertain generalisation abilities.

Barschdorff (1991) states that the use of ANNs can significantly improve symptom interpretation in scenarios of malfunctions of mathematically difficult to describe systems and processes.

6.4.   Artificial Neural Networks and Fault Diagnosis

The possibility of incorporating ANNs in engine health monitoring has recently been the subject of much research after its successful application to other endeavours of life such as medicine (diagnosis of diseases), finance (prediction of stocks) amongst others. ANNs have been applied by a number of authors to fault diagnostic activities. Such areas include:

- **Sensor(s) faults**. Single sensor fault diagnosis for industrial power plants (Simani and Fantuzzi, 2000). Single sensor fault diagnosis for a space shuttle main engine (Guo and Nurre, 1991). Prediction of a failed sensor and actuators in automobile engines (Dong et al., 1997).
- **GT faults**. Aeroengine fault and sensor bias detection (Kobayashi and Simon, 2001; Zedda and Singh, 1998). Fault diagnosis of fleet engines (Eustace and Merrington, 1995). Faulty sensor and component isolation for a single spool GT (Kanelopoulos et. al., 1997). Jet engine parameter trending and engine malfunction prediction (Denney, 1993). Diagnosis and prognosis for the fuel system faults of an AGT-1500 military tank's GT (Illi et al., 1994).

- **Jet and rocket engines.** Detection of bearing failure and fuel interruptions in real time as well as stipulating the severity and duration of the fault (Dietz *et al.*, 1989).
- **Nuclear power plant.** Nuclear power plant diagnostics (Guo and Uhrig, 1992; Parlos *et al.*, 1994; Tsai and Chou, 1996), signal validation (Upadhyaya and Eryurek, 1992; Fantoni and Mazzola, 1996), control (Jous and Williams, 1990; Bakal *et al.*, 1995), plant state identification (Barlett and Uhrig, 1992; Tsoukalas, 1994), prediction of plant parameters (Sofa *et al.*, 1990) and optimisation (Fukuzaki *et al.*, 1992).
- **Mechanical damage.** Detection of rotating machinery gearbox and bearing housing faults (Paya *et al.*, 1997). Prediction of propulsion system rotor unbalance (Huang *et al.*, 2001), GT blade fault diagnosis (Angelakis *et al.*, 2001).

Some developed GT diagnostic approaches involving the use of ANNs include the following reviewed works.

-Zedda and Singh (1998) proposed the use of a modular based diagnostic framework for a twin spool turbofan GT with low bypass, thermodynamically similar to the Garret TFE 1042. In their work, the authors considered the possibility of using multiple nets in the detection and quantification of faults within three of the four (FAN, HPC, HPT and LPT) components of this GT unit. Seven sensors were considered for the isolation of fault in eight performance parameters. The analysis considered a single operating point and component faults were split into two categories – soft and hard, which required that a different diagnostic path be traversed for the detected category. Single component faults were also considered. The diagnostic procedure modules consisted of preclassification, classification, data validation, training set selection and net training. The results were reportedly encouraging by the authors.

Kobayashi and Simon (2001) proposed a hybrid neural network - genetic algorithm technique for engine performance diagnostics. A General Electric simulation programme for the XTE46 – a scaled unclassified representation of an advanced military twin spool turbofan engine – was used to generate data for constructing the diagnostic process. Faults were modelled by adjustments to efficiencies and/or flow coefficient scalars of the fan (FAN), booster (BST), high pressure compressor (HPC), high pressure turbine (HPT) and low pressure turbine (LPT). This gave nine health parameters to be estimated. The authors chose twelve sensed parameters to monitor the engine and compute the health parameters. In their approach, a neural network estimator was designed to estimate the engine health parameters from sensor measurements while the genetic algorithm was applied to the sensor bias detection task. The authors claimed that the approach of incorporating genetic algorithms would reduce the size of the network training set significantly while inferring that ANN will not perform well if sensor bias is present in the measurements used to train it. In general, the results showed good estimation capabilities of the designed system with estimation errors below the 30% level considered by the authors to be their satisfactory mark. The authors suggested that an area of further work would require a systematic way of selecting and/or locating sensors for health estimation, as simply increasing the number of sensors does not guarantee improved estimation performance.

Kanelopoulos *et al.* (1997) applied multiple neural networks in the simulation of performance and qualitative diagnosis of faults in a single shaft GT. The authors suggested that two networks with the first used to isolate sensor faults and the subsequent one to isolate component faults would provide better results than applying a single network for the combined task. This work amongst others gave impetus to the idea of using a specialised network for a specialised task.

Eustace and Merrington (1995) applied a probabilistic neural network to diagnose faults in any engine within a fleet of 130 engines. This idea is interesting especially when one considers the fact that even for healthy engines, measured parameters vary naturally from engine to engine within a fleet. The General Electric F404 low-bypass-ratio afterburning turbofan engine was chosen for consideration. This engine has six modules – fan, compressor, HPT, LPT and afterburner/final nozzle section. The authors used a statistical correlation technique to select five from eight available engine-monitoring parameters as inputs to the network. Residuals obtained from the difference of a measured parameter and its baseline – which was computed from correlative relationship with another parameter - were used to train the network. Faulty data were generated by fault implantation on a single engine and superimposed linearly on the fault-free data of the fleet, of which 60 were used to generate the network and 70 to test the network. This superimposition was done to reduce the time and cost involved in fault implant tests. Implanted faults were in the form of off-nominal adjustments to both the compressor variable geometry (CVG) and exhaust nozzle final area. Results from the network tests showed that an average accuracy of 87.6% was achieved with test patterns of about 4900. Considering the variability in the baseline used, the obtained result can be deemed acceptable.

Cifaldi and Chokani (1998) discussed the use of ANN with the backpropagation and delta learning rule in predicting the performance of six components (diffuser, compressor, burner, turbine, nozzle and mechanical shaft) of a turbojet engine while simultaneously giving an overview of its possible application to vibration-related faults. Ten thousand training patterns were generated with the simulation programme and another twenty-five patterns were used to test the trained network. Each of these patterns represented an operating point. The result of their study showed that the mechanical, burner, compressor and turbine efficiency trends were well predicted while the efficiency trends of the diffuser and nozzle were poorly predicted. The authors attributed this poor performance to the choice of the instrumentation.

Green and Allen (1997) discussed the need to incorporate ANNs with other AI tools to obtain a cognitive (awareness), ontogenetic (learning organism), engine health monitoring (EHM) system or COEHM with estimation of lifing, diagnostic and prognostic capabilities.

Guo *et al.* (1996) applied an autoassociative neural network (AANN) for sensor validation. The authors in their analysis assumed a redundancy in the instrumentation set. This may imply that a nonredundant instrumentation set cannot be successfully applied with AANN for sensor validation since according to the authors, the number of neurons in the bottleneck must not be less than the minimum number of sensors required to generate all sensor estimates in case of a detected failure.

Napolitano *et al.* (1996) while comparing the approaches of Kalman filters (KF) and ANN for sensor failure detection, isolation and accommodation (SFDIA), used units without physical redundancy in the sensory capabilities. Basing their analysis on soft failures/faults, the authors applied multiple ANNs in the form of main and decentralised networks (MNN, DNNs) to perform SFDIA. The application of multiple nets makes it possible to infer that if errors are to be minimised for this and other complex applications, then more than one net need be employed with each, applied to a specific aspect of the problem.

Weidong *et al.* (1996) and Lu *et al.* (2000) used the relativity of inputs and outputs of an ANN to detect the presence, or otherwise, of faults in sensors, with the output said to represent a better approximation of the sensors' correct measurements. This network output can then be fed to other networks, probably, for component fault diagnosis.

In the present analysis, however, we intend to develop a methodology for fault diagnostics of the gas path of a two-shaft gas turbine. We shall consider faults that affect the components (turbines and compressor) as well as the sensors, using ANNs. Table 6.1 shows some of the strengths of ANNs that are juxtaposed with their perceived weaknesses. The strengths make ANNs very useful for integration in engine diagnostics, while the weaknesses create challenges that will need solutions as more research is focussed on improving ANN applications to diagnostics systems.

Table 6.1.   Comparison of the strengths and weaknesses of ANNs in engine diagnostics

ANN STRENGTHS	ANN WEAKNESSES
• It has the ability to handle nonlinear relationships, which are characteristics of engine parameter interrelationships. This feature can be extended to include such cases where ANN is applied to represent relationships where no analytical model exists. • It is tolerant to measurement nonrepeatability problems or noise. • It can operate satisfactorily even in the presence of limited information. • It can be applied online due to its extremely fast convergence when in the recall mode.	• The optimal network structure for a given problem is generally not known. • The criteria for the validation of a network are not well defined. • The criteria for the selection of the best training algorithm for fast convergence of given or new patterns is not understood. • The rules for selecting the amount and type of data for training as to improve quality of network are minimal. • The convergence of training algorithms is not guaranteed. • Long training/ adaptation times. • Data effusive, which could be difficult to obtain in some actual situations.

6.5.   Measurable Parameters and Measurement Uncertainties/Errors

It is obvious that the ability to accurately determine engine health largely depends on the accuracy of measurements available. Many sensors installed on the engine operate in very hostile environments at extremes of temperature and/or pressure. Unfortunately, sensor measurements are often distorted by noise and bias, thereby masking the true condition of the engine and leading to incorrect estimation results. This creates the situation where sensor reliability may be lower than component reliability, and causes incorrect component fault diagnosis.

Measurement errors may be broken down into two distinct components, a random error and a fixed error (Abernethy and Thomson, 1973). Random error is the difference in values between repeated measurements of the same item. This can be described as instrument nonrepeatability or precision error, and can be of the same order of magnitude as changes induced by a real engine fault. The fixed error is called the sensor bias and remains constant. In repeated measurements, each measurement will have the same amount of bias. Sensor failures can be viewed as either hard catastrophic failures or soft uneasy-to-detect failures. Hard failures are generally assumed to be easy to detect. Soft failures may generally not degrade the system performance for some time but if left undetected can eventually cause catastrophic results. An undetected sensor bias can either point to a nonexistent fault or point to a fault in an engine component.

For simplicity, and to be able to communicate the level of uncertainty associated with a measurement, an "uncertainty" term may be used to describe the measurement instrument. The most widely used convention is a hybrid of bias and precision error. Uncertainty may be centred about the measurement and is defined as:

$$U = \pm (B + t_{95}s) \tag{4}$$

where B is the bias limit, s is the precision error index (standard deviation of the sampled population) and t_{95} is the 95th percentile point for the two-tailed "t" distribution (Figure 6.7).

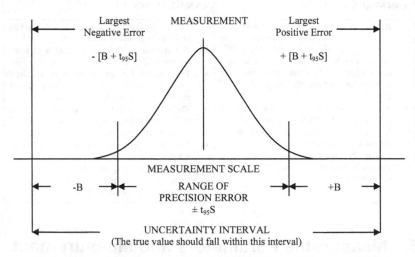

Figure 6.7.   Instrument uncertainties (Abernethy and Thomson, 1973).

Six measurable parameters (the process of determining them is presented later) are used in the current analysis, and their precision values are given in Table

6.2, together with the levels of deviations for which they could be considered as producing faulty readings. The precision values were applied to all simulated data before introduction to the ANN programme for training and testing purposes.

Table 6.2.   Measurable parameters nonrepeatability errors

Sensor		Description	Precision Values (% span)	Fault Level Considered (%)
1	N1	Gas generator relative shaft speed	0.03	$\pm$ (0.06 to 10)
2	WFE	Gas generator fuel flow	1	$\pm$ (2 to 10)
3	P2	Gas generator compressor delivery total pressure	0.1	$\pm$ (0.2 to 10)
4	T2	Gas generator compressor delivery total temperature	0.4	$\pm$ (0.8 to 10)
5	P4	Gas generator exhaust pressure	0.1	$\pm$ (0.2 to 10)
6	T4	Gas generator exhaust temperature	0.4	$\pm$ (0.8 to 10)

6.6. Case Study

Gas path faults can occur during the operation of a gas turbine, and because they affect performance and life, it is necessary to diagnose and correct them. It is important to note that in addition to component faults, measurement noise and sensor bias are other sources of parameter changes in the gas path of a gas turbine. A stochastic approach would therefore seek not to undermine this fact. Application of artificial neural networks has the capability to deal with inaccuracies of conventional diagnostic tools. Such inaccuracy effects include undermodeling (where a simplified model is used for convenience to appropriate the real system), linearization errors and measurement noise. Figure 6.8 presents a first level schematic of the diagnostic strategy being proposed. The procedures adopted include:

(1)   Obtaining an aerothermodynamic model of the engine from which simulation data would be generated for training and testing the networks. This approach was applied because it is extremely expensive to sacrifice actual engines for such an analysis and the probability of obtaining erroneous data from actual fault implantations cannot be ruled out.

(2)   Determining the sensors to be monitored. This can be done by making use of the sensor information available for the given engine or applying such techniques as gas path analysis to determine the optimum combinations that would be effective to diagnose the desired faults (Ogaji and Singh, 2002b). The latter approach was used.

(3)   Implanting faults in the engine model and generating data to cover all the possible fault scenarios as well as the required operating conditions defined by the power setting parameter and ambient conditions.

(4)   Training and testing various network architectures and determining the best data flow framework for the required diagnostic purpose.

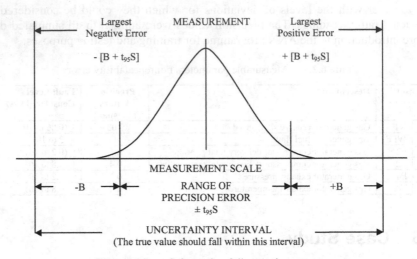

Figure 6.8.   Schematic of diagnostic strategy.

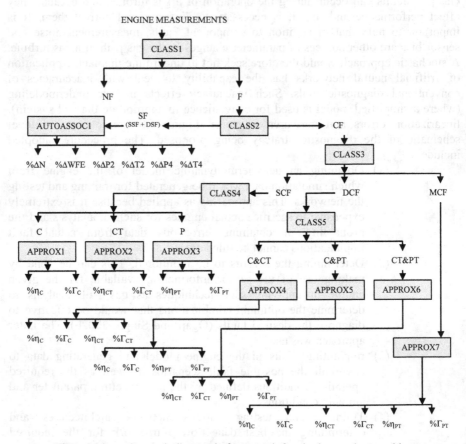

Figure 6.9.   Gas path diagnostic framework for single-spool gas turbine.

The diagnostic framework (ANN model from Figure 6.8) applied is shown in Figure 6.9, and its functioning is given below:

- Measured patterns from the engine sensors are fed into the first classification network denoted by CLASS1. These patterns are classified into either faulty (F) or not faulty (NF).

- If there is no fault detected in the patterns and if the network is sufficiently accurate, then there is no need for further diagnostic checks. If a fault is detected, the patterns are passed on to CLASS2 where they are classified into either sensor faults (SF) or component faults (CF). The sensor faults considered in this case are single (SSF) and dual (DSF).

- If a sensor fault is detected, the pattern is passed on to an autoassociative network (AUTOASSOC1), whose output has been constrained during training, to give nonfaulty results. Thus the percentage deviation between input to this network and its output provides an indication of the amount of bias/fault or even noise present in each of the sensors.

- Alternatively, if the pattern from CLASS2 is classified as a CF, then the patterns are passed on to another classification network called CLASS3 which classifies the patterns into any of the three categories: single-component faults (SCF), dual-component faults (DCF) and multi-component faults (MCF). It necessary to note that the engine under consideration has four basic components – one compressor, one combustor and two turbines. The combustor is excluded in this analysis because its efficiency is relatively stable with time (Diakunchak, 1992) and thus its performance deterioration does not provide sufficient information from the measurable parameters which is a requirement for assessing its health using our technique.

- A pattern identified as SCF is passed on to another network, CLASS4, which attempts to isolate the affected component, which could be the compressor (C), compressor turbine (CT) or power turbine (PT). If the faulty component is successfully isolated, the pattern is passed on to an approximation network that assesses the extent of fault by determining the changes in efficiency (η) and flow capacity (Γ). Interpretation of the nature of the fault is left to the user.

- The approach to DCF and MCF fault assessment is similar to that of SCF described above.

The anatomy and results of these networks as well as results obtained from tests carried out are presented in the next section. A possible alternative diagnostic structure to that shown in Figure 6.9 is also presented.

6.7.   Network Anatomy and Results

In Table 6.3 a summary of the classification networks developed in this work is presented including results obtained in terms of correctly classified test patterns. The network type is the probabilistic neural network (PNN), which can be set up in less than two minutes when data is available. This network requires no "training," but its hidden layer takes up processing units or neurons equal to the number of training patterns while the input and output layers are respectively equal, in terms of the number of neurons, to the number of sensors and the expected output groups. The PNN was applied to all pattern classification tasks except CLASS3, because in addition to the quick setup time, it also has the basic advantage of novelty detection (assigning previously unseen patterns to the most probable fault class). Appendix 2 offers a succinct description of the networks used in this work including the PNN.

Table 6.3.   Anatomy of classification networks and results

NETWORK	Type	TTRP/TTP	RESULTS (%CCP)		
CLASS1	PNN	13526	NF 100	F 99.9	
CLASS2	PNN	12026	SF 100	CF 99.7	
CLASS3	PNN	9926	SCF 99.1	DCF 90.1	MCF 76.3
CLASS4	PNN	1330	C 100	CT 100	PT 100
CLASS5	PNN	4096	C&CT 98.6	C&PT 96.8	CT&PT 97.2

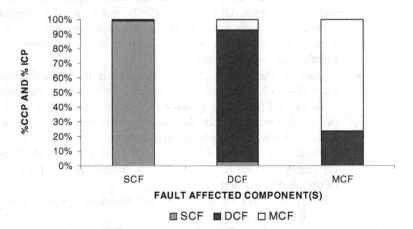

Figure 6.10.   Distribution of classification results from CLASS3 using a PNN.

CLASS1 data set comprised representations from all the possible fault scenarios, thus patterns in all the other CLASS networks are also members of CLASS1. The classification accuracy of CLASS1 is very high which indicates the network's ability to adequately distinguish between a faulty (F) and nonfaulty (NF) engine. The philosophy of first ascertaining the condition of an engine before diagnosing its fault is considered a novel development.

Generally, all classification networks performed well except CLASS3 where some DCFs were misclassified as either SCF or MCF. This is because when one or both components included in the DCF are lightly affected by fault, the fault pattern becomes basically similar to that of an SCF and is classified as such. If both components in the DCF are heavily affected by fault, the pattern created becomes very similar to that of an MCF and is thus classified as such. Also, most of the MCFs were classified as DSF for the same reason (Figure 6.10). This problem led to application of a trained network to this aspect of the diagnostic framework. Using a fully connected feedforward network with architecture 6-35-35-3, resilient backpropagation (RB) as training algorithm and tanh sigmoid transfer function (Demuth and Beale, 2001) on all nodes, we obtained improved classification accuracy for this class (Table 6.4). The lesson to be derived here is that a modular diagnostic structure like the one proposed in Figure 6.8 allows for optimisation of each aspect of the structure, by using the best network configuration suitable for that aspect.

Table 6.4.   Comparison of classification from PNN and RB for CLASS3

NETWORK TYPE	SCF	DCF	MCF
PNN (%CCP)	99.10	90.06	76.31
RB (%CCP)	98.95	95.00	90.44

An alternative to the classification section of the ANN framework proposed in Figure 6.9 is shown in Figure 6.11. Here, a CLASSΩ network created on the PNN principle is used to diagnose any of the nine possible engine conditions, a task hitherto performed by five CLASS networks. The classification accuracy achieved (Table 6.5) is similar to that from Figure 6.9 when the percentages are compounded down the chain, but the possibility of optimising any section of the classification network structure is ruled out as is possible with Figure 6.8.

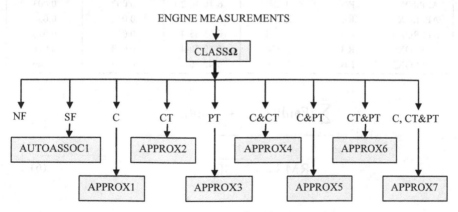

Figure 6.11.   Alternative classification structure.

Table 6.5.   Classification accuracy for alternative structure

FC	NF	SF	C	CT	PT	C+CT	C+PT	CT+PT	MCF
%CCP	100.00	99.62	99.82	98.42	98.42	89.06	87.76	86.72	76.02

The implanted component faults ranged from a 0.5% to 3.5% drop in efficiency while various levels of flow capacity changes were combined with each level of efficiency drop depending on the type of fault being simulated. This is expected to cover the range of faults of interest during engine operation. Test patterns were generated at positions between the training patterns that account for the equality of test and training patterns. In Table 6.6, a summary of the approximation networks is presented. It should be recalled that approximation networks are created to quantify the amount of changes in independent variables for component(s) diagnosed to be faulty. The sizes of network deemed optimal from the number of networks trained for each category are also shown. All the networks here were trained with RB training algorithm (Demuth and Beale, 1992) with the transfer function for all nodes tan sigmoid. The last two columns of Table 6.6 show the MSE obtained from training and testing these networks. The MSE and RMS defined by Eqs. 5 and 6 respectively are the statistical parameters used to examine the performance of the networks as well as make comparisons with other diagnostic techniques in this work.

The very low MSE obtained during training and testing of the APPROX networks vis-à-vis the close similarity between the MSE from the training and testing process in the presence of measurement noise indicates the high estimation quality of the networks for the faults being diagnosed.

Table 6.6.   Anatomy of approximation networks and results

NETWORK	NTRALG	TTRP/TTP	SIZE	MSE (TRAINING)	MSE (TEST)
APPROX1	RB	1830	6-15-15-2	0.009	0.010
APPROX2	RB	1220	6-10-10-2	0.003	0.003
APPROX3	RB	1220	6-10-10-2	0.002	0.003
APPROX4	RB	23064	6-30-30-4	0.032	0.032
APPROX5	RB	23064	6-35-35-4	0.018	0.018
APPROX6	RB	15376	6-30-30-4	0.018	0.018
APPROX7	RB	20736	6-40-40-6	0.137	0.146

$$\text{MSE} = \frac{\sum_{i=1}^{n}\left(\text{Fault}_{implanted} - \text{Fault}_{Detected}\right)^2}{n} \tag{5}$$

$$\text{RMS} = \sqrt{\text{MSE}} \tag{6}$$

Table 6.7. Correlation of APPROX4 test output with target and analysis of prediction error

Parameter	Correlation Coefficient (r)
η_c	0.9721
Γ_c	0.9993
η_{ct}	0.9787
Γ_{ct}	0.9992

		$?\eta_c$	$?\Gamma_c$	$?\eta_{ct}$	$?\Gamma_{ct}$
	Mean Error	0.01	0.00	0.01	0.00
% of points within the given std.	σ	0.21	0.18	0.18	0.14
	1σ	75	70	81	69
	2σ	95	95	95	95
	3σ	99	99.5	98	99.5

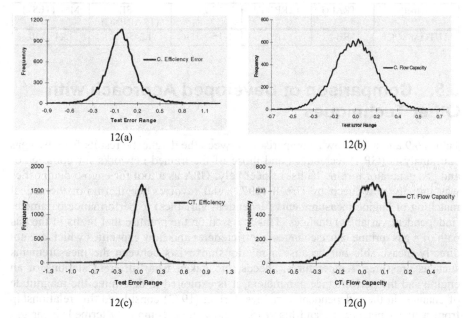

12(a)　　　　12(b)

12(c)　　　　12(d)

Figure 6.12. Distribution of actual error in ANN prediction of compressor turbine performance parameters

    A close view at one of these approximation networks presented in Table 6.6, say APPROX4, shows that it has architecture of 6-30-30-4 with 23,064 patterns used for training while another 23,064 patterns were involved in the testing of the network. This network was designed to assess the amount of DCF present in the compressor and compressor turbine. Figure 6.12a-d shows the prediction error distribution from testing of this network. Considering the level and complexity of the faults being diagnosed, especially with the level of noise added, this degree of accuracy is satisfactory even in actual applications. From the correlation coefficients (Table 6.7, left), we show the degree of matching obtained from the ANN predicted fault level and the target or true values for each of the independent variables. From Table 6.7, right, it is shown that over 70% of the test patterns fall within one standard deviation of the mean error, with the mean effectively equal to zero in this case.

Other networks showed similar performance to those presented above, but generally, as the complexity of the problem being addressed increased, the degree of accuracy of the network in addressing the problem decreased.

In Table 6.8, the anatomy of the autoassociative network used to determine changes from a working baseline for sensor fault(s) is shown. The MSE error, both for training and testing of the network here, again, indicate a very high level of prediction accuracy. The amount of sensor noise that may be present is also determined.

Table 6.8.   Anatomy of autoassociative network and results

Label	NTRALG	TTRP/TTP	SIZE	MSE (TRAINING)	MSE (TEST)
AUTOASSOC1	RB	2100	6-15-3-15-6	1.245E-10	1.245E-10

6.8.   Comparison of Developed Approach with Other Techniques

Tables 6.9 and 6.10 show a comparison between the diagnostic results from two gas path analysis (GPA) techniques and those of the trained networks for compressor and gas generator turbine faults, respectively. GPA as a tool for engine diagnostics was initially introduced by Urban (1972) and involves the thermo-mathematical matching of engine measurements (dependent variables) to performance parameter (independent variables) changes. This is based on the premise that faults in the gas path of a gas turbine cause changes in efficiencies and flow capacities which are not directly measurable but because a relationship exists between the measurements such as pressures, temperatures, speeds, etc. taken from different stations of an engine and the performance parameters, it is exploited to determine the magnitude of changes in the independent variables. Urban (1972) considered this relationship from a linear perspective and his work is now more commonly termed linear gas path analysis (LGPA). In reality, gas turbine parameter interrelationships are highly nonlinear, hence, Escher and Singh (1995) developed an iterative approach to the problem with the principles based on Urban's formulation. This new approach is termed nonlinear gas path analysis (NLGPA).

In Table 6.9, the implanted fault in the compressor component and the diagnostic results from three diagnostic techniques, LGPA, NLGPA and ANN, are compared. It should be noted that the presence of a fault is indicated by a change in the independent variables which would thus affect the measurements taken from the engine. The ANN module involved in estimating the fault in this component is APPROX2 (see Figure 6.9). The mean RMS errors from the three techniques show that the estimation accuracy depreciates from NLGPA through ANN to LGPA; in fact the mean error from the ANN is twice that from NLGPA. A similar conclusion can be drawn from Table 6.10, where APPROX2 is called to estimate compressor turbine fault from the ANN module in Figure 6.9. In Table 6.10, however, NLGPA failed to converge on some fault scenarios. This nonconvergence is due to a convergence feature in the NLGPA algorithm that causes instability when it is perceived that a solution is not possible with the current instrumentation suite. This is in contrast with the ANN results, which show that the instrumentation suite is sufficient. In addition, the results from the GPA techniques (LGPA and NLGPA) do not include measurement noise, unlike those from ANN. Had noise been included in the NLGPA measurements, the ANN diagnostic results may have compared favourably with those from NLGPA, or even better since no noise filtering algorithm exists in the NLGPA tool.

Table 6.9. Comparison between ANN and GPA diagnostic results for compressor

IMPLANTED FAULTS		LINEAR GPA			NONLINEAR GPA			ANN		
η_c	Γ_c	η_c	Γ_c	RMS	η_c	Γ_c	RMS	η_c	Γ_c	RMS
-0.5	-0.5	-0.81	-0.33	0.251	-0.50	-0.47	0.022	-0.59	-0.50	0.062
-0.5	-1.0	-0.83	-0.86	0.253	-0.50	-1.00	0.003	-0.53	-0.94	0.045
-0.5	-1.5	-0.92	-1.50	0.299	-0.50	-1.55	0.037	-0.55	-1.49	0.034
-0.5	-2.0	-1.22	-1.69	0.555	-0.62	-1.53	0.340	-0.59	-2.04	0.071
-1.0	-1.0	-1.62	-0.65	0.503	1.00	-0.98	0.012	-1.04	-1.00	0.030
-1.0	-2.0	-1.66	-1.72	0.506	-1.00	-2.00	0.002	-0.80	-1.83	0.189
-1.0	-3.0	-2.07	-2.52	0.832	-1.13	-2.49	0.373	-1.01	-3.03	0.020
-1.0	-4.0	-2.46	-3.42	1.111	-1.01	-3.97	0.025	-1.02	-4.04	0.032
-1.5	-1.5	-2.46	-0.88	0.811	-1.50	-1.47	0.019	-1.34	-1.40	0.130
-1.5	-3.0	-2.46	-0.88	1.647	-1.49	-3.00	0.007	-1.54	-3.04	0.042
-1.5	-4.5	-3.13	-3.81	1.251	-1.50	-4.48	0.015	-1.35	-4.35	0.151
-1.5	-6.0	-3.72	-5.11	1.693	-1.51	-5.99	0.006	-1.81	-6.29	0.302
-2.0	-2.0	-3.51	-0.80	1.365	-2.00	-1.99	0.008	-1.79	-1.87	0.177
-2.0	-4.0	-3.49	-3.09	1.236	-2.08	-3.73	0.201	-1.81	-3.85	0.170
-2.0	-6.0	-4.19	-5.11	1.673	-2.00	-6.00	0.005	-1.93	-5.99	0.048
-2.0	-8.0	-5.01	-6.88	2.270	-2.01	-7.99	0.012	-1.91	-7.93	0.080
-2.5	-2.5	-4.30	-1.02	1.648	-2.50	-2.48	0.015	-2.74	-2.74	0.243
-2.5	-5.0	-4.24	-4.07	1.393	-2.53	-4.96	0.038	-2.59	-5.10	0.097
-2.5	-7.5	-5.28	-6.24	2.156	-2.50	-7.49	0.010	-2.62	-7.55	0.090
-2.5	-10.0	-6.33	-8.69	2.862	-2.52	-9.99	0.014	-2.48	-9.87	0.093
-3.0	-3.0	-5.25	-0.98	2.138	-3.01	-2.99	0.006	-2.81	-2.97	0.137
-3.0	-6.0	-5.09	-4.85	1.690	-3.04	-5.96	0.039	-3.14	-6.05	0.107
-3.0	-9.0	-6.37	-7.45	2.623	-3.01	-8.99	0.009	-3.08	-9.00	0.054
-3.0	-12.0	-7.60	-10.41	3.440	-2.99	-11.99	0.006	-3.06	-12.05	0.057
		Mean Error		1.425	**Mean Error**		0.051	**Mean Error**		0.102

Table 6.10.   Comparison between ANN and GPA diagnostic results for compressor turbine module

IMPLANTED FAULTS		LINEAR GPA			NONLINEAR GPA			ANN		
η_{CT}	Γ_{CT}	η_{CT}	Γ_{CT}	RMS	η_{CT}	Γ_{CT}	RMS	η_{CT}	Γ_{CT}	RMS
-0.5	0.5	-0.99	0.38	0.358	-0.51	0.47	0.021	-0.53	0.55	0.038
-0.5	1.0	-1.01	0.86	0.373	-0.51	0.97	0.023	-0.53	1.13	0.098
-0.5	1.5	-1.04	1.30	0.403	-0.51	1.44	0.041	-0.60	1.61	0.109
-0.5	2.0	-1.06	1.75	0.434	-0.49	1.97	0.023	-0.59	1.97	0.065
-1.0	1.0	-2.11	0.69	0.814	-1.01	1.01	0.007	-1.00	1.06	0.040
-1.0	1.5	-2.17	1.13	0.866	-0.99	1.48	0.014	-1.06	1.59	0.075
-1.0	2.0	-2.37	1.55	1.021	-1.00	1.99	0.008	-0.94	1.96	0.053
-1.0	2.5	-2.58	1.95	1.184	-1.00	2.50	0.003	-0.94	2.39	0.085
-1.5	1.5	-3.96	1.01	1.775	-1.51	1.50	0.004	-1.47	1.49	0.020
-1.5	2.5	-4.32	1.73	2.069	-1.67	2.48	0.118	-1.50	2.45	0.033
-1.5	3.5	-4.36	2.46	2.152	-1.52	3.48	0.023	-1.53	3.53	0.028
-1.5	4.5	-4.65	3.16	2.421	-1.49	4.49	0.008	-1.44	4.38	0.097
-2.0	2.0	-5.45	1.17	2.507	-2.01	2.00	0.006	-2.04	1.95	0.042
-2.0	3.0	-5.76	1.89	2.770	-2.02	2.99	0.013	-2.00	3.06	0.041
-2.0	4.0	-6.07	2.58	3.048	-2.01	4.00	0.006	-2.01	4.02	0.018
-2.0	4.5	-6.22	2.91	3.190	-2.01	4.49	0.011	-1.91	4.39	0.096
-2.5	2.5	-6.82	1.34	3.166	NC	NC	-	-2.42	2.39	0.097
-2.5	3.0	-7.01	1.69	3.318	NC	NC	-	-2.43	2.95	0.061
-2.5	3.5	-7.18	2.03	3.469	NC	NC	-	-2.56	3.55	0.059
-2.5	4.5	-7.79	2.69	3.951	NC	NC	-	-2.55	4.56	0.055
-3.0	3.0	-11.53	1.42	6.134	NC	NC	-	-2.95	3.07	0.057
-3.0	3.5	-12.23	1.70	6.648	NC	NC	-	-3.04	3.63	0.095
-3.0	4.0	-11.44	1.98	6.139	NC	NC	-	-3.02	4.16	0.111
-3.0	4.5	-12.37	2.21	6.822	NC	NC	-	-2.99	4.61	0.081
		Mean Error		2.710	Mean Error		0.021	Mean Error		0.065

6.9. Conclusion

A hierarchical approach to gas path diagnostic for a two-shaft simple gas turbine involving multiple neural networks has been presented. The described methodology has been tested with data not used for training, and generalisation is found to be appropriate for actual application of this technique. In addition, the level of accuracy achieved by this decentralised application of ANNs shows derivable benefits over techniques that require just a single network to perform fault detection, isolation and assessment. The technique presented, combined with inference tools such as expert system or fuzzy logic, could be expanded to produce an engine health monitoring scheme since ANNs also have the ability to fuse data from other associated performance monitoring techniques such as vibration and oil analysis.

Generally, as the number of simultaneously faulty components is increased, the reliability of the network to accurately assess the fault decreases. One way of improving this reliability would be the increase of sensory information by considering data at different operating points, otherwise known as multiple operating point analysis (MOPA).

The ANN structure described above forms a part of the diagnostic tool that includes other aspects involved in parameter corrections, as well as aspects that provide linguistic information on the nature and type of fault, since ANNs only give qualitative and quantitative results without any explanation for their significance.

References

1. Abernethy RB and Thomson JW Jr (1973) Uncertainty in Gas Turbine Measurements. In: Proceedings of the AIAA/SAE 9th Propulsion Conference, 5-7 November, Las Vegas, NV, USA, AIAA 73-1230

2. Agrawal RK, MacIsaac BD and Saravanamuttoo HIH (1978) An Analysis Procedure for Validation of On-Site Performance Measurements of Gas Turbines. ASME Journal of Engineering for Power, paper no. 78-GT-152

3. Aker GF and Saravanamuttoo HIH (1989) Prediction Gas Turbine Performance Behaviour Due to Compressor Fouling Using Computer Simulation Techniques. ASME Journal of Engineering for Gas Turbines and Power 111:343-350

4. Angelakis C, Loukis EN, Pouliezos AD and Stavrakakis GS (2001) A Neural Network Based Method for Gas Turbine Blading Fault Diagnosis. International Journal of Modelling and Simulation 21(1)

5. Bakal B, Adali T, Fakory R, Sonmez MK and Tsaoi O (1995) Neural Network Simulation of Real Time Core Neutronic Model. In: Proceedings of the SCS Simulation Multiconference, Phoenix, AZ, USA

6. Barlett EB and Uhrig RE (1992) Power Plant Status Diagnostics Using Artificial Neural Network. Nuclear Technology 97:272-281

7. Cifaldi MI and Chokani N (1998) Engine Monitoring Using Neural Networks. American Institute of Aeronautics and Astronautics, AIAA-98-3548

8. Demuth H and Beale M (1992) Matlab Neural Networks Users Guide Ver. 4. MathWorks

9. Denney G (1993) F16 Jet Engine Trending and Diagnostics with Neural Networks. SPIE Applications of Artificial Neural Networks IV 1965:419-422

10. Diakunchak IS (1992) Performance Deterioration in Industrial Gas Turbines. ASME Journal of Engineering for Gas Turbines and Power 114:161-168

11. Dietz WE, Kiech EL and Ali M (1989) Jet and Rocket Engine Fault Diagnosis in Real Time. Journal of Neural Network Computing 1(1):5-18

12. Dong DW, Hopfield JJ and Unnikrishnan KP (1997) Neural Networks for Engine Fault Diagnostics. In: Proceedings of the 1997 IEEE Workshop, pp. 636-644

13. Escher PC and Singh R (1995) An Object-Oriented Diagnostics Computer Program Suitable for Industrial Gas Turbines. In: Proceedings of the United 21st International Congress on Combustion Engines (CIMAC), Interlaken, Switzerland, 15-18 May

14. Eustace R and Merrington G (1995) Fault Diagnosis of Fleet Engines Using Neural Networks. In: Proceedings of the Twelfth International Symposium on Air Breathing Engines, Melbourne, Australia , September 10-15, paper no. ISABE 95-7085

15. Fantoni PF and Mazzola A (1996) Multiple Failure Signal Validation in Nuclear Power Plants Using Artificial Neural Networks. Nuclear Technology 113(3)

16. Fukuzaki T, Ohga Y and Kobayashi Y (1992) Feasibility Studies on Applying Neural Network Techniques in Nuclear Power Plants. In: Proceedings of the OECD-NEA/IAEA International Symposium on NPP Instrumentation and Control, Tokyo, Japan

17. Green A and Allen D (1997) Artificial Intelligence for Real Time Diagnostics and Prognostics of Gas Turbine Engines. In: Proceedings of the 33rd AIAA/ASME/SAE/ASEE Joint Propulsion Conference and Exhibition, Seattle, WA, 6-9 July, paper no. AIAA 97-2899

18. Guo Z and Uhrig RE (1992) Use of Artificial Neural Networks to Analyze Nuclear Power Plant Performance. Nuclear Technology 99:36-42

19. Guo T-H and Nurre J (1991) Sensor Failure Detection and Recovery by Neural Networks. International Joint Conference on Neural Networks, Seattle, Washington, 8-12 July, paper no. NASA-TM-104484

20. Guo T-H, Saus J, Lin C-F and Ge J-H (1996) Sensor Validation for Turbofan Engines Using an Autoassociative Neural Network. AIAA Guidance Navigation and Control Conference, San Diego, CA, 29-31 July, paper no. AIAA-96-3926

21. Haykin S. (1999) Neural networks. A comprehensive foundation. Prentice-Hall

22. Huang H, Vian J, Choi J, Carlson D and Wunsch D (2001) Neural Network Inverse Models for Propulsion Vibration Diagnostics. In: Proceedings of SPIE 4390:12-21

23. Illi OJ, Greitzer FL, Kangas LJ and Reeve TJ (1994) An Artificial Neural Network System for Diagnosing Gas Turbine Engine Fuel Faults. In: Proceedings of the 48th Meeting of the Mechanical Failure Group, April 19-21. Wakefield, MA, paper no. MFPG 48

24. Jouse WC and Williams JG (1990) Neural Control of Temperature and Pressure during PWR Start-up. American Nuclear Society Transactions 61:219-220

25. Kanelopoulos K, Stamatis A and Mathioudakis K (1997) Incorporating Neural Networks into Gas Turbine Performance Diagnostics. In: Proceedings of the International Gas Turbine and Aeroengine Congress and Exhibition, Orlando, Florida, June 2-5, paper no. 97-GT-35

26. Kobayashi T and Simon DL (2001) A Hybrid Neural Network-Genetic Algorithm Technique for Aircraft Engine Performance Diagnostics. In: Proceedings of the 37th AIAA/ASME/SAE/ASEE Joint Propulsion Conference and Exhibit, Salt Lake City, Utah, paper no. AIAA-2001-3763

27. Lakshminarasimha AN, Boyce MP and Meher-Homji CB (1994) Modelling and Analysis of Gas Turbine Performance Deterioration. ASME Journal of Engineering for Gas Turbines and Power 116:46-52

28. Lu P, Hsu T, Zhang M and Zang J (2000) An Evaluation of Engine Faults Diagnostics Using Artificial Neural Networks. In: Proceedings of ASME Turbo Expo 2000: Land, Sea and Air, Munich, Germany, 8-11 May, paper no. 2000-GT-0029

29. Napolitano M, Windon D, Casanova J and Innocenti M (1996) A Comparison between Kalman Filter and Neural Network Approaches for Sensor Validation. In: Proceedings of the AIAA Guidance Navigation and Control Conference, San Diego, CA, July 29-31, paper no. AIAA-96-3894

30. Ogaji SOT and Singh R (2002a) Advanced Engine Diagnostics Using Artificial Neural Networks. In: Proceedings of the IEEE International Conference on

Artificial Intelligence Systems, 5-10 September, Gelendzhik, Black Sea Coast, Russia, pp. 236-241

31. Ogaji SOT and Singh R (2002b) Study of the Optimisation of Measurement Sets for Gas Path Fault Diagnosis in Gas Turbines. In: Proceedings of ASME Turbo Expo 2002, Amsterdam, The Netherlands, 3-6 June, paper no. GT-2002-30050

32. Ogaji SOT, Singh R and Probert SD (2002a) Multiple-sensor fault-diagnoses for a 2-shaft stationary gas-turbine. Applied Energy 71:321-339

33. Ogaji S, Sampath S and Singh R (2002b) Gas Turbine Faults: Detection, Isolation and Assessment Using Neural Networks. In: Proceedings of the Sixth International Conference on Knowledge-Based Intelligent Information & Engineering Systems, 16-18 September, Crema, Italy, pp. 141-145

34. Parlos AG, Muthusami J and Atiya AF (1994) Incipient Fault Detection and Identification in Progress Systems Using Accelerated Neural Network Learning. Nuclear Technology 105(2): 145-161

35. Paya BA, Esat II and Badi MNN (1997) Artificial Neural Network Based Fault Diagnostics of Rotating Machinery Using Wavelet Transforms as a Pre-processor. Mechanical Systems and Signal Processing 11(5): 751-765

36. Simani S and Fantuzzi C (2000) Fault Diagnosis in Power Plant Using Neural Networks. Information Sciences 127:125-136

37. Singh R (1999) Managing Gas Turbine Availability, Performance and Life Usage via Advanced Diagnostics. In: Proceedings of the 44th Gas Turbine Users Association Annual Conference, Dubai, UAE, 9-14 May

38. Singh R (2001) Managing Gas Turbine Availability, Performance and Life Usage Via Advanced Diagnostics. In: Proceedings of the Symposium for Diesel and Gas Turbine Engineers (IDGTE), Milton Keynes, United Kingdom, September 27-28

39. Sofa T, Eryurek E, Uhrig RE, Dodds HL and Cook DH (1990) Estimation of HFIR Core Flow Rate Using a Backpropagation Network. American Nuclear Society Transactions 61

40. Tsai TM and Chou HP (1996) Recurrent Neural Networks for Fault Detection and Isolation. In: Proceedings of the 1996 American Nuclear Society International Topical Meeting on Nuclear Plant Instrumentation, Control and Human-Machine Interface Technologies, Pennsylvania, USA, pp. 921-926

41. Tsoukalas LH (1994) Virtual Measurement and Prediction in Human-Centered Automation. In: Proceedings of the Topical Meeting on Computer-Based Human Support Systems: Technology, Methods, and Future, The American Nuclear Society's Human Factors Division, Pennsylvania, USA, pp. 235-241

42. Upadhyaya BR and Eryurek E (1992) Application of Neural Networks for Sensor Validation and Plant Monitoring. Nuclear Technology 97(2):170-176

43. Urban LA (1972) Gas Path Analysis Applied to Turbine Engine Condition Monitoring. In: Proceedings of the AIAA/SAE 8th Joint Propulsion Specialist Conference, New Orleans, Louisiana, paper no. AIAA-72-1082

44. Weidong H, Kechang W and Qizhi C (1996) Sensor Failure Detection and Data Recovery Based on Neural Network. In: Proceedings of the 32nd AIAA/ASME/SAE/ASEE Joint Propulsion Conference, Lake Buena Vista, FL , July 1-3, paper no. AIAA-96-2932

45. Zaita AV, Buley G and Karlsons G (1998) Performance Deterioration Modelling in Aircraft Gas Turbine Engines. ASME Journal of Engineering for Gas Turbines and Power 120:344-349

46. Zedda M and Singh R (1998) Fault Diagnosis of a Turbofan Engine Using Neural Networks: A Quantitative Approach. In: Proceedings of the 34th AIAA/ASME/SAE/ASEE Joint Propulsion Conference & Exhibit, Cleveland, OH, 13-15 July, paper no. AIAA 98-3602

Appendix 1

Nomenclature

η	Component efficiency
Γ	Component flow function/capacity
σ	Standard deviation
n	Number of measured patterns

Abbreviations

APPROX	Function approximation network
AUTOASSOC	Autoassociative neural network
C	Compressor
CBM	Condition based maintenance
CCP	Correctly classified patterns
CF	Component fault
CLASS	Pattern classification network
CT	Compressor turbine
DCF	Dual component fault
DSF	Dual sensor fault
EHM	Engine health monitoring
F	Fault
FC	Fault class
GT	Gas turbine
ICP	Incorrectly classified patterns
MCF	Multicomponent fault
MSE	Mean square error
NC	No convergence
NF	No fault
NTRALG	Network training algorithm
PNN	Probabilistic neural network
PT	Power turbine
RB	Resilient backpropagation network training algorithm
RMS	Root mean square
SCF	Single component fault
SF	Sensor fault
SSF	Single sensor fault
TTP	Total test patterns

TTRP	Total training patterns

**Glossary of terms
(including jargon)**

Advanced diagnostic technique (ADT)	A diagnostic approach that applies state-of-the-art tools.
APPROX	A network that is designed to provide quantitative estimates.
Architecture	A graph describing the layout of a neural network.
Artificial neural network (ANN)	A collection of mathematical models that emulates some of the observed properties of biological nervous systems and draws on the analogies of adaptive biological learning.
Bias	A fixed component of measurement error, which remains constant no matter how many times the measurement is taken.
CLASS	A network that is designed to provide qualitative results.
Dimensionality	The number of independent units contained in a given layer of a network.
Epoch	The presentation of a set of training (input and/or target) vectors to a network and the calculation of the new weights.
Expert system (ES)	A computer program that contains a *knowledge base* and a set of *algorithms* or rules that infer new facts from that knowledge and from incoming data.
Feedforward network	A form of network connectivity in which outputs go to following but not preceding neurons.
Fuzzy logic (FL)	A form of algebra applied in decision making with imprecise data. It employs a range of values between extremes of perfection, i.e., "true" or "false."
Gas path analysis (GPA)	A commonly used term for performance analysis.
Gas path faults (GPF)	Faults that affect the working fluid's flow path in a gas turbine. They include fouling and erosion.
Gas path fault diagnostics (GPFD)	The process of isolating and assessing faults in an engine's gas path.
Generalisation	The ability of a network to produce a required output from an input vector, similar to its training set.
Kalman filter (KF)	An algorithm for producing best estimates of the component changes and sensor biases that produced an observed set of gas-path measurement differences from expectation.
Noise	A random component of measurement error caused by numerous small effects, which cause disagreements between repeated measurements of the same parameter.
Pattern	A vector of inputs.
Testing	The process of ascertaining the generalisation ability of a trained network.
Training	A procedure whereby a network is adjusted to do a particular job.

Appendix 2 – Neural Network Structures

Figure 6.13 shows a typical probabilistic neural network (PNN) with m hidden layer neurons and k output classes. PNNs are simple on design, and with sufficient data are guaranteed to generalize well in classification tasks. When a pattern is introduced to the network, distances are computed between the inputs and the training patterns. The sum of each contribution is obtained and arranged into a vector of probabilities by the radial basis layer (middle layer). This vector of probabilities is then passed as an argument to a compete transfer function which allocates a one to the class of the candidate with the highest probability, because it has the maximum probability of being correct while other classes are allocated zero. A drawback, however, is that PNN networks are slower to operate in the recall mode because more computations are required each time they are called.

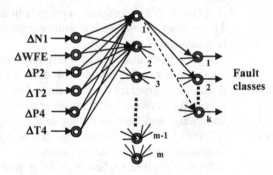

Figure 6.13.   Probabilistic neural network

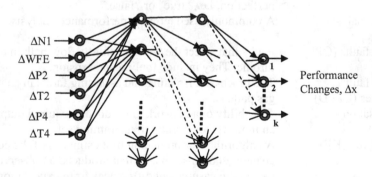

Figure 6.14.   Two-hidden-layer feed forward network.

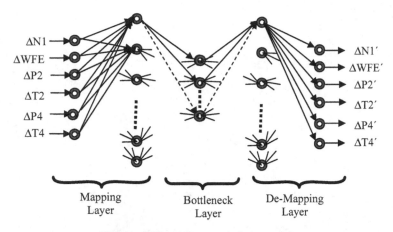

ΔN1
ΔWFE
ΔP2
ΔT2
ΔP4
ΔT4

ΔN1′
ΔWFE′
ΔP2′
ΔT2′
ΔP4′
ΔT4′

Mapping
Layer

Bottleneck
Layer

De-Mapping
Layer

Figure 6.15. Autoassociative network.

Figures 6.14 and 6.15 show typical supervised network architectures that require training before application in the recall mode for the intended purpose. Previous works by Ogaji and Singh (2002a) and Ogaji et al. (2002a) show that engine parameter estimation tasks are best handled by a two-hidden-layer network. Because of its speed of convergence during training, and efficiency in memory usage, resilient backpropagation training algorithm was used for our entire network training process. Also, because gas turbine parameter relationships are inherently nonlinear, a tangent sigmoid transfer function, which takes input in the range of plus and minus infinity and squashes the output to the range {-1, 1}, is used for all network nodes. This transfer function is differentiable and thus suitable for engine diagnostic purposes.

The autoassociative network presented in Figure 6.15 has been shown to perform well in sensor fault detection and isolation (Guo et al., 1996; Lu et al., 2000; Zedda and Singh, 1998; Ogaji et al., 2002b). This network has three hidden layers with the central layer called a bottleneck. The network requires that the number of neurons in the bottleneck be greater than or equal to the number of principal components required in constructing the output in the case of failed sensor(s) or noisy inputs. Also, in this kind of network, the dimensionality of the input and output patterns is the same, and various input sets may be required to give a particular output pattern. This makes it distinct from the hetero-associative networks, where various input patterns are mapped into various output sets, with the dimensionality of the input and output not necessarily being identical.

Figure 6.15 ...

7. Two-Stage Neural Networks Based Classifier System for Fault Diagnosis

Arūnas Lipnickas

This chapter gives a description of a two-stage classifier system for fault diagnosis of industrial processes. The first-stage classifier is used for fault detection and the second one is used for fault isolation and identification. The first stage classifier operates as primary fault detection unit, and it is used to distinguish between normal operating state and abnormal operating states. In order to reduce the number of false alarms, a penalizing factor is introduced in the training error cost function. The second-stage classifier is used to differentiate between different detectable faults. In order to increase the reliability of fault identification, the probabilities of classification performed by this classifier are averaged within the fault duration time. The performance of the proposed approach is validated by application to a valve actuator fault diagnosis problem.

7.1. Introduction

In today's highly complex industrial systems, one of the main problems is the occurrence of faults in equipment. These faults usually have a significant economical impact due to loss of productivity and breakdown of the equipment. In extreme cases occurrence of faults may even endanger human lives. Recently, early fault detection has received increasing attention, as it is connected with the rising demand for higher performance as well as for more safety and reliability of industrial systems.

The most commonly used fault diagnosis approach is based on building the model of the real system in order to provide estimates of certain measured signals. Then, the estimates of the measured signals are usually compared with the real measured signals, i.e., differences between real signals and their estimates are used to form residual signals (Figure 7.1). These residuals are eventually employed for fault detection and isolation (FDI) (Calado *et al.*, 2001; Isermann, 1997; Frank and Ding, 1997; Chiang *et al.*, 2001; Lipnickas and Korbicz, 2004; Angeli and Chatzinikolaou, 2004). The successful detection of a fault is followed by a fault isolation procedure whose aim is to classify the fault. The fault diagnosis performance is degraded if the identified model is not accurate.

However, in many FDI problems, the information encoded by residual signals is sufficient for robust fault detection, but it is insufficient for fault isolation and identification. Therefore, pattern recognition techniques seem to be an alternative solution for the model-based FDI.

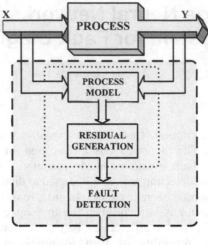

DECISION: *Normal behaviour* **OR** *Faulty state*

Figure 7.1.   General scheme for process model-based fault detection.

The data space with measured process signals and heuristic symptoms provided by experienced human operators is called features space. A diagnosis task consists of transforming the quantitative information from the features space into a qualitative statement about the cause of a given disturbance (Chen and Patton, 1999). The assignment of the proper category to each point in the features space is basically one of the tasks of pattern recognition.

Various classification techniques might be used for pattern recognition and classification. A wide variety of approaches have been taken towards the classification task. According to Raudys (2001), the number of classification algorithms already published exceeds two hundred.

The artificial neural networks (NNs) are powerful tools for handling complex pattern recognition problems. One of the most important advantages of feedforward NNs is their ability to implement nonlinear transformations for function approximation problems, i.e., given a sufficiently large number of hidden nodes, any continuous function from input to output can be approximated arbitrarily well by an NN (Bishop, 1996; Duda *et al.*, 2000; Narendra and Parthasarthy, 1990; Wang, 1992).

Neural networks have been extensively used in many engineering domains and one of the application fields is fault diagnosis (see Chen and Patton (1999) for a list of references). According to Chen and Patton (1999) NNs are properly aimed at processes that are ill defined, complex, nonlinear and stochastic. Therefore, neural networks have many advantages and can be used in a number of ways to tackle fault diagnosis of nonlinear dynamic systems.

From the theoretic point of view, data classification represents a static non-linear mapping between inputs and outputs. Without modifications, an NN classifier cannot be used to represent dynamic systems. Therefore, for identification of dynamic systems, classifiers need to have some dynamic elements involved in the structure (Patton *et al.*, 1999). The most common way of dynamics identification is the use of tapped delay lines (TDL) such as the Nonlinear Auto Regressive (NARX) model with exogenous input (Narendra and Parthasarthy, 1990).

This chapter describes a two-stage classifier system for fault diagnosis of small and medium-size FDI problems. The first classifier is trained to distinguish normal operating state of the analyzed process from malfunctioning states. Notice that this classifier performs the three main FDI tasks (Figure 7.1) for fault detection in the "black box" manner, i.e., identifying process model, residual generation, and detection of changes into residuals. However, due to neural networks' "black box" characteristics, the identified model is not explicit. In the case when recognizing one of the process operating states *normal* or *malfunction* is more important than recognizing the other one, a penalizing factor in the classifier training cost function is proposed. To build a reliable fault detection unit, a calculation methodology for false alarm reduction is proposed.

When the first-stage classifier detects a fault occurrence, then the second-stage classifier is used to identify the type and the strength of the fault. In order to increase the reliability of the fault identification unit the probabilities of classification performed by this classifier are averaged within the fault duration time.

The performance of the proposed approach is validated by applying the proposed methodology to a valve actuator fault diagnosis problem, i.e., the multi disciplinary and complementary EU Research Training Network project DAMADICS. The project is focused on development and application of methods for actuator fault diagnosis in industrial control systems.

The chapter is organized as follows. In Section 7.2, the background on data classification and on the MLP classifier is given. Section 7.3 presents the background on the proposed two-stage classifiers FDI. The case study, DAMADICS benchmark, is described in Section 7.4. The experimental results are presented in Section 7.5. Finally, Section 7.6 presents some conclusions.

7.2. Pattern Recognition and Data Classification

Pattern recognition is the research area that studies the operation and design of systems that recognise and classify patterns in data. The classification decision in such systems is made on the basis of observed attributes or features, and each datum is assigned to one class from a set of predefined classes. In the following, a few basic classification techniques, i.e., statistical or Bayesian classifiers, classification by decision trees and neural networks are reviewed.

Statistical approaches are generally characterised by having an explicit underlying probability model, which provides a probability of being in each class rather than simply a classification. One of the statistical approaches is building a classifier based on Bayes decision theory, i.e., the Bayesian classifier. Bayes' formula, used for classification, allows one to calculate *a posteriori* class probabilities $P(c_j \mid \mathbf{x})$ of input pattern $\mathbf{x}$ based on the *a priori* class c_j probabilities $P(c_j)$ and the conditional class densities distribution $p(\mathbf{x} \mid c_j)$:

$$P(c_j \mid \mathbf{x}) = \frac{p(\mathbf{x} \mid c_j)P(c_j)}{\sum_j p(\mathbf{x} \mid c_j)P(c_j)} \tag{1}$$

For the classification problem, the classification is done by choosing the class c_j with the highest *a posteriori* probability $P(c_j \mid \mathbf{x})$.

The classifiers based on Bayes' formula, are optimal, i.e., no other classifiers have a lower expected classification error rate. However, in practise this error rate is nearly unattainable because the classifier assumes that complete information is known about the statistical distributions in each class. Statistical procedures try to supply the missing information on distribution of class probabilities in a variety of ways, but there are two main directions: *parametric* and *nonparametric*. Parametric methods make assumptions about the nature of the distributions (commonly it is assumed that the distributions are Gaussian), and the problem is reduced to estimating the parameters of the distributions (means and covariance matrices in the case of Gaussians). Nonparametric methods make no assumptions about the specific distributions involved and, therefore, they can be described more accurately as distribution-free.

There are two basic approaches to nonparametric estimation for pattern classification: in one the class densities are estimated (and then used for classification), in the other one the class is chosen directly (direct estimation of the *a posteriori* probabilities). The former approach may be exemplified by Parzen windows, which are implemented in the probabilistic neural networks (PNNs) (Bishop, 1996). The latter approach may be exemplified by the k-nearest-neighbours algorithm (Bishop, 1996; Duda *et al.*, 2000), in which the k nearest prototypes are used to label an unknown pattern. If the size of the training data set used increases towards infinity, the nearest-neighbour classifier is almost as good as a Bayes classifier, and its error rate is bounded from above by twice as much as the Bayes error rate (Duda *et al.*, 2000). In spite of the merits of the k-nearest-neighbours methodology, the technique is very time consuming for large data sets and especially when $k>1$ (Duda *et al.*, 2000; Michie *et al.*, 1994).

The other non-parametric technique, which is not based on the formalism of Bayes decision theory, is the decision tree approach. This approach can be easily used to classify objects characterised by continuous and/or discrete features. Such situations arise often in real applications.

The decision tree classifier is particularly useful for nonmetric data where all of the questions can be answered in a "yes/no," "true/false" or "value from a set of values" style that does not require any notion of metric. The classification is carried out through a sequence of questions about object features, in which the next question asked depends on the answer to the current question.

Such a sequence of questions can be displayed in a directed decision tree or simply tree, where by convention the first or root node is displayed at the top, connected by successive (directional) links or branches to other nodes. These are similarly connected until terminal or leaf nodes are reached, which have no further links. The growing procedure for decision trees is based on logical operations, which learn a task from a series of examples.

The simple decision tree in Figure 7.2 illustrates one benefit of trees over many other classifiers, i.e., *interpretability*. It is straightforward to render the information contained by such trees under the form of logical expressions built using logical conjunctions and disjunctions. For instance, the tree shows **Apple** = (*green* AND *medium*) OR (*red* AND *medium*) or simplified rule **Apple** = (*medium* AND NOT *yellow*).

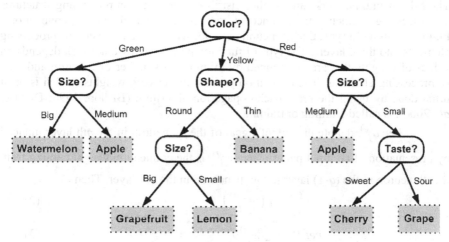

Figure 7.2.   An example of decision tree for fruit classification.

In practice, the decision tree is useful when the classification problem is fairly simple, the training set is small and expert knowledge might be incorporated.

The neural network approach for classification is one of the most competent in terms of performance, and it is preferred over the other classification approaches due to its nonparametric adaptive learning and high nonlinearity. In general, a neural network consists of layers of interconnected nodes, each node producing a nonlinear function of its input. The input to a node may come from other nodes or directly from the input data (Figure 7.3). Also, some nodes may be identified with the output of the network. The complete network therefore represents a very complex set of interdependencies, which may incorporate any degree of nonlinearity, allowing any kind of function to be modelled. Given a sufficiently large number of hidden nodes, any continuous function from input to output can be approximated arbitrarily well by such a network (Duda *et al.*, 2000).

For this reason, the multilayer perceptron (MLP) neural networks are used in the study.

Unfortunately, there are two main drawbacks in the use of neural network techniques: complexity adjustment and selection of neural network model. The input feature space and number of predefined classes define the number of inputs and outputs, respectively. Therefore, the total number of weights or parameters in the network depends on the number of nodes in the hidden layer. If too many free parameters (hidden nodes) are used, generalisation will be poor; conversely, if too few parameters are used, the training data will not be learned adequately. Usually neural network-based modelling involves trying multiple networks with different architectures, learning techniques, and training parameters in order to achieve "acceptable" model accuracy. Typically, one of the trained networks is later chosen as "the best," while the rest are discarded.

7.2.1. The MLP Neural Networks Used in the Study

The MLP neural networks are parallel-distributed information processing structures of processing elements interconnected via signal channels called connections. Figure 7.3 shows a typical MLP neural network with explicit division of processing elements into three layers. The type of function performed by a network depends on values of weights that are determined by minimising some error function and type of processing elements. The estimation process of network weights, which is most often done by using the error backpropagation algorithm (Bishop, 1996; Duda *et al.*, 2000), is called learning or training.

Let $o_j^{(q)}$ denote the output signal of the jth neuron in the qth layer induced by presentation of an input pattern, and $w_{ij}^{(q)}$ is the connection weight coming from the ith neuron in the $(q-1)$ layer to the jth neuron in the qth layer. Then

$$o_j^{(q)} = f\left(net_j^{(q)}\right) \tag{2}$$

$$net_j^{(q)} = \sum_{i=0}^{n_{q-1}} w_{ij}^{(q)} o_i^{(q-1)} \tag{3}$$

where $net_j^{(q)}$ stands for the activation level of the neuron, n_{q-1} is the number of neurons in the q-1 layer and $f(net)$ is a neuron's transfer function.

In most often applications, the sigmoid neuron's activation function is used:

$$f(net) = 1/(1 + \exp(-\lambda\ net)) \tag{4}$$

where λ is a slant parameter.

When an augmented input vector $\mathbf{x} = [1, x_1, x_2, ..., x_n]^t$ is given in the input ($0th$) layer, the output signal of the jth neuron in the output (Hth) layer is given by

$$o_j^{(H)} = \psi(\mathbf{x}) = f\left(\sum_i w_{ij}^{(H)} f\left(\sum_k w_{ki}^{(H-1)} f\left(...(\sum_t w_{tm}^{(1)} x_t)\right)\right)\right) \tag{5}$$

When the output values $o_{nj}^{(H)}$ induced by presentation of a particular input pattern $\mathbf{x}_n$ are compared with the desired output values d_{nj}, a mean squared output error cost function is formed as

$$E_o = \sum_n E_{on} = \frac{1}{2} \sum_{n=1}^{N} \sum_{j=1}^{Q} \left(d_{nj} - o_{nj}^{(H)}\right)^2 \tag{6}$$

where N is the number of learning samples and Q is the number of classes.

During the network *training*, the actual output of the network is compared to the required output or target, and the error is backpropagated through the network such that the weighted connections between all the units are adjusted in the right direction. Training the network is done by minimising the error function (Eq. 6).

During the network *testing*, the weights are no longer adjusted and the performance of the network can be tested by presenting new data, and comparing the actual outputs with the desired ones. The ability of the network to produce a correct response to the new (unseen) data is called *generalisation*. The generalisation is poor when the network overfits (or underfits) the training data.

The degree to which network overfits (underfits) the training data is related to the number of training patterns and the number of parameters in the model. In general, with a fixed number of training patterns, overfitting can occur when the model has too many parameters (too many degrees of freedom). Or, for the selected model of network, the number of training data is too small. Haussler (1992) has shown that, for nonlinear regressors, the required number of training examples necessary for good generalization is $\theta*\log(\theta)$, where θ is the total number of weights in the model. According to the exhaustive experiments reported in the literature, for the MLP network it is sufficient to have at least the $3*\theta$ training data.

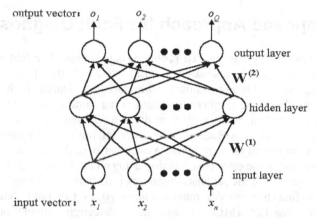

Figure 7.3.   A feedforward multilayered neural network with one hidden layer, where $\mathbf{W}^{(1)}$ is the weight vector between the input and the hidden layer and $\mathbf{W}^{(2)}$ is the weight vector between the hidden and the output layer.

However, neural network models produce only static input-output mapping. In order to maintain dynamic system modelling, the tapped delay lines (TDL) should be introduced to the neural network model (Figure 7.4) (Calado *et al.*, 2001; Patton *et al.*, 1999). Unfortunately, this kind of network has an input space dimensionality problem. This problem is overcome if the order of the process to be modelled is known and all necessary inputs/outputs are fed to the NN. Otherwise the input space of the network becomes very large (depending on the past history horizon). The essential features extraction or input features selection should be introduced before neural network design. The literature on features reduction is very rich (Bishop, 1996; Jollife, 1986; Baldi and Hornik, 1989; Teeuwsen *et al.*, 2002; Verikas and Bacauskiene, 2002). Only a few works are related to the dimensionality reduction problem for time-series data, for an example see (De Mers and Cottrell, 1993). The reduction of the dimensionality of neural network input space is an important task. It leads to better generalisation and less computational task.

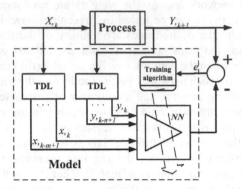

Figure 7.4.   Process modelling using feedforward NNs and tapped delay lines (TDL).

7.3.   Proposed Approach for Fault Diagnosis

A two-stage classifier system for FDI problems is proposed. The first NN classifier is trained to distinguish normal operating state of the process from the malfunctioning state. During training, the classifier learns both the system behavioural model and the adaptive threshold at the same time. In the case a fault occurrence is detected, then and only then the second-stage unit is engaged for the fault identification and classification. When recognizing one operating state of the system is more important than recognizing the other one, the first-stage classifier is trained by minimizing the error cost function using an additional penalizing factor.

The structure of the proposed approach is depicted in Figure 7.5. As shown in Figure 7.5 first the process measurements go to the fault detection block consisting of classifier (MLP_1) and fault detection calculation procedure (*Primary-Fault-Detection* and *Final-Fault-Detection*). In the case the plant is operating in normal state (NS), then classifier MLP_1 indicates the state NS. If a fault occurred and the plant is operating in the faulty state, MLP_1 indicates the occurrence of a faulty state (FS). Sequentially, the proposed procedure calculates the frequency of fault occurrences in predefined time window. When the number of fault occurrences exceeds the threshold, then the *final-fault-detection* signal is triggered and process measurements from the fault detection moment are passed to the second-stage classifier (MLP_2).

The MLP_2 is trained to identify and classify system faults. To increase the reliability of the fault identification and isolation, the probabilities of classification by MLP_2 are averaged within the fault duration time. A detailed description of the approach is given in the following sections.

7.3.1.   Fault Detection Unit

To train first-stage classifier MLP_1, the data is collected from process data operating in NS stage and in all possible malfunction stages (FS). The trained MLP_1 classifier is further used as the primary fault detection (PFD_k) component.

The dashed lines in Figure 7.5 show the possible getaway from the FS to the NS in the fault disappearance case. Practically, every noisy process measurement in such fault detection system might cause false alarms. Therefore, in order to reduce the amount of false alarms the final-fault-detection (FFD_k) system based on two sliding windows is introduced. The FFD_k computes the occurrence of the PFD_k binary signal within a prespecified time window. The final fault decision signal FFD_k is produced when the number of PFD_k overcomes a constant value γ:

$$FFD_k = \begin{cases} 1 \ (FS), & \text{if } \sum_{i=1}^{T_{w1}} PFD_{k-i} > \gamma - \sum_{j=1}^{T_{w2}} FFD_{k-j} \\ 0 \ (NS), & \text{otherwise} \end{cases} \qquad (7)$$

where k is the process time index, T_{w1} is the size of the time window for the PFD_k signal, γ is a constant and T_{w2} is the size of the time window for FFD_k. The PFD_k is computed in such manner that it eliminates false alarms and increases the successful fault detection with proper values of γ, T_{w1} and T_{w2}. Thus values are dependent on the performance of the MLP 1 and are determined experimentally with the property $T_{w1} \gg T_{w2}$. The time interval T_{w2} serves as a holdout of alarm and in the case of fault disappearance ($PFD_k=0$ for the time period $\sim T_{w1}$), the FFD_k signal will be switched off.

The final fault detection rule is written as:

if $FFD_k > 0$ then {Fault occurred at moment k} $\qquad (8)$

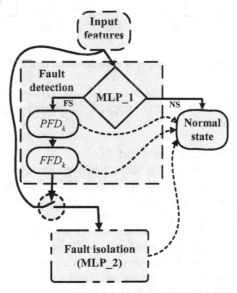

Figure 7.5. Fault detection.

An example performance of the fault detection unit is demonstrated in Figure 7.6. The panel depicts the PFD signal generated by MLP_1 classifier with the binary values "0" for the normal state (NS) and "1" for the faulty state (FS). Necessary values of parameters to calculate FFD were set as following: $T_{w1} = 80$ s, $T_{w2} = 6$ s and $\gamma = 8$. The middle panel presents calculations of the inequality in Eq. 7;

the dotted line gives the calculation for the left-hand site and the solid line for the right- hand side. As is seen, till the moment k=190 s the system operation was treated as *normal* state but with the increased *primary fault detection* occurrences the system state has been changed to *faulty* and later, after the disappearance of *PFD* occurrences, the fault detection unit has switched the system status back to *normal* state.

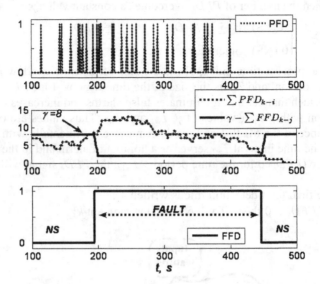

Figure 7.6.   Performance demonstration of fault detection unit with T_{w1} =80 s, T_{w2}=6 s and γ=8.

The successful fault detection triggers the second-stage unit, used for fault isolation and classification.

7.3.1.1. Proposed Error Cost Function

A false alarm is an indication of a fault, when no fault has occurred. A missed detection is no indication of fault occurrence. For fault detection, there is an intrinsic trade-off between minimisation of the false alarms and missed detection rate. In the statistical hypothesis theory, the tight classification threshold of an instance would result in high false alarm and low fault misdetection rate, while limits which are too spread, for normal state, will result in a low false alarm and a high misdetection rate. Consider the case with two classes: normal state (NS) and faulty state (FS). Using a certain given threshold value, the statistical hypothesis theory might be applied to predict NS and FS states based on statistical properties of the collected training data (Figure 7.7). The conditional class densities distribution $p(x|c_{NS})$ and $p(x|c_{FS})$ are calculated from normal and faulty states data, respectively. Using Bayesian decision theory (Section 7.2) and appropriate threshold value the faulty state can be detected. As seen in Figure 7.7, increasing the threshold (shifting the threshold to the right) decreases the false alarm rate but the rate of misdetection is increased. This is the trade-off between false alarms and misdetection rate (Trunov and Polycarpou, 2000).

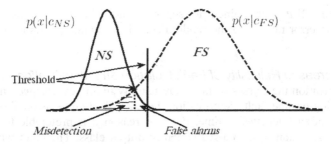

Figure 7.7.   The conditional class densities distributions of two classes, normal state and faulty state. By moving the threshold value from left to right, the *false alarm* rate is decreased while at the same time the *misdetection* rate is increased.

The nonparametric classifiers such as neural networks do not estimate conditional class densities distributions, but try to find appropriate classification hyperplanes based on the applied training error cost function. Usually, such an error function is equally weighted for all classes.

Most often in practice, one operating state of the plant is more important than the other one due to safety requirements or due to unreliable ways of collecting data for one of the operating states. For these reasons, a penalizing factor might be introduced in the training cost function (Lipnickas *et al.*, 2004). Then the neural network classifier is trained through minimisation of the classification error rate with a penalising factor:

$$E = \sum_{p=1}^{P} \beta_p e_p \tag{9}$$

where e_p is classification error of data point p and β_p is the penalising factor defined as:

$$\beta_p = \begin{cases} 1, & \text{if } e_p = 0 \\ \alpha, & \text{if } e_p = 1 \text{ AND misclassified } C\_1 \\ 1, & \text{if } e_p = 1 \text{ AND misclassified } C\_2 \end{cases} \tag{10}$$

The penalising factor is equal to 1 if classification is correct, to the constant α for misclassified class C_1, and to "1" for misclassified C_2. When $0<\alpha<1$ then misclassification of class C_1 is less important than misclassification of C_2 and in the case $\alpha>1$ the class importance is the opposite.

7.3.2. Fault Isolation and Identification

The second-stage classifier (MLP_2) is trained to operate for the fault isolation and identification purpose. The training data used correspond only to the faults detected by MLP_1. The detectable faults might not be separable based on the input measurement; therefore some additional heuristic symptoms should be found and added to the original data measurements. When several different faults behave identically and there is no way to distinguish them then these faults must be grouped into the same class. Each collected datum must be labelled with class numbers standing for individual faults or groups of them.

The MLP_2 is trained to separate the labelled data by minimising classification error rate using the random search technique (Verikas and Gelzinis, 2000).

7.3.2.1. Increased Reliability of Fault Isolation and Identification

In real application the classes of faults are usually highly overlapped and therefore by performing on-line fault identification the classification decision about detected faults most often fluctuates in time. For that reason it is preferable to use a time window for selection of the most frequently output class. The other way is to use class probability averaging within a prespecified time window.

Wan (1990) has shown that MLP neural networks for classification are able to approximate the Bayes optimal discriminant function (Bayes a *posteriori* probabilities) on given training data. Therefore, in order to increase the fault identification reliability of MLP_2 classifier, the averaged probability for every classified datum is computed starting with fault detection time j, FFD_j. The computations of the averaged class probabilities are finished and they are reset to zero from the moment when FFD_k signal goes to zero (NS state). The averaged class probabilities are computed according to the formula:

$$P_{c_i}(t+1) = \frac{P_{c_i}(t)t + p_{c_i}^{MLP-2}(t+1)}{t+1}, \quad t = 0,... \text{ until the end of fault} \qquad (11)$$

where i is an index of considered class with class probability $p_{c_i}^{MLP-2}$. $P_{c_i}(t)$ is the averaged class probability with the property $P_{c_i}(0) = 0$, $\forall c_i$ and c_i is the class label.

The class label c of the measured data at a time t is then determined as follows:

$$c(t) = \arg\max_i P_{c_i}(t) \qquad (12)$$

where $P_{c_i}(t)$ is the averaged class probability and i is class index.

7.4.   Case Study: DAMADICS Benchmark

DAMADICS – Development and Application of Methods for Actuator Diagnosis in Industrial Control Systems – is a Research Training Network funded by the European Commission under Framework V.

The studied valve actuator block can be considered as a four-input and two-output system, as shown in Figure 7.8. Data sampling and storage is performed using a 1s sampling interval. The input measurements x_k at time moment k are defined as follows:

$$x_{[1,2,3,4,5,6],k} = (CV; P1; P2; T1; F; X) \qquad (13)$$

where process variables are: CV - control value, $P1$ - pressure at the inlet of the valve, $P2$ - pressure at the outlet of the valve, $T1$ - juice temperature at the inlet of the valve, F - juice flow at the outlet of the valve, and X - servomotor rod displacement.

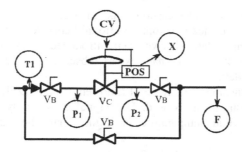

Figure 7.8. The actuator block.

Table 7.1. Set of faults specified for benchmark. Incipient faults – *I*. Abrupt faults: *S* - small, *M* - medium, *B* - big

Fault	Description	S	M	B	I
f1	Valve clogging	*	*	*	
f2	Valve plug or valve seat sedimentation			*	*
f7	Medium evaporation or critical flow	*	*	*	
f8	Twisted servomotor's piston rod	*	*	*	
f10	Servomotor's diaphragm perforation	*	*	*	
f11	Servomotor's spring fault			*	*
f12	Electropneumatic transducer fault	*	*	*	
f13	Rod displacement sensor fault	*	*	*	*
f14	Pressure sensor fault	*	*	*	
f15	Positioner feedback fault			*	
f16	Positioner supply pressure drop	*	*	*	
f17	Unexpected pressure change across the valve			*	*
f18	Fully or partly opened bypass valves	*	*	*	*
f19	Flow rate sensor fault	*	*	*	

Within the DAMADICS project, the valve actuator simulator has been developed under MATLAB Simulink. This tool makes it possible to generate normal operating mode data, as well as faulty data for 19 faults. The considered faults are presented in Table 7.1. The faults can be considered either as abrupt or incipient. The asterisks denote combinations of faults and failure modes that have physical backgrounds and are specified for benchmark. A comprehensive description of DAMADICS benchmark is available at http://www.eng.hull.ac.uk/research/control/damadics1.htm.

7.5. Experimental Investigation

In the case of flow valve diagnosis, the only information about system state is available from measurements generated by the sensors. In this work a 3s TDL sliding window ($\mathbf{X}_k=[\mathbf{x}_k, \mathbf{x}_{k-1}, \mathbf{x}_{k-2}]$) of the original measurements has been used. The initial input vector consists of 18 measured signals.

Besides the original measurements, in order to increase the accuracy of fault isolation and identification, four additional heuristic fault symptoms derived from the process input data x_k have been introduced. These heuristic symptoms have been derived through human expert observation and inspection of the behaviour of faulty data.

To detect the abrupt increase of fluid temperature $DT1$, the value $T1_k=x_{[4],k}$ from the input measurements is used. This signal is used only for isolating the $f7$. $DT1=1$ when the fluid temperature is higher than the maximum admission temperature T_{adm}:

$$DT1_k = \begin{cases} 1, & if \ T1_k > T_{adm} \\ 0, & otherwise \end{cases} \tag{14}$$

To detect the unexpected abrupt pressure change across the valve case, the values of upper stream pressure $P1_k=x_{[2],k}$ and downstream pressure $P2_k=x_{[3],k}$ are used. The derived signals are used only for isolating the $f17$: when pressure drops rapidly then $DP2=1$,

$$DP2_k = \begin{cases} 1, & if \ P1_k - P2_k > P_{const} \\ 0, & otherwise \end{cases} \tag{15}$$

In the case of incipient fault $f17$ development the symptom $DP2in$ will be set to "1". For the incipient fault $f17$ detection a symptom extracted by the line approximation $y_k^{P2} = a_k^{P2} * x_{[3],k} + b_k^{P2}$ in sliding time window $T_{wP2}=50$ s has been used. The parameters a_k^{P2} and b_k^{P2} are computed by least-squares method:

$$DP2in_k = \begin{cases} 1, & if \ a_k^{P2} > a_{const}^{P2} \\ 0, & otherwise \end{cases} \tag{16}$$

Finally, another heuristic symptom is calculated as the derivative of *Rod displacement* and it marks the rapid changes in the measurement of *Rod displacement*. For fault isolation and identification purposes, the most informative is the sign of the computed derivative. This symptom is very sensitive to noise and therefore a detection threshold has to be used:

$$Spike\_POZ_k = \begin{cases} 1, & until \ k+250; \ if \ x_{[6],k} - x_{[6],k-1} \geq Xdt_{const} \\ 0, & until \ k+250; \ if \ x_{[6],k} - x_{[6],k-1} \leq -Xdt_{const} \\ 0, & otherwise \end{cases} \tag{17}$$

$$Spike\_NEG_k = \begin{cases} 1, & until \ k+250; if \ x_{[6],k} - x_{[6],k-1} \leq -Xdt_{const} \\ 0, & until \ k+250; if \ x_{[6],k} - x_{[6],k-1} \geq Xdt_{const} \\ 0, & otherwise \end{cases} \tag{18}$$

One important feature of *Rod displacement* spikes is that such spikes are never equal to 1 at the same time k, i.e., $Spike\_POZ_k=1 \neq Spike\_NEG_k=1$.

The positive spike ($Spike\_POZ$) is relevant for faults $f11$ and $f13$. This helps to distinguish such faults from all other faults, but the amplitude of the spike is very large only in the "Big" fault case.

The negative spike of *Rod displacement* (*Spike_NEG*) is relevant to faults *f7*, *f10*, and *f17*. Faults *f7* and *f17* are identified by other additional signals and the *Spike_NEG* signal is redundant for them. The *Spike_NEG* signal is useful to distinguish "Medium" and "Big" cases for fault *f10* {M,B}.

The usage of *Rod displacement* derivative is related to real spikes in the process measurements. Therefore a 250s time interval has been selected to keep spike signal "*ON*" unchanged, hoping that this time interval will be sufficient for fault isolation and fault maintenance, but not too long so that to cause *false* fault identification (in the case of noise spike in the process measurement).

The values of the constants used in the study have been found to be as follows: T_{adm} =0.75 (150°C), P_{const}=0.2 (0.8 MPa), and Xdt_{const}=0.5 (50% of rod displacement motion amplitude). It is noteworthy that these values are object and process dependent.

7.5.1. Fault Detection

The first classifier MLP_1 for fault detection is trained to classify the labelled data corresponding to plant operating states NS and FS. For this task, an MLP with one hidden intermediate layer has been trained. The training and testing data sets consisted respectively of 2000 samples (50%) for NS and another 2000 samples (50%) for FS. The FS data set consists of all faults specified within the DAMADICS benchmark. The MLP network structure has been chosen according to the author's experience together with a trial-and-error procedure. The optimal number of hidden neurons with a logarithmic sigmoid transfer function has been found to be 15.

The MLP_1 network has been first trained to minimise the classification error of the training data. With the chosen structure, the classifier was able to separate the operation states with 13.0% error for the training set and 14.3% for the testing set. The confusion matrix obtained after performing the test is shown in Table 7.2. The diagonal elements of the matrix represent data that has been correctly classified. The results in nondiagonal places show the classification errors. An approximately equal percentage of classification error has been obtained for both classes. This means that the fault detection system will cause frequent false alarms during normal operating state. Therefore, for the second trial the network has been trained with the proposed error cost function (Eq. 9). The penalising factor α (Eq. 10) was set to "0.75" to penalise the network performance more for the misclassified NS and less for the misclassified FS.

The idea behind the penalising factor in Eqs. 9 and 10 is that recognising the system operation in normal state is more important than recognising its operation in faulty state. This is also due to the way the data points from different system behavioural states have been collected, i.e., some faults in DAMADICS benchmark are only dynamically detectable and the system response in FS state to the static control value is identical to the NS behaviour.

With the same structure of MLP neural network, but introducing the penalising factor, the classifier MLP_1 is able to separate the two operation states with 14.1% error for the training set and 15.3% for the testing set. The confusion matrix obtained after performing the test is shown in Table 7.3. The performance of fault detection is a little bit worse, but the amount of misclassification of NS is drastically reduced.

Table 7.2.   The confusion matrix of MLP_1

	NS	FS
NS	84.8	13.2
FS	15.2	86.8

Table 7.3.   The confusion matrix of MLP_1 trained with the proposed error cost function

	NS	FS
NS	98.7	29.3
FS	1.3	70.7

The MLP_1 classifier trained with the proposed error cost function is further used as the primary fault detection (PFD_k) unit (Figure 7.5). For the final fault detection (Eq. 1) the values of constants have been searched for within the ranges: $T_{w1} \in [50,...,150]$, $T_{w2} \in [4,...,10]$ and $\gamma \in [4,...,10]$ and the values found are $T_{w1}=80$ s, $T_{w2}=6$ s, and $\gamma =8$. The set of faults detectable by FFD is shown in Table 7.4. Faults $f8$ and $f14$ are undetectable because the effect of the faults is at the same level as the uncertainty in the MLP_1 and fault $f16$ ("Small" and "Medium" cases) is only dynamically detectable.

The increased NS recognition performance in Table 7.3 compared to Table 7.2 is not surprising since, from Table 7.4, it is obvious that about 15% of the collected data from FS are undetectable. Undetectable means that the behaviour of the analysed process in FS state is almost equivalent to NS and therefore this data might be considered actually mislabelled. By forcing the classifier to minimise the proposed error cost function, the influence of the mislabelled data is reduced.

7.5.2. Fault Isolation and Identification

The purpose of this section is to investigate the possibilities of isolating the faults that are successfully detected, i.e., faults denoted by "D" in Table 7.4. The detected faults have been grouped into 20 classes according to the authors' experience together with a trial-and-error procedure. Equally shaded squares in Table 7.4 mean that faults have similar symptoms and without additional process measurements cannot be properly distinguished, i.e., faults $\{f13S, f13M, f18S, f18M\}$ form one class and the other larger class consists of the group of faults $\{f1S, f10S, f12S, f12M, f12B\}$. The dotted squares denote classification of incipient faults. These faults are a special class of slowly developing faults and they can be detected only after fault strength signal passes a certain value.

For fault identification task the MLP_2 network with one hidden intermediate layer has been trained through minimisation of classification error. The optimal number of hidden neurons for MLP_2 with a logarithmic sigmoid transfer function has been found to be 15. The data set consisted of at least 200 samples per class. The whole data set has been split into two equal parts for training and testing the classifier.

With the chosen structure the classifier MLP_2 was able to classify the occurred faults with 11.0% error for the training set and 11.3% classification error for the testing set. The worst fault identification is for fault $f18$B, approximately 36% of data is assigned to the class with $f18$S and $f18$M. This is not a serious problem since classifier correctly identifies the fault type and only misses the identification of the fault strength. Fault $f7$M has been found to be in a similar situation: 37% of data is misidentified as smaller ($f7$S) or larger ($f7$B) strength of the same fault.

7.5.3. On-Line FDI Application

The proposed two-stage classifiers FDI has been applied to detect and identify faults on-line using the methodology detailed in section 7.2.1.

It was found that the MLP_2 classifier is unable to recognise dynamically developing faults. This is not surprising, since the data for MLP_2 training was collected from the static parts of the faults. Therefore it has been proposed to suspend fault identification during dynamic behaviour of faults. The short time of dynamic fault development is observed in the cases of occurrence of faults $f7$, $f10$, $f11$, $f13$, and $f17$. The fault dynamic is based on the physical processes within actuator valve (see DAMADICS website). For instance in the case of $f7$ fault, the temperature of the fluid is so high that during the first moments when fault occurs the fluid possesses physical characteristics similar to the steam. Later the characteristics change back to fluid characteristics. Similar behaviour is observed for fault $f10$ (pneumatic servomotor's diaphragm perforation). The abrupt perforation of diaphragm causes fast changes in valve rod displacement (*Spike_NEG*). Until the moment when pressure outflow in the servomotor's chamber equals the pressure flow income, the fault has the dynamic characteristics for about 25 seconds (Figure 7.10).

In the case a fault is detected along with a spike occurrence (*Spike_POZ* or *Spike_NEG*), the fault identification system is triggered only 25s after the fault detection moment. Such a situation is demonstrated in Figures 7.9 and 7.10. The real fault occurred at the time moment 100s and the FFD_k reports fault occurrence (*FS*) at the moment 106s. Due to the detected spike, fault identification by MLP_2 is forced to suspend the output by 25 s. Later MLP_2 produces outputs with stable and correct fault identification.

In the case a spike has not occurred, MLP_2 identifies a fault as soon as the fault is detected by fault detection system (FFD_k). Such a situation is demonstrated in Figure 7.11 for incipient fault $f13$. The fault occurred at the time moment 100s, the FFD_k reported the occurrence of fault (*FS*) at the moment 178s, and the correct fault identification has been obtained starting with at the moment 420s. As may be seen from Figure 7.11, the occurred incipient fault changes its characteristics all the time and it is continuously misidentified till the moment fault reaches a specific fault kernel. It is obvious that the more time is given for the development of incipient fault the better fault identification is obtained.

Table 7.4.   Results of fault detection (D - detectable, N - not detectable) for abrupt faults: S - small, M - medium, B - big, and I - incipient

Fault	S	M	B	I
f1	D	D	D	
f2			D	D
f7	D	D	D	
f8	N	N	N	
f10	D	D	D	
f11			D	D
f12	D	D	D	
f13	D	D	D	D
f14	N	N	N	
f15			D	
f16	N	N	D	
f17			D	D
f18	D	D	D	D
f19	D	D	D	

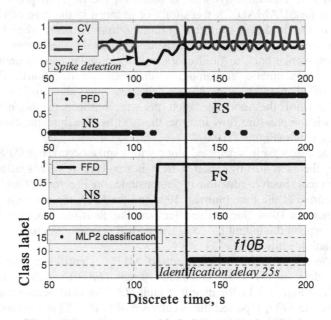

Figure 7.9.   Symptoms of fault *f10*B and its classification.

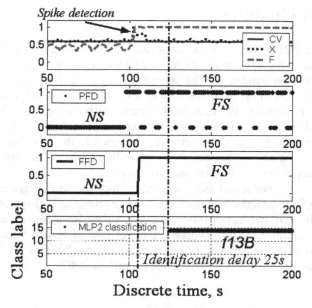

Figure 7.10. Symptoms of fault *f13B* and its classification.

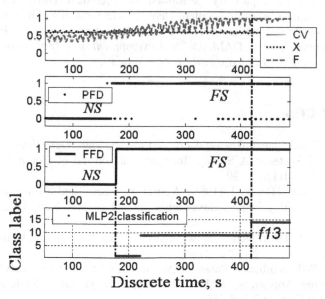

Figure 7.11. Symptoms of incipient fault *f13* and its classification.

7.6.   Conclusions

The proposed FDI system is based on a two-stage classification system: the first classifier is used for fault detection and the second one for fault identification. In order to reduce the number of false alarms during fault detection, the penalising factor is introduced in the error cost function for MLP_1 network training. Also, a methodology to compute the final fault occurrence is introduced. The simulation results have shown that a satisfactory fault detection rate is obtained. Therefore, the proposed technique provides an alternative approach to the model-based FDI. The approach in this study has been applied for on-line fault identification in order to examine the capabilities of the proposed technique.

It is well known that analytical redundancy of the FDI system can ensure more reliable fault detection and isolation. For the proposed FDI system, it might be used an additional two-out-of-three voting system (Isermann *et al.*, 2002) for triggering an alarm, in order to obtain a lower rate of misclassification. Also a committee of classifiers might be applied to ensure better fault identification (Lipnickas and Korbicz, 2004; Verikas and Lipnickas, 2002).

Acknowledgements

This work has been partially performed at Technical University of Lisbon (Portugal), Instituto Superior Tecnico, Dept. of Mechanical Engineering under the supervision of Prof. J. Sá da Costa and it has been funded by EU FP 5 Research Training Network project DAMADICS: *Development and Application of Methods for Actuator Diagnosis in Industrial Control Systems.*

References

1.   Angeli C and Chatzinikolaou A (2004) On-Line Fault Detection Techniques for Technical Systems: A Survey. International Journal of Computer Science & Applications 1(1):12 - 30
2.   Baldi P and Hornik J (1989) Neural networks and principal component analysis: learning from examples without local minima. Neural Networks 2:53–58
3.   Bishop CM (1996) Neural Networks for Pattern Recognition. Clarendon Press, Oxford
4.   Calado JMF, Korbicz J, Patan K, Patton RJ and Sa da Costa JMG (2001) Soft Computing Approaches to Fault Diagnosis for Dynamic Systems. European Journal of Control 7:248-286
5.   Chen J and Patton RJ (1999) Robust Model-based Fault Diagnosis for Dynamic Systems. Kluwer Academic Publishers, London
6.   Chiang LH, Russell EL and Braatz RD (2001) Fault Detection and Diagnosis in Industrial Systems. Springer Berlin

7. DeMers D and Cottrell GW (1993) Non-linear dimensionality reduction. In: Giles CL, Hanson SJ and Cowan JD (eds) Advances in Neural Information Processing Systems 5, Morgan Kaufmann, San Mateo, CA, pp. 580-587
8. Duda RO, Hart PE and Stork DG (2000) Pattern Classification. John Wiley & Sons, New York, 2nd Edition
9. EC FP5 Research Training Network DAMADICS Development and Application of Methods for Actuator Diagnosis in Industrial Control Systems, http://www.eng.hull.ac.uk/ research/control/damadics1.htm
10. Frank PM and Ding X (1997) Survey of robust residual generation and evaluation methods in observer-based fault detection systems. Journal of Process Control 7(6):403-424
11. Haussler D (1992) Decision theoretic generalisations of the PAC model for neural net and other learning applications. Information and Computation 100:78-150
12. Isermann R (1997) Supervision, fault-detection and fault-diagnosis methods – an introduction. Control Engineering Practice 5(5):639-652
13. Isermann R, Schwartz R and Stoltz S (2002) Fault-Tolerant Drive-By-Wire Systems. IEEE Control Systems Magazine 22(5):64-81
14. Jollife IT (1986) Principal Component Analysis. Springer Series in Statistics. Springer-Verlag, New York
15. Lipnickas A, Korbicz J (2004) Adaptive Selection of Neural Networks for a Committee Decision. International Scientific Journal of Computing 3(2):23-30.
16. Lipnickas A, Sa da Costa J and Bocaniala C (2004) FDI based on two stage classifiers for fault diagnosis of valve actuators. Application to DAMADICS benchmark. In: Proceeding of the 11th International Conference EPE-PEMC'2004, 2-4 September, Riga, Latvia, vol. 3, pp. 147-153
17. Michie D, Spiegelhalter DJ and Taylor CC (1994) Machine Learning, Neural and Statistical Classification. Ellis Horwood, New York
18. Narendra KS and Parthasarthy K (1990) Identification and control of dynamical systems using neural networks. IEEE Transactions on Neural Networks 1(1):4-27
19. Patton RJ, Lopez-Toribio CJ, Uppal FJ (1999) Artificial intelligence approaches to fault diagnosis for dynamic systems. International Journal of applied mathematics and computer science 9(3):471-518
20. Raudys Š (2001) Statistical and Neural Classifiers: An Integrated Approach to Design. Advances in Pattern Recognition. Springer Berlin
21. Teeuwsen SP, Erlich I and El-Sharkawi MA (2002) Feature reduction for neural network based small-signal stability assessment. In: Proceedings of the 14th PSCC, Sevilla, 24-28 June, session 14
22. Trunov A and Polycarpou M (2000) Automated Fault Diagnosis in Nonlinear Multivariable Systems Using a Learning Methodology. IEEE Transactions on Neural Networks 11(1):91-101
23. Verikas A and Bacauskiene M (2002) Feature selection with neural networks. Pattern Recognition Letters 23:1323-1335
24. Verikas A and Gelzinis A (2000) Training neural networks by stochastic optimisation. Neurocomputing 30: 153-172

25. Verikas A and Lipnickas A (2002) Fusing neural networks through space partitioning and fuzzy integration. Neural Processing Letters 16(1):53-65
26. Wan E (1990) Neural network classification: A Bayesian interpretation. IEEE Transactions on Neural Networks 1(4):303-305
27. Wang LX (1992) Fuzzy systems are universal approximators. In: Proceedings of IEEE Fuzzy Systems Conference, pp. 1163-1170

8. Soft Computing Models for Fault Diagnosis of Conductive Flow Systems

Viorel Ariton

This chapter focuses on the fault diagnosis of artefacts often met in industry, but not only, that execute various functions involving conductive flows of matter and energy, i.e., multifunctional conductive flow systems (MCFSs). The proposed MCFS abstraction is close to the human diagnostician way of conceiving entities and relations on physical, functional and behavioural structures. Diagnosis reasoning, performed by human diagnosticians, is intrinsically abductive reasoning. This chapter presents the abduction by plausibility and relevance in a connectionist approach. The case study on a hydraulic installation of a rolling mill plant gives examples on the knowledge elicitation process and on the diagnostic expert system building and running.

8.1. Introduction

Fault diagnosis of complex systems is often a difficult task, due to the incomplete, imprecise and uncertain knowledge on behaviours and interactions encountered in the real-life context. Diagnostic reasoning is abductive reasoning, thus it is different from the common (deductive) reasoning. The latter starts from causes and leads to effects, hence the "explanation" is based on a definite space of causes to a definite set of effects, while the first starts from effects to reveal causes. Hence, the "explanation" is based on a presumed space of causes with many-to-many links to a (reduced) space of effects. In real life, the diagnosis itself proceeds differently for similar target systems running in different contexts. On top of those difficulties, one may notice that computer applications for fault diagnosis face the modelling and the parameter identification burdens, both after a challenging knowledge elicitation effort on the target area.

Consequently, fault diagnosis of complex systems often relies on human diagnosticians, who usually perform knowledge acquisition on faulty behaviours, later used to "recognize" faults from (some) instance effects. In a simple view, they use a mapping of faults to effects, for searching causes possibly linked to the instance effects, and sequentially refining the diagnostic based on knowledge in the area and from practice.

The artificial intelligence community concerned with diagnosis obtains the mapping either by methodical experiments – exhausting the faults' space and collecting the effects – or by means of some knowledge of human experts from practice. However, the computational models for fault diagnosis also require methods to reduce the many-to-many relations of the reverse mapping from effects to faults, which commonly are known as human diagnostician's deep knowledge.

The diagnostic is then obtained: (1) using a matching procedure from actual effects to possible faults – as in the case-based diagnosis or in the neural/causal network-based diagnosis, (2) using a transformed effects space regarding the difference from the expected and the actual behaviour labelled with faults – as in the model-based diagnosis, or (3) using an "intelligent" look up procedure performed through a combined effects space, according to human diagnostician knowledge on phenomena specific to the target system in normal and faulty running – as in knowledge-based fault diagnosis.

Computational models of the above approaches have shortcomings at both phases above, most of them revealed when the target system runs in a real context:

a)   For the faults-to-effects mapping phase: cases (1) and (2) above involve experiments which are barely possible for (all) faults, hence no complete mapping is possible, while in case (3), the mapping involves additional structures on causal relations between faults and effects, coming from some explanations of phenomena taking place.

b)   For the diagnostic decision phase: in cases (1) and (2), the computational models are simpler but the diagnostic not entirely reliable, while in case (3) the backward chaining from effects to faults is applied in specific ways to the various running contexts.

Knowledge handled in cases (1) and (2) is often identified as "shallow knowledge," while that in case (3) is considered "deep knowledge." In usual cases, target systems involve flow conduction; hence the effects propagate throughout the (entire) system and thus make the diagnosis much more difficult. In that case, the combinatorial growth of the faults-effects mapping – cases (1) or (2), and because the deep knowledge refers to the model of the entire system – case (3). However, for systems in real life, neither the complex mapping nor the (many) complex models are possible, and that's why the human diagnostician's role is crucial. It is worth noting that running contexts of real systems are of greatest importance, while identical systems may behave differently – due to age, environment, maintenance.

The present chapter first states some considerations on the diagnosis as an abduction problem solving which exhibits an intrinsic connectionist nature: the many-to-many relations of the effects to causes may get forward (excitatory) links meant for activation of plausible causes, then relevant causes result from competition between the plausible ones. The artificial neural network (ANN) implementation of the connectionist model is enriched with specific architectural features (structures of neural sites) meant to solve all types of abduction problems met in the literature.

The nodes of the connectionist model are manifestations, symptoms and faults. Human diagnosticians handle such concepts in a discrete and qualitative way. In order to obtain a sound representation of the concepts and their qualitative relations, the chapter develops the analysis on modelling means that lead to discrete knowledge pieces and their relations, as human diagnosticians handle, regarding normal and faulty behaviour of a target system.

The chapter focuses on the class of conductive flow systems that perform more functions at a time; such systems are most encountered in technical and economical domains, and due to their multifunctional and flow conduction natures they are termed *multifunctional conductive flow systems* (MCFS). Sections 8.4 and

8.5 develop appropriate knowledge elicitation schemes, in a multi-modelling approach, to discriminate concepts and relations, as knowledge pieces involved in fault diagnosis.

All concepts and relations take part in appropriate Computational Intelligence models which combine human diagnosticians' deep and shallow knowledge on the target system behaviour, based on *fuzzy logic and possibilistic modelling* of incomplete and imprecise deep knowledge on manifestations, and based on *neural network* blocks for abductive problem solving of both fault diagnosis and next best test policy in refining the diagnostic.

The neural networks embed the shallow knowledge as data sets from practice and experiments for the plausibility links between faults and manifestations. Deep knowledge helps finding the relevant causes (from the plausible ones), and it is embedded in the neural sites of the specific abduction problems on manifestations and faults in the target system. Also, it is embedded in the links between faults and their specific symptoms corresponding to the four "orthogonal transport anomalies" (first introduced in (Ariton, 2003)). Additionally, the deep knowledge on the physical structure of the target system is embedded as the projection structure of neural blocks, each corresponding to a Bond Graph junction of the flow conduction system (Ariton, 2001).

Whilst deep and shallow knowledge are combined and embedded in the neural network, the training does not require exhaustive experiments on faults in the complex target system (which are barely possible in real life), and the diagnosis exploits the common view on the whole system as an interconnection of modules; to each module a neural network block is attached, thus easier to handle and train. The architectural features that embed the deep knowledge allow a better and comprehensive diagnostic, and also offer the opportunity to generate dedicated diagnosis applications for each concrete complex target system and its real-life running context. That opportunity is of most importance for the diagnosis task while two identical target systems may behave differently. While for the control task of a system it is natural to provide all homeostatic conditions to obtain the intended aim, the diagnosis task deals with the system as it is, in its real context and local conditions.

8.2. Diagnostic Problem Solving by Abduction

Abductive reasoning is a challenge for philosophy, science and practice. Abduction is sometimes creative while it puts effects before causes (Bylander *et al.*, 1991; Schurz, 2002). Computer applications require effective computational models, commonly focusing on the connectionist nature of the abduction problems (Peng and Reggia, 1990; Ayeb *et al.*, 1998).

8.2.1. Abduction Problems in Diagnosis

In the real world, fault diagnosis involves *open spaces* of manifestations and faults, while both are not completely known in real contexts. Unlike deductive reasoning , which focuses a definite aim and may consider the targeted part isolated from the whole, abductive reasoning (e.g., in diagnosis) may not ignore causes (and effects) without corrupting the result (i.e., the diagnostic). For example, if the excessive heat of the air around a hydraulic installation is neglected, one may assert that abnormal running is due to a faulty component – which may be false; a similar case arises when ignoring the quality of the mineral oil flow.

In fault diagnosis, the *cause* may represent one or more faults occurring at a moment, and the *effects* are subsequent deviations from the normal running that appear. A huge number of causes come from combinations of various faults and various external events, so the set of all possible causes is never taken into consideration (it is not realistic). On the other hand, some effects are observed and become *manifestations*, and some are not "visible" – due to the lack of information (e.g., no sensors).

Both aspects presented in the previous paragraph are facts of the intrinsic knowledge incompleteness of the diagnosis, actually of abductive reasoning in general. So, diagnosis always deals with open spaces of causes and effects; moreover, it deals with imprecise and uncertain knowledge of human experts on the real behaviour of the target system. However, for feasibility reasons, both the space of causes and the space of effects should be closed spaces. In this respect, special classes of causes and effects should be introduced – e.g., the "normal" situation or "unknown" causes.

Studies of Bylander *et al.* (1991) on abductive reasoning reveal four categories of abduction problems:

a)   *independent* abduction problems – no interaction exists between causes;

b)   *monotonic* abduction problems – an effect appears at cumulative causes;

c)   *incompatibility* abduction problems – pair of causes are mutually exclusive;

d)   *cancellation* abduction problems – pair of causes cancel some effects, otherwise explained separately by one of them.

Ayeb *et al.* (1998) have a sound approach in this respect. They introduce a fifth category:

e)   *open* abduction problems – when observations consist of three sets: present, absent and unknown observations.

The discrimination of the abduction problem type is specific to the particular behaviour of the target system and it is a matter of deep knowledge of the human diagnostician on causes and effects in the local context. For each type of abduction problem, Section 8.2.4.2 presents a suitable architectural feature, which may enter the neural network implementation for the abductive problem solving.

8.2.2. Abductive Reasoning through Plausibility and Relevance

Direct causal links between effects and causes may represent *plausibility criteria* (Bylander *et al.*, 1991). From the set of all plausible causes, only a subset represent actual causes, usually obtained through a parsimonious principle. Konolige (1992) considers the minimum cardinality as a *relevance criterion*, and applies it to the set of plausible faults to obtain the diagnostic subset.

In the presented approach the concept of relevance gets a specific representation, namely, it assumes some grouping of plausible causes – following specific points of view, then selecting the most relevant causes from a group – following competition or sorting/choosing procedures (Ariton and Ariton, 2000). In the connectionist implementations, plausibility links get direct representations as forward links between specific effects to specific causes As a concept, the "relevance" is not often discussed in the literature, so below a special attention is given to the subject.

A *relevance group* is a set of causes that are hardly likely to occur the same time – e.g., the set of faults for a particular component in the target system; in other words, a faulty component may exhibit only a small number of faults at a time (usually, only one). The point of view from which causes may enter a relevance group is the *relevance scope*, and it reflects the human diagnostician's deep knowledge on the faulty behaviour of the target system. The *relevance criterion* is the method used in selecting relevant cause(s). In order to perform selection, a quantitative quotient (e.g., "certainty" or "activation") is provided to rank causes. Following the relevance criterion (usually "minimum cardinality"), the selection of "most relevant" causes proceeds, e.g., by competition inside the group – for the connectionist implementation, or by choosing the cause with greatest activation. Other relevance criteria may state specific order of causes or specific quantitative relations between activations.

In the case of fault diagnosis, the minimum cardinality is usually applied as a relevance scope for the single fault diagnosis, disregarding it refers to a component or to the whole target system. However, the concept of relevance may be extended to the selected aspects met in real-life situations, i.e., to other "relevance features." For example, in conductive flow systems, a group of faults may indicate "leakage" symptom, so they all form a relevance group; if some of such faults in the group are plausible, the most relevant will be the one exhibiting the maximum relevance feature (in that case "leakage").

The abduction problem solving proceeds by applying plausibility and relevance criteria to the sets of all effects and causes, as further described; the input is the set of instance effects and the output is the set of plausible and relevant causes – which form the diagnostic. In Sections 8.2.4 and 8.2.5, the plausibility and the relevance get connectionist models adequate to computational implementation.

8.2.3. Connectionist Approach to Abduction

Many-to-many causal relations between faults and manifestations get reversed when reasoning by abduction. However, no inverse exists for the complex relations when real problems are under concern – e.g. fault diagnosis of a real complex installation. In such a case, one fault evokes many manifestations and the same manifestation is evoked by many faults. Moreover, manifestations may enter conjunction grouping to one fault, whereas disjunction grouping for others.

8.2.3.1. Qualitative Plausibility and Quantitative Relevance

It is worth noting two interesting characteristics of the above concepts: *plausibility is qualitative* and *relevance is quantitative*. So, in order to find:

- plausible causes, one should use some qualitative processing to select all causes complying with the observed current situation, e.g., asserting the faults related to the instance manifestations that appeared;
- relevant causes, one should use some quantitative processing to select only causes exhibiting a certain degree (e.g., greater than a given threshold value) from the set of plausible ones.

The practical conclusions on issuing a connectionist model for abductive reasoning by plausibility and relevance are:

- the activation mechanisms involved in plausibility criteria should allow a "logical overload" of numbers toward the qualitative processing on causes;
- the competition mechanisms for relevance criteria should assess (numerical) *degrees* which enter the quantitative processing on relevance of causes.

The logical overload is meant for affecting "quantities" (e.g., numbers) in order to become "qualities" (i.e., meanings) thus suited for plausibility criteria; the meaning is attached to each range of values, corresponding to the significance of that range taken from the deep knowledge of domain experts. The simplest logical overload attaches two complementary meanings for the two ranges of numerical values obtained after splitting the whole domain based on a border value (i.e., a threshold) with certain significance for the variable.

That simplest logical overload is actually used in the neural network implementation of the plausibility: if the link strength to a fault-neuron, coming from a manifestation-neuron, is greater than 0.5 (the doubt threshold), then the link is "important" and gets that meaning. Therefore, it has to pass the gates into the fault-neuron, i.e., enter the input function (the stimuli sum). Otherwise, it is "not important" and hence the gate to the fault-neuron is blocked, i.e., the input stimulus does not enter the input function (actually, the input value is set to 0). Practical examples on how to use the logical overload in specific abduction problems in neural network implementation are presented in the next subsections.

8.2.3.2. Parallel Plausibility and Sequential Relevance

Relations between causes and effects (in this direction) correspond to the deductive explanations and indicate which causes determine which effects. The many-to-many relations between effects and causes (in the reverse direction) show which effects may evoke which causes, but instance effects do no indicate instance causes (that really occurred), while no inverse of the direct relations exists. Therefore, in the general case, complex relations between effects and causes naturally lead to a *connectionist model* which, in an artificial neural network (ANN) implementation, will present excitatory links for the plausibility and competition links for relevance.

In a general approach, abduction problem solving proceeds by multiple applications of the following functions (Ariton and Ariton, 2000):

- *plausibility(P_CRITERIA, EFFECTS)* – which originates the plausibility of each element from the set of *CAUSES*, based on the set of instance *EFFECTS*, and according to plausibility criteria *P_CRITERIA*.
- *relevance(R_CRITERIA, CAUSES)* – which yields the subset of *CAUSES* selected from the set of plausible ones, observing *R_CRITERIA* specific to each relevance grouping resulted from the relevance scopes.

Note that entities in *CAUSES* and *EFFECTS* sets exhibit values in [0,1] interval. The above functions apply to each entire set of entities: first, all instance *EFFECTS* contribute to activation of plausible causes (so they attain nonzero values), then the entire set of *CAUSES* enters the relevance competition (repeatedly) while the less plausible causes already have near-zero values, thus eliminated. That assures a "classical" connectionist implementation in the ANN approach.

P_CRITERIA refer to deep knowledge of human experts (related to known causal relations between effects and causes) or they refer to shallow knowledge after the ANN train, following data collected from experiments on causes and effects. Plausibility may operate in parallel on EFFECTS to activate the related.

R_CRITERIA refer solely to deep knowledge of human experts on the various cases where causes show specific relations between them, specific links to running contexts or particular behaviours. Relevance processing is repeatedly (sequentially) applied, until a final definite set of causes (i.e., the diagnostic) achieve the highest stationary activation. In single fault diagnosis, the cardinality accepted for the diagnostic set is 1, in multiple fault diagnosis cardinality is greater than 1. How sequential diagnosis proceeds is presented in Section 8.7.3.

8.2.4. Neural Models of Plausibility for the Abduction Problems

In the neural network model, plausibility refers to forward (excitatory) links between effects and causes. A cause (e.g., fault) becomes the output neuron F_i and an effect (e.g., manifestation) becomes an input neuron M_j. The activation of a cause is the result of cumulative action effects associated to it, and it may be expressed by the well-known neural activation function applied to inputs M_j:

$$F_i = f(\sum_{j=1}^{|M|} w_{ij} \, M_j + \theta_i)$$

(1)

i.e., each manifestation from the set M (with $|M|$ the cardinality) evokes, in a specific measure (i.e., weight) w_{ji}, the fault F_i, if the sum becomes greater than the threshold θ_i.

However, human diagnosticians often take into account a manifestation linked to a fault in a simple, "logical manner" (Ariton and Palade, 2004): manifestation M_j is "valid" (as a witness) for a fault F_i only if its activation is greater than a threshold, specific to the given manifestation-to-fault link. In the simplest way, if any two neurons M and F have activations in [0, 1] and the weight on their link is w, the maximum contribution of M to F is w (when $M=1$) and it is still "valid" when $M>0.5$ (when M is above the doubt value) – i.e., its contribution is greater than $w/2$.

The logical overload consists in attaching certain linguistic attributes to the generic input I of a cause neuron, e.g., exceeding the doubt level, $w/2$:

$$\textit{if } I > w/2 \textit{ then } I = \text{"valid" } \textit{else } I = \text{"not valid"} \tag{2}$$

This way, each link's strength is logically overloaded, and it makes possible the logical aggregation of effects to (evoked) causes, as required by each type of abduction problem.

8.2.4.1. Neural Sites and Specific Logical Aggregation

The ANN computational model of abduction for plausibility of the logical aggregation of input-effects to cause-neurons is performed by means of dedicated "neural sites," as specific architectural features that may embed deep knowledge in the connectionist model, beside the native shallow knowledge – which is embedded by training. The logical aggregations envisaged are (Ariton and Palade, 2004):

> i) *disjunctive aggregation*, performed by the "disjunctive site" through the default cumulative processing (that is already the input function of the "classical" neuron), i.e., all m inputs cumulate their activation I_j:

$$O = \sum_{j=1}^{m} I_j \tag{3}$$

> ii) *conjunctive aggregation*, performed by the "conjunction site," whose output O obeys the rule given by Eq. 4. After the logical overload, the inputs I_1, I_2 are aggregated according to the truth table from Figure 8.1f:

$$\textit{if } I_1 > w_1/2 \textit{ AND } I_2 > w_2/2 \textit{ then } O = I_1 + I_2 \textit{ else } O = 0 \tag{4}$$

> iii) *negation*, performed by the "negation site". The output O is obtained from input I according to Eq. 5 and the truth table in Figure 8.1g:

$$O = w - I \tag{5}$$

Note that the logical aggregation upon links' strengths modifies only the input value of the cause-neuron; it does not affect the usual processing inside the neurons in the original neural network (i.e., input or activation neuron functions). So, the training and the recall procedures do not change (e.g. for perceptron or counterpropagation neural networks).

8.2.4.2. Structures of Sites and Neurons for Different Abduction Problems

Each type of abduction problem in Section 8.2.1 is solved through a specific structure of neural sites, involving forward links from effects to causes as follows:

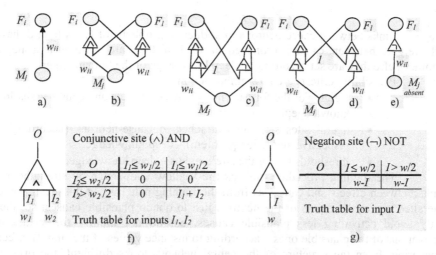

Figure 8.1.   Various abduction problems solved by neural network features using logical overload of the links between neurons.

a) For *independent* abduction problems – excitatory links apply directly from the effect M_j to the corresponding cause F_i (see Figure 8.1a). If there also exists a conjunction grouping of the effects to the cause, conjunction site(s) are used at the input of the cause-neuron. Note that, by default, the neuron implements a disjunctive grouping of inputs through its input (sum) function (Eqs. 1 and 3).

b) For *monotonic* abduction problems – the causes F_i and F_l both evoke the same effect M_j, hence they suffer conjunction with one another and with the common effect through conjunction sites, as shown in Figure 8.1b, and expressed by the rule:

$$F_i \leftarrow F_l \; AND \; M_j, \; F_l \leftarrow F \; AND \; M_j \tag{6}$$

c) For *incompatibility* abduction problems – the pair F_i and F_l of causes are mutually exclusive (i.e., they are not both active at the same time), both evoking the same effect M_j. Each of them suffers conjunction with the negation of the other cause and with the common effect, as shown in Figure 8.1c, and expressed by the rule:

$$F_i \leftarrow NOT \; F_l \; AND \; M_j, \; F_l \leftarrow NOT \; F_i \; AND \; M_j \tag{7}$$

d) For *cancellation* abduction problems – the pair of causes F_i and F_l reduce the effect M_j when both occurred, although each of them evokes it separately. They suffer conjunctions as in Figure 8.1d, according to the following rule:

$$F_i \leftarrow F_l \; AND \; NOT \; M_j, \;\; F_l \leftarrow F_i \; AND \; NOT \; M_j \tag{8}$$

e) For *open* abduction problems – the difficulty is dealing with absent effects, so the cause F_i is activated if no effect M_j exists (Figure 8.1e), according to the rule:

$$F_i \leftarrow NOT\ M_j \tag{9}$$

Links between cause-neurons in abduction problems of types b, c, d, have all weights between cause-neurons equal to 1 if they are symmetric (one to another), else they are set according to deep knowledge of the human expert.

Plausibility criteria are now embedded in:

- weights of the forward links between effects and causes – shallow knowledge;
- neural sites structures attached to cause-neurons (according to respective abduction problem) – deep knowledge;
- thresholds set for the site's inputs – deep knowledge.

The training procedure embeds the shallow knowledge by strengthening links between effects and causes as from the training patterns. At the recall phase, the sites trigger the inputs of the neurons just to obtain plausible causes; so, they only avoid activating less plausible causes, but do not modify the values of activations of the plausible ones – according to instance values of the (input) effects appearing. Even the structure of the neural network looks different, the original training procedure of the (two-layer) neural network does not change (no matter the type of the neural network used – e.g., perceptron, counterpropagation).

8.2.5. Neural Models of Relevance and Layered Modularization

The neural model of the relevance is competition. Relevance assumes a numerical value attached to causes, and the relevant cause(s) have the highest values that also exceed a given threshold. The cardinality of the relevant set of causes is 1 if "winner takes all" competition applies, or greater (if a relaxed competition applies). So, the relevant causes observe the minimum cardinality condition.

Relevance is a sequential processing: each relevance criterion is applied one after another in a given order, each criterion assuming the following steps:

  i) Consider plausible causes in the current relevance group whose values exceed the given threshold.

  ii) Start *competition* between causes inside the relevance group.

  iii) *Select* relevant cause(s) observing the given cardinality (1 for single fault diagnosis).

Both pieces of information, the order of the relevance criteria applied and the causes belonging to each relevance group, are a matter of the human diagnostician's deep knowledge on refining the diagnostic. The numerical values involved in competition and the selection of causes come from the plausibility processing of causes based on instance effects.

Due to the fact that plausibility activates in various degrees the causes, competition always proceeds on the whole relevance group of cause (not only on the plausible ones); less plausible have lower (or zero) values and are easily eliminated, so the computational procedure is applied identically.

8.2.5.1. Relevance Scope

Any cause should enter a relevance group, i.e. no cause is relevant by itself while it is either already known or permanent. A relevance group usually consists of causes that share the same characteristics (Ariton and Ariton, 2000). For example, faults occurring at a given component form a relevance group, faults exhibiting "leakage" symptom at a given module form a relevance group, etc. Note that one cause (e.g. fault) may take part in more relevance groups, due to its properties.

The groups of causes are actually obtained by performing some modularisation on the entire set of causes observing relevance criteria that fall into one of the following categories:

- Scope on *physical structure* – concerning the physical units as locations for causes: all the faults at the module level form a relevance group, and all the faults at the component level form a relevance group;

- Scope on *functional structure* – concerning the specific running contexts (i.e., activities or process phases) in which causes are "visible": all the faults whose effects appear only when the piston of a hydraulic cylinder is moving form a relevance group;

- Scope on *generic effects* – usually concerning the same symptom: all faults evoking "leakage" symptom form a relevance group, while those evoking "clogged" symptom form another relevance group.

The relevance criterion is usually the minimum cardinality on plausible causes, meaning that causes are *unlikely to appear simultaneously*. It is applied at the various unit levels (physical or functional). Other relevance criteria are: *faults more likely* to occur (due to component's age or state – as from human diagnostician's experience), *faults requiring further observations* (by means of human operator tests), etc. In such cases, to each cause is attached a numerical value necessary in the processing presented above.

8.2.5.2. Layered Modularisation of Causes

A cause may enter various relevance groups of the same set of causes, in a *layered modularisation*. Each layer refers to a scope – regarding the modularisation of the set of causes, for each relevance scope obtaining two (or more) "relevance groups." For example, some layers refer to the physical structure: one layer contains groups of causes associated to modules and another one to components; other layers refer to generic symptoms associated to faults: those producing "leakage" and those producing "obstruction." For each layer a specific modularisation occurs, corresponding to the scope it represents.

Suppose that the layered modularisation of causes is performed according to n relevance scopes, so n-times partitioning of the same set of causes is obtained. Each layer L of relevance induces a specific modularisation of causes and has a specific weight W^L in the economy of the diagnosis. A layer (and its scope) may be more relevant than another, provided weights are normalized, i.e.:

$$\sum_{L=1}^{n} W^L = 1 \tag{10}$$

The relevance criteria, scopes and layers, groups and weights of layers all come from the deep knowledge of human diagnosticians, and they are indicated during knowledge elicitation time. The competition that takes place over causes in a relevance group, is independent of the forward plausibility processing in the neural network structure, no matter what ANN implementation is chosen. So, the relevance may be added without altering the original neural network functioning to an appropriate feedforward ANN architecture.

8.2.5.3. Relevance of the Faulty Situation Against the Normal Situation

A component is the final location in fault isolation, corresponding to the set of all faults as possible causes of some faulty behaviour of that component. However, the space of faults should be completed with the "normal" situation. The neural network output layer will contain $F_0, F_1, \ldots, F_{n-1}$ neurons indicating faults, and the F_n neuron indicating the normal situation.

The F_n cause (and neuron) is of capital importance, while the *NORMAL* situation enters the relevance competition along with the *FAULTY* situation. So, before fault isolation proceeds, the fault detection attests the *FAULTY* situation against the *NORMAL* one. The relevance group is the set of $F_0, F_1, \ldots F_n$ causes, and the relevance criterion (Eq. 11) asserts the *FAULTY* situation:

$$if \ \exists \, Fi > 0.5 \ (\,i = 0,1,\ldots,n\text{-}1\,) \wedge \sum_{i=0}^{n-1} Fi > n \cdot Fn \ \ then \, FAULTY \qquad (11)$$

In other words, if any of the activated faults has a truth value greater than the "doubt value," and the relative level of the *NORMAL* situation is greater than all current (activated) faults, then the *FAULTY* situation is credited.

In conclusion, the connectionist model for abduction problem solving, using plausibility and relevance presented in this paper, is fully functional for all categories of abduction problems, as well as for disjunctive and conjunctive groupings of effects to a cause.

The proposed neural network model for abduction is a two-layer feed-forward neural structure, similar to perceptron or counterpropagation, that is completed with neural site structures for plausibility and relevance grouping / competition for relevance. The presented approach is more natural and simpler than the unified connectionist model for abduction presented by Ayeb *et al.* (1998). It also allows various "classic" ANN implementations, if appropriate feedforward and competition links are provided.

8.3.   Aspects of Human Knowledge Usage in Fault Diagnosis

Fault diagnosis deals with concepts as fault, fault mode, manifestation, symptom or anomaly. The diagnostic problem solving is commonly conceived in two stages: Fault Detection, then Isolation of the actual faults (Palade *et al.*, 2002; Uppal *et al.*, 2002; Bocaniala *et al.*, 2004; 2005). The literature in the field defines the above concepts slightly different from one researcher to another, depending on the approach or the actual implementation or method proposed. Diagnosis (DX) approaches deal with Artificial Intelligence (AI) and Cognitive Sciences concepts (Cordier *et al.*, 2000) and are closer to the human diagnostician way of acting.

In real life, fault diagnosis faces three types of inconveniences with respect to the faulty behaviour of a target complex system (Davis, 1993):

- *Incomplete knowledge* – the set of all (single or multiple) faults, effects and relations between them is not completely known. Diagnosis relies on a small set of causal relations (deductive) and empirical associations between faults and causes, and on a vague idea on how to proceed in FDI. Some manifestations are not known, while the human operator may supply information from test points, if required. When propagated effects exist, they increase the uncertainty on the faulty behaviour (e.g., in conductive flow systems (Ariton, 2001)).

- *Imprecise knowledge* – there is perpetually a drift in any measured value of a variable, the human expert having only a clue on abnormal ranges of values for each variable.

- *Uncertain knowledge* – when they have occurred, manifestations may not be entirely "abnormal"; that is, faults and manifestations occur "with some degree," they have truth values attached.

Aiming the computational modelling, the present approach is pragmatic: it considers definite meanings for the concepts above, allowing the representation of knowledge incompleteness, imprecision and uncertainty, assuming it comes from human diagnosticians' deep and shallow knowledge on faulty behaviour of a target real-world system.

8.3.1. Knowledge Pieces Involved in Diagnosis

Human diagnosticians' deep knowledge refers to the structure of the system under diagnosis and to the expected normal behaviour, while shallow knowledge refers to faulty behaviour at module and/or component levels. The structure of the target system consists of modules and components, as units conceived by designers, and accepted by diagnosticians to master the system's complexity. Modules and components are usually conceived as functional units. In the literature, the module is a structure of components, but the component does not have a clear meaning. It may suffer further decompositions (see Section 8.6.2.1), but nevertheless a component is conceived as the final location for faults or manifestations.

In the following definitions, we make use of the term *piece of knowledge*, stressing that the concept defined is obtained through an appropriate processing on the physical reality to extract (discrete) objects and logical meanings. A cognitive neutral numerical value X_k gets meanings (depending on the value range or particular situations) that are expressed by truth values $X_k \in [0,1]$, where $X_k = 1$ means that the concept is certain or complete. The concept may be a state (expressed by a noun) or a grade (expressed by an adjective or an adverb).

8.3.1.1. Component
A component is "a piece of equipment accepted by the human diagnostician as being sufficient for fault isolation" (Ariton and Ariton, 2000). Of course, it is a convention how much "detailed" a component is, while the human diagnostician decides what unit exhibits "pointed" causes for abnormal behaviours. After all, it is a matter of troubleshooting: deciding the location of the cause is the first step in removing the faulty unit (for further removing the disorder). How "small" (or how "low") the components are is a decision of the elicitation made upon the system under the diagnosis, when the fault isolation granularity is established.

8.3.1.2. Disorder
A disorder refers to nonconformities in the actual behaviour of the target system, against the expected one – which is designed and considered "normal." In order to obtain a feasible diagnosis system, the space of causes has to be a closed space, so it includes: disorders taking place at *components* (e.g., damages or ill tuning), *flow* (e.g., bad quality), *environment* (e.g., abnormal surrounding conditions) and *human operation* (technological discipline). Note that environment includes all neighbour systems: technical systems ambient atmosphere, etc., which may affect the target system's running.

8.3.1.3. Fault
A fault is a simple *piece* of knowledge regarding a physical nonconformity located at a component. Fault is a human concept with intrinsic discrete and logical natures: it has a name, usually expressed as a proposition about the disorder, and a degree of uncertainty – usually expressed in terms of a truth value $F_l \in [0,1]$. If $F_l \geq 0.5$, then it is above doubt that fault F_l occurred. From the human diagnostician point of view, the truth value is a *measure of plausibility* of a fault. The set F of all "known" faults should be decided at the elicitation time, each for a specific disorder or for a class of disorders, and reflecting the open space of effects induced by the incomplete knowledge. Open spaces should be closed by completing with generic "disorders" of the kind "not known" or "undecided," also with locations of the kind "out of target system limit." The *fault mode* refers to a specific disorder induced by a certain fault in a given process phase.

8.3.1.4. Manifestation
A manifestation is a simple piece of knowledge attesting to an abnormal value of an observed variable, during a certain running context of the target system. In the entire set M of manifestations, some may reach the diagnosis system by sensors (from continuous or binary variables), and others by human operator tests on observed variables in the process (from human senses – as adjectives, or from test points – as numbers). The manifestation's truth value $M_r \in [0,1]$ indicates how certain is the state or a grade exhibited, and it reflects our knowledge imprecision and uncertainty.

8.3.1.5. Symptom
A symptom is a complex piece of knowledge that refers to a certain behaviour coming from the deep knowledge on the target system and the domain. Symptoms

evoke classes of faults and induce some partition S on the entire set of faults F. Some symptoms provoke disjunctive partitions (e.g., faults in the "leakage" class/symptom do not belong to the "clogged" class/symptom), others provoke non-disjunctive partitions. A fault that evokes more than one nondisjunctive symptom cumulates its plausibility (it is more relevant). The primary and secondary effects, witnessed in conduction flow systems, are symptoms: primary effect is the one located at the faulty component, secondary effect is the one located at the nonfaulty component due to propagated deviations of variables values (deviations from the expected "normal" values).

8.3.1.6. Process

Process phase is a complex piece of knowledge that refers to a certain state of the process, with certain duration in the functioning of the target system. From the human diagnostician point of view, a process phase characterizes the context in which the diagnosis takes place. While in the real system's running the process phase is "expected" to happen, its truth value P asserts the degree to which the context is really known, during the current slice of time in the process evolution. Process phases induce partitions on the set M of all manifestations and on the set S of all symptoms.

All the "evaluations" made by the (automated) diagnosis system to obtain truth values for manifestations, symptoms, process phases, and faults evoke some processing performed on observed variables' values (Calado *et. al.*, 2001). Note that the human diagnostician deals with "linguistic variables" when referring to manifestations and symptoms. By default, knowledge pieces are *discrete* and *qualitative* in nature, the latter reflecting knowledge imprecision or knowledge incompleteness regarding the human diagnostician view on the (faulty) behaviour of the target system. Therefore, any processing should comply with these aspects.

8.3.2. Observed Variables

Let us consider now a computerized diagnosis system that deals with manifestations and faults with graded values of truth as described above. If the observations made upon the target system's behaviour are linguistic or binary variables, they already have a "logical meaning" – present/absent. The observations made upon the target system come to the diagnosis system from the human operator (thus meaningful) or from sensors, as numerical values, thus cognitivly neutral. To obtain a common denominator, they should undergo some processing to become manifestations, so they undergo some "intelligent encoding" indicated by Cherkassky and Lari-Najafi (1992) as being crucial in diagnosis.

The preprocessing performed by the diagnosis system on the raw acquired values depends on the observed variable's type:

  a) Binary variable from digital sensor – no processing required. By default, such a variable has two values, attached to a logical meaning (e.g., present/absent, open/shut). The manifestation results immediately, and $M_r \in \{0,1\}$.

  b) Continuous variable from analogical sensor/device – processing required. To obtain some discrete piece of knowledge (manifestation with some truth value $M_r \in [0,1]$) from primary data, the continuous signal supplied by the sensor is sampled and the series of values undergoes some processing according to the current process phase.

c) Discrete variable from human operator tests – no processing required. For example, the linguistic variable "noisy" is by default a logical variable with two values; thus manifestation results immediately: $M_r \in \{0,1\}$. Note that variables like "not hot," "hot," "very hot" should be reduced to more manifestations of the same type $M_r \in \{0,1\}$.

d) Continuous variable from human operator test performed in a test-point – processing required. The numerical pointwise value, entered by the human operator, should be evaluated if normal or not. Abnormal situation results as a (discrete) manifestation, according to the current process phase (e.g., fuzzification of point-wise numerical values, obtaining a fuzzy attribute with a graded value of truth $M_r \in [0,1]$).

So, intelligent encoding depends on the type of observed variables. The specific processing brings them to a uniform representation. Knowledge incompleteness, imprecision and uncertainty, specific to human diagnostician qualitative way of thinking, come from the abstractions made on the real continuous running of the target system (Mosterman and Biswas, 2002) and from the complexity of real phenomena. These aspects of human knowledge are melted into discrete and logical representations of manifestations, both useful in the neural network approach of the diagnosis, further presented in this chapter.

8.3.3. Semiqualitative Encoding of Manifestations

Fuzzy logic deals with associating logical meanings to numbers. It copes with the qualitative way of thinking of human experts, and quantities become sets, or intervals with imprecise edges, but specific meanings. In the present approach, a manifestation is a fuzzy attribute of an observed *continuous variable V* during the process phase *P*, i.e., it is a fuzzy subset over its universe of discourse $\Omega(V)$, as shown in Figure 8.2.

8.3.3.1. Prototype Manifestations

The attributes refer to the qualitative subdomains related to the abnormal values "too low" (*lo*) and "too high" (*hi*) in the current running context. Fuzzification is chosen as the "intelligent encoding" meant for manifestations. In Figure 8.2, the subdomains between *landmarks Lm(no) - Lm(lo)* and *Lm(no) - Lm(hi)*, respectively, refer to the qualitative subdomains of Kuipers's approach (Kuipers, 1994) on quantifying values of a variable, in qualitative physics.

Pairwise neighbour subdomains form the fuzzy attributes "too low" and "too high" for the generic manifestations *lo* and *hi* corresponding to the given variable *V* and the given process phase *P*. Note that the fuzzy attribute "normal" (*no*) refers to the range of "expected values" for the observed variable, which indicates a normal behaviour; it is essential for obtaining a closed space of causes.

The overlapped intervals of the fuzzy attributes (see Figure 8.1) reflect the knowledge incompleteness and imprecision of the human diagnostician, which is linked to the specificity of the manifestation (Turksen, 1996).

The attributes *lo* or *hi* – as triangular membership functions in the semi-qualitative representation – are *prototype manifestation* set by the human diagnostician at knowledge elicitation on the system under the diagnosis.

The effective landmarks and the fuzzy subsets for generic manifestations *lo, no, hi* are provided at elicitation time. The knowledge engineer uses deep knowledge from the domain expert to assign qualitative landmarks for each observed variable from sensors. In this case, the CAKE (Computer Aided Knowledge Elicitation) tool is useful for the human diagnostician (see Section 8.6).

The triangular membership functions of the generic manifestations fit well to the *semiqualitative representation* usually encountered by human diagnosticians (Kruse *et al.*, 1994). Due to the linear and baricentric encoding, such representation offers some advantages for logical processing in a human-like way, also for fuzzy arithmetic with ranges when assessing propagated effects (Ariton, 2003). That simple semiqualitative representation best captures the human diagnostician's knowledge on manifestations of any kind, when the system is faulty.

8.3.3.2. Handling Uncertainty on Instance Manifestations

The manifestations linked to a continuous variable (type b or d from the above classification) actually refer to the pointwise value v that enters the diagnosis system during a process phase P. After fuzzification, each attribute *lo, no, hi* gets a truth value.

The *instance manifestations* obtained reflect the uncertainty of the situation occurring when for example both truth values $\mu_{hi}(v)>0$ and $\mu_{no}(v)>0$ appear (see Figure 8.2) – the last one reflecting the opinion on "normal" behaviour of the current situation. The preprocessing block of the diagnosis system should assert, for any variable instance, the appearing manifestations and their extent (the truth value).

8.3.3.3. Types of Manifestations

The set of all instance manifestations M^P for a given process phase P comprises: the instance manifestations for all sensor-observed continuous variables M_C^P (truth values in $[0,1]$), the instance manifestations for all sensor-observed binary variables M_B^P (truth values in $\{0,1\}$) and the instance manifestations for all human operator-observed variables M_O^P (truth values in $\{0,1\}$).

Taking into consideration all variables of any kind, and for all process phases, will lead to the set M of all manifestations as distinct knowledge pieces. It comprises the set MM of manifestations obtained by permanent measurements through sensors mounted in the process:

$$MM = \{ M_C^P \cup M_B^P \mid \text{for all process phases } P \} \qquad (12)$$

and the set OM of manifestations obtained by human operator observations:

$$OM = \{ M_O^P \mid \text{for all process phases } P \} \qquad (13)$$

Hence, the set M of all discrete manifestations entering the diagnosis system is:

$$M = MM \cup OM \qquad (14)$$

and comprises all pieces of knowledge of the kind *lo, no, hi* for manifestations at continuous variables, or *present / absent* for binary variables.

Overall, the cardinality of the set of all observed variables is lower than the cardinality of the set of manifestations *M*, since the sensor-observed binary variables may have two "pieces of knowledge" (i.e., one manifestation of type "present" and, afterwards, one of type "absent"), and the human operator-observed variables may have three "pieces of knowledge" (i.e., two manifestations *lo, hi* and one of type *no* – as "absent" or "normal"). Some "absent" manifestations are quite important in diagnosis (see below), as they require a specific type of abduction problems to be solved.

Some continuous operator-observed variables may be "measurements on the fly," i.e., they are not permanently observed by sensors, but supplied occasionally by the human operator when required, following a best next test procedure (de Kleer and Kurien, 2003). In this case, the diagnosis system should perform the fuzzification or other processing, after the operator supplies the required value. This is a usual approach to finding logical meanings for manifestations (with truth values), and the obtained unified and discrete representation will be used in the connectionist implementation for diagnosis described in the next sections.

8.3.4. Intelligent Encoding of Instance Manifestations

Depending on the source of the observation, the obtained manifestation requires more complex or simpler processing, for example when observation comes from analogical sensors or from binary sensors, respectively. In the latter case, values as close/shut are already discrete and have a meaning – thus no processing required.

For an observed pointwise value *v* the truth value results from regular fuzzification (Kruse *et al.*, 1994) – e.g., in Figure 8.2 the instance manifestations *hi* and *no* get truth value $\mu_{hi}(v)$ and $\mu_{no}(v)$. The representation is semiqualitative while it exhibits qualitative attributes (i.e., *lo, no, hi*) and truth (numerical) values for each. However, human diagnosticians judge manifestations for the activity as a whole, hence the instance manifestation refers to the set of values (not the pointwise one) acquired during the current process phase *P*. Thus, straight fuzzification is not suited to encode manifestations (Dubois and Prade, 1998). An appropriate processing is further used.

8.3.4.1. Instance Domain for an Observed Variable

The sampling and the conversion of the *V* variable during τ^P time period of the *P* activity produce N^P binary numbers, further denominated *instance domain* (see the solid line in Figure 8.3a). A pointwise (quantified) value v_i appears η^P_i times in the instance domain. If divided by N^P, it becomes the frequency of v_i during τ^P, with a maximum η^P_m at value v_m: $\eta^P_m = \max_i \eta^P_i$. The value v_m is a meaningful value but it

does not evoke a manifestation, while it does not refer to the entire set of values, hence a special encoding scheme is needed, which is further presented.

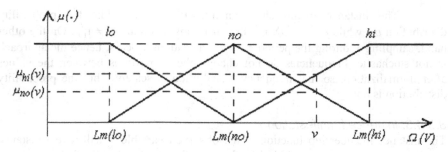

Figure 8.2. Semiqualitative representation of generic manifestations expected at a sensor-observed variable V.

The frequency distribution η^P_V for all values is the collection:
$$\eta^P_V = \{ \eta^P_i \mid i = 0 .. N^P \} \qquad (15)$$
and the normalized frequency distribution (to the maximum η^P_m) – see Figure 8.3a – is:
$$\mu^P_V = \{ \eta^P_i / \eta^P_m \mid i = 0 .. N^P \} \qquad (16)$$

8.3.4.2. Instance Membership Function for Series of Acquired Values
Instead of a pointwise value, the diagnosis system will use the normalized frequency distribution μ^P_V to assert manifestations for the variable V over the process phase P, as shown below. So, the instance domain (solid line in Figure 8.3a) may be seen as a fuzzy set in the statistical approach (as from (Kruse *et al.*, 1994)), and μ^P_V is the actual *instance membership function*.

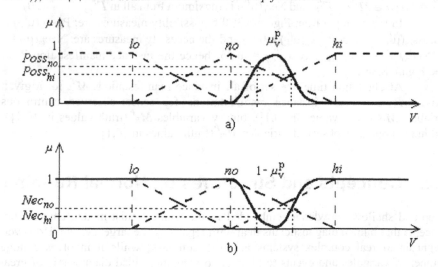

Figure 8.3. Possibility measure (a) and necessity measure (b) of the instance membership function upon the prototype manifestations for the continuous variable V, during the activity P

The instance membership function μ_V^P is not like the probability distribution p_V, while $p_V = \eta_i^P / \Sigma\, \eta_i^P$, thus it is obvious that $p_V \neq \eta_V^P$. On the other hand, sampling V during the period t^P is not a random process, hence the approach is not stochastic. Frequencies do not change the proportions between the values after normalization, so that frequency distribution is scalable, but the probability distribution is not.

8.3.4.3. Instance Manifestation

The instance membership function of the observed variable V will reveal instance manifestations that appeared during the actual activity P. Manifestation is an attribute $a \in \{lo, no, hi\}$, which results from the possibility and the necessity measures (Ayeb *et al.*, 1998) of the instance membership function over the partition in Figure 8.3a:

$$\text{Poss}_V(a) = \sup_{v \in a} \mu_v^P, \ \text{Nec}_V(a) = 1 - \text{Poss}_V(a) = \inf_{v \notin a} (1 - \mu_v^P) \qquad (17)$$

Inference of the instance manifestations proceeds as follows:

    i) Calculate the membership function μ_V^P of the V variable's instance domain.

    ii) Calculate the set $\boldsymbol{\Pi}_V^P$ of *possible manifestations*:

$$\boldsymbol{\Pi}_V^P = \{\, a \mid a \in \{lo, no, hi\} \text{ and } \text{Poss}_a(\mu_V^P) > 0.5\} \qquad (18)$$

    iii) Calculate the set $\boldsymbol{\Gamma}_V^P$ of *necessary manifestations*:

$$\boldsymbol{\Gamma}_V^P = \{\, a \mid a \in \{lo, no, hi\} \text{ and } \text{Nec}_a(\mu_V^P) > 0\} \qquad (19)$$

    iv) Assert which *instance manifestation* M_V^P actually occurred, applying:

$$M_V^P = \{\, a \mid a \in \boldsymbol{\Pi}_V^P \cap \boldsymbol{\Gamma}_V^P \text{ and } \text{Nec}_a(\mu_V^P) \text{ is maximum from all in } \boldsymbol{\Gamma}_V^P\} \qquad (20)$$

In the example from Figure 8.3, the possibility measures are: $\text{Poss}_{lo}(\mu_V^P) = 0$, $\text{Poss}_{no}(\mu_V^P) = 0.75$, $\text{Poss}_{hi}(\mu_V^P) = 0.55$ and the necessity measures are: $\text{Nec}_{lo}(\mu_V^P) = 0$, $\text{Nec}_{no}(\mu_V^P) = 0.45$, $\text{Nec}_{hi}(\mu_V^P) = 0.25$, hence the instance manifestation is *no* (see Figure 8.3b).

At elicitation time, the set of all instance manifestations M^P, for a given activity P, comprises: instance manifestations for sensor-observed continuous variables M_C^P (truth values in [0,1]), binary variables M_B^P (truth values in $\{0,1\}$), and human operator-observed variables M_O^P (truth values in $\{0,1\}$).

8.4.   Concepts and Structures on Normal Running

Deep and shallow knowledge, embedded in the connectionist model, comes from concepts that human diagnosticians deal with regarding the target system. However, diagnosis of real complex systems is a difficult task, while it involves a huge number of variables and events to handle, so computer-aided diagnosis is of great help.

The following section presents some principles on discriminating the concepts and their relations for the fault diagnosis following a human-like diagnosis, and using connectionist models for abduction. In that endeavor, means-end modelling approach seems best suited for the analysis and representation of physical and functional structures. The approach makes use of bond graph models, adapted to cope with human-like qualitative view on the faulty behaviour of conductive flow systems, and also to the modular way of thinking when isolating faults.

8.4.1. Means-End Abstractions of Physical and Functional Structures

Real systems are multifunctional systems, while they perform many functions at the same time. Functions refer to tasks performed by modules and components toward specific utilities envisaged by the artefact. Each module performs a sequence of activities, and all modules perform activities in parallel – each module one activity at a time, during the given slice of time in the whole installation running. As a term, "multifunctional" is introduced in (O'Brien, 1970) on complex systems' safety, and it is used in fault diagnosis in (Okuda and Miyasaka, 1991; Shibata *et al.*, 1991).

Most encountered systems in technical or economical domains are *conductive flow systems* (CFSs) (Cellier, 1995) – i.e., they transport matter, energy and information as flows passing through pipe-like paths. Through the effects propagation, same effects may appear at many faults, located at faulty and non-faulty units. In such cases, the human diagnostician deals with primary and secondary effects, i.e., effects located at the faulty component and effects spread to nonfaulty components, respectively.

Means-end modelling approach is a view on artefacts from the utility perspective: the ends (concrete goals of the artefact) are those structuring the means (functional structures) supported by physical components. In (Larsson, 1992) a component performs a "flow function" (and a module a network of flow functions) – acting upon the flow.

8.4.1.1. Multifunctional Systems
A multifunctional system (MFS) under the diagnosis is the 5-tuple $\langle C, G, S, T, H \rangle$:

C is the set of all physical components, each component meant as the final location for fault isolation, each completing certain functions;

G is the set of functions components may accomplish;

S is the set of ends, each end characterized by performance of a certain utility that the system must accomplish;

T is the set of time durations in accomplishing (each of all) ends;

H is the set of modules, each module h_i comprising a subset C_i of components and accomplishing a subset S_i of ends.

An elementary end s_{ik} is achieved during (and corresponds to) an *activity* – from the Discrete Event System abstraction of the h_i module's running. A module may accomplish more ends. For example, a hydraulic conveyor executes four activities corresponding to the four ends of the actuator (the hydraulic cylinder): still left, move left-to-right, still right, move right-to-left, each being a function of the actuator component.

The set of modules H is a disjunctive partition upon the set S of ends, each module accomplishing a specific subset of ends S_i but only one end s_{ik} at a time. In the example above, the module comprises components as pipes, control valve, damper, hydraulic cylinder. The ends are the "move" or "stay still" services, and the durations in accomplishing those ends are either specified – e.g., the expected duration for each movement of the piston, or derived – e.g., the stay-still duration (between movements). The relations between cardinalities $|S|=|T|$ and $|S|>|H|$ hold; in other words, each end has a certain duration (in normal and abnormal situations) and a module exhibits at least two activities (idle/active) to a certain end.

8.4.1.2. Multifunctional Conductive Flow Systems

Multifunctional conductive flow system (MCFS) is the 7-tuple $\langle C,G,S,T,U,H, \leqslant\leqslant \rangle$:

$\quad$ C, G, S, T are as above;

$\quad$ U is the set of flow types; a certain flow type u_t is processed by components of a module toward a specific end by means of specific functions of components;

$\quad$ H is as above, but restricted to the subset C_i of components that act upon the same flow type u_t .

$\quad$ $\leqslant\leqslant$ is the weak upstream relation taking place between components c_{ij}, and between modules h_i along the flow paths in the conductive flow system.

$\quad$ The (matter/energy) flow conduction is ruled by specific laws that are not captured in the definition above but will be discussed later (see Section 8.4.2) in the discrimination of primary from secondary effects at faults.

$\quad$ Note that upstream relations of neighbour components depend on the activity; for example, the "hydraulic cylinder" has an upstream relation with a component when the piston moves left-to-right (filling its left chamber) and downstream relation with the same component when the piston moves right-to-left (filling its right chamber).

$\quad$ In the proposed approach, MCFS appears as a multiple layered structure of conductive flow systems, each of them handling a certain type of flow and acting toward some definite ends on the same set of components. For example, the "mineral oil flow" in the hydraulic installation of a rolling mill plant is an auxiliary flow beside the "long steel plate flow" meant for the (main) technological end – plate extrusion.

8.4.1.3. Means-End Abstraction on Functions

Each component c_{ij} fulfills a certain flow function during a certain activity, upon a certain type of flow u_t, but it may fulfill simultaneously more flow functions, each upon different flow types "passing" through the component. For example, a control valve in a hydraulic system may complete a "barrier" flow function (when blocking the flow for "piston stay-still" end) or a "transport" flow function (when letting through flow for "piston move" end); on the other side, the control valve always exhibits a "transport" flow function for the electric current through the control coil of the valve.

$\quad$ Each module $h_i \in H$ achieves a certain end by means of the functions g_{ij} specific to the components in the set C_i of the given module. Other aspects of the flow functions follow:

$\quad\quad$ a) the component c_{ij} fulfills a unique "flow function" upon a certain flow type, during a certain activity of the module h_i (according to Larsson (1992));

b) the end s_{ik} of a module is accomplished by the set C_i of components by means of the "network" of "flow functions" (Larsson, 1992);

c) the module is actually a functional unit, comprising only components that process the same u_t flow type (in the presented approach).

8.4.1.4. Qualitative View on Flow Functions

The detailed flow functions (transport, barrier, distribution, etc.) in (Larsson, 1992) may be reduced to three qualitative functions, sufficiently relevant for the diagnosis task, while it is somehow simpler and more qualitative than the control task. In (Opdahl and Sindre, 1994) three orthogonal operational facets of real-world systems are proposed, as in Table 8.1.

Table 8.1. Functional orthogonal facets of real-world systems

Concept	Process	Flow	Store
Activity	Transformation	Transportation	Preservation
Aspect	Matter	Location	Time

The concepts refer to physical or chemical processing (see *Process*), the space location change (see *Flow*) and the time location change (see *Store*), i.e., time delay.

The activities associated with the three concepts suggest three primary flow functions, suited to the qualitative modelling of components' faulty behaviours. For each concept in Table 8.1 the corresponding primary flow function is:

i) flow processing function (*fpf*) – like chemical or physical transformation of the piece of flux (to a certain utility);

ii) flow transport function (*ftf*) – like space location change of the piece of flux (by pipes, conveyors, etc.);

iii) flow store function (*fsf*) – like time delay of the piece of flux, by accumulation of mass or energy in some storing or inertial components.

A real component achieves several primary flow functions, but solely one during a given activity. Note that components that directly accomplish ends of the target system, fulfill processing (*fpf*) and store (*fsf*) primary flow functions; most components fulfill transport (*ftf*) primary flow function. Flow function's misbehaviour is easily associated with some generic anomalies that may appear at faults (see Section 8.5.2).

8.4.2. Bond-Graph Modelling and MCFS's Structures

Conductive flow modelling of real systems observes Kirchkoff's laws, no matter the type of flow (matter, energy or information). Bond graphs are appropriate and general modelling tools for conductive flow systems, with the great advantage of Kirchkoff's laws applied in a modular way, and not for the whole system as in the classical way (Cellier, 1995; Mosterman *et al.*, 1995). Moreover, bond-graph modelling offers general concepts useful for behavioural abstractions of the flow functions for every type of flow (see below).

8.4.2.1. Modularisation by Bond Graph Junctions in the Target MCFS

Bond graph modelling deals with flow power variables: the intensive (pressure like) and the extensive (flow-rate like) variables, called *effort* (*e*) and *flow* (*f*), respectively (Cellier, 1995).

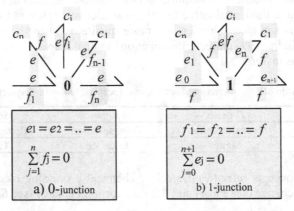

Figure 8.4.   The bond graph 0-junction (a), and 1-junction (b).

Components, along flow paths in CFS, form bond graph junctions:
- type 1 junction – that corresponds to a loop of interconnected components,
- type 0 junction – that corresponds to a node of interconnected components.

Each junction's common variables are: effort in 0-junction and flow in 1-junction; the noncommon power variable is specific to each component and all enter a sum (e.g., the flow in the 0-junction), as in Figure 8.4a,b.

In the present approach, the 1-junction corresponds to a given activity of a module, i.e., the 1-junction is the bond graph model of the activity, so it may play the role of the "module" – in the multifunctional abstraction (Ariton, 2003). The 1-junction is already a network of flow functions – complying with the means-end point of view.

The conclusions above are useful in knowledge elicitation of modules, during MCFS hierarchical decomposition. In this view, the 0-junction is the interconnection of modules, and the structure of the whole target system is made of 0-junctions.

8.4.2.2. Primary Flow Functions and Bond-Graph Components

The large generalization specific to the bond graph approach is synthetically illustrated in the tetrahedron of state in Figure 8.5 (Cellier, 1995). Variables on flow conduction may have specific meanings to specific domains: the effort *e* may correspond to force (in mechanics), to voltage (in electricity), to pressure (in hydraulics), flow f may correspond to velocity, to current, to volume flow rate (in the respective domains). Other general concepts in bond graph modelling approach are: the generalized momentum p (momentum in mechanics, flux in electricity, etc.), and the generalized displacement q (distance, charge, etc.).

The presented approach extensively uses the concepts of *bond graph components*:

- power flow components: Resistance R, Capacitance C, Inductance I, corresponding to dissipative, storage and inertial elements, respectively;
- power transfer components: transformer TR (effort-effort and flow-flow ratios) and gyrator GY (effort-flow and flow-effort ratios).

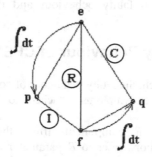

Figure 8.5.   The tetrahedron of state and the bond graph components R, C, I.

Components of MCFSs have projections on bond-graph and means-end perspectives:

- R component corresponds to transport function (ftf);
- C and I components correspond to storing function (fsf);
- TR and GY components correspond to processing function (fpf).

This result is useful in the faulty behaviour modelling (see Sections 8.5.1 and 8.5.2) and in the hierarchical decomposition of the target system toward components (see Section 8.6.2.1).

8.4.2.3. Upstream Relations between Modules and Components

The bonds (half-arrows in Figure 8.4) indicate the flow but do not refer to the upstream/downstream relations between components. Those relations are important in locating the effects along flow paths (see Section 8.5.3.3).

In Figure 8.4 the indices $j \leq 1 \leq n$ show the components' upstream order between components $c_{i1}, c_{i2}, c_{i3} \in h_i$ (belonging to the same module) and direct neighbours (which input / output ports are directly coupled). Neighbour modules also exhibit upstream relations.

The upstream relation is strong ($<<$) at 1-junction: $c_{i1} << c_{i2} << c_{i3}$ when the order of two neighbours is strict, while they are output-input coupled and the flow strictly gets out from one component and gets in the neighbour one.

The upstream relation is weak ($\leqslant\leqslant$) at 0-junction: $c_{i1}\leqslant\leqslant c_{i2} \leqslant\leqslant c_{i3}$ when two neighbour components' ports are input-input or output-output coupled, so for both neighbour components the flow either gets out or gets in the coupled ports.

The two bonds of indices 0 and $n+1$ of the 1-junction indicate effort at the input and at the output of the series of components, and actually represent links to the upstream and downstream 0-junctions, respectively.

8.5.   Concepts and Structures on Faulty Running

Elicitation defines knowledge pieces (some of them discriminated above) but also prepares corresponding data for further processing. The chapter introduces knowledge pieces related to faulty behaviour and their representation for the computational model.

8.5.1.   Generic Faulty Behaviour of CFS's Components

Following the above approach, the faulty behaviour of components of the target CFSs is conceived as human-like symptoms attached to various faults of the real components:

- Faults in R component affect the transport function (*ftf*); manifestations refer to R parameter changes, and the symptoms refer to propagation of power deviations along the paths in the system (discussed in Section 8.5.2.2).
- Faults in C and I components affect the storing function (*fsf*); manifestations refer to changes in time delays in the process running.
- Faults in TR and GY components affect the processing function (*fpf*); manifestations and symptoms are specific to each end of flow processing.

Faults may occur at any components but only R components are involved in power propagation along the system. Consequently, deviations of the power variables e and f propagate from the faulty component to other components, where they indirectly affect specific parameters – for example the delay for C and I, or the transferred effort and flow for TR and GY.

An important conclusion is drawn from the statements above: the anomalies of R bond-graph components are primary effects, and they provoke secondary effects by means of flow power variables deviations propagated throughout the flow path in the target CFS. Another important conclusion, from the point of view of diagnosis, is that the discrimination of primary effects from secondary effects leads to fault isolation.

The TR and GY components correspond to actuators in the target system, and they decouple flows or modules. Hence, the two components are, usually, the final components in the network of flow functions, i.e., they are components at the border between two modules. For example, the carrier of a conveyor is not part of the module, while the hydraulic cylinder is a transformer from the effort of the mineral oil towards displacement (of the carrier). Actually, the carrier and its load are part of another module, decoupled by the hydraulic cylinder (as a transformer). So, the b) item from the Section 8.4.1.3 is observed.

8.5.2. Anomalies Related to Primary Flow Functions

Anomaly is a piece of knowledge indicating a class of abnormal behaviours; it is another word for symptom, which is used in the present approach to restrict the meaning of the symptom to a deviation from the expected behaviour of one of the three primary flow functions defined above. The anomaly is located at the faulty unit, i.e., it is a "primary effect." This way, the fault isolation procedure benefits from some additional information useful when the location of the fault is of concern.

8.5.2.1. Anomalies and Primary Flow Functions

Flow process anomaly, flow store anomaly and flow transport anomaly are disorders of respective flow functions, located at the faulty component or module:

a) Process anomaly (*AnoP*) appears at the actuator components – bond-graph gyrator *GY* or transformer *TR* components. Process anomalies refer to abnormal values of performance parameters of the end envisaged.

b) Store anomaly (*AnoS*) appears at storage or inertial components – bond-graph capacitance *C* and inductance *I* components. The store anomaly refers to abnormal values of the time delay appearing at faults in storage or inertial elements.

c) Transport anomaly (*AnoT*) appears at dissipative component, in the bond-graph view resistance *R* components. In fault diagnosis literature and practice "leakage" or "clogged pipe" are usual terms for such anomalies.

8.5.2.2. Transport Anomalies

Ariton (2003) introduces four orthogonal transport anomalies that completely cover the faulty behaviour of a component involved in the flow transport, namely:

d) *Obstruction (Ob)* – consists in change (increase) of the transport *R* parameter of a component, without flow path modification (e.g., clogged pipe).

e) *Tunnelling (Tu)* – consists in change (decrease) of the transport *R* parameter of a component, without flow path modification (e.g., broken-through pipe).

f) *Leakage (Le)* – consists in *structure* changing (output flow too low) of a flow transport component, involving flow path modification.

g) *Infiltration (In)* – consists in *structure* changing (output flow too high) of a flow transport component, involving flow path modification.

Transport anomalies are orthogonal (see Figure 8.6): inside the pair and between pairs. In Figure 8.6 the axes' names indicate the "main" power flow variable for the pair, the one mainly involved in the effect at the respective pair of transport anomalies. Note that the effort for *Ob/Tu* pair is meant at the input, and the flow for *In/Le* pair is meant at the output of the given flow transport unit (component or module), so the signs depicted in Figure 8.6 are specific to those situations.

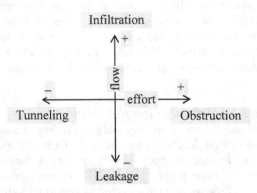

Figure 8.6.   Orthogonal transport anomalies.

Solely, one transport anomaly may appear at a time vis-à-vis a faulty component.

The four transport anomalies are effective concepts in the qualitative modelling of faulty behaviour and in effects propagation. As later shown, transport anomalies are of seminal importance in the discrimination of primary effects from secondary ones, in detection and isolation of faults.

Various components in real systems are involved in flow transport, i.e., they act as *R* bond-graph components and may exhibit transport anomalies at faults.

The transport anomalies *Ob/Tu* are symptoms similar to events as "clogged paths" or broken-through paths, and *In/Le* are symptoms similar to flow exchange with the environment. The first pair observes the (expected) flow balance equations, while the second does not. Transport anomalies play a central role in fault detection, while they have the meaning of "primary effects" – i.e., effects located at the faulty component (or module). Asserting a transport anomaly means detecting a fault and also isolating the fault – while the transport anomaly location is asserted.

Process anomalies *AnoP* and store anomalies *AnoS* may appear as *secondary effects* when induced by the flow power deviations propagated through components with flow transport functions, along the flow paths, while the deviations appeared at the location of a transport anomaly *AnoT* that occurred as a *primary effect*.

8.5.3. Qualitative Deviations Induced by Transport Anomalies

The following study focuses on deviations of the effort e and the flow f of bond-graph power variables at faulty and nonfaulty bond-graph R type components.

8.5.3.1. Qualitative Behaviour of R Components

The qualitative relation between the power variables for a nonfaulty component is $e = M^+ \cdot f$, according to the general qualitative Ohm's law (Struss, 1997). The flow variables' deviations from expected values at the input port comply:

$$\Delta e = M^+ \cdot \Delta f \qquad (21)$$

where M^+ is a class of increasing monotonic functions (according to qualitative physics and notations from (Kuipers, 1994)). Δe and Δf refer to power variable finite deviations (due to some external causes of the nonfaulty component. The qualitative relation Eq. 21 also holds for the flow variables at the output port (note that no concern exists in the extent of the relation).

8.5.3.2. Power Deviations at Faulty and Non-faulty R Components

As presented in Section 8.5.2.2, the faulty flow transport components induce one of the four orthogonal symptoms (transport anomalies) shown in Table 8.2.

The deviations of effort and flow variables from the expected (normal) values are specific to R bond-graph component for the given transport anomaly (Ob/Tu, In/Le). The deviations' signs (i.e., the qualitative values) simply result from the affected parameters of R and of the main variable in the context of the transport anomaly.

Table 8.2.   Flow power variables' deviations at input and output ports of R bond-graph components for each transport anomaly occurrence

Transport anomaly	"Main" variable deviation for the anomaly class	Effort deviation at the input (output) ports	Flow deviation at the input (output) ports	Qualitative effort-flow relations
Obstruction (Ob)	$e_{in\text{-}out} > 0$	$\Delta e_{(in)} > 0$ ($\Delta e_{(out)} < 0$)	$\Delta f_{(in)} < 0$ ($\Delta f_{(out)} < 0$)	M^- (M^+)
Tunneling (Tu)	$e_{in\text{-}out} < 0$	$\Delta e_{(in)} < 0$ ($\Delta e_{(out)} > 0$)	$\Delta f_{(in)} > 0$ ($\Delta f_{(out)} > 0$)	M^- (M^+)
Infiltration (In)	$f_{out} > 0$	$\Delta e_{(in)} > 0$ ($\Delta e_{(out)} > 0$)	$\Delta f_{(in)} < 0$ ($\Delta f_{(out)} > 0$)	M^- (M^+)
Leakage (Le)	$f_{out} < 0$	$\Delta e_{(in)} < 0$ ($\Delta e_{(out)} < 0$)	$\Delta f_{(in)} > 0$ ($\Delta f_{(out)} < 0$)	M^- (M^+)

As shown in the last column of Table 8.2, the qualitative relation between the deviations of flow variables at the input port is:

$$\Delta e = M^- \Delta f \qquad (22)$$

where M^- is a class of negative monotonic (decreasing) functions. It seems that the relation does not comply with the general Ohm's law; note that Eq. 22 refers to deviations from *expected values*, so it is not the Ohm's law in question but variables' deviations.

Equations 21 and 22 are the basis of the qualitative modelling for the effects' propagation along the flow paths in the conductive flow system.

8.5.3.3. Signatures of Qualitative Deviations at Flow Transport Anomalies

The transport flow function reflected by R bond-graph generic component is involved in the propagation of flow power and also in propagation of the deviations of the flow power variables when faults occur. The propagated flow power deviation reaches a neighbour nonfaulty component involved in the flow transport, and affects the effort (at input port) and the flow (at output port) values depending on the bond-graph junction they share.

Table 8.3 presents the signatures of manifestations for the effort and flow variables corresponding to each transport anomaly and to each type of bond-graph junction. The signatures are patterns expressed in terms of qualitative deviations (*lo* – "too low" and *hi* – "too high") for the flow variables at a nonfaulty component sharing the same bond-graph junction with the faulty one. Note that both (faulty and nonfaulty) components are flow transport (R bond-graph) components; hence they are both involved in the flow power deviation's propagation (from the *AnoT* "cause" location).

Table 8.3.   Signatures of the transport anomalies as effort-flow manifestations at the input-output ports (respectively), in each type of bond-graph junction

	1-junction	0-junction $1 \gg 2$ $\underset{3 \quad 4}{\leq\leq}$		0-junction $1 \gg 2$ $\underset{3 \quad 4}{\geq\geq}$	
Transport anomaly (*AnoT*)	$1\gg2\gg3$ shadowed item is AnoT (the faulty component)	fault downstream (of Kirchkoff's node)		fault upstream (of Kirchkoff's node)	
	$1 \gg 2$ $3 \ll 2$	$1 \gg 2$	$4 \geq\geq 2$	$2 \ll 1$	$3 \leq\leq 1$
Obstruction (*Ob*)	*hi-lo* *lo-lo*	*hi-hi*	*hi-lo*	*lo-hi*	*lo-lo*
Tunneling (*Tu*)	*lo-hi* *hi-hi*	*lo-lo*	*lo-hi*	*hi-lo*	*hi-hi*
Infiltration (*In*)	*hi-lo* *hi-hi*	*hi-lo*	*hi-lo*	*lo-hi*	*hi-hi*
Leakage (*Le*)	*lo-hi* *lo-lo*	*lo-lo*	*lo-lo*	*hi-hi*	*lo-lo*

If the flow power deviation reaches the location of GY/TR bond-graph (actuator) component, or of C/I (store/inertial) bond-graph component, a secondary effect appears, expressed by the *AnoP* or *AnoS* anomalies. Those effects actually reflect the *AnoT* anomaly propagated as power flow deviations along the flow paths throughout the target system.

Manifestations at nonfaulty components are expressed in terms of qualitative deviation of the effort – at the input port, and of the flow – at the output port, in pairs (*hi-lo*, *lo-lo*, etc.), and they result from the qualitative relations of the flow power variables at faulty (Eq. 22) and nonfaulty (Eq. 21) components (Ariton,

2003), in the corresponding behaviour contexts (the triplet: junction type, upstream relation, transport anomaly).

The signatures with manifestations at the components upstream/downstream from the faulty one are specific to the transport anomaly (*AnoT*) and the junction type; the only exceptions are Tunnelling and Infiltration in 0-junction (column 3 of the Table 8.3), which cases should be decided based on relations in neighbour 1-junction(s). Note that weak relations ($\leq\leq$ / $\geq\geq$) are equivalent for the meant study of qualitative signatures.

8.6. Knowledge Elicitation and the CAKE Tool

Diagnosis performed by human experts involves deep knowledge and shallow knowledge on a real target system comprising many modules and components, many activities, many faults, manifestations and symptoms.

It is difficult to manage the huge amount of information if no adequate instrument exists, i.e., a Computer Aided Knowledge Elicitation (CAKE) tool. Such a tool assists the human diagnostician in the knowledge acquisition phase and in managing the information on the concrete target system. Therefore, the knowledge acquisition is performed more easily and the computational model is easily adapted to specific situations on the place. The CAKE (software) tool takes the place of the knowledge engineer, who is the essential human expert in the design phase of a dedicated diagnosis system. So, human diagnosticians and human operators do not need a knowledge engineer to build their own diagnosis system (for the target system) but they simply put all the information into it guided by the software tool.

8.6.1. Elicited Concepts with the Aim of Fault Diagnosis

The concepts' representation involves a combination of models presented above and concisely noted below, along with their role and use:

a) *Means-end* modelling of hierarchical structures for the multifunctional aspect:

   i. role – identifies deep knowledge on physical and functional structures (components and simplified functions, modules and ends);

   ii. use – define behavioural patterns at faults based on proposed primary flow functions.

b) *Discrete event* modelling of the running context for the multifunctional aspect:

   i. role – identifies deep knowledge on activities toward ends of modules;

   ii. use – determines current activity of a module and its time limits.

c) *Bond-graph* modelling of components for the flow conduction aspect:

   i. role – identifies deep knowledge on flow conduction as bond-graph junctions and components;

        ii. use – associates functions to bond-graph components and generic anomalies observing effects propagation.

d) *Qualitative* modelling of concepts and relations for the faulty behaviour:

        i. role – describes deep knowledge on faulty behaviour: faults (at component level), symptoms (as generic anomalies), observations and manifestations (with prototype and instance attributes);

        ii. use – detects faults (by instance manifestations and symptoms) and hierarchically isolate faults (at module and then component levels) by recognizing cause-effects as from deep and shallow knowledge of human diagnosticians.

The models follow the human expert's common view on diagnosis: items a and b cover the discrete view on the structure and the behaviour in normal situations, while item d covers the discrete view on the behaviour in faulty situations. Item c. covers the continuous view on fault effects propagation by flow conduction. The paper proposes a qualitative view on faulty behaviour of components and a procedure to assert primary effects from the propagated (secondary) effects.

The data on real running of the target system have a close representation to the human diagnostician's view, through:

e) *Fuzzy logic* – for the "intelligent encoding" of observations to manifestations:

        i. role – encodes "prototype manifestations" as meaningful intervals according to the deep knowledge of human diagnostician;

        ii. use – obtains "instance manifestations" from the actual values collected from sensors during installation running.

The diagnosis follows modular and incremental procedures, carried out by:

f) *Inference engine* – for fault detection and sequential diagnostic refinement:

        i. role – detects abnormal behaviour (symptoms) and sequentially performs diagnosis for temporal sliding windows and for newly observed variables;

        ii. use – locates a transport anomaly at module level, then starts the neural network recognition process for further fault isolation.

g) *Artificial Neural Networks* – for recognition of the faults:

        i. role – embeds shallow knowledge from practice and experiments as links between manifestations and symptoms to faults;

        ii. use – isolates faults by recognizing patterns of manifestations and anomalies.

The diagnostic is obtained by recognizing patterns of manifestations and symptoms associated with faults. Items e to g are computational models that emulate the human diagnostician's way of acting, and directly embed human concepts in their native form. The diagnosis proceeds incrementally, following the sequence of activities of the modules during the target system's running and adding new observation meant to refine the diagnostic.

The knowledge pieces for diagnosis involve a large amount of data that should enter the diagnosis expert system (Patton *et al.*, 2000). Each concept addresses a set of specific information:

- module – name, ends, activities, specific set of components, up-stream relations to neighbour modules, junctions and signatures for each   transport anomaly identification, nonspecific observations (e.g., mud);
- activities – code, next activity, time limits;
- component – name, primary flow function and bond-graph component for each activity of the host module, set of specific faults, component and module located manifestations;
- fault – name, (deep knowledge) links from manifestations and anomalies of the flow function in the host component, abductive relations to causes from the target system or environment, (shallow knowledge) links from other manifestations in the host module;
- manifestation – name, source type (sensor or human operator observations), prototype attributes and ranges of values (specific to the activity of the host module), abductive relations to causes;
- anomaly – type (*AnoP, AnoS, AnoT*), host component or module, end parameters values for abnormal behaviour, etc.

Knowledge elicitation will provide data for building the structures of ANN blocks (e.g., data on layers of neurons for manifestations and faults, for the abductive links between them, for training with patterns). Knowledge elicitation provides data for the inference engine of the diagnosis expert system: the series of activities for each module, order of 0-junction for which signatures of neighbour modules identify the transport anomaly, etc.

The knowledge pieces enter the Knowledge Base for consistency checking and for storing concrete data in the appropriate representation. After elicitation, the training of ANN blocks follows, then the diagnosis expert may be generated as a dedicated software for the given target MCFS.

All knowledge pieces, presented in previous sections, are specific knowledge structures that the CAKE tool deals with. The structures refer, for example, to the physical and functional units of the target system, to the systems interconnected with the targeted one, to all situations that may disturb or originate faulty situations.

The feasibility condition, meant for the computational model of the fault diagnosis system, is to assure closed spaces for causes and effects. Abnormal behaviours are not only caused by faults at components but also by any other abnormal situation inside the target system or coming from outside. To cope with such cases, the concept of *disorder* is introduced. Disorder refers to any cause that will induce an abnormal situation: human operator mishandling (e.g., ill tuning, infringement of technological rules, etc.), ill state of matter or energy flows (e.g., the quality), abnormal conditions in the environment (e.g., too hot or too cold), and negative influences from the neighbour systems.

Fault diagnosis deals with various aspects of the target system, each of them identified as a subsystem:

a) *Physical Subsystem* – refers to all physical units (e.g., modules and components) and hierarchical structures (e.g., the whole installation and the modules) as means for achieving the ends of the system. Regarding the diagnosis, they represent the locations for faults.

b) *Functional Subsystem* – refers to all functional units (primary flow functions) and hierarchical structures (process phases and activities), which actually achieve the ends of the system. Regarding the diagnosis, they represent locations for the behavioural aspects of the target system.

c) *Behavioural Subsystem* – refers to all concepts related to the abnormal running of the target system: observations, manifestations, symptoms and faults, along with their links.

d) *Operational Subsystem* – refers to the human operator actions that may provoke an abnormal situation.

e) *Flow Subsystem(s)* – all types of matter or energy flow that may induce abnormal situations (e.g., the "foaming oil" in a hydraulic installation).

f) *Environment* – refers to all systems out of the diagnosis contour (i.e. the target system): the ambient atmosphere, the mounting conditions, and the neighbour systems.

All knowledge pieces become entities related to each other that should be indicated by the knowledge engineer and should enter the computational model for fault diagnosis, as further presented. The structures of knowledge pieces are further presented in the entity-relationship diagrams that follow.

8.6.2. Elicitation Aspects on Normative and Faulty Models

The normative model consists of physical and functional structures that support the ends' achievement. They comprise entities specific to their corresponding subsystems, presented in the previous sections.

The diagrams in Figures 8.7 and 8.8 are UML representations of entities relations elicited for the corresponding subsystems. Having in mind fault diagnosis, in each diagram will appear the two entities *Disorder* and *Fault* – the last inheriting the first one. The dashed ellipses indicate borders of the other subsystems.

8.6.2.1. The Physical Subsystem

The entities involved in the Physical Subsystem are `Component` (the entire set *C*), `Module` (the entire set *M*), and `Installation`; all of them are locations of faults. However, there are disorders that may produce similar effects as faults, which are located in other systems (Flow, Operational or Neighbour systems).

The discrimination of the physical units proceeds from the means-end view (as MFS) and from the bond-graph view (as CFS), following the hierarchy of physical/functional units. For each flow type u_t, the knowledge engineer should assert the end of the modules, then the primary flow functions of the comprised components along with the associated bond-graph generic component. So,

- Modules – result from ends (and activities) accomplished towards products / services achieved, and correspond to bond-graph 1-junctions.
- Components – result from primary flow functions completed in each activity, and correspond to certain bond-graph components.

Fault *isolation granularity* is the extent of the decomposition of the physical structures into components, hence the cardinality of C. The fault isolation granularity reflects human diagnostician's troubleshooting pragmatism regarding the sufficient location of disorders for their removal; it also reflects the incompleteness of human knowledge on physical structures and on the environment. Usually, a component may exhibit more faults, so C induces a disjunctive partitioning over F.

The discrimination of physical components – sufficient for fault isolation – follows the hierarchical structure of the target system, and proceeds to a combined decomposition observing the physical and the functional structures:

i.   from the entire Installation – which is also the whole Process,

ii.   decomposition proceeds to Modules – each referring to a Subprocess with two or more Activities,

iii. then each Activity is decomposed in primary Flow Functions – each being attached to a Component.

The relations between entities – with the corresponding multiplicity attached to each relation – are illustrated in Figure 8.7 and they represent:

- Association «loc» (located to) directs to the location of the Disorder;
- Dependency «evo» (evokes) directs to the anomaly evoked by the Disorder;
- Inheritance Fault from Disorder;
- Composition of Component to Module, and to Installation.

The physical units (in the physical structures) present hierarchical relations and also upstream >> (strong) and ≥≥ (weak) relations, depending on the bond-graph junction the physical units enter. Upstream and downstream relations appear in the diagrams representing the bond-graph junctions of the target system, for each combination of activities of the participating modules, and for the components inside the module. While specific, those diagrams are not shown here.

8.6.2.2. The Functional Subsystem

The functional structure is also a hierarchical structure: activities (of each module) comprise flow functions (of each component) and each flow function is linked to a specific faulty behaviour. All knowledge on physical and functional structures is deep knowledge, while it comes from human experts' acquaintance with the domain and with the design issues of the target MCFS.

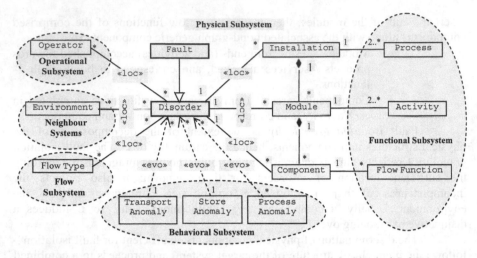

Figure 8.7.   The UML diagram for entities and relations of the Physical Subsystem.

The entities of the Functional Subsystem are: `Process` and `Subprocess` (as general concepts related to the running of the whole `Installation` and of each `Module`). `Activity` is defined in Section 8.4.1.1, and – from the means-end point of view – corresponds to the network of flow functions for the components that leads to a certain (processing) end of the module. The `Process phase` is the current set of activities existing at a moment during the whole installation running. The `Operational Mode` indicates a state of the `Component` that leads to a primary flow function or to another, depending on the control action meant for the components (e.g., valve is open or shut). The fact that a `Disorder` depends on the `Activity` it appears, is represented by the constraint {and} upon the respective relations (note that {} stands for {and}, reduced because of the limited space).

8.6.2.3. The Behavioural Subsystem

The human diagnostician's view on manifestations and symptoms concerns:
> i) deviations of the observed variables from the expected ("normal") values – where observations may refer to ends, effort and flow variables, linguistic values from human operator;
> ii) deviations of functions that lead to abnormal ends – anomalies in the end's accomplishment, in the flow store or flow transport;
> iii) propagation of the effects from the fault location – deviations of flow variables appear as primary effects (transport anomalies) and provoke secondary effects.

Entities on the faulty behaviour come from the deep knowledge of human experts in the domain and on the target MCFS, as presented in Section 8.5.

The relation «evo» indicate that a `Manifestation` evokes a `Disorder`, while «rev» indicates that an `Observation` reveals a `Manifestation`.

The {and} constraints between respective dependencies and associations indicate that the `Disorder` is specific to the `Anomaly` *and* the `Activity` that appear.

A causal relation that has an explanation represents deep knowledge. Relations that come from experiments or practice represent shallow knowledge that is embedded in the Artificial Neural Network (ANN) blocks. Shallow knowledge is embedded into the diagnosis expert system during the training procedures, based on known patterns acquired from practice (off line) or from experiments (on-line).

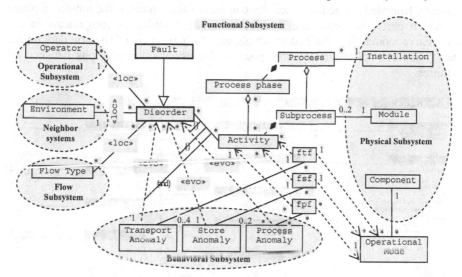

Figure 8.8. The UML diagram for entities and relations of the Functional Subsystem.

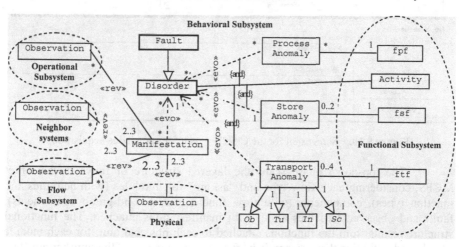

Figure 8.9. The UML diagram for entities and relations of the Behavioural Subsystem.

8.6.3. The CAKE Tool

Knowledge elicitation and knowledge acquisition are assisted by the Computer Aided Knowledge Elicitation (CAKE) software tool, which actually replaces the knowledge engineer who is involved in the design and implementation of the diagnosis expert system (Ariton and Baciu, 2002).

Knowledge elicitation proceeds by asking the operator about entities, values and relations, namely, on specific concepts of the subsystems in the target system. Knowledge elicitation activity consists of three phases: the top-down phase – which performs means-end discrimination of modules to components in the normative model, then the bottom-up phase – for collection of specific data on the faulty model, and finally the join phase – for establishing relations between all entities.

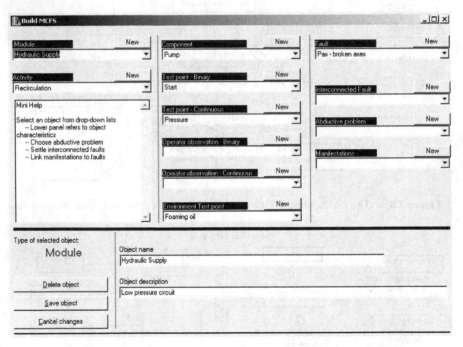

Figure 8.10. Screenshot for the CAKE screen for knowledge acquisition.

The top-down phase scans the layered structure of flows in the target MCFS, considering each flow type and "asking" for: modules (with activities and junction types), components (with flow functions and bond-graph components), faults and observed variables along with manifestations attached. The functional structure results from the functions attached to each physical unit: for each module – ends and activities they accomplish, for each component – the appropriate flow functions and the corresponding bond-graph generic component for each activity.

The bottom-up phase scans in the reversed order the physical and the functional structures, attaches faults to components, performs intelligent encoding of manifestations, attaches manifestations to appropriate faults (from the shallow knowledge), and finally attaches anomalies to faults (from the deep knowledge).

The join phase puts together the existing modules in the respective bond-graph junctions (as from deep knowledge), attaches signatures to each junction, and indicates specific tasks for the inference engine (e.g., the order of bond-graph junctions to scan for transport anomalies).

The knowledge acquisition in the three phases refers to all knowledge pieces and relations for the target MCFS. The information is stored in the CAKE tool's Knowledge Base, which is specific to the target system. This way, data are prepared for the generation of a dedicated diagnosis application. Figure 8.10 shows a screenshot of the CAKE tool for MCFS building involved in the second phase.

The result of the knowledge acquisition is the complete description of the target system as text and data stored in the knowledge base. Following the text description and the knowledge base, the CAKE tool generates the code for a dedicated diagnosis expert system. The "Fault Isolation" (neural) blocks are later trained with faults-manifestations and faults-symptoms patterns, based on previously collected data from practice and/or experiments.

8.7. Fault Diagnosis System by Abduction

As already shown, the human diagnostician combines deep and shallow knowledge on the target system, and then isolates faults following hierarchical decomposition and incremental procedures in refining the diagnostic (i.e., finally locating the fault). The deep knowledge is more compact and it rapidly reduces the searching space based on laws from the domain ("explanations"). However, deep knowledge captures only general causal links and hardly refers to the diversity of effects and causes in the real running. So, shallow knowledge comes to describe the detailed behaviour in the uncertain and incomplete context of the complex real system.

8.7.1. Diagnosis Expert System's Structure

In Figure 8.11 is depicted the block structure of the Diagnosis Expert system and the place of the CAKE tool – which, actually, is not part of the diagnosis system. The diagnosis approach mainly focuses the knowledge regarding the faulty behaviour of the target MCFS, while knowledge regarding the normative model is only meant for the physical and the functional structures that will support the behavioural model in locating anomalies and faults.

All knowledge enters the "Knowledge Base" block, which in the proposed approach is simply a data base, while the normative and the faulty models are sets of behavioural units with parameters and links between them.

The "Knowledge Base" is the central block of the diagnosis expert system; data structures come from the "Knowledge elicitation" block (the CAKE tool included).

The actual data (values) come from the "Target MCFS" through the "Data acquisition and pre-processing" block which performs scanning, sampling and intelligent encoding of data from sensors and from human operators; data channels are depicted as ⇨ in Figure 8.11.

The "Incremental diagnosis" block is the inference engine of the expert system; it controls the other blocks through control channels (depicted as simple arrows → in Figure 8.11). The inference engine's tasks are presented in Section 8.7.2.3.

The "Fault isolation" blocks are Artificial Neural Networks (ANN) dedicated and trained each for a given module faults recognition, based on patterns of manifestations and anomalies. The ANN blocks are connectionist models for abduction of faults from effects that embed deep knowledge on "abductive problems" of causes and effects (see (Ariton and Palade, 2004)), and also shallow knowledge on effects-to-causes pattern relations.

The "Human operator interface" block interacts with the human operator by asking and providing operator observations to "Data acquisition and pre-processing" block (arrow ∿ in Figure 8.11) and displays the diagnostic.

The "Knowledge elicitation and acquisition" block provides the knowledge (see ⇨ in Figure 8.11) for the "Knowledge Base" block, prototype manifestations for the "Data acquisition and pre-processing" block and faults-manifestations patterns for the ANN blocks. The "Knowledge elicitation and acquisition" is the CAKE tool (see Section 8.6) and it is actually the subject of the present work.

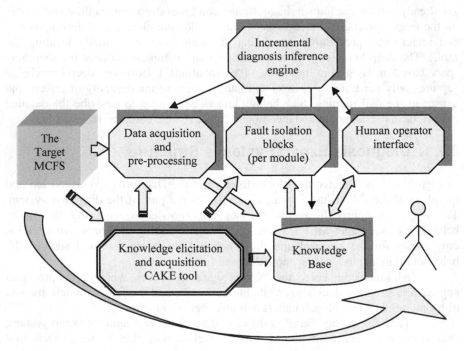

Figure 8.11.   Diagnosis expert system and the place of the CAKE tool.

8.7.2. Modular and Incremental Diagnosis

Diagnosis proceeds by locating faults hierarchically, like the human diagnostician does:

- first discriminating the module with a transport anomaly,
- then recognizing fault(s) inside the module.

The transport anomaly is detected using signatures of manifestations on effort and flow variables at each module's input/outputs – see Table 8.3 – which leads to isolation of the faulty module. The existence of the transport anomaly is a confirmation of the faulty state and valuable information for further isolation of the concrete faults inside the module.

At the module level, it is possible to proceed the same way, i.e., to locate the faulty component detecting it by signatures of power variables' deviations. However, it is hardly the case that effort and flow are measured at every component in real installations. So, at the module level, fault isolation is performed by recognizing "pattern faults" from "pattern manifestations and symptoms," based on a dedicated ANN block provided for the module.

8.7.2.1. Parallel Processing for Modular Diagnosis

Manifestations (i.e., *lo, no, hi* linguistic values at the observed variables) and symptoms (i.e., process, store and transport anomalies) are input neurons and the faults are the output neurons of the ANN. All concepts have the appropriate representations as presented above: discrete (i.e., linguistic) knowledge and logical meanings (i.e., truth values). This way, the abductive reasoning of the human diagnostician may be described by the connectionist model proposed in Section 8.2.3.

The main advantage of the presented connectionist approach in diagnosis is the embedding of the human diagnostician's shallow knowledge by ANN training, using manifestations-to-faults patterns as from the actual behaviour of each module in the target system. It is worth mentioning that it is unrealistic to use a unique ANN block for an entire real system, while it deals with enormous numbers of combined causes and training patterns. By using the modular approach presented, the combination of manifestations-to-faults patterns is drastically reduced, and the fact that the human expert's shallow knowledge usually refers to the module level, even experiments on site or in laboratory conditions are conducted at the module level.

8.7.2.2. Testing Policy as an Abduction Problem Solving

The testing policy aims to indicate the best next test the result of which allows the optimal diagnostic refining, in other words the shortest path (as steps) to the diagnostic.

The "next best test problem" can be formulated as an abduction problem, and it can be solved in the same way as the diagnosis itself, i.e., as a connectionist implementation of plausibility and relevance of the next test to follow. Testing is performed stepwise, and takes part of the sequential diagnostic refinement.

The testing procedure requires human operator observations, but only a few are useful given the current situations (faults occurred, process phase, etc.), and given the entire set *OM* of human observed manifestations (see Section 8.3.3.3).

The current set of instance manifestations used at the training phase of the ANN block includes those observed by human senses (or portable measurement devices) and they should be provided as required at the time of diagnosis. In reverse, the embedded knowledge may be used to find out which is the plausible and relevant observation that the human operator should supply to advance the optimal diagnosis.

In this way, the next best test is obtained as the solution of the abduction problem solving, using plausible and relevance criteria as follows:

- *plausibility(P_CRITERIA, EFFECTS, CAUSES)* – whose outcome is the set of operator-observed manifestations *OM* (hence variables to be tested), based on the set of manifestations joined with the set of plausible faults obtained at the current step in the diagnosis.
- *relevance(R_CRITERIA, OM)* – whose outcome is the set of relevant operator observations out of the plausible ones, that satisfy *R_CRITERIA*.

The abduction problem is solved by means of a neural network implementation, and indicates the most plausible and relevant operator observation (if the competition is strict), or a set of observations (if the competition is relaxed), for which the human operator will supply data.

8.7.2.3. Incremental Processing for the Diagnostic Refining

The inference engine of the expert system with the same name, sequentially and repeatedly fulfills the following tasks:

i) Start data acquisition from the Target MCFS by means of the "Data acquisition and pre-processing" block, which also performs the „intelligent encoding."

ii) Identify the activities of all modules, during the current process phase (note that a process phase lasts between any two transitions of activities for any of the modules entering the same 0-junction).

iii) Detect faults – by identifying process and store anomalies.

iv) Detect transport anomalies and the faulty module – by identifying signatures of manifestations of effort and flow variables from Table 8.3.

v) Isolate fault(s) inside the faulty module(s), by means of manifestations and anomalies patterns, applied at the inputs of "Fault isolation block per module"; recognize fault using the dedicated ANN for the module.

vi) Evaluate the truth value of the "faulty" state versus the "normal" state for the entire target system.

vii) If "faulty" is greater than "normal" but no diagnostic exists (i.e., truth value of all activated faults is under a given threshold) ask human operator for additional observations and go to step i.

viii) If a diagnostic exists ("normal" and "unknown" included) and no further additional observations requested, display the diagnostic.

The inference engine cycle is standard but embedded knowledge and data are specific to the target system under the diagnosis.

8.7.3. Aspects of the Sequential Diagnosis

In the presented approach, sequential diagnosis involves three aspects:

a) Abduction by plausibility and relevance proceeds stepwise: first, plausible causes are obtained through feed-forward activations according to instance manifestations; second, the relevant faults are discriminated from the relevance groups, each group as a specific modularisation of faults, one modularisation applied at a time.

b) Process phases arise one after another, each process phase exhibiting specific plausibility criteria; consequently, the connectionist abduction is performed according to the (expected) current process phase.

c) Additional observations required from and supplied by human operator get into the diagnosis system, until no test is required – i.e., until the diagnostic is obtained (even if it is "no fault" or "unknown fault").

For aspects a and b above, an example of sequential diagnosis is presented in the previous section; item c refers to the next best test policy formulated as an abduction problem, and solved by plausibility and relevance implemented by neural networks. Note that "unknown fault" that occurs in the real running is finally decided by the human operator of the diagnosis system – when a faulty situation exists but no diagnostic provided.

8.7.3.1. Diagnosis by Plausibility and Relevance Criteria Sequentially Applied

Let us consider the diagnosis performed for a process phase P. After applying the plausibility criteria $P\_CRITERIA$ upon the set of $EFFECTS$, the set F^* of all plausible causes is deducted (i.e., the set comprising all causes with a positive activation). The "mass activation" of plausible faults is, by notation, ΣF_i, as given in Eq. 23, where F^* is the set of plausible causes.

$$\Sigma F_i = \sum_{F^*} F_i = \sum_{F} F_i \qquad (23)$$

The sum is performed over the set F^* of plausible causes but it actually is the same if performed over the entire set F of causes, while nonplausible causes exhibit zero activation. So, the computational procedure always deals with the entire set F of causes, hence simple implementation.

Applying the relevance criteria $R\_CRITERIA$ upon the set of $CAUSES$ will increase the activation of a plausible and relevant cause F_i^*, according to the layer's weight W^L (see Section 8.2.5.2). The increase will affect the numerical value of F_i^*, according to the mass activation ΣF_i of all faults and to the weight W^L of the current modularisation layer:

$$\Delta F_i^* = W^L \cdot \frac{F_i}{\sum_i F_i} \tag{24}$$

In the proposed approach, the order of the relevance criteria applied is important, because the activation mass changes accordingly. The best order is the one of increasing weights W^L, so the activation mass $\sum F_i$ is updated only once, before the current layer processing. Each layer induces a graded increase of respective cause(s) activation, the last layer of modularisation inducing the highest increase.

After applying all relevance criteria, the relevance of faulty situation is determined (see Section 8.2.5.3) and the diagnostic is issued as the most relevant causes resulted, including faults with activation over the doubt level.

8.7.3.2. Testing Policy by Plausibility and Relevance Criteria Sequentially Applied

The next test is required after each diagnostic obtained. The diagnosis system "asks" the human operator to provide a certain variable value; he or she supplies the value, and so diagnosis based on plausibility and relevance restarts.

The most plausible and relevant operator-observed variable(s), for the given situation, result as an abduction problem solving according to Section 8.2.3. The next best observation (i.e., test) is indicated by the ANN block provided for each module, based on current faults and instance manifestations activated.

Now, the activation of plausible fault F_i^* changes according to new manifestations provided and, additionally, the activation is affected by the weight W^O attached to the operator-observed variable provided at the current step:

$$\Delta F_i^* = W^O \cdot \frac{F_i}{\sum_i F_i} \tag{25}$$

The human diagnostician sets up weights for the operator-observed manifestations according to the deep knowledge in the domain, provided $\sum W^O = 1$ for the set of operator-observed manifestations in the relevance group. The human operator supplies the observed values (manifestations) in the reverse order of weights W^O. That is, the values of the most important variables are provided first.

In the economy of the diagnosis by next best test, the most important role is played by Eq. 11, which starts the next test procedure if the *FAULTY* situation prevails over the *NORMAL* one. It is possible to stop asking for new operator-observed variables if a predefined faulty situation threshold is surpassed, e.g.,

$$\frac{\sum_{i=0}^{n-1} F_i}{n \cdot F_n} > \alpha \tag{26}$$

where $\alpha = 9$ means that the faulty situation is 90% certain as the normal one.

8.7.4. Neural Network Architecture for Diagnosis and Testing

The neural network architecture for diagnosis using a testing policy comprises two neural networks, each dedicated to the abduction problem solving: one for the diagnosis – DNN (Diagnosis Neural Network), the other for indicating the next observations to be made – TNN (new Test Neural Network), as shown in Figure 8.12.

Both neural network blocks contain feed-forward links for plausibility, between the input and the output neurons; for DNN, between input neurons of the type *OM* (Operator-observed Manifestations), *MM* (permanent Monitored Manifestations), *SY* (SYmptoms detected) and output neurons *F* (Faults); for TNN, between *F* (Faults) and *OM* (Operator-required Manifestations – identical as set with the Operator-observed Manifestations set). Forward links are represented as arrows between input and output layers of neurons, and competition links are represented by horizontal arrows between the output neurons (*F* and *OM*, respectively).

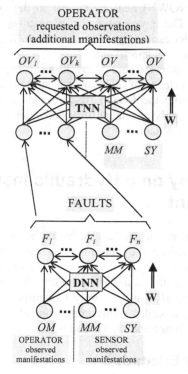

Figure 8.12. Neural network architecture for fault diagnosis by abduction, with additional observations from human operator.

The input of the DNN block consists of permanent observed manifestations *MM* and operator-observed manifestations *OM* – the last ones passing through the network as long as they are triggered and supplied by the operator. Plausible faults at the output of the DNN block become inputs of the TNN block, along with the current manifestations *MM*, to produce most plausible and relevant observations to be tested by the human operator. The entire set of neuron outputs of the DNN block are passed to the input of the TNN block, while only plausible faults get activated and count for the abduction towards the next test indicated to the operator.

Diagnosis proceeds stepwise. At each step, the observations become first manifestations by "intelligent encoding," then most plausible and relevant faults result by abduction at the output of the DNN block, along with required operator-observed variables indicated at the output of the TNN block. The set of most plausible and relevant faults at each step is a partial result with attached values of *FAULTY* and *NORMAL* situations, as from Eq. 14. The final diagnostic is obtained when the *FAULTY* situation surpasses a given threshold and no operator observations are required. Depending on the number of relevant faults resulting from competition, single or multiple fault diagnosis is in concern.

The "closed world assumption" is satisfied if all situations that may appear during the diagnosis have a result; hence the "no fault" (NORMAL) as well as "unknown fault" (UNKNOWN) neurons appear in the output layer of the DNN neural network block. The processing for plausibility and relevance roughly corresponds to general phases in diagnostic reasoning: "hypotheses generation" and "hypotheses discrimination," respectively.

The neural network is the core of the diagnosis expert system, and it deposits the deep and shallow knowledge of the human diagnostician. The way the diagnosis proceeds also complies with the human diagnostician's way of acting, i.e., it is performed sequentially, applying plausibility and relevance criteria step by step, until the final diagnostic is obtained.

8.8.   Case Study on a Hydraulic Installation in a Rolling Mill Plant

The case study is performed on the simple hydraulic installation shown in Figure 8.13. It comprises two hydraulic cylinders (for a carrier and a brake), two control valves, the mineral oil tank, the pump with a pressure valve, and two long pipes. To master the complexity of the installation under diagnosis, the installation was divided into modules: the Hydraulic supply (containing tank, pump and pressure valve) and two driving modules (containing control valve, cylinder, damper – Drossel) – the Hydraulic brake and the Hydraulic conveyor.

8.8.1. Knowledge Elicitation

The information regarding the physical and the behavioural subsystems consists of knowledge pieces presented in Table 8.4. The whole set of disorders considered consists of: faults, the *NORMAL* situation, and the nonconformities at flow, human operator and neighbour systems.

For each component, the numbers of faults are: 2 at the tank, 4 at the pump, 3 at the pressure valve, 2 at the pipes, 3×2 at the control valves, 2 at the damper, 2×2 at the cylinders.

There exist 6 disorders that refer to nonconformities: 2 for the mineral oil (i.e., "too many suspensions" and "foamy oil"), 1 at the environment ("too hot"), 3 for operating errors (Olu "no oil in the tank" – see below, "carrier load too heavy," "pump velocity ill tuned"). So, the disorders consist of 23+1 faults ($NORMAL$ added), and 6 nonconformities, i.e., $|F| = 30$.

Line 4 in Table 8.4 shows the types of manifestations and the number of data according to the activities in line 2; for example, the number of the fuzzy attributes for the Supply module is (6 variables)·(3 landmarks)·(2 activities) = 36 manifestations of type lo, no, hi.

The measured manifestations refer to $|MM| = 48$ pieces that are variables expressed as single neurons (for the binary variables), or triple neurons (for the continuous variables with lo, no, hi attributes), each neuron with a graded value of truth. The observed variables come from analogical sensors for 2 input/output flow-rates, 3 input/output/damper pressures, 4 temperatures (control valves, pump and tank), from contacts for 4 operator commands (brake on/off, carrier on/off), for 5 positions (of type left/right, open/shut) of the two pistons and of the pressure valve. The 4 durations of the pistons' movements (left/right – for the two cylinders) enter also as measured manifestations.

In the set of the $|OM| = 14$ operator-observed variables, there are 5 of type "noise" (2 for the pump, 3 for the pressure and the control valves), 6 "oil leakage" (all except the damper) and also there are 3 anomalies outside the hydraulic system (brake/carrier mechanical blockage, no pump power).

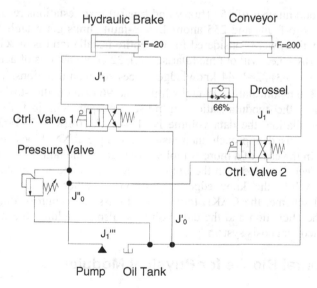

Figure 8.13. Hydraulic installation under elicitation case study.

Running contexts of the target hydraulic installation refer to each discrete position or motion of the pistons in the two cylinders, as well as to the two states of the control valve. So, we find the activities for each of the three modules: 2 activities for the supply module and 4 activities for each driving module. The total number of process phases is 2+4×4=18. Even for such a simple installation, the numbers of process phases is quite large, provided that for each of them the knowledge engineer should develop experiments to assess the specific manifestations and their links to faults, hence plausibility criteria and the DNN block training. Instead, each module's specific behaviour was studied separately when faulty. The simulated faults and the manifestations that had appeared were collected for each separate module, concerning only the 2 activities of the supply module and the 4 activities of each driving module, respectively.

Table 8.4.   Inventory of the knowledge pieces involved in the fault diagnosis

Module / Entity	Hydraulic Supply	Hydraulic Brake	Hydraulic Conveyor
1. Components	pump, tank, pressure valve, pipes	control valve, cylinder	control valve, self, cylinder
2. Activities / Faults	2 / 11	4 / 5	4 / 7
3. Sensors (observed variables)	Analogical 6, Digital 7	Analogical 5, Digital 8	Analogical 3, Digital 8
4. Manifestations	Fuzzy 6·3·2, Binary 7·2	Fuzzy 5·3·4, Binary 8·2	Fuzzy 3·3·4, Binary 8·2
5. AnoP, AnoS, AnoT	2, 1, 4	2, 2, 4	2, 2, 4

A total number of 155 (fuzzy and binary) manifestations result, hence 888 manifestations-to-faults and 255 anomalies-to-faults links get established. If faults and manifestations were considered for the entire installation (as in "classic" ANN-based diagnosis – i.e., without modularisation), 32 combinations of activities result, hence (6·3+5·3+3·3)·32=1344 knowledge pieces for manifestations, which require 30·1344=40320 manifestation-to-faults links, and 9600 anomalies-to-faults links.

Using the modularisation in presented approach, just for the simple hydraulic installation, the data volume is (1344+40320)/(888+255)=36 times less for the modularised approach than using a unique ANN block for the entire installation. In the case of a more complex installation, the ratio is much bigger, and embedding deep knowledge in the links between faults and manifestations is quite impossible. While the knowledge acquisition is rather difficult even for the modularised scheme, the CAKE tool comes to assist the human diagnostician in managing the elicitation and the data volumes, also in yielding the data structures for a dedicated diagnosis system.

8.8.2. Neural Blocks for Physical Modules

The diagnosis was meant for three distinct process phases, namely, the one with the control valve open (for faults at the supply module) and those with moving pistons (for the two driving modules). No symptoms were considered on the installation behaviour. The faults–to-manifestations patterns, used in the training of the DNN and TNN neural network blocks for each module, were partly acquired from human diagnostician practice, partly from experiments.

Again, the modularisation represents an advantage in the implementation of the diagnosis system. So, instead of considering the process phases for the whole installation as the running contexts (which determine the specific faulty behaviour), it is now possible to consider only the activities of modules interconnected in the same bond-graph junction. Furthermore, the neural sites for the abduction problems were easier to build separately for each module.

The structure of the neural network block for the supply module is depicted in Figure 8.14, where:

- Faults are: *Pax* (pump – axis broken), *Pai* (pump – clogged admission), *Pne* (pump – ill joints), *Puz* (pump – worn out), *Tne* (tank – worn-out filter);
- Manifestations are: *P1* (oil pressure at the tank outlet: "too low" *lo*, "too high" *hi*), *D1* (oil flow rate at the tank outlet: "too low" *lo*, "too high" *hi*), *T2* (oil temperature "high" in the tank);
- Manifestations requested from the human operator are: *Z1* (whistling noise at pump), *Z2* (jerky noise at pump), *M1* (oil mud at pump), *M2* (oil mud at tank);
- Nonconformities from flow and from human operator: *Uim* (dirty oil), *Usp* (foaming oil), *Olu* (tank empty), *Otm* (pump angular velocity ill tuned).

As shown in Figure 8.14, there are two monotonic faults (*Pne* and *Puz*), two monotonic operator-observed variables (*Z1* and *Uim*), and two conjunction sites (for *Pax* and *Otm*). The negation sites for operator-observed variables prevent further demand of the variables already requested and supplied.

8.8.3. Plausibility and Relevance

For each running context, the plausibility links between faults and manifestations were set up according to the human diagnostician's deep knowledge, but also systematically linking all manifestations to faults in a module.

The neural network model used for the DNN and TNN blocks is the perceptron; it supports the feed-forward plausibility criteria with modified structure, suited to abduction problem solving (see Figure 8.14).

Plausibility criteria refer to different abduction problems implemented as neural sites and to trained faults-to-manifestations patterns from simulated experiments, on each target module, for fault, "normal" and "unknown" cases.

Competition is added over the set of fault neurons regarding the following relevance grouping:

1. faults at the same component (physical structure scope) – minimum cardinality criterion;
2. faults which are obvious only in specific activities of the respective module (e.g., control valves "blocked parallel" and "blocked crossed" are obvious only when the piston is moving in the hydraulic cylinder);

3. faults in the module provoking leakage and those provoking clogged symptoms for mineral oil flow.

For each functional module i, it corresponds to a neural network module with two blocks, DNN^i and TNN^i. Additional relevance criteria discriminate between the diagnostics at module level, in order to issue the diagnostic at the level of the whole installation. The relevance criteria at installation level are based on symptoms and on Eq. 11; the relevance criterion of minimum cardinality was considered.

The training of the neural network block DNN^1 (associated with module 1 – the oil supply module presented above) is performed using the standard learning algorithm for the perceptron. The NORMAL situation for the entire supply module is trained using normal values (see Figure 8.15): no for P1 and D1, and normal states of the other manifestations. The UNKNOWN situation is trained by means of patterns, randomly generated but consistent with those used for plausibility of faults and the normal situation.

As it is difficult to gather all the necessary details for the NN structures for all modules, a CAKE (Computer Aided Knowledge Elicitation) instrument was build and used to describe and automatically generate the DNN and TNN structures at the module level.

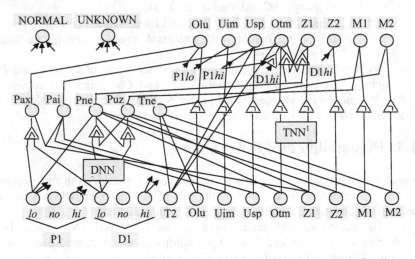

Figure 8.14.   The neural network structure for the first (oil supply) module for diagnosis.

8.8.4. Sequential Diagnosis for the Supply Module

Figure 8.16 illustrates the four steps in which the diagnosis regarding the supply module is performed, with respect to a fault that occurred in the pump, namely, *Pai* (short name for the fault "oil tank pipe is clogged"). Each window shows a step during the diagnosis refinement, including the partial diagnostic and the operator-observed variables required from the human operator. For the simulated fault – marked by x – the diagnostic is obtained in four steps, after eliminating other causes

– see in the third window *Olu* (short name for the non-conformity "oil tank empty").

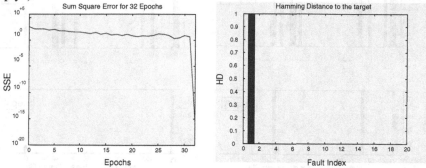

Figure 8.15. Training of the NORMAL situation for the oil supply module, in 32 epochs.

The Y axis indicates the truth value of a specific item from the X axis, which shows discrete knowledge pieces from 0 to 50.

The three sections of the X axis represent: the 31 disorders mentioned above, the 6 nonconformities (in the section "Non-cf"), and the 14 observations needed from the human operator. Faults' truth values, as resulted from the diagnosis, are indicated as bars at the index position of each fault (0 to 30).

The 6 nonconformities and the 14 operator-observed manifestations are also indicated as bars, but their meaning is now a demand to the human operator, i.e., a confirmation required for a possible nonconformity indicated as a bar, or a value required from the operator for the observed variable indicated as a bar, at its specific index on X axis. As a response, the human operator has to indicate if that environment nonconformity is present, or the current value for the operator-observed variable, respectively. In the sections for nonconformities and for operator observations, the height of a bar indicates how stringent is the respective item, so the human operator may choose the highest one(s) for supplying the confirmation or the value.

Additional observations required from the human operator in the current step appear in the *Non-cf.* section and in the *Operator Observations* section on the X axis. The window in each step shows the current diagnostic. Activated observations from the human operator decrease to 0 after the value is supplied.

The diagnostic is strongly dependent on the coverage of faulty behaviours for each module with faults or classes of faults. The data on the behaviour of the hydraulic installation come from simulated experiments. The diagnosis system always produced a diagnostic in a finite number of steps, and the average accuracy of the diagnosis was 96%. Additional observations supplied by the human operator require some steps in the diagnostic refinement that hinders real-time diagnosis.

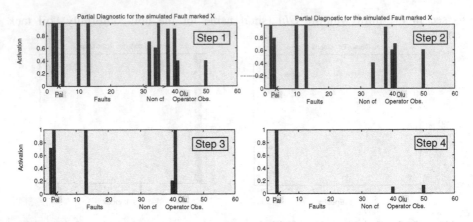

Figure 8.16.   Sequential diagnosis in 4 steps for the fault *Pai*, with additional Operator Observations.

8.9.   Conclusions

Fault diagnosis of complex systems involves deep and shallow knowledge of human diagnosticians, since diagnosis in the reallife deals with incomplete, imprecise and uncertain knowledge on the behaviour of target systems. The aim of the chapter is to describe a diagnostic system that emulates the human diagnostician's way of acting, in order to build dedicated diagnosis systems for concrete target systems. The automated fault diagnosis is based on computational intelligence models: fuzzy and possibilistic logic, artificial neural networks.

The chapter focuses on the fault diagnosis of artefacts often met in industry (and not only), that executes more functions at the same time based on conductive flows of matter and energy, i.e., multifunctional conductive flow systems (MCFSs). The proposed MCFS abstraction is close to the human diagnostician's way of conceiving entities and relations on physical, functional and behavioural structures.

Diagnosis reasoning is intrinsically abductive reasoning. The chapter presents the abduction by plausibility and relevance, in a connectionist approach. Plausibility criteria become feed-forward links from manifestations to faults – as from the shallow knowledge acquired in practice or experiments. Relevance criteria become competition between the elements of various groups of causes (be they faults or other kind of disorders), put together according to the deep knowledge on physical, functional and behavioural structures of the target system.

In order to solve all types of abduction problems (according to Bylander *et al.*, 1991), specific architectural features are added to the neural network. The features refer to plausibility criteria and affect the feed-forward links between manifestation and fault neurons, also between fault neurons. This way, the abduction problem solving is straightforward and easier implemented in various neural network types than other approaches (e.g., Ayeb *et al.*, 1998).

Deep knowledge refers to physical and functional structures, as means for achieving the ends of the target system. Also, deep knowledge refers to the sets of faults, manifestations and symptoms along with some behavioural hints regarding primary and secondary effects useful for locating faults. Shallow knowledge refers to (unexplained) links of faults to manifestations or to symptoms, from the human diagnostician's practice or experiments.

The embedding of the deep and shallow knowledge requires appropriate representations of physical, functional and behavioural concepts, observing the discrete and qualitative nature of human knowledge. In this respect, means-end and qualitative modelling approaches are adapted to obtain a unified representation of various behavioural entities. The faults' effects propagation is modelled using four orthogonal transport anomalies related to the bond-graph model of components and bond-graph junctions for modules for the entire target system.

The concepts and relations involved in human-like diagnosis get appropriate representations by computational intelligence paradigms. All concepts and relations enter the connectionist models of the abduction problem solving, and their representation is also meant for the systematic knowledge acquisition on concrete target systems. All knowledge pieces involved in fault diagnosis enter appropriate elicitation models addressing human diagnosticians' way of acting, and lead to structures useful for the computational model of the diagnosis system.

The decision on the next best test, aiming the diagnostic refining, is also seen as an abduction problem, and it is solved based on plausibility and relevance criteria in the connectionist implementation. The diagnosis on the whole is performed as a sequential application of plausibility and relevance criteria, applied incrementally, and completed with new tests until the final diagnostic is found.

Fault diagnosis of real systems involves a great amount of data. Therefore, knowledge acquisition, knowledge representation and data management tasks require appropriate tools to assist human diagnosticians in building the diagnosis system. The Computer Aided Knowledge Elicitation (CAKE) software tool assists the human diagnostician, or even the human operator, in the design and generation of the dedicated diagnosis system for the concrete target system envisaged. So, the CAKE tool replaces the knowledge engineer and the software designer. Moreover, specific knowledge on the concrete target system is embedded in the diagnostic expert system, exploiting the human diagnostician's practice and knowledge on the running conditions of the target real system.

The case study on a hydraulic installation of a rolling mill plant gives examples on the knowledge elicitation process and on the diagnostic expert system building and running.

References

1. Ariton V, Ariton D (2000) A General Approach for Diagnostic Problems Solving by Abduction. In: Proceedings of IFAC-SAFEPROCESS, Budapest, Hungary, pp. 446-451
2. Ariton V (2001) Abstraction Levels for the Fault Isolation in Multifunctional Conductive Flow Systems. In: Proceedings of the 9th IFAC/IFORS/IMACS/IFIP/

Symposium on Large Scale Systems-Theory and Applications, Bucharest, Romania, pp. 386-391

3.   Ariton V, Baciu C (2002) Knowledge Elicitation and Case Tool for Fault Diagnosis in Multifunctional Conductive Flow Systems. In: Proceedings of SCI2002 - 6th World Multiconference on Systemics, Cybernetics and Informatics, Orlando, Florida, USA, July 14-18, vol. XXII, pp. 345-350

4.   Ariton V (2003) Deep and shallow knowledge in fault diagnosis. In: Palade V, Howlett RJ, Lakhmi J (eds) Knowledge-Based Intelligent Information and Engineering Systems, 7th International Conference, KES 2003, Oxford, UK, September 3-5, Proceedings, Springer-Verlag, pp.748-755

5.   Ariton V, Palade V (2004) Human-like fault diagnosis using a neural network implementation of plausibility and relevance. Neural Computing & Applications (Springer-Verlag) 14(2):149-165

6.   Ayeb B, Wang S, Ge J (1998) A Unified Model for Abduction-Based Reasoning. IEEE Transactions on Systems, Man and Cybernetics - Part A: Systems and Humans 28(4):408-424

7.   Bocaniala CD, Sa da Costa J, Palade V (2004) A Novel Fuzzy Classification Solution for Fault Diagnosis. International Journal of Fuzzy and Intelligent Systems 15(3-4):195-206

8.   Bocaniala CD, Sa da Costa J, Palade V (2005) Fuzzy-based refinement of the fault diagnosis task in industrial devices. International Journal of Intelligent Manufacturing 16(6): 599-614

9.   Bylander T, Allemang D, Tanner MC, Josephson JR (1991) The Computational Complexity of Abduction. Artificial Intelligence 49:25-60

10.   Cherkassky V, Lari-Najafi H (1992) Data Representation for Diagnostic Neural Networks. IEEE Expert 7(5):43-53

11.   Cellier FE (1995) Modelling from Physical Principles. In: Levine WS (ed) The Control Handbook. CRC Press, Boca Raton, pp.98-108

12.   Calado JMF, Korbicz J, Patan K, Patton RJ, Sa da Costa MG (2001) Soft Computing Approaches to Fault Diagnosis for Dynamic Systems. European Journal of Control 7(2-3):248-286

13.   Cordier MO, Dague P, Dumas M, Lévy F, Motmain J, Staroswiecki M, Travé-Massuyès L (2000) AI and Automatic Control Approaches of Model-Based Diagnosis: Links and Underlying Hypotheses. In: Proceedings of IFAC-SAFEPROCESS, Budapest, Hungary, pp. 274-279

14.   Davis R (1993) Retrospective on "Diagnostic Reasoning Based on Structure and Behaviour". Artificial Intelligence 59:149-157

15.   Dubois D, Prade H (1998) Possibility Theory: Qualitative and Quantitative Aspects. In: Gabbay DM, Smets P (eds) Handbook of Defeasible Reasoning and Uncertainty Management Systems, vol 1, pp. 120-159, Kluwer Academic Publishers, New York

16.   de Kleer J, Kurien J (2003) Fundamentals of Model-Based Diagnosis. Proceedings of IFAC-SAFEPROCESS, Washington, USA, pp. 1-12

17.   Konolige K (1992) Abduction Versus Closure in Causal Theories. Artificial Intelligence 53:255-272

18.   Kruse R, Gebhardt J, Klawon F (1994) Foundations of Fuzzy Systems. John Wiley & Sons, New York

19. Kuipers BJ (1994) Qualitative Reasoning: Modelling and Simulation with Incomplete Knowledge. MIT Press, Cambridge, MA, USA

20. Larsson JE (1992) Knowledge-based methods for control systems. PhD Thesis, Lund

21. Mosterman PJ, Biswas G (2002) A Hybrid Modelling and Simulation Methodology for Dynamic Physical Systems. In: SIMULATION: Transactions of the Society for Modeling and Simulation International, 78(1):5-17

22. Mosterman PJ, Kapadia R, Biswas G (1995) Using bond graphs for diagnosis of dynamical physical systems. In: Proceedings of the Sixth International Conference on Principles of Diagnosis, pp. 81-85

23. O'Brien T (1970) Reliability of Multifunction Structures. New York University

24. Okuda K, Miyasaka N (1991) Model based intelligent monitoring and real time diagnosis. In: Isermann R (ed) Preprints of SAFEPROCESS '91

25. Opdahl AL, Sindre G (1994) A taxonomy for real-world modelling concepts. Information Systems 19(3): 229-241

26. Palade V, Patton RJ, Uppal FJ, Quevedo J, Daley S (2002) Fault diagnosis of an industrial gas turbine using neuro-fuzzy methods. In: Proceedings of the 15th IFAC World Congress, 21–26 July, Barcelona, pp. 2477–2482

27. Patton RJ, Frank PM, Clark RN (2000) Issues of Fault Diagnosis for Dynamic Systems. Springer-Verlag, London

28. Peng Y, Reggia J (1990) Abductive Inference Models for Diagnostic Problem Solving. Springer-Verlag, London

29. Schurz G (2002) Models of Abductive Reasoning. TPD Preprints Annual 2002, no.1, University of Düsseldorf, Germany

30. Shibata B, Tateno S, Tsuge Y, Matsuyama H (1991) Fault diagnosis of the chemical process utilizing signed directed graph. In: Isermann R (ed) Preprints of Fault Detection Supervision and Safety for Technical Processes - SAFEPROCESS '91, pp.381-386

31. Struss P (1997) Model-based and qualitative reasoning: An introduction. Annals of Mathematics and Artificial Intelligence 19: 355-381

32. Turksen IB (1996) Non-Specificity and Interval-Values Fuzzy Sets. Fuzzy Sets and Systems 80:87-100

33. Uppal FJ, Patton RJ, Palade V (2002) Neuro-Fuzzy Based Fault Diagnosis Applied to an Electro-Pneumatic Valve. In: Proceedings of the 15th IFAC World Congress, 21–26 July, Barcelona, Spain, pp. 2483-2488

9. Fault Diagnosis in a Power Generation Plant Using a Neural Fuzzy System with Rule Extraction

Kok Yeng Chen, Chee Peng Lim, Weng Kin Lai

In this chapter, the Fuzzy Min-Max (FMM) neural network is integrated with a rule extraction algorithm, and the resulting network is applied to fault diagnosis tasks in a power generation plant. With the rule extraction capability, the FMM network is able to overcome the "black-box" phenomenon by justifying its predictions with fuzzy if-then rules that are comprehensible to the domain users. To assess the effectiveness of the FMM network, real sensor measurements are collected and used for diagnosing the heat transfer and tube blockage conditions of the Circulating Water (CW) system in a power generation plant. The FMM network parameters are systematically varied and tested. Bootstrapping is used to statistically ascertain the stability of the network performance. In addition, the extracted rules are found to be compatible with the domain information as well as the opinions of the experts who are involved in the maintenance of the CW system. Implications of the FMM network with the rule extraction facility as an intelligent and useful fault diagnosis tool are discussed.

9.1. Introduction

Fault diagnosis is a research area that is becoming increasingly important owing to the complexity of modern industrial systems and growing demands for quality, cost efficiency, reliability, and safety (Al-Najjar, 1996). In order to maintain the competitive edge, factory operators and manufacturers often have to ensure that their machines and processes are set at optimal operating conditions. Fault diagnosis systems support this objective by predicting failures and, if a failure had occurred, by identifying the reasons behind the failure. In a complex process, fault diagnosis systems normally deal with the management and maintenance of a whole chain of actions to detect and diagnose abnormal events. Early prediction of possible fault states allows maintenance work to take place before a machine/system breaks down, that may cause damages and obstructions to the overall operation, hence improving the level of plant safety and, at the same time, reducing production downtime and productivity loss.

When developing a fault diagnosis system, the basic a priori condition needed is a set of failures and the relationship between the observations (symptoms) and the faults. There are a variety of approaches for devising process fault detection and diagnosis systems. Venkatasubramanian et al. (2003a,b,c) through a series of systematic and comparative study of various diagnostic methods from different perspectives have shown that process fault detection and diagnosis methods may be categorised into three general categories, namely, quantitative model-based methods, qualitative model-based methods, and process history-based methods. Quantitative model-based methods correspond to modelling the physical process by using some mathematical functional relationships of the inputs and outputs of the process. Qualitative model-based methods deal with modelling the physical process by expressing the model equations in terms of qualitative functions centred on different units of the process. In contrast to model-based methods where a priori knowledge (either quantitative or qualitative) about the process under scrutiny is needed, process history-based methods (data-based methods) utilise the availability of a large amount of historical process data for modelling the physical process, either implicitly or explicitly.

In general, data-based fault diagnosis approaches involve a wide range of actions which can consist of measuring data, processing the data, comparing new data with the original data, evaluating the data, and coming to a conclusion on the general health condition of the process. In this aspect, computational intelligence approaches, including neural network (NN) models, have emerged as an alternative to design and develop robust fault diagnosis tools (Venkatasubramanian et al., 2003c). Indeed, NN models have been adopted as intelligent learning systems owing to their intrinsic parallelism, adaptability, and ability to handle noisy data. They can learn complex associations and relationships directly from data. They can also handle fusion of multiple sources of data and information. With these attractive features, NN-based systems increasingly have been employed as intelligent fault diagnosis tools to identify and to distinguish between faulty and normal operating conditions in complex processes (Polycarpou and Helmicki, 1995).

From the literature review, there is evidence that NN-based systems are effective in handling fault diagnosis tasks. For example, NNs and fuzzy logic were utilised to provide intelligent diagnosis of a turbine engine (Kuo, 1995). Similarly, NN models were employed to model the critical parameters in the gas turbine engine, and the differences between the modelled and actual parameters were used to accurately predict engine malfunction (Denny, 1993). In (Kuo, 1995), a multiple NN system was applied to fault diagnosis of a diesel engine, while NN-based fault diagnostic systems were adopted to monitor jet and rocket engines in (Dietz et al., 1989). An approach based on NN models was developed for helicopter gearbox fault detection (Dellomo, 1999). Other examples include use of the backpropagation network and the Radial Basis Function network, respectively, to detect fault conditions in pneumatic control valve actuators (de Freitas et al., 1999) and to classify rolling element bearing faults (Jack et al., 1999).

Nonetheless, most of the NN-based diagnostic systems suffer from the so-called "black-box" phenomenon, i.e., it is difficult to extract domain knowledge encoded in a trained network to explain its predictions. Users, who need symbolic knowledge and reasoning in order to be convinced of the predicted outcome, are often reluctant to use such a system if the NN model is unable to provide an explanatory facility to justify how a prediction is reached. Such a drawback can be a barrier to a wider acceptance of NN applications in real environments, especially in mission-critical operations such as those in a power generation plant.

In rule learning and extraction research, a lot of effort has been devoted to the integration of symbolic, rule-based knowledge and NN models. There are many techniques available for rule extraction from trained NNs, e.g., the KT rule extraction algorithm (Fu, 1994), rule-extraction-as-learning technique (Craven and Shavlik, 1994), and DEDEC approach (Tickle *et al.*, 1996). According to (Andrews *et al.*, 1995), there are three main approaches in the aspect of translucency of NN rule extraction techniques, namely, the decompositional, pedagogical, and eclectic approaches. The main idea of the decompositional approach (e.g., the KT rule extraction algorithm) is to extract rules at the level of individual hidden and output nodes by analysing the weight vector associated with each local node in the trained NN models. The pedagogical approach (e.g., the rule-extraction-as-learning technique) views the trained NN models at the minimum possible level of granularity. The network is treated as a black box in which the extracted rules map the inputs directly to the outputs. The eclectic approach (e.g., the DEDEC methodology) is the combination of both decompositional and pedagogical approaches. In this approach, knowledge about the internal architecture and/or weight vectors in the trained NN models are used to complement a specific symbolic learning algorithm.

In this chapter, the applicability of the Fuzzy Min-Max neural network (Simpson, 1992) (hereafter referred to as FMM) to fault diagnosis tasks in a power generation plant is described. In order to overcome the "black-box" phenomenon, FMM is further enhanced with a rule extraction capability. There are two main reasons that motivate the use of FMM with rule extraction. First, it has the capability of learning in a single pass through the data samples and is able to build and fine-tune the decision boundaries of different classes without retraining. Second, the proposed rule extraction procedure, which can be categorised as a decompositional approach, is able to extract knowledge and rules from FMM in a straightforward manner for justifying its predictions.

This chapter is organized as follows. In section 9.2, the architecture and dynamics of FMM are introduced. The rule extraction algorithm is explained in section 9.3. A case study on fault diagnosis in a power generation plant is described in section 9.4. Conclusions are drawn in section 9.5.

9.2. The Fuzzy Min-Max Neural Network

FMM is a type of neural network model that builds decision boundaries by creating hyperboxes in the pattern space. The hyperboxes are defined by pairs of minimum and maximum points and their corresponding membership functions are used to create fuzzy subsets in the n-dimensional pattern space. One of the important properties of FMM is that it learns incrementally in a single pass through the data. It refines the existing pattern classes as new information is received. It also has the ability to add new pattern classes online. The learning process in FMM is mainly concerned with proper placement and adjustment of hyperboxes in the pattern space. If overlapping hyperboxes of different classes occurred in the pattern space, contraction will be performed to eliminate the overlapping areas. Thus, the learning dynamics are comprised of *compare*, *add*, and *subtract* operations that fine-tune the boundaries of the pattern classes.

Figure 9.1 illustrates the aggregation of several hyperboxes in a two-dimensional pattern space for a binary classification problem. Definition of the fuzzy set for each hyperbox, B_j, is as follows.

$$B_j = \left\{ X, V_j, W_j, f\left(X, V_j, W_j\right) \right\} \quad \forall X \in I^n \tag{1}$$

where X = input pattern, $X = (x_1, x_2, ..., x_n)$, V_j = minimum point for B_j, $V_j = (v_{j1}, v_{j2}, ..., v_{jn})$, and W_j = maximum point for B_j, $W_j = (w_{j1}, w_{j2}, ..., w_{jn})$.

Notice that the pattern space is an n-dimensional unit cube I^n. Using the above definition, the collective fuzzy set that characterises the kth pattern class C_k is defined as

$$C_k = \bigcup_{j \in K} B_j \tag{2}$$

where K is the index set of the hyperboxes associated with class k. Note that the union operation is typically the maximum of all of the associated fuzzy set membership functions.

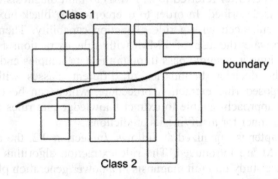

Figure 9.1. An example of fuzzy min-max hyperboxes placed along the boundary of a two-class problem. Note that the hyperboxes corresponding to the two classes are nonoverlapping between classes.

The learning algorithm of FMM allows overlapping hyperboxes from the same class. However, it eliminates the overlapping between hyperboxes that represent different classes. The membership function of the jth hyperbox $b_j(A_h)$, $0 \le b_j(A_h) \le 1$, measures the degree to which the hth input pattern A_h falls outside hyperbox B_j. Equation 3 shows the measurement of how far each component is greater (lesser) than the maximum (minimum) point value along each dimension. If $b_j(A_h) \rightarrow 1$, the point should be more "contained" by the hyperbox. Note that $b_j(A_h) = 1$ represents complete hyperbox containment. The function that meets all these criteria is the sum of two complements, i.e., the average amount of maximum point violation and the average amount of the minimum point violation. The resulting membership function is defined as

$$b_j(A_h) = \frac{1}{2n} \sum_{i=1}^{n} [\max(0, 1 - \max(0, \gamma \min \quad (1, a_{hi} - w_{ji}))) + \max \quad (0, 1 - \max(0, \gamma \min(1, v_{ji} - a_{hi})))] \tag{3}$$

where $A_h = (a_{h1}, a_{h2}, \cdots, a_{hn}) \in I^n$ is the hth input pattern, $V_j = (v_{j1}, v_{j2}, \cdots, v_{jn})$ is the minimum point for B_j, $W_j = (w_{j1}, w_{j2}, \cdots, w_{jn})$ is the maximum point for B_j, and γ is the sensitivity parameter that regulates how fast the membership values decrease as the distance between A_h and B_j increases.

Figure 9.2 shows a three-layer FMM neural network. Each $F_B = (b_1, b_2, \cdots, b_m)$ node represents a hyperbox fuzzy set where the F_A to F_B connections are the min-max points and the F_B transfer function is the hyperbox membership function (as defined in Eq. 3). The input layer $F_A = (a_1, a_2, \cdots, a_n)$ has n processing elements, one for each of the n dimensions of the input pattern A_h. After the learning process, all the minimum points and maximum points created are stored in matrix V and matrix W, respectively. These connections are adjusted using the learning algorithm that will be presented later. The connections between F_B and F_C nodes are binary valued and stored in matrix U, which is defined as

$$u_{jk} = \begin{cases} 1 & \text{if } b_j \text{ is a hyperbox for class } c_k \\ 0 & \text{otherwise} \end{cases} \tag{4}$$

where b_j is the jth F_B node and c_k is the kth F_C node.

Each F_C node represents a class, and the output of the F_C node represents the degree to which the input pattern A_h fits within the class k. The transfer function for each of the F_C nodes performs the fuzzy union of the appropriate hyperbox fuzzy set values, i.e.,

$$c_k = \max_{j=1}^{m} b_j u_{jk} \tag{5}$$

There are two ways to utilise the outputs of the F_C nodes. If a soft decision is required, the output is utilised directly. However, if a hard decision is required, the winner-takes-all approach (Kohonen, 1984) is utilised, i.e., the F_C node with the highest value is selected and its output node value will be set to 1 to indicate that it is the closest pattern class and the remaining F_C node values are set to 0.

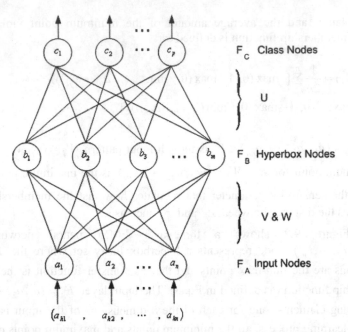

Figure 9.2.   A three-layer Fuzzy Min-Max neural network.

9.2.1. Learning in the Fuzzy Min-Max Neural Network

The learning algorithm in FMM comprises an expansion/contraction process. Assume that training set D consists of a set of M ordered pair $\{X_h, d_h\}$, where

$X_h = (x_{h1}, x_{h2}, \cdots, x_{hn}) \in I^n$ is the input pattern and $d_h \in \{ 1, 2, \cdots, m \}$ is the index of one of the m classes. The expansion/growth process allows decision boundaries that are nonlinearly separable to be formed. It allows existing classes to be refined over time, and new classes to be added without retraining. The expansion process will lead to overlapping among hyperboxes. Thus, elimination of hyperboxes will commence using the contraction process if overlapping hyperboxes from different classes occurred. Nevertheless, it is not a problem when overlapping occurs for the same class.

In summary, the FMM learning algorithm comprises a three-step process:

1.   *Expansion*: Identify expandable hyperboxes and expand them. If an expandable hyperbox cannot be found, a new hyperbox for that class will be added. For hyperbox B_j to expand and to include X_h, the following constraint must be met:

$$n\theta \geq \sum_{i=1}^{n} \left(\max (w_{ji}, x_{hi}) - \min (v_{ji}, x_{hi}) \right) \tag{6}$$

where $0 \leq \theta \leq 1$ is a user-defined value that determines the maximum size of a hyperbox.

2.   If the expansion criterion is met, the minimum and maximum points of the hyperbox are adjusted as follows.

$$v_{ji}^{new} = \min(v_{ji}^{old}, x_{hi}) \ \forall_i, i = 1, 2, \cdots, n \tag{7}$$

$$w_{ji}^{new} = \max(w_{ji}^{old}, x_{hi}) \ \forall_i, i = 1, 2, \cdots, n \tag{8}$$

3. **Overlapping Test**: Determine if any overlapping exists between hyperboxes from different classes. For all dimensions, if at least one of the following four cases is satisfied, then overlapping exists between two hyperboxes. Assuming $\delta^{old} = 1$ initially, the four test cases and the corresponding minimum overlap value for the ith dimension are as follows.

$$\text{Case 1}: v_{ji} < v_{ki} < w_{ji} < w_{ki}, \ \delta^{new} = \min(w_{ji} - v_{ki}, \ \delta^{old}) \tag{9}$$

$$\text{Case 2}: v_{ki} < v_{ji} < w_{ki} < w_{ji}, \ \delta^{new} = \min(w_{ki} - v_{ji}, \ \delta^{old}) \tag{10}$$

$$\text{Case 3}: v_{ji} < v_{ki} < w_{ki} < w_{ji}, \delta^{new} = \min(\min(w_{ki} - v_{ji}, w_{ji} - v_{ki}), \delta^{old}) \tag{11}$$

$$\text{Case 4}: v_{ki} < v_{ji} < w_{ji} < w_{ki}, \delta^{new} = \min(\min(w_{ji} - v_{ki}, w_{ki} - v_{ji}), \delta^{old}) \tag{12}$$

where j = hyperbox B_j that expanded in the previous step, and k = hyperbox B_k represents another class and is being tested for possible overlapping.

4. **Contraction**: If overlapping between hyperboxes of different classes exists, eliminate the overlapping by minimally adjusting each of the hyperboxes. If all dimensions of the two hyperboxes do overlap, only one of the n dimensions that has minimum overlapping is adjusted to keep the hyperbox size as large as possible. To make the proper adjustment, the same four cases are examined where Δ is the selected dimension to contract.

$$\text{Case 1}: v_{j\Delta} < v_{k\Delta} < w_{j\Delta} < w_{k\Delta}, \ w_{j\Delta}^{new} = v_{k\Delta}^{new} = \frac{w_{j\Delta}^{old} + v_{k\Delta}^{old}}{2} \tag{13}$$

$$\text{Case 2}: v_{k\Delta} < v_{j\Delta} < w_{k\Delta} < w_{j\Delta}, \ w_{k\Delta}^{new} = v_{j\Delta}^{new} = \frac{w_{k\Delta}^{old} + v_{j\Delta}^{old}}{2} \tag{14}$$

$$\text{Case 3a}: v_{j\Delta} < v_{k\Delta} < w_{k\Delta} < w_{j\Delta}, \ (w_{k\Delta} - v_{j\Delta}) < (w_{j\Delta} < v_{k\Delta}) \text{ and}$$
$$v_{j\Delta}^{new} = w_{k\Delta}^{old} \tag{15}$$

$$\text{Case 3b}: v_{j\Delta} < v_{k\Delta} < w_{k\Delta} < w_{j\Delta}, \ (w_{k\Delta} - v_{j\Delta}) > (w_{j\Delta} < v_{k\Delta}) \text{ and}$$
$$w_{j\Delta}^{new} = v_{k\Delta}^{old} \tag{16}$$

$$\text{Case 4a}: v_{k\Delta} < v_{j\Delta} < w_{j\Delta} < w_{k\Delta}, \ (w_{k\Delta} - v_{j\Delta}) < (w_{j\Delta} < v_{k\Delta}) \text{ and}$$
$$w_{k\Delta}^{new} = v_{j\Delta}^{old} \tag{17}$$

$$\text{Case 4b}: v_{k\Delta} < v_{j\Delta} < w_{j\Delta} < w_{k\Delta}, \ (w_{k\Delta} - v_{j\Delta}) > (w_{j\Delta} < v_{k\Delta}) \text{ and}$$
$$v_{k\Delta}^{new} = w_{j\Delta}^{old} \tag{18}$$

9.3.   Rule Extraction from the Fuzzy Min-Max Neural Network

Owing to the "black-box" phenomenon, rule extraction plays an important role for the acceptance of NN systems as an intelligent and useful fault diagnosis tool. With an explanatory facility, the predictions from NN systems can be justified with if-then rules. This will enable domain users to gauge the NN predictions, thus overcoming the suspicion from non-NN experts to utilise this technology in their work.

With respect to FMM, out of all the hyperboxes created, some of them are rarely used during prediction. To reduce the complexity of FMM, an algorithm for network pruning and rule extraction, as proposed in (Carpenter and Tan, 1995), is incorporated into FMM. The main objective of network pruning is to remove those hyperboxes that have low confidence factors while preserving a high accuracy rate of the prediction. A hyperbox is eliminated when its confidence factor is lower than a user-defined pruning threshold, τ. The confidence factor of each hyperbox is expressed as

$$CF_j = \lambda \ U_j + (1 - \lambda) \ A_j \qquad (19)$$

where U_j and A_j are Usage and Accuracy of the jth hyperbox, respectively, while $\lambda \in [0, 1]$ is a weighting factor. Parameter U_j is defined as the fraction of the number of training patterns coded by hyperbox b_j (C_j) that predicts a particular outcome over the maximum number of training patterns coded by any hyperbox that predict the same outcome, i.e.,

$$U_j = \frac{C_j}{\max \ [C_j]} \qquad (20)$$

Accuracy A_j is defined as the fraction of the percentage of prediction patterns predicted by hyperbox j (P_j) over the maximum percentage of prediction patterns predicted by any hyperbox that predicts the same outcome, i.e.,

$$A_j = \frac{P_j}{\max \ [P_j]} \qquad (21)$$

By using the above approach, it is possible to equip FMM with rules that have interpretation in consequence of the min-max points of the hyperboxes. To further facilitate the rule interpretation in a comprehensible form, weight quantisation by truncation (Eq. 19) is applied. This method divides the range between 0 and 1 into Q intervals, and assigns a quantisation point to the lower bound of each interval, i.e.,

$$V_q = \frac{(q - 1)}{Q} \qquad (22)$$

for $q = 1, 2, \cdots, Q$, where Q is the quantisation level. By using weight quantisation, the extracted rules can be interpreted in accordance with fuzzy linguistic terms. For example, with $Q = 5$, the consequent part of the if-then rules can be translated into *very low*, *low*, *medium*, *high*, and *very high*. As a result, the rules from FMM can be elucidated in human linguistic terms that are easily comprehensible to the domain users.

9.4. Fault Diagnosis in a Power Generation Plant

Power generation is a mission-critical service in a country. It is imperative to ensure that the process of power generation is conducted in an efficient manner such that continual supply of energy is guaranteed. In general, power generation involves complex processes and equipment, and effective and intelligent fault diagnosis tools are of vital importance to a power generation facility. As a result, a research project has been conducted to investigate the applicability of FMM with rule extraction to fault detection and diagnosis tasks in collaboration with a power generation plant in Penang, Malaysia.

A case study pertaining to the Circulating Water (CW) system in the Prai power generation plant, Malaysia, has been carried out. The function of the CW system is to supply a sufficient and continuous amount of cooling water to the main turbines condenser to condense steam from the turbine exhaust and other steam flows into the condensers. Figure 9.3 shows a simplified diagram depicting the main components of the CW system. In reality, the CW system includes all piping and equipment (such as condensers and drum strainer) between intake of sea water and the outfall of the system where sea water is discharged back to the sea.

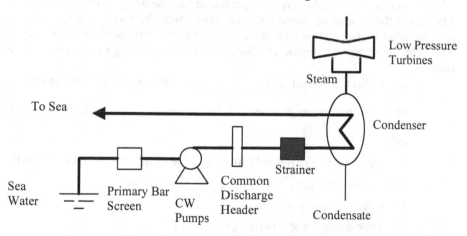

Figure 9.3. The Circulating Water system.

As shown in Figure 9.3, sea (circulating) water enters the plant from the sea through a primary bar screen at the pump house. The bar screen is used to prevent large-sized debris, such as timber and clumps of seaweed, from entering the CW system. In the pump house, the CW pumps draw sea water from the suction chamber to a common discharge header through a hydraulic discharge valve. From the common discharge header, sea water flows into the CW inlet culvert through a drum strainer, which acts as a filter to remove fine debris, such as shells and seaweed. Circulating water flows through the culvert up to the turbine condensers, where circulating water is used to condense steam being exhausted from the low-pressured turbine. After passing through a pair of outlet valves, circulating water enters a concrete outlet culvert before it is discharged back to sea.

Data relating to a targeted power output of 80 MW was collected. Two experiments were conducted to evaluate the applicability of FMM as an intelligent fault diagnosis tool. Before describing the experiments and the results, a discussion on bootstrapping, a statistical method used to evaluate the performance, is presented in the next section.

9.4.1. The Bootstrap Method

The performance indicator used in the experiments was accuracy, i.e., ratio of the correct number of predictions for the test samples to the total number of test samples. In addition, the bootstrap method (Efron, 1979; Efron and Tibshirani, 1993) was employed to compute the estimated confidence bounds for accuracy. Estimation of confidence bounds is important in order to ascertain the statistical variation of accuracy, owing to the uncertainty of the network performance when different initialisation conditions were used.

Bootstrapping is useful for estimating the confidence interval of parameters when the underlying distribution function of the parameter is unknown. It involves generating subsets of data on the basics of random sampling with replacements as data are sampled. This method has no constraints upon the number of times that a data sample may be represented in generating a single resampling. The size of the resampling subsets may be fixed arbitrarily which is independent of the parameter of the experimental design, and may even exceed the total number of data. The algorithm to estimate confidence intervals by using bootstrapping is as follows.

1. Collect a sample $(x_1, x_2,..., x_n)$ with mean $\hat{\alpha}$ that defines a discrete distribution function $\hat{G}$ having mass $\frac{1}{n}$ at each of n sample points.

2. Draw a sample randomly from $\hat{G}$. The distribution of each x^{*i1} in the bootstrap sample is $\hat{G}^{*i1}$, i.e., $x_1^{*i1}, x_2^{*i1},..., x_n^{*i1} \sim \hat{G}^{*i1}$.

3. Calculate the new mean $\hat{\alpha}^{*i}$.

4. Repeat step 2 and 3 m times to obtain $\hat{\alpha}^{*i1}, \hat{\alpha}^{*i2},..., \hat{\alpha}^{*im}$.

5. Sort the bootstrap mean values in ascending order, $\hat{\alpha}^{*i1} < \hat{\alpha}^{*i2} <...< \hat{\alpha}^{*im}$.

6. Calculate the confidence intervals from the sorted list. The confidence interval is (COF_{c1}, COF_{c2}), where $COF_{c1} = \frac{ma}{2}$ (upper confidence interval), and $COF_{c2} = m - COF_{c1} + 1$ (lower confidence interval), when a is the confidence level (e.g., 0.95 for 95% confidence interval).

9.4.2. Experiment I – Heat Transfer Conditions

The turbine condensers use circulating water to remove rejected energy (heat) from the low-pressured steam and, at the same time, to keep the turbine backpressure (condenser vacuum) at the lowest possible yet constant level. Heat transfer conditions in the condenser have a significant effect on the condenser backpressure, in which an efficient heat transfer process will assist in maintaining the condenser backpressure at a low level. With a satisfactory level of condenser backpressure, a high turbine work efficiency to generate power can be maintained. On that account, factors such as pressure and temperature of the exhaust steam and the cooling water have a profound influence on the performance of the condenser in the process of condensation.

The data set used in this experiment contained 2439 samples. Each data sample consisted of 12 features comprising the temperature and pressure measurements at various inlet and outlet points of the condenser, as well as other important parameters as shown in Table 9.1. The heat transfer conditions were classified into two categories, i.e., the process of heat transfer was accomplished either efficiently or inefficiently. From the database, there were 1224 data samples (50.18%) that showed inefficient heat transfer condition, whereas 1215 data samples (49.82%) showed efficient heat transfer condition in the condenser. The data samples were equally divided into three subsets for training, prediction and test.

Table 9.1.   List of sensor parameters used in the experiments

No.	Parameter	Description
1	LPT A	Low Pressure Cylinder Exhaust Temperature A
2	LPT B	Low Pressure Cylinder Exhaust Temperature B
3	GEN	Generator
4	CWIT A	Condenser Circulating Water Inlet Temperature A
5	CWIT B	Condenser Circulating Water Inlet Temperature B
6	CWOT A	Condenser Circulating Water Outlet Temperature A
7	CWOT B	Condenser Circulating Water Outlet Temperature B
8	CWIP A	Condenser Circulating Water Inlet Pressure A
9	CWOP A	Condenser Circulating Water Outlet Pressure A
10	CWIP B	Condenser Circulating Water Inlet Pressure B
11	CWOP B	Condenser Circulating Water Outlet Pressure B
12	VAC	Condenser Vacuum

During the experimental study, some important FMM parameters were varied systematically to investigate the network performance. Table 9.2 shows the test accuracy rates subject to varying θ from 0.01 to 0.10, with the sensitivity parameter $\beta = 5$. The highest accuracy rate achieved was 97.66%, and was produced by setting $\theta = 0.04$. Bootstrapping was applied to the results to determine the 95% confidence intervals of accuracy, and the results are shown in Table 9.3. Notice that the difference between the lower and upper limits of the confidence bounds was small, suggesting that the network performance was stable.

Table 9.2.   Test results for Experiment I

θ	Test Accuracy (%)	θ	Test Accuracy (%)
0.01	97.17	0.06	96.06
0.02	97.05	0.07	96.06
0.03	97.66	0.08	95.33
0.04	97.66	0.09	94.34
0.05	95.85	0.10	95.08

Table 9.3.   Bootstrapped results for Experiment I

Number of Resamplings	Confidence Intervals		Mean (%)
	Lower (%)	Upper (%)	
200	96.695	97.301	97.030
400	96.686	97.285	97.007
600	96.694	97.310	97.020
800	96.686	97.309	97.007
1000	96.685	97.301	97.009

Table 9.4.   Pruning results for Experiment I

τ	Test Accuracy (%)	No. of Hyperboxes
0.0	97.66	499
0.1	97.05	205
0.2	97.05	196
0.3	97.05	196
0.4	96.93	194
0.5	96.93	194
0.6	96.68	192
0.7	96.06	100
0.8	79.09	27

Network pruning was performed to remove those hyperboxes that had a low confidence factor. The pruning threshold, τ, was varied from 0.0 to 0.8, with $\theta = 0.04$. Table 9.4 shows the test accuracy and the number of hyperboxes after pruning. The result for $\tau = 0.7$ was selected for rule extraction because of the high test accuracy rate with a smaller network size.

Table 9.5 shows six rules from each class that have the best confidence factor while Table 9.6 shows an interpretation of the first positive rule and the second negative rule. The heat transfer conditions can be ascertained by monitoring certain parameters such as LPT A, LPT B, CWIT A, CWIT B, CWOT A, CWOT B and VAC. Notice that VAC for most of the positive rules ranged from 3 (medium) to 4 (high) while for the negative rules it ranged from 1 (very low) to 2 (low). Indeed, in order to have efficient heat transfer in the condensers, the condenser vacuum should be preserved at a low level. If CWIT A and CWIT B increased, the steam temperatures (LPT A and LPT B) exiting the turbine would increase to establish the needed differential temperature for continuous heat transfer during power generation. This situation can be identified in most of the extracted rules, where LPT A and LPT B were less than 2 (low) while CWIT A and CWIT B ranged from 2 (low) to 3 (medium) for the negative rules. On the other hand, if LPT A and LPT B increased from 3 (medium) to 4 (high), CWIT A and CWIT B would increase from 3 (medium) to 5 (very high) in most positive rules. The rules extracted were found to be compatible with domain knowledge as well as the experts' opinions in maintaining the CW system.

9.4.3. Experiment II – Tube Blockage Conditions

In this experiment, the objective was to predict the occurrence of tube blockage in the CW system. The cleanliness of the condenser tubes has a significant impact on the ability of the condenser to transfer heat from the exhaust steam to the cooling water. One of the most common causes of blockage is tube fouling. Occasionally, there are mud and small solid materials, such as seaweed, shells, and sand, which have inadvertently escaped the filtering process of the CW system. As a consequence, these solid materials enter the CW piping system, which includes the condenser tubes. They may block the tubes and affect the efficiency of the condenser in cooling exhaust steam. Thus, the second experiment focused on blockage detection in the condenser tubes and nearby pipes. The conditions of the condenser tubes were categorized into two classes: significant blockage and insignificant blockage.

The same data set as used in Experiment I was employed. From the set, a total of 1313 samples (53.83%) showed significant blockage and the remaining showed insignificant blockage in the condenser tubes. The data samples were again equally divided into three subsets for training, prediction and test. A number of tests were conducted by varying θ from 0.01 to 0.95 with the sensitivity parameter $\beta = 5$. Table 9.7 shows the results from $\theta = 0.09$ to $\theta = 0.50$ as setting $\theta < 0.09$ would result in overspecific rules while setting $\theta > 0.50$ would result in too common rules. Notice that FMM was able to achieve perfect score (100% accuracy) in this experiment.

Table 9.5.   Example of the extracted rules for Experiment I, where positive (+) and negative (–) rules, respectively, indicate inefficient and efficient heat transfer conditions

Rule	Parameters												CF	Test	
	1	2	3	4	5	6	7	8	9	10	11	12		No	Acc
+	3-4	3-4	3	3	2	2-3	3	1	1	2	1	3	1.000	19	1.00
+	3	3	4	3	2	2-3	3	1-2	1	2	1	3-4	0.900	19	1.00
+	3	3	3-4	3	2	2	3	2	1-2	2	1	3	0.900	24	1.00
+	3	3	3-4	3	2	2	3	1	1	2	1	3-4	0.950	15	1.00
+	3	3	3	5	4	3-4	4	2	3-4	2	3	2	0.850	19	1.00
+	3	2-3	3	4	3	3	3	1-2	3	1	1	3	0.800	19	1.00
–	2	2	4	4	2	2	2	3	4	2	1	2	1.000	17	0.94
–	1-2	1	3-4	3	1	2	1	3	4	2	1	2	0.943	21	1.00
–	1	1-2	3	2	2-3	1	3	2	2	2	5	2	0.943	16	1.00
–	2	2	3-4	3	2	2	1-2	3	4	2-3	1	1-2	0.943	17	1.00
–	1	1	4	2-3	1	1	1	2	4	2	1	1-2	0.886	20	1.00
–	1	1	3	3	1	1	1	3	4	2-3	1	1	0.829	26	1.00

Table 9.6.   Interpretation of the first positive rule and the second negative rule

IF	IF
LPT A = medium to high	LPT A = very low to low
LPT B = medium to high	LPT B = very low
GEN = medium	GEN = medium to high
CWIT A = medium	CWIT A = medium
CWIT B = low	CWIT B = very low
CWOT A = low to medium	CWOT A = low
CWOT B = medium	CWOT B = very low
CWIP A = very low	CWIP A = medium
CWOP A = very low	CWOP A = high
CWIP B = low	CWIP B = low
CWOP B = very low	CWOP B = very low
VAC = medium	VAC = low
THEN Heat transfer is not efficient	*THEN* Heat transfer is efficient

To facilitate rule extraction, network pruning was conducted to remove those hyperboxes that had a low confidence factor. Table 9.8 summarises the results obtained by varying τ from 0.0 to 0.8, with $\theta = 0.15$. It can be seen that setting $\tau = 0.7$ resulted in a reasonably high test accuracy rate with a small network size. Bootstrapping was applied to the pruned results to determine the 95% confidence intervals of the network accuracy. The bootstrapped results are tabulated in Table 9.9. Again, the results indicate that the network performance remained stable after pruning.

Table 9.10 shows the extracted rules and examples of their interpretation are shown in Table 9.11. Notice that CWOP B was at 1 (very low) for all the positive rules. On the contrary, CWOP B for all the negative rules ranged from 3 (medium) to 4 (high). In addition, CWOP A for the positive rules can achieve 1 while CWOP A for the negative rules ranged from 3 (medium) to 5 (very high). In fact, there is a close relationship between the flow rate and the pressure of the CW system. The low outlet pressure is actually a sign of insufficient flow of circulating water in the condenser tubes. Insufficient flow can also be traced by a low CW inlet pressure. This is clearly shown by CWIP A and CWIP B of the first, third, fourth, and sixth positive rules, where the rules ranged from 1 (very low) to 3 (medium). The extracted rules, again, were found to be compatible with domain information as well as the experts' opinions.

Table 9.7. Test results for Experiment II

θ	Test Accuracy (%)	θ	Test Accuracy (%)
0.09	100.00	0.30	99.88
0.10	100.00	0.35	100.00
0.15	100.00	0.40	100.00
0.20	99.88	0.45	99.88
0.25	99.02	0.50	99.88

Table 9.8. Pruning results for Experiment II

τ	Test Accuracy (%)	No. of Hyperboxes
0.0	97.66	499
0.1	97.05	205
0.2	97.05	196
0.3	97.05	196
0.4	96.93	194
0.5	96.93	194
0.6	96.68	192
0.7	96.06	100
0.8	79.09	27

Table 9.9. Bootstrapped results for Experiment II

Number of Resamplings	Confidence Intervals		Mean (%)
	Lower (%)	Upper (%)	
200	92.848	96.023	94.398
400	92.463	96.121	94.410
600	92.841	95.941	94.471
800	92.865	96.203	94.531
1000	92.913	96.146	94.466

Table 9.10.   Example of the extracted rules for Experiment II, where positive (+) and negative (–) rules, respectively, indicate significant and insignificant tube blockage in the CW system

Rule	Parameters												CF	Test	
	1	2	3	4	5	6	7	8	9	10	11	12		No	Acc
+	3-4	3-4	1-4	3-4	2	2-3	2-3	1-2	1-2	2	1	3-4	1.000	109	1.00
+	1	1	2-4	2-3	1-2	1	1	2-3	4	2-3	1	1-2	0.914	64	1.00
+	2-3	2	4-5	3-4	2	2-3	2	1-2	3	1-2	1	2-3	0.875	73	1.00
+	1-2	2	3-4	3-4	2	2	2	1-3	3-4	1-3	1	2	0.796	71	1.00
+	2-3	2-3	2-4	5	4	3	3	2-3	3-4	2-3	1	2-3	0.843	53	1.00
+	3	2-3	2-5	4	2-3	3	2-3	1-2	3	1	1	3-4	0.741	24	1.00
–	2-3	2	2-4	4-5	3-4	2-3	2-3	3	4	3	3-4	1-2	1.000	107	0.94
–	2-3	2-3	2-3	4-5	3-4	3	3-4	2-3	4	2-3	3	2-3	0.952	95	1.00
–	5	5	2-4	5	5	5	5	3	5	2	3	4-5	0.782	19	1.00
–	3-4	3	2-3	5	4-5	3-4	4	2-3	3-4	2	3	2-3	0.782	40	1.00
–	2	2	3-4	3-5	2	2	2-3	2	3-4	2	3	1-2	0.758	37	1.00
–	3	2-3	1-4	5	4	3	3-4	3-4	4	3	3	2-3	0.746	24	1.00

Table 9.11.   Interpretation of the first positive rule and the first negative rule

IF	IF
LPT A = medium to high	LPT A = low to medium
LPT B = medium to high	LPT B = low
GEN = low to high	GEN = low to high
CWIT A = medium to high	CWIT A = high to very high
CWIT B = low	CWIT B = medium to high
CWOT A = low to medium	CWOT A = low to medium
CWOT B = low to medium	CWOT B = low to medium
CWIP A = very low to low	CWIP A = medium
CWOP A = very low to low	CWOP A = high
CWIP B = low	CWIP B = medium
CWOP B = very low	CWOP B = medium to high
VAC = medium to high	VAC = very low to low
Then **Significant blockage**	**Then** **Insignificant blockage**

9.5. Summary

In this chapter, FMM is endowed with a rule extraction algorithm. With the rule extraction algorithm, FMM is able to explain its predictions using fuzzy if-then rules, thus overcoming the "black-box" phenomenon as suffered by most NN models. Applicability of FMM to fault diagnosis tasks in a power generation plant has been examined. The potential of FMM in learning and predicting faults in complex processes as well as in providing a comprehensible explanation for its predictions has been demonstrated in two experiments. The proposed rule extraction algorithm is able to yield a comprehensible rule set. The extracted rules have been verified as meaningful and are in line with the domain knowledge as well as experts' opinions. Further research work will concentrate on the aspects of implementation, validation, and verification of FMM as a useful, robust, and intelligent fault diagnosis tool in a variety of application domains.

Acknowledgements

The effort and time of staff at TNB Prai Power Generation Plant in providing guidelines and advice for this research project are highly appreciated. The corresponding author gratefully acknowledges the research grants provided by Universiti Sains Malaysia, and the Ministry of Science, Technology, and Innovations Malaysia (No. 06-02-05-8002 & 04-02-05-0010) that have in part resulted in this chapter.

References

1. Al-Najjar B (1996) Total quality maintenance: An approach for continuous reduction in costs of quality products. Journal of Quality in Maintenance Engineering 2:2-20
2. Andrews R, Diederich J and Tickle AB (1995) A survey and critique of techniques for extracting rules from trained artificial neural networks. Knowledge Based Systems 8:373-389
3. Carpenter GA and Tan AH (1995) Rule extraction: From neural architecture to symbolic representation. Connection Science 7:3 -27
4. Craven MW and Shavlik JW (1994) Using sampling and queries to extract rules from trained neural networks. In: Machine Learning: Proceedings of the Eleventh International Conference, San Francisco, CA, USA
5. Dellomo MR (1999) Helicopter gearbox fault detection: a neural network based approach. Journal of Vibration and Acoustics 121:265-272
6. Denny G (1993) F16 jet engine trending and diagnostics with neural networks. In: Proceedings of SPIE, vol. 1965, pp. 419-412
7. Dietz WE, Kiech EL and Ali M (1989) Jet and rocket engine fault diagnosis in real time. Journal of Neural Network Computing 1: 5-18
8. de Efron B (1979) Bootstrap Methods. Another Look at the Jackknife. The Annals of Statistics 7:1-26
9. Efron B and Tibshirani RJ (1993) An introduction to the bootstrap. Chapman & Hall
10. Freitas JFG, MacLeod IM and Maltz JS (1999) Neural networks for pneumatic actuator fault detection. Transactions of the SAIEE 90:28-34
11. Fu LM (1994) Rule generation from neural networks. IEEE Transactions on Systems, Man, and Cybernetics 28: 1114-1124
12. Jack LB, Nandi AK and McCormick AC (1999) Diagnosis of rolling element bearing faults using radial basis function networks. EURASIP Journal on Applied Signal Processing 6:25-32

13. Kuo RJ (1995) Intelligent diagnosis for turbine blade faults using artificial neural networks and fuzzy logic. Engineering Applications of Artificial Intelligence 8:25-34

14. Polycarpou MM and Helmicki AJ (1995) Automated fault detection and accommodation: A learning system approach. IEEE Transactions on System, Man, and Cybernetics 25:1447-1458

15. Simpson P (1992) Fuzzy Min-Max Neural Networks–Part 1: Classification. IEEE Transactions on Neural Networks 3:776-786

16. Sharkey JC, Chandroth JO and Sharkey NE (2000) A multi-net system for the fault diagnosis of a diesel engine. Neural Computing and Applications9:152-160

17. System description and operating procedures, Prai Power Station Stage 3, vol. 14, 1999

18. Tickle B, Orlowski M and Diederich J (1996) DEDEC: A methodology for extracting rule from trained artificial neural networks. In: Proceedings of the Rule Extraction from Trained Artificial Neural Network Workshop, Society for the Study of Artificial Intelligence and Simulation of Behaviour Workshop Series (AISB'96), University of Sussex, Brighton, UK, pp. 90-102, 1996

19. Venkatasubramanian V, Rengaswamy R, Yin K and Kavuri SN (2003a) A review of process fault detection and diagnosis. Part I: Quantitative model-based methods. Computers and Chemical Engineering 27:293-311

20. Venkatasubramanian V, Rengaswamy R, Yin K and Kavuri SN (2003b) A review of process fault detection and diagnosis. Part II: Qualitative models and search strategies. Computers and Chemical Engineering 27:313-326

21. Venkatasubramanian V, Rengaswamy R, Yin K and Kavuri SN (2003c) A review of process fault detection and diagnosis. Part III: Process history based methods. Computers and Chemical Engineering 27:327-346

22. Kohonen T (1984) Self-Organization and Associative Memory. Springer-Verlag Berlin

10. Fuzzy Neural Networks Applied to Fault Diagnosis

João Calado and José Sá da Costa

In this chapter, after a brief state-of-the-art of the use of ANNs in industrial applications, the authors describe a fault diagnosis approach based on Fuzzy Neural Networks (FNNs) that combines the advantages of both fuzzy reasoning and neural networks. Fuzzy reasoning is capable of handling uncertain and imprecise information, while an ANN is capable of learning from examples. In contrast to conventional feed-forward ANNs, FNNs have an additional layer that converts the increment in each on-line measurement into fuzzy sets. Thus, on-line measurement data are compressed into qualitative values whose semantics are represented by fuzzy sets and, hence, the training of the FNN and the diagnosis of the faults can be carried out more efficiently.

However, fault symptoms concerning multiple simultaneous faults are harder to learn than those associated with single faults. Furthermore, the larger the set of faults, the larger the set of fault symptoms will be and, hence, the longer and less certain the training outcome. In order to overcome this problem, the proposed approach comes forward with a hierarchical structure of three levels, where several fuzzy neural networks are used. Thus, a large number of patterns are divided into many smaller subsets so that the classification can be carried out more efficiently. The adoption of a hierarchical structure of several FNNs for fault diagnosis aims at developing an architecture that can localize abrupt and incipient as well as single and multiple faults correctly, or at least with a minimum misclassification rate, and be easily trained using only single abrupt fault symptoms. In such an architecture, measurements or faults act as antecedents from which we can infer a classification of the pattern input that is diagnosis.

In order to test the performance and robustness of the current fault diagnosis approach, a pneumatic servomotor actuated industrial control valve has been used as test bed, and the analysis of results will be presented, as well as conclusions drawn.

10.1. Introduction

Nowadays, control systems are becoming more and more complex and control algorithms more and more sophisticated. Therefore, on-line fault detection and isolation (FDI) is one of the most important tasks in safety-critical and intelligent control systems. A major goal of intelligent control systems is to achieve high performance with increasing reliability, availability and automation of maintenance procedures. In many applications, increased requirements on productivity and performance lead to plants operating near design limits for much of the time. This may often result in system failures, which are typically characterised by critical changes in the inherent dynamics of the process. Process failures can potentially result not only in the loss of productivity but also in the loss of expensive equipment and, ultimately, of human lives. For these reasons, there is a growing need for on-line FDI approaches in order to increase reliability of such safety-critical industrial processes.

In dynamical systems, faults may be divided in two main classes: abrupt faults and incipient faults. The incipient faults affect the process behaviour slowly and may take a long time before being detected. Conversely, abrupt faults give rise to jumps in the process parameters or model, resulting in an appreciable deviation from normal behaviours. Abrupt faults are easy to detect, while incipient faults are more difficult to detect since they could resemble the transient behaviour of the process under normal regulation.

Thus, early detection and isolation of process faults, i.e., before they seriously degrade or affect safety as well as economic and environmental factors, is becoming an important consideration in effective plant supervision and control. In this context, fault detection and isolation and subsequent diagnosis of the degree of fault severity, likely causes, has been increasing in importance. Precise diagnostic information must be generated quickly to protect the plant from shutdown and provide operators with appropriate process status information to help them to take the correct decisive actions not only when faults become serious but also when faults that are developing become difficult to detect (incipient faults).

FDI systems based on conventional techniques are usually supported by linear process model (Patton *et al.*, 1994). For nonlinear processes, the traditional approach is to linearise the process model around the process operating point. This approach is effective for many nonlinear processes if the operating range is limited and the FDI system has been designed to be robust enough to tolerate small perturbation around the operating point. However, for processes with a high nonlinearity and a wide operating range, the linearised approach fails to give satisfactory results. One solution is to use a large number of linearised models corresponding to a range of operating points which is not yet very practical for real-time applications (Chen, 1995). On the other hand, the difficulty associated with diagnosing multiple faults based on classical linear mathematical models like the state space model arises from the need to have a very accurate model and the extensive calculations required. If there are errors in the model, they manifest themselves as faults, yielding false alarms. Furthermore, dealing with incipient faulty scenarios, where faults evolve gradually instead of suddenly occurring abrupt faults, is a major limitation of some techniques used in the conception of current FDI systems.

The increased number of international conferences and workshops including the FDI topic demonstrates the great attention given by the scientific community to the development of related methodologies. Such a research topic can be grouped into three main areas: quantitative, qualitative approaches or a mix of both (Patton *et al.*, 2000). The quantitative approaches are typically based on a mathematical model of the process (differential equations – white box model) or on a model based on artificial neural networks (black box model). On the other hand, the qualitative approaches are typically based on qualitative models of the processes, like fuzzy models or other qualitative techniques (Calado *et al.*, 2003). The third group of FDI approaches includes the coupling between qualitative and quantitative methodologies.

As pointed out by several authors (Patton *et al.*, 1999; Calado *et al.*, 2001), the application of different methods depends on our knowledge about the process and/or about the main objectives needed to be achieved. However, choosing between one or other methodology to implement a specific FDI system is often not an easy task since, according to the type of faults that such a system has to cope with, each method is characterized by some advantages and some disadvantages. As previously mentioned, the quantitative methods based on mathematical models are normally simplified (linear models) because the real processes are normally very complex and nonlinear, hence, hard to model. The quantitative methods that use artificial neural networks depend on the data that can be acquired from the process and it is also a very hard task to obtain faulty data from real processes. Usually, the data contain only the steady-state behaviour of the processes. On the other hand, the qualitative approaches (like fuzzy systems) depend on the knowledge and experience available about the process. So, the best solution is the combination between the two approaches, where the advantages of both methodologies could be combined compensating the disadvantages.

Thus, this chapter will be concerned with the application of fuzzy neural networks for fault isolation purposes and is organized as follows: in the next section a brief introduction to the artificial neural networks topic is given, as well as some industrial applications of multilayer perceptron and some applications of fuzzy neural networks are pointed out; section 10.3 describes the application of artificial neural networks to on-line fault detection and isolation (FDI) and a specific methodology based on a hierarchical structure of fuzzy neural networks is presented; section 10.4 presents the results achieved with the application of the methodology presented in the previous section to fault isolation of a pneumatic servomotor actuated industrial control valve; in section 10.5 some concluding remarks are presented.

10.2. Artificial Neural Networks

Artificial Neural Networks (ANNs) share their origins with the infancy of machine-based information processing, when McCulloch and Pitts first showed that a network of interconnecting threshold units could replicate any Boolean function. These units are modelled on the response of neural cells in biological nervous systems, hence the evocative name given to this field.

Therefore, ANNs grew out of research in Artificial Intelligence; specifically, attempts to mimic the fault-tolerance and capacity to learn of biological neural systems by modelling the low-level structure of the brain (Patterson, 1996). The main branch of Artificial Intelligence research in the 1960s to 1980s proposed the Expert Systems. These are based upon a high-level model of reasoning processes attempting to mimic the concept that human beings reasoning processes are built upon manipulation of symbols. It became rapidly apparent that these systems, although very useful in some domains, failed to capture certain key aspects of human intelligence. In order to reproduce intelligence, it would be necessary to build systems with a similar architecture.

The brain is mainly composed of a very large number (about 10,000,000,000) of *neurons*, massively. Each neuron is a specialized cell that can propagate an electrochemical signal. The neuron has a branching input structure (the dendrites), a cell body, and a branching output structure (the axon). The axon of one cell connects to the dendrites of another via a synapse. When a neuron is activated, it *fires* an electrochemical signal along the axon. This signal crosses the synapses to other neurons, which may in turn fire. A neuron fires only if the total signal received at the cell body from the dendrites exceeds a certain level known as the firing threshold. The strength of the signal received by a neuron and, hence, its chances of firing, critically depends on the efficacy of the synapses. Each synapse actually contains a gap, with neurotransmitter chemicals poised to transmit a signal across the gap. One of the most influential researchers into neurological systems (Donald Hebb) postulated that learning consisted mainly in altering the "strength" of synaptic connections. Recent research in cognitive science, in particular in the area of no conscious information processing, has further demonstrated the enormous capacity of the human mind to infer ("learn") simple input–output covariations from extremely complex stimuli (Lewicki *et al.*, 1992).

Thus, from a very large number of extremely simple processing units (each performing a weighted sum of its inputs, and then firing a binary signal if the total input exceeds a certain level), the brain manages to perform extremely complex tasks. Of course, there is a great deal of complexity in the brain which has not been discussed here, but it is interesting that ANNs can achieve some remarkable results using a model not much more complex than this.

ANN models, as an approximation scheme, are normally viewed as a composition of many non-linear computational elements operating in parallel and arranged in certain patterns. These models attempt to achieve good performance via dense interconnections of simple computational elements. The parameters associated with each interconnection are determined during a training period whatever the topological structure of the neural network models. However, all are aimed at approximating complex nonlinearities by linear combination of a simple nonlinear function.

Thus, ANNs witnessed an explosion of interest over the last few years, and are being successfully applied across a broad range of problem domains, in areas as diverse as finance, medicine, engineering, geology and physics. Indeed, anywhere there are problems of prediction, *classification* or control, ANNs are being introduced. This sweeping success can be attributed to a few key factors:

- ANNs are parallel systems used for solving regression and classification problems (Bishop, 1995). They estimate a function without requiring a mathematical description of how the output functionally depends on the input: they learn from examples. In particular, ANNs are *nonlinear* systems. For many years *linear modelling* has been the commonly used technique in most modelling domains, since linear models have well-known optimisation strategies. Where the linear approximation was not valid, which was frequently the case, the models suffered accordingly. ANNs also keep in check the *curse of dimensionality* problem that bedevils attempts to model nonlinear functions with large numbers of variables.

- ANNs *learn by examples*. The ANN user gathers representative data, and then invokes *training algorithms* to automatically learn the structure of the data. Although the user does need to have some heuristic knowledge of how to select and prepare data, how to select an appropriate neural network, and how to interpret the results, the level of user knowledge needed to successfully apply ANNs is much lower than would be the case using some more traditional nonlinear statistical methods.

ANNs are also intuitively appealing as they are a crude low-level model of biological neural systems. In the future, the development of this neurobiological modelling may lead to genuinely intelligent computers.

ANNs are applicable in virtually every situation in which a relationship between the predictor variables (inputs) and predicted variables (outputs) exists, even when that relationship is very complex and not easy to articulate in the usual terms of "correlations" or "differences between groups." A few representative examples of problems to which neural network analysis has been applied successfully are:

- **Detection of medical phenomena.** A variety of health-related indices (e.g., a combination of heart rate, levels of various substances in the blood, respiration rate) can be monitored. The onset of a particular medical condition could be associated with a very complex (e.g., nonlinear and interactive) combination of changes on a subset of the variables being monitored. ANNs have been used to recognize this predictive pattern so that the appropriate treatment can be prescribed.

- **Stock market prediction.** Fluctuations of stock prices and stock indices are another example of a complex, multidimensional, but in some circumstances at least partially-deterministic phenomenon. ANNs are being used by many technical analysts to make predictions about stock prices based upon a large number of factors such as past performance of other stocks and various economic indicators.

- **Credit assignment.** A variety of pieces of information are usually known about an applicant for a loan. For instance, the applicant's age, education, occupation, and many other facts may be available. After training an ANN on historical data, the ANN could be used to classify applicants as good or bad credit risks.

- **Monitoring the condition of machinery.** ANNs can be instrumental in cutting costs by bringing additional expertise to scheduling the preventive maintenance of machines. An ANN can be trained to distinguish between the normal operational conditions of a machine versus when it is on the verge of a problem. After this training period, the expertise of the network can be used to warn a technician of an upcoming breakdown, before it occurs and avoid costly unforeseen "downtime."

- **Engine management.** ANNs have been used to analyze the input of sensors from an engine. The ANN controls the various parameters within which the engine functions, in order to achieve a particular goal, such as minimizing fuel consumption.

As a matter of fact, neural computation is a highly interdisciplinary field, touching upon such diverse disciplines as statistics, neuroscience, psychology, physics or linguistics. As mentioned above, what unites the field is the original motivation behind neural networks to abstractly model the function of neurons and neuron assemblies in the brain. Starting from this motivation, and the number of models that have been developed, the field has moved outwards into several directions, and continues to move today.

In the next two subsections, some industrial applications of artificial neural networks, are reported.

10.2.1. Industrial Applications of Multilayer Perceptron

In engineering and physics, the classical approach to describe the behaviour and functioning properties of real systems and to obtain mathematical models to represent them relies on the use of algebraic and differential equations. The use of parameter estimation techniques and accurate knowledge of the physical system dynamics are required by such approaches together with numerical calculations to emulate the system operation. However, due to the complexity of the physical system, uncertainties are always present, making the corresponding mathematical model inaccurate, or even nonrealistic. Hence, in practice, approximate analysis is used and linearity assumptions are usually made.

To overcome the above difficulties, as mentioned in the last section, ANNs implement algorithms that attempt to achieve a neurological related performance, such as learning from experience, making generalizations from similar situations and judging states when poor results were achieved.

In recent years, many real-world industrial problems have been solved by applying ANNs. Such approaches include functional predictions and systems modelling when the physical systems are not well understood or are highly complex, pattern recognition and robust classifiers, with the ability to generalize while making decisions about imprecise input data.

Nowadays, many different types of ANNs are known. However, some of the more popular include multilayer perceptron (MLP), which is generally trained with the backpropagation learning algorithm, learning vector quantization, radial basis function (RBF), Hopfield and Kohonen networks, to name a few. Depending on how data is processed through the artificial neural network, they can be divided in two main groups. One of those groups is concerned with feedforward ANNs while the other includes the recurrent ANNs (i.e., implement feedback). Another way of classifying ANNs is related to the learning (or training) method used, as some ANNs employ supervised learning, while others are referred to as unsupervised or self-organizing learning methodologies.

Control engineers are often faced with engineering problems exhibiting knottiness, nonlinearities and uncertainties (Fukuda and Shibata, 1992). ANNs have been proven to be a powerful methodology providing accurate solutions for such classes of problems and overcoming the difficulties associated with the classical methods to deal with those problems. They are suitable to cope with such complexities due to the following features: learning from training data used for physical system identification by finding a set of connection strengths that will allow the network to carry out the desired computation (Rumelhart et al., 1994); generalisation from inputs not previously presented during the training phase by accepting an input and producing a plausible response determined by the internal ANN connection structure, which makes the overall system robust against noisy data and features exploited in industrial applications (Jung and Hsia, 1998); mapping of nonlinearities making them suitable for identification in process control applications (Rahman et al., 2000); parallel processing capabilities, allowing fast processing for large-scale dynamical systems; applicable to multivariable systems, since they naturally process many inputs and have many outputs; used as a black-box approach and implemented on compact processors for space-and-power constrained applications with no prior knowledge about the physical system being modelled.

The Multilayer Perceptron (MLP) is the most used model in classification problems; it is an artificial neural network with a topology where each neuron output is connected to every neuron in subsequent layers, connected in cascade with no feedback connections or connections between neurons in the same layer. Such an approach has been used in several industrial applications reported by many authors. Some examples are automatic wood surface inspection (Lampinen et al., 1998), speed control of DC motors (Rubaai and Kotaru, 2000; Venayagamoorthy and Harley, 1999), diagnostics of induction motor faults (Chow et al., 1991, 1993; Filippetti et al., 1995, 2000), induction motor control (Burton and Harley, 1998; Burton et al., 1995; Huang et al., 1999; Wishart and Harley, 1995), and current regulator for pulsewidth-modulation (PWM) rectifiers (Cichowlas et al., 2000). Maintenance and sensor failure detection was reported by Naidu et al. (1990), check valves operating in a nuclear power plant (Ikonomopoulos et al., 1992; Tsoukalas and Reyes-Jimenez, 1990), and vibration monitoring in rolling element bearings (Alguindigne and Uhrig, 1994). It has been widely applied in feedback control (Carelli et al., 1995; Er and Liew, 1997; Hashimoto et al., 1992; Jung and Hsia, 1998; Ozaki et al., 1991; Payeur et al., 1995; Sun et al., 2001; Sundareshan and Askew, 1997) and fault diagnosis of robotic systems (Vemuri and Polycarpou, 1997). The MLP was used in modelling chemical processes (Bhat et al., 1990), to produce quantitative estimation of concentration of chemical components (Liu et al., 1993), and to select powder metallurgy materials and process parameters (Cherian et al., 2000). It was used in a turbo generator controller (Venayagamoorthy and Harley, 1999), digital current regulation of inverter drivers (Buhl and Lorenz, 1991), modelling and control of a welding process (Andersen et al., 1990; Cook et al., 1995). An optimisation tool applied to the gas industry was reported by Martineau et al. (2002), as well as a tool to predict daily natural gas consumption needed by gas utilities (Khotanzad et al., 2000). Such artificial neural network was also used in a temperature control system (Khalid and Omatu, 1992;

Khalid *et al.*, 1995), monitoring feedwater flow rate and component thermal performance of pressurised water reactors (Kavaklioglu and Upadhyaya, 1994), and fault diagnosis in a heat exchanger continuous stirred tank reactor system (Sorsa *et al.*, 1991).

The MLP is indeed the most used ANN structure and spread out across several disciplines, like identification and defect detection on woven fabrics (Sardy *et al.*, 1993), automatic detection of damages on a critical conveyor belt transporting 60 million tons of coal per annum (Alport *et al.*, 2002), prediction of paper cure in the papermaking industry (Edwards *et al.*, 1999), controller steering backup truck (Nguyen and Widrow, 1990), and modelling of plate rolling processes (Gorni, 1997).

The majority of the reported applications involve fault detection and diagnosis, quality control, pattern recognition and adaptive control (Boger, 1995; Fogel, 1990; Liu *et al.*, 1993; Uhrig, 1994). All the mentioned MLP applications demonstrate adaptability features with the industrial problem, thus becoming part of the industrial processes.

In the next subsection some applications of a special type of artificial neural networks called fuzzy neural networks are presented.

10.2.2. Applications of Fuzzy Neural Networks

A major reason for the widespread application of fuzzy systems in industry is that they have the ability to handle problems not well defined, including nonlinearity and uncertainty, are easy to understand, are easy to apply quickly, and reduce development costs. However, fuzzy systems can express knowledge but cannot learn to adapt themselves. ANNs have the ability to learn, so the two methods complement each other. From an engineering point of view much of the interest in ANNs and fuzzy systems has been for dealing with difficulties arising from uncertainty, imprecision and noise. Fuzzy reasoning is capable of handling uncertain and imprecise information, while an ANN is capable of learning from examples. Thus, fuzzy neural networks (FNNs) intend to combine the advantages of both fuzzy reasoning and ANNs (Buckley and Hayashi, 1994a).

The name *fuzzy neural networks* suggests that it refers to artificial neural networks that are fuzzy, which means that some kind of fuzziness has been introduced to standard artificial neural networks. Therefore, as pointed out by Rutkowska and Hayashi (1999), such a name is most suitable for the neural networks obtained by direct fuzzification of signals and/or weights, as well as artificial neural networks composed of fuzzy neurons. Artificial neural networks, fuzzified by introducing fuzzy signals, weights, activation functions, etc., have been reported by several authors (Hayashi *et al.*, 1993; Ishibuchi *et al.*, 1995). Fuzzy neurons and fuzzy neural networks were first introduced by Lee and Lee (1975). Their fuzzy neurons were understood as a fuzzy generalisation of the McCulloch-Pitts neuron model (McCulloch and Pitts, 1943), which was historically the first neuron model proposed for classical artificial neural networks (Zurada, 1992; Anderson, 1995). Much later, the classical perceptron (Rosenblatt, 1958) was considered with the addition of membership functions; it was called the *fuzzy perceptron* (Keller and Hunt, 1985). A survey paper of Takagi (1990) discussed the fusion of artificial neural networks and fuzzy logic. However, very little research on fuzzy neural networks was done by then.

Fuzzy set theory has long been considered a suitable framework for pattern recognition, especially classification procedures because of the inherent fuzziness involved in the definition of a class or of a cluster (Lin and Lee, 1996). On the other hand, fuzzy set theory has been introduced to cope with uncertainty in other steps of the pattern recognition process, as for instance, to cope with the fuzziness involving the feature or the classification space.

In recent years, the concept of incorporating fuzzy logic into an ANN has grown into a popular research topic (Chen and Teng, 1995; Wang, 1997; Lin *et al.*, 1999, 2001). Fuzzy logic and artificial neural networks are complementary technologies (Lin and Lee, 1996). In contrast to classical ANNs or fuzzy systems, Fuzzy Neural Networks (FNNs) possess both their advantages. They combine the capability of fuzzy reasoning in handling uncertain information with the advantages of artificial neural networks, such as learning abilities, optimisation abilities, generalisation abilities and connectionist structures. Thus, one of the merits of the fuzzy neural approach is faster convergence speed with smaller network size as compared to the classical ANN (Kiguchi and Fukuda, 1997; Farag *et al.*, 1998).

Moreover, in many real-world applications, partial knowledge is available, but not a complete set of rules. What is needed is a technology that can work with a partial knowledge base and can learn from the additional data in order to perform the task correctly. Fuzzy logic handles the explicit knowledge, whereas the artificial neural networks handle the knowledge implicit in the data. A fusion of these two models into one model provides a better way of resolving problems that neither approach can solve separately.

An FNN can process both numerical information from measuring instruments and linguistic information from experts. In addition to fuzzy rule-based neural networks, which are also called neuro-fuzzy networks whose aims are mainly to process numerical relationships (Horikawa *et al.*, 1992; Jang, 1993; Chakraborty *et al.*, 2002), another class of FNNs that has attracted researchers attention is feedforward fuzzified neural networks, which are defined from conventional feedforward artificial neural networks by including fuzzified neurons, or by substituting crisp neurons with fuzzified ones (Buckley and Hayashi, 1994b; Liu and Wang, 1999; Liu, 2000). This second class of FNNs have been successfully applied to many real problems that are inherently uncertain and imprecise, involving adaptive control, system identification and pattern classification (Ishibuchi *et al.*, 1995; Feuring *et al.*, 1999; Ishibuchi and Nii, 2001).

Furthermore, according to Buckley and Hayashi (1994a), for an artificial neural network to be called a fuzzy neural network, the signals and/or weights must be fuzzy sets. They also consider three groups of FNNs. The first group includes the FNNs having real number signals but fuzzy set weights. In the second group the FNNs have fuzzy signals and real number weights. In the last group, FNNs have both fuzzy signals and fuzzy weights.

Some examples where fuzzy neural networks have been applied aiming at the automation of many different tasks are model reference control methodology based on fuzzy neural networks (Chen and Teng, 1995) and position and force control of industrial robot manipulators (Kiguchi and Fukuda, 1997).

In the next section, the use of fuzzy neural networks for fault detection and isolation will be presented. Furthermore, a detailed description of a hierarchical structure of fuzzy neural networks developed for fault isolation purposes will be provided.

10.3. Fuzzy Neural Networks Applied to FDI

Recently, the use of FNN for FDI purposes has received increasing attention in both research and application (Garcia *et al.*, 1997; Leonhardt and Ayoubi, 1997; Patton *et al.*, 1999; Calado and Sá da Costa, 1999; Patton *et al.*, 2000; Koscielny and Syfert, 2000; Calado *et al.*, 2001; Mendes *et al.*, 2002; Kowal *et al.*, 2002; Calado *et al.*, 2003). These reported studies have demonstrated that FNNs could be used to overcome the difficulties of conventional fault isolation techniques to deal with nonlinear behaviours. Establishing an appropriate training set allows the fuzzy neural networks to learn and generalize for operating with unseen input data. However, fault symptoms concerning multiple simultaneous faults are harder to learn than those associated with single faults. Furthermore, the larger the set of faults, the larger the set of fault symptoms will be and, therefore, the longer and less certain the training outcome.

Hence, in order to overcome the difficulties previously mentioned, the authors will present an approach based on a hierarchical structure of three levels where several FNNs are used. Thus, a large number of patterns are divided into many smaller subsets so that the classification can be carried out more efficiently. The adoption of a hierarchical structure of FNN approach for fault isolation aims at development of an architecture that can localise abrupt and incipient single and multiple faults correctly, or at least with a minimum misclassification rate and be easily trained, from only single abrupt fault symptoms.

Therefore, the current fault isolation approach consists of a hierarchical structure with three levels (lower, medium and upper) where the lower and the medium levels use one or more FNNs and the upper level is a fuzzy OR decision block, as depicted in Figure 10.1. It can be seen that the fuzzy neural networks have been achieved by adding a fuzzification layer to the conventional feedforward artificial neural networks (Haykin 1999).

In previous applications using the current fault isolation methodology (Calado *et al.*, 2001; Mendes *et al.*, 2002), the inputs to the hierarchical structure of fuzzy neural networks (HSFNN) used for fault isolation purposes have been based on the differences of the process measurement variables values, as expressed by Eq. 1:

$$dMV_k = MV_k - MV_{k-i} \tag{1}$$

where MV is the measured variable and k the sampling time. Further studies have been performed and the fault isolation approach based on the HSFNN has been applied for fault isolation purposes of a pneumatic servomotor actuated industrial control valve, as described in the next section. It has been observed during the mentioned design that such type of input variables has disadvantages, if they are applied to slowly developing incipient faults. In these cases, it is almost impossible to distinguish the fault symptoms from the measurement noise without using a high value of index i. However, since the FDI system should be able to isolate faults in a very early stage of their development as already mentioned, the index i has to be relatively small. One way to overcome such a problem will be to consider as inputs of the HSFNN the time derivative of the measured variables instead of their differences as given by Eq. 1.

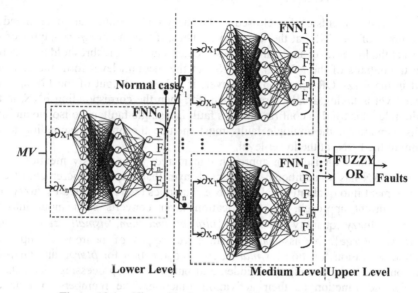

Figure 10.1. Hierarchical structure of fuzzy neural networks.

However, since the measurement variables are affected by noise, it is necessary to exercise some caution on how the estimated derivative is obtained. Thus, the derivatives are estimated by means of linear regression, being given by the following formula:

$$a_k = \frac{\sum\limits_{j=0}^{i-1} t_{k-j} MV_{k-j} - \left(\sum\limits_{j=0}^{i-1} t_{k-j} \right) \left(\sum\limits_{j=0}^{i-1} MV_{k-j} \right) / i}{\left(\sum\limits_{j=0}^{i-1} t_{k-j}^2 \right) - \left(\sum\limits_{j=0}^{i-1} t_{k-j} \right)^2 / i} \tag{2}$$

In Eq. 2 the following notation is used: a_k is the slope of the line at instant k; t stands for time; MV is the measured variable; and i is the number of points used for fitting the line. In the case study detailed in the next section, 15 points have been used for linear regression purposes ($i=15$).

According to Figure 10.1 the lower level of the HSFNN consists of one FNN_0 where all derivatives of the measured variables are used as inputs. The medium level uses a number of FNNs (structurally identical or different) that is equal to the number of single fault scenarios considered. Each FNN_i at the medium level is also fed with all the measurement variables and each one is associated with an output of the FNN_0 at the lower level, corresponding to a particular single fault. The upper level consists of a fuzzy OR operation on the FNN_i outputs at the medium level. There are different fuzzy OR operators available (Klir and Folger, 1988), but in the current approach we use the max-min operations to construct the fuzzy OR, represented by Eq. 3. Thus, the final fault vector is the result of this operation, which means the maximum values of each fault for all outputs from the medium level.

$$F_i = \max \left[\mu \left(F_i^{FNN_1} \right), ..., \mu \left(F_i^{FNN_n} \right) \right], \ i \geq 1 \tag{3}$$

The elements of the set used in the fuzzy OR operation are determined by the outputs of the FNN_0 at the lower level. Thus, if the i-th and j-th outputs of the FNN_0 at the lower level are taking values greater than 0.5, the threshold considered, then the outputs of the i-th and j-th FNN_i at the medium level form the elements used in the fuzzy OR operation. However, if only one output of the FNN_0 at the lower level is taking a value greater than 0.5, then the corresponding FNN_i in the medium level is used to confirm that this fault is a single fault, or to isolate multiple faults. Obviously, the multiple faults must include the one corresponding to the output of the FNN_0 at the lower level.

In the fault isolation approach considered, as previously mentioned, the adopted FNN has an additional fuzzy input layer that maps the increment of each measurement into qualitative values whose semantics are represented by fuzzy sets. In the current approach, the fuzzification layer converts each input into the following fuzzy quantity space, $Q_f = \{nlarge, nmedium, nsmall, zero, psmall, pmedium, plarge\}$, by association with seven types of neurons (complement sigmoid activation function for $nlarge$, sigmoid function for $plarge$ and Gaussian function for all the others). The hidden and output layers processing elements use the sigmoid function as their activation function. The membership functions associated with the neurons in the fuzzification layer could be determined by using the c-mean clustering algorithm (Bezdek, 1981) applied to the vectors used to train the neural networks. Both the lower level and the medium level networks are made up of three layers. The neural networks used in the case study described in the next section were trained using the Newton method combined with the Levenberg-Marquardt method (Marquardt, 1963). The training goal was to obtain a mean squared error smaller than 10^{-3}.

The FNN_0 (lower level) training data will be obtained from the process single abrupt fault simulation. In general and in order to cope with different fault strengths, the same fault will be simulated with several different intensities. Thus, the number of training patterns used to train the FNN_0 is equal to the number of single abrupt faults times the number of fault strengths considered plus a number of training patterns corresponding to the normal operational conditions. In general, Table 10.1 shows the training data associated with the lower level FNN, considering only one fault intensity.

On the other hand, the FNN_i (medium level) will be trained using the data for one single abrupt fault (the fault associated with the corresponding FNN_i) and for all possible double abrupt faults that the FNN_i will be able to diagnose. This training data is obtained by adding the data for the corresponding single abrupt faults considered, as shown in Table 10.2 and in Eq. 4:

$$\delta e_1^{1+2} ... \ \delta e_m^{1+2} = \delta e_1^1 + \delta e_1^2 ... \ \delta e_m^1 + \delta e_m^2 \tag{4}$$

Table 10.1. Training data for single abrupt faults

Vectors	FNN inputs	FNN outputs	Fault diagnosed
1	$\delta e_1^0 \dots \delta e_m^0$	0 0 0 ... 0	Normal
2	$\delta e_1^1 \dots \delta e_m^1$	1 0 0 ... 0	F_1
.	.	.	.
.	.	.	.
.	.	.	.
n-1	$\delta e_1^{n-1} \dots \delta e_m^{n-1}$	0 0 ....1 0	F_{n-1}
n	$\delta e_1^n \dots \delta e_m^n$	0 0 0 ... 1	F_n

Table 10.2. Training data for double abrupt faults

Vectors	FNN inputs	FNN outputs	Faults diagnosed
1	$\delta e_1^{1+2} \dots \delta e_m^{1+2}$	1 1 0 ... 0	$F_1 F_2$
2	$\delta e_1^{1+3} \dots \delta e_m^{1+3}$	1 0 1 ... 0	$F_1 F_3$
.	.	.	.
.	.	.	.
n-1			
n	$\delta e_1^{(n-1)+n} \dots \delta e_m^{(n-1)+n}$	0 0 ... 1 1	$F_{n-1} F_n$

In order to cope with process transient behaviours due to normal set point regulations, the current fault isolation approach should be coupled with a fault detection system, as for instance in the approach proposed by Calado *et al.* (2003).

Thus, when quantitative models are not readily available, a correctly trained artificial neural network can be used as a nonlinear dynamic model of the process. However, the neural network does not easily provide insight into model behaviour; the model is explicit rather than implicit in form. This main difficulty can be overcome using qualitative modelling or rule-based inference methods. For example, fuzzy logic can be used together with state-space models or neural networks to enhance FDI diagnostic reasoning capabilities (Lopez-Toribio *et al.*, 1999).

In the next section, the fault isolation approach described above will be applied to a pneumatic servomotor actuated industrial control valve and the results achieved will be provided.

10.4. Case Study

Faults are usually the main cause of loss of productivity in the process industry. One of the most important types of equipment present in the process industry is the flow control valve. A fault in a flow control valve may lead to a halt in production for long periods of time. Apart from these economic considerations faults may also have security implications. A fault in an actuator may endanger human lives, as in the case of a fault in an elevator's emergency brakes or in the stems position control system of a nuclear power plant. The occurrence of faults can be reduced through preventive maintenance; however, they cannot be fully eliminated. If a fault is detected in its early stages a quick intervention can often prevent serious consequences to the ongoing process. Therefore, there is a need for fault diagnosis systems that detect and isolate a fault as soon as it occurs (Chen and Patton, 1999; Patton *et al.*, 2000). The design and performance testing of fault diagnosis systems for industrial process often requires a simulation model since the actual system is not available to generate normal and faulty operational data needed for design and testing, due to the economic and security reasons that they would imply.

One of the most common types of actuators in the process industry is the flow control valve. Their numbers can run up to the thousands in process industries, such as oil refineries and the food industry. These flow control valves are widely used to control the distribution of process fluids as water and steam. The processes in which this kind of valve finds its most common application are characterized by high time constant, like thermal regulation and slow chemical reactors and evaporators. In all these cases, it is necessary to ensure the flow to be constant at a specified set point for a long period, while the transient time to reach the control value is usually of minor interest. These devices are subject, relatively often, to faults and malfunctions due to harsh environment conditions, which cause a decrease in production or even an installation shutdown. Recently, the application of fault diagnosis systems to industrial valve actuators has been studied under the European research training network DAMADICS (http://diag.mchtr.pw.edu.pl/damadics/) where a benchmark problem was defined. In this chapter the performance of the fault isolation technique described in the previous section will be demonstrated on this industrial benchmark valve actuator used to control the flow of the feeding water of a steam generator boiler. This benchmark problem will be described next.

10.4.1. Flow Control Valve

Figure 10.2 shows a view and the schematics of a typical industrial flow control valve. The flow control valve is a final control device that acts on the controlled process. Most of these valves are pneumatically actuated, consisting of three main parts: body of the valve, actuator (e.g., spring-and-diaphragm pneumatic servomotor) and positioner controller. The valve body is the component that determines the flow through the valve. The fluid enters the valve by port 1, it flows across the restricted section 2 and it exits the valve by port 3. The plug 4 can translate along its axis 5 in order to change the area of the restricted section. A change of the restricted area in the valve regulates the flow. There are many types of valve bodies; the differences between them relate to the form by which the restricted flow area changes. Here, the globe valve case will be adopted.

The flow through the valve body mainly depends on the valve opening, which is a function of the position of the stem, and on the pressure difference across the valve. The actuator sets the position of this stem. There are many types of servo actuators: electrical motors, hydraulic cylinders, spring-and-diaphragm pneumatic servomotor, etc. The most common type of actuator is the spring-and-diaphragm pneumatic servomotor due to its low cost. This actuator consists of a stem that has, at one end, the valve plug and at the other end the plate. The plate is placed inside an airtight chamber and connects to the walls of this chamber by means of a flexible diaphragm. This assembly is supported by a spring, as shown in Figure 10.2. Compressed air is admitted in chamber 6 and it acts on diaphragm 7. The spring 8 is compressed and it develops a force proportional to the deflection that opposes the force developed by the air on the diaphragm. The position of the stem is proportional to the pressure inside the airtight chamber.

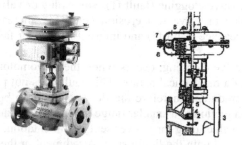

Figure 10.2.   Industrial flow control valve and schematics.

The positioner, shown in Figure 10.3, determines the flow of air into the chamber.

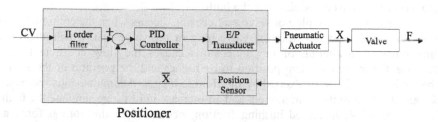

Figure 10.3.   Positioner controller.

The positioner is the control element that performs the position control of the stem. It receives a control reference signal (setpoint) from a computer controlling the process, passes it through a second-order filter, in order to get rid of noise and abrupt changes of the reference signal, prior to the PID control action that leads the stem's position to that reference signal. The positioner comprises as well a position sensor and an electrical-pneumatic (E/P) transducer. The first determines the actual position of the stem so that the error between the actual and desired position (reference signal) can be obtained. The E/P transducer receives a signal from the PID controller transforming it into a pneumatic valve-opening signal that adds or removes air from the pneumatic chamber. This transducer is also connected to a pneumatic circuit and to the atmosphere. If the controller indicates that the stem should be lowered, the chamber is connected to the pneumatic circuit. If, on the other hand, the stem should be raised, the connection is established with the atmosphere, thus allowing the chamber to be emptied.

10.4.2. Faults

The control valve may be affected by a number of faults (Koj, 1998). These faults are grouped into four major categories: valve faults, actuator faults, positioner faults and general/external faults. Here only abrupt or incipient faults are considered.

Valve faults are faults that affect the valve body. There are six different faults for this type: valve clogging (fault f1), valve plug or valve seat sedimentation (fault f2), valve plug or valve seat erosion (fault f3), increased bushing friction (fault f4), external leakage (fault f5) and internal leakage or fault in valve tightness (fault f6).

Fault f1, valve clogging, occurs when the servomotor stem is blocked by an external event of a mechanical nature. This fault does not permit the stem to go above a certain position and therefore the flow cannot drop below a certain value. Restricting the stem motion to a smaller range simulates this fault.

Fault f2, valve plug or valve seat sedimentation, occurs when solid particles that are mixed with the liquid start to sediment in the valve plug or in the valve seat reducing the orifice dimensions. The altering of the dimensions causes the K_v to decrease, the maximum stem position (x_{max}) to be smaller and the position of the stem to change because the force exerted by the fluid is smaller. A simultaneous decrease of the flow coefficient K_v, an alteration of the stem motion, and a decrease in its range simulate the fault.

Fault f3, valve plug or valve seat erosion, occurs when the continuing flow starts to remove material from the valve plug or the valve seat, which alters their dimensions. The altering of the dimensions causes the flow coefficient K_v to increase, the maximum stem position to be higher and the position of the stem to change because the force exerted by the fluid is bigger. A simultaneous increase of K_v, an alteration of the stem motion, and an increase in its range simulate the fault.

Fault f4, increased bushing friction, occurs when the normal force and static friction coefficient on the valve stem packing box increases due to corrosion, sedimentation, pollution, etc. This causes the hysteresis that already occurs in the stem to be increased. This fault is simulated by an increase in the hysteresis of the stem motion.

Fault f5, external leakage, occurs when the valve has a leakage, caused by corrosion, mechanical wear or poor assembly. This fault entails a loss of flow to the environment. This fault is simulated by a reduction in the flow at the output of the valve.

Fault f6, internal leakage, occurs when there is a loss of valve plug–valve seat tightness due to erosion, corrosion or mechanical wear. This fault is simulated by an increase of the flow coefficient K_v.

The actuator faults affect the pneumatic servomotor. There are four faults that fall into this category: twisted servomotor stem (fault f7), servomotor housing tightness (fault f8), diaphragm perforation (fault f9), and spring fault (fault f10).

Fault f7, twisted servomotor stem, may occur when the stem is bent due to external or internal forces parallel to the stem's axis. This will cause the normal force on the valve stem-packing box to increase and therefore cause an increase in hysteresis. This fault is simulated by an increase in the hysterisis that affects the stem motion.

Fault f8, servomotor housing tightness, occurs when there are air losses due to the lack of tightness of the pneumatic chamber. These air losses have an influence on the chamber pressure. This fault is simulated by a reduction in the airflow into or from the pneumatic chamber.

Fault f9, diaphragm perforation, occurs when the flexible diaphragm is punctured due to fatigue of the material. This causes a loss of air from the pneumatic chamber to the atmosphere, which alters the chamber pressure. This fault is simulated by a reduction in the airflow into or from the pneumatic chamber and in the area of the flexible diaphragm.

Fault f10, spring fault, occurs when the spring, which supports the stem, has a fault due to corrosion and/or fatigue of the spring's material. This fault is simulated by reducing the spring constant K.

There are three main faults that affect the positioner: E/P transducer fault (fault f11), stem displacement sensor fault (fault f12) and positioner feedback fault (fault f13).

Fault f11, E/P transducer fault, occurs when the characteristics of the transducer are changed due to coil damage or mechanical fault. This fault is simulated by changing the output of the E/P transducer, which will affect the airflow into or from the chamber.

Fault f12, stem displacement sensor fault, occurs when the potentiometric sensor responsible for supplying the measurements of the stem's position is faulty, due to wear of the materials or wire breaks due to fatigue. This fault is simulated by an increase, or decrease, in the readings of the position sensor.

Fault f13, positioner feedback fault, is caused by fault of a spring cancelling the clearance in the positioner mechanical lever feedback system. This fault is simulated introducing hysteresis in the feedback portion of the control loop, not affecting the sensor reading.

General/external faults are faults whose origin is not in the flow control valve system but rather in the plant installation, but may affect the valve's performance. There are four main faults that fall into this category: positioner supply pressure drop (fault f14), unexpected pressure change across the valve (fault f15), opened bypass valve (fault f16) and flow sensor fault (fault f17).

Fault f14, positioner supply pressure drop, occurs when the pressure of the pneumatic circuit that connects with the positioner drops. This causes the airflow into the chamber to be altered. This fault is simulated by a reduction of the pressure of the pneumatic circuit.

Fault f15, unexpected pressure change across the valve, occurs when, for some reason related to the system where the valve is placed, the pressure difference across the valve is altered. It causes changes in the flow and in the stem position. This fault is simulated by a change in the values of the upstream pressure or the values of the downstream pressure.

Fault f16, opened bypass valve, occurs when the valve of a bypass circuit, used to allow the control valve to be changed without stopping the flow, is opened, either due to employee mishandling or to a fault in this valve. This fault will lead to a greater flow at the exit of the circuit than what would be expected. The fault is simulated by an increase in the flow through the valve.

Fault f17, flow sensor fault, occurs when the sensor responsible for measuring the flow is faulty due to electronics or wiring failure. This causes the flow measurements to be biased. This fault is simulated by an increase, or decrease, in the flow readings.

A complete description of the faults and the way they affect the valve can be found in (Louro, 2003).

10.4.3.   Flow Control Valve Benchmark Simulator

An efficient parameterized MATLAB/SIMULINK simulator was developed that allows the simulation of normal and faulty conditions of the flow control valve. The faults are parameterized by defining the starting time, the type of fault (single, multiple, abrupt or incipient), the fault intensity, and the fault settling time (if the fault is incipient). Results can be assessed by an appropriate graphic interface and data files.

The simulator's inputs are the stem position reference signal (CV), the upstream and downstream pressures (P_{us} and P_{ds}) and the fluid temperature (T), given by the actual measurements from the plant. The outputs of the model are the stem position (X) and the flow (F) through the valve, as well as the previously mentioned inputs. The difference between the values given as inputs and the outputs referring to those values is that noise is added to them in order to simulate an actual sensor reading. Noise is assumed to be white with uniform distribution with sinusoidal mean and variance set by the user, being the seed generated randomly.

The developed simulator was compared with the data originating from an actual industrial system and it was concluded that the simulator provides a response that is very similar to the one of the actual system.

Some faults were introduced on purpose in the real system and the measurements compared with the data generated by the simulator for the same faults. The faulty data generated by the simulator was not as close to the real system as it had been for the normal operation. However, it is close enough for the intended purpose of fault diagnosis design and testing.

10.4.4. Fault Isolation

To test the efficiency of the fault isolation (FI) system based on the HSFNN previously described, four rates of change of the measurement variables have been defined as input data to the fault isolation system: dF_i – rate of change of the flow sensor measurement, dX_i – the rate of change of the rod displacement, dT_i – the rate of change of the fluid temperature and dP_i – the rate of change of the pressure difference across the valve.

To achieve a fault or faults isolation in the process under supervision, an analysis of the output values from the FNN at the lower level of the hierarchical structure is necessary. If the number of nonzero outputs (output ≥ 0.5) in FNN_0 is equal to 0, then it is assumed that no fault occurred in the process under consideration. Otherwise, the result of the fault isolation system is considered to be the result of a fuzzy OR operation (upper level) on several FNN_i outputs in the medium level, as previously described.

In the FI system considered all FNNs are equal, with a fuzzification layer consisting of 28 processing elements arranged in 4 groups, corresponding to the four rates of change of the measurement variables, where each group contains 7 neurons corresponding to the respective fuzzy sets (Figures 10.4 and 10.5). The number of neurons in the hidden layer is determined by the complexities of the relationships between the faults and the fault symptoms. During the design stage, following a trial and error procedure, it was found that 7 hidden processing elements give satisfactory performance for the fault isolation system under consideration. However, further research could be conducted in order to optimize the FNN topology by using ANN pruning algorithms. Moreover, since to test the current FI system, only 8 relevant single abrupt faults have been considered (F2, F7, F10, F11, F13, F17, F18 and F19), the output layer of each network is up to 8 neurons, each one corresponding to a fault. Besides the previously mentioned set of single faults, all possible double fault scenarios corresponding to an AND operation in the single fault space have also been considered.

The training of the FI system has been accomplished by using data relative to the normal behaviour of the process and all eight abrupt faults, at one specific operating point (CV=0.5), considering only one fault intensity (fs=0.75), giving a total of 8 time series containing the faulty information plus 1 time series containing the data relative to the normal behaviour of the process. The 9 time series are used for training the lower level network. For training the medium level networks the data relative to one of the faults is added with the data relative to the other faults in order to form data relative to double faults. Only the time series pertaining to the same operating point and fault intensity are added, which means that for training each medium level network there is a total of 8 operating points, 1 pertaining to the fault to which the network is associated and 7 pertaining to multiple faults. The membership functions associated with the fuzzy sets in the fuzzy layer of the FNN are estimated by applying the fuzzy c-mean clustering algorithm to the training data. The membership functions obtained can be seen in Figures 10.4 and 10.5.

The testing set contains information relative to normal operation conditions and to all eight faults, with two operating points (CV=0.65 and CV=0.75) and with three fault intensity values (fs=0.25, fs=0.5 and fs=0.75) for the case of abrupt faults, according to what has been defined for benchmark purposes. Table 10.3 shows the results achieved. From these results it can be concluded that for abrupt faults the HSFNN provides a good generalization capability as a fault isolation system. This is a very important aspect as far as the performance of the fault isolation system is concerned, since only single abrupt fault symptoms at one operating condition and for one fault intensity are considered during the training task.

Incipient faults are a type of faults where the magnitude of the fault intensity does not change instantaneously but rather develops through time. It is difficult to know the shape of the evolution since it depends on the case study and the type of fault. For the present case study, it is assumed that the fault intensity varies linearly from 0, at an instant called fault starting time, to 1, at an instant called fault settling time. After the simulation has reached the fault settling time, the fault intensity remains at 1 during the remaining simulation. The testing set for incipient faults is composed of data relative to all four faults shown in Table 10.3, considering two operating points (CV=0.65 and CV=0.75). Table 10.4 contains the times used for simulating these incipient faults.

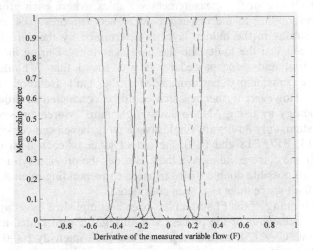

Figure 10.4.   Membership functions applied to the derivative of F and T.

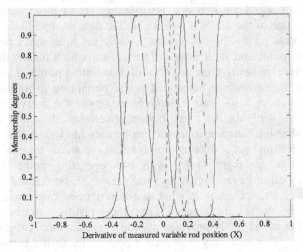

Figure 10.5.   Membership functions applied to the derivative of X and P.

Table 10.3.   FI results for single abrupt and incipient faults

Fault	Description	Abrupt			Incipient
		Small	Medium	Big	
F1	Valve clogging	▓▓▓▓▓▓▓▓▓▓▓▓▓▓▓▓▓▓▓			
F2	Valve plug or valve seat sedimentation			100%	0%
F3	Valve plug or valve seat erosion			███	
F4	Increase of valve or bushing friction			███	
F5	External leakage (leak bushing, covers, terminals)			███	
F6	Internal leakage (valve tightness)			███	
F7	Medium evaporation or critical flow	100%	100%	100%	
F8	Twisted servomotor's piston rod	███████████			
F9	Servomotor's housing or terminal tightness			███	███
F10	Servomotor's diaphragm perforation	100%	100%	100%	
F11	Servomotor's spring fault			100%	0%
F12	Electro-pneumatic transducer fault	▓▓▓▓▓▓▓▓▓▓▓▓▓▓▓▓▓▓			
F13	Rod displacement sensor fault	100%	100%	100%	0%
F14	Pressure sensor fault	█████████		▓▓▓	
F15	Positioner feedback fault	█████████		▓▓▓	
F16	Positioner supply pressure drop	███	▓▓▓▓▓▓▓▓		
F17	Unexpected pressure across the valve			100%	0%
F18	Fully or partly opened bypass valves	100%	100%	100%	███
F19	Flow rate sensor fault	100%	100%	100%	

███	Undetectable faults or faults only dynamically detectable, hence, the fault isolation system is not triggered
▓▓▓	Fault isolation system is not able to cope with such faulty scenarios
Xxx%	Percentage of correct isolated faults
	Not used for benchmark purposes

Under these incipient faulty scenarios, Table 10.3 shows that unsuccessful results have been achieved. One of the reasons for the bad performance of the fault isolation system under incipient faulty scenarios is concerned with the very slow evolution of the symptoms associated with such faults, as can be seen from Table 10.4. The changes observed in the measurement variables are so small that it is impossible to distinguish the fault effects from the noise that affects the process. As an example, Figures 10.6 and 10.7 illustrate the situation when fault F19 is considered as an incipient fault. Fault F19 has no effect on the measurement variables T and P. Furthermore, it is worth noting that only 15 points are used to evaluate the derivatives of the measurement variables, which are the inputs of the fault isolation system. Another reason that makes it very difficult to isolate the incipient faults simulated with a very low fault development speed is concerned with the pneumatic servo-motor actuated industrial control valve used, which has a position controller that compensates the influence of some faults in the process. The controller action could mask the fault effect in the process and, hence, the incipient fault symptoms will be substantially different from the abrupt fault symptoms used to train the FNNs.

Table 10.4.   Times that characterize incipient faults

Fault	Simulation Starting Time (s)	Fault Starting Time (s)	Fault Settling Time (s)	Simulation Ending Time (s)
F2	0	50	84050	100000
F11	0	50	84050	100000
F13	0	50	650	1200
F17	0	50	3650	5000

The double simultaneous abrupt faults used to test the FDI system have been achieved through an AND operation in the single fault space. For all double simultaneous abrupt faults considered the fault detection system was able to detect a hypothetical fault and, therefore, the fault isolation system has been triggered. The results achieved by the FI system under double simultaneous abrupt faults considering only the situations where the abrupt faults are simulated with big intensity and the two operating points mentioned above are shown in Table 10.5.

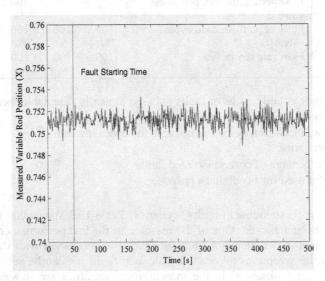

Figure 10.6.   Effect of incipient fault F19 on the rod position.

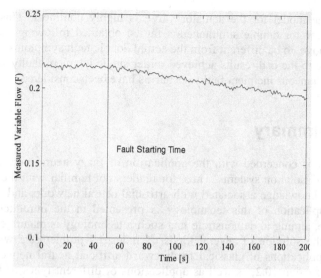

Figure 10.7. Effect of incipient fault F19 on the flow.

From Table 10.5 it can be seen that the performance of the FI system under double simultaneous faulty scenarios is not good for some faults. Several misclassification problems have been observed. The poor isolation results for double abrupt faults have two main causes. Firstly it may not be possible to distinguish single and double abrupt faults, especially when the isolation task is based on only one time instant thus ignoring the faults' dynamic characteristics. The double abrupt faults may not be distinguishable from the single faults. For instance, the symptoms of fault F10 are symmetric to the symptoms of fault F11. This means that the symptoms of the double simultaneous abrupt faults, F10+F11, will be very similar to those of a single abrupt fault. In this case, single abrupt fault F10 and double simultaneous abrupt fault, F10+F11, have identical symptoms.

Table 10.5. FI results for double simultaneous abrupt faults

Double Faults	Description	Abrupt Big
F2 + All other faults (1)	Valve plug or valve seat sedimentation	67%
F7 + All other faults (1)	Medium evaporation or critical flow	80%
F10 + All other faults (1)	Servo-motor's diaphragm perforation	68%
F11 + All other faults (1)	Servo-motor's spring fault	17%
F13 + All other faults (1)	Rod displacement sensor fault	0%
F17 + All other faults (1)	Unexpected pressure across the valve	83%
F18 + All other faults (1)	Fully or partly opened bypass valves	0%
F19 + All other faults (1)	Flow rate sensor fault	0%

Another cause for the poor isolation results may be the fact that the double fault symptoms are computed from the single abrupt fault symptoms as previously described. Such a methodology assumes that the relation between the symptoms is linear and has provided good results in cases where the HSFNN strategy was applied to linear systems or systems with small nonlinearities (Calado *et al.*, 2001).

However, the model for the actuator valve is highly nonlinear. This causes the training vector for double simultaneous faults, obtained following the procedure described above, to be different from the actual double fault symptoms.

Due to the bad results achieved under single incipient faulty scenarios, no double simultaneous incipient faulty scenarios have been considered.

10.5. Summary

This chapter is concerned with the application of fuzzy neural networks to fault detection and isolation systems. Thus, for readers not familiar with the subject, the background knowledge associated with artificial neural networks and the potential fields of application of this technology is presented in the introduction section. Furthermore, aiming to demonstrate that such a technology is mature enough to be applied in the solution of several kinds of industrial problems, a wide range of industrial applications of classical feedforward artificial neural networks are also reported in section 10.2, as well as applications of different types of fuzzy neural networks.

Section 10.3 is concerned with the development of FDI approaches based on fuzzy neural networks and a specific fault isolation system based on a hierarchical structure of several fuzzy neural networks is described in detail. The robustness and performance of such a fault isolation system has been assessed in section 10.4 by using a test bed consisting of a pneumatic servomotor actuated industrial control valve. Different kinds of faults have been considered, which has been assumed to occur in an abrupt or incipient manner, or by affecting the measurement variables in the process under supervision in an abrupt way or, instead, by affecting the process behaviour slowly (incipient faults).

The results presented in section 10.4 have shown that, under abrupt faults, the HSFNN provides very accurate results and is characterized by a good generalization capability as a fault isolation system. Under incipient or multiple simultaneous faulty scenarios, the performance of the proposed methodology depends on the fault development speed and/or on the system nonlinearities.

Acknowledgements

The authors acknowledge funding support under the EC FP5 contract (HPRN-CT-2000-00110) DAMADICS Human Potential Research Training Network. Thanks are expressed to the management and staff of the Lublin sugar factory, Cukrownia Lublin SA, Poland for their collaboration and provision of manpower and access to their sugar plant.

References

1. Alguíndigue IE and Uhrig RE (1994) Automatic fault recognition in mechanical components using coupled artificial neural networks. In: Proceedings of IEEE World Congress on Computational Intelligence, June–July, pp. 3312–3317

2. Andersen K, Cook GE, Karsai G and Ramaswamy K (1990) Artificial neural networks applied to arc welding process modeling and control. IEEE Transactions on Industry Applications 26:824–830

3. Anderson JA (1995) An Introduction to Neural Networks. MIT Press

4. Alport M, Mhlongo A, Naicker J and Plumb S (2002) Application of Neural Networks to Solve Industrial Problems: Bridging in Practice. Physica Scripta T97:118-121

5. Bezdek JC (1981) Pattern Recognition with Fuzzy Objective Function Algorithms. Plenum Press, New York

6. Bhat NV, Minderman PA, McAvoy T and Wang NS (1990) Modeling chemical process systems via neural computation. IEEE Control Systems Magazine 10:24–30

7. Bishop CM (1995) Neural Networks for Pattern Recognition. Oxford University Press.

8. Buckley JJ and Hayashi Y (1994a) Fuzzy Neural Networks. In: Yager RR and Zadeh LA (eds) Fuzzy Sets, Neural Networks, and Soft Computing. Van Nostrand Reinhold, New York, pp. 233-249

9. Buckley JJ and Hayashi Y (1994b) Can fuzzy neural nets approximate continuous functions, Fuzzy Sets and Systems 61(1):43-51

10. Buhl M and Lorenz RD (1991) Design and implementation of neural networks for digital current regulation of inverter drives. In: Proceedings of Conf. Rec. IEEE-IAS Annual Meeting, pp. 415-423

11. Burton B and Harley RG (1998) Reducing the computational demands of continually online-trained artificial neural networks for system identification and control of fast processes. IEEE Trans. on Industry Applications 34:589–596

12. Burton B, Kamran F, Harley RG, Habetler TG, Brooke M and Poddar R (1995) Identification and control of induction motor stator currents using fast on-line random training of a neural network. In: Proceedings of Conf. Rec. IEEE-IAS Annual Meeting, pp. 1781–1787

13. Boger Z (1995) Experience in developing models of industrial plants by large scale artificial neural networks. In: Proceedings of the Second New Zealand International Two-Stream Conf. Artificial Neural Networks and Expert Systems, pp. 326–329

14. Calado JMF and Sa da Costa JMG (1999) An Expert System Coupled with a Hierarchical Fuzzy Neural Network Approach for Multiple Fault Diagnosis. International Journal of Applied Mathematics and Computer Sciences 9(3): 667-687

15. Calado JMF, Korbicz J, Patan K, Patton RJ and Sa da Costa JMG (2001) Soft computing approaches to fault diagnosis for dynamic systems. European Journal of Control 7(2-3):169-208

16. Calado JMF, Carreira FPNF, Mendes MJGC, Sa da Costa JMG and Bartys M (2003b) Fault Detection Approach Based on Fuzzy Qualitative Reasoning Applied

to the DAMADICS Benchmark Problem. In: Proceedings of the 5th IFAC Symposium on Fault Detection, Supervision and Safety of Technical Processes, SAFEPROCESS'2003, Washington, D. C., USA, June 9-11, pp. 1179-1184

17. Carelli R, Camacho EF and Patiño D (1995) A neural network based feed forward adaptive controller for robots. IEEE Trans. on Systems, Man and Cybernetics 25: 1281–1288

18. Cichowlas M, Sobczuk D, Kazmierkowski MP and Malinowski M (2000) Novel artificial neural network based current controller for PWM rectifiers. In: Proceedings of the 9th Int. Conf. on Power Electronics and Motion Control, pp. 41–46

19. Chakraborty S, Pal K and Pal NR (2002) A neuro-fuzzy framework for inference. Neural Networks 15:247-261

20. Chen J (1995) Robust Residual Generation for Model-Based Fault Diagnosis of Dynamic Systems. PhD Thesis, Department of Electronics, University of York, UK

21. Chen J and Patton RJ (1999) Robust Model Based Fault Diagnosis for Dynamic Systems. Kluwer Academic Publishers, New York

22. Chen YC and Teng CC (1995) A model reference control structure using a fuzzy neural network. Fuzzy Sets and Systems 73:291-312

23. Cherian RP, Smith LN and Midha PS (2000) A neural network approach for selection of powder metallurgy materials and process parameters. Artificial Intelligence Engineering 14:39–44

24. Chow MY, Mangum PM and Yee SO (1991) A neural network approach to real-time condition monitoring of induction motors. IEEE Trans. on Industrial Electronics 38:448–453

25. Chow MY, Sharpe RN and Hung JC (1993) On the application and design of artificial neural networks for motor fault detection—Part II. IEEE Trans. on Industrial Electronics 40: 189–196

26. Cook GE, Barnett RJ, Andersen K and Strauss AM (1995) Weld modelling and control using artificial neural network. IEEE Trans. on Industry Applications 31:1484-1491

27. Edwards PJ, Murray AF, Papadopoulos G, Wallace AR, Barnard J and Smith G (1999) The application of neural networks to the papermaking industry. IEEE Trans. on Neural Networks 10: 1456–1464

28. Er MJ and Liew KC (1997) Control of adept one SCARA robot using neural networks. IEEE Trans. on Industrial Electronics 44: 762–768

29. Farag WA, Quintana VH and Torres GL (1998) A genetic-based neuro-fuzzy approach for modelling and control of dynamical systems. IEEE Trans. on Neural Networks 9: 756-767

30. Feuring T, Buckley JJ and Hayashi Y (1999) Fuzzy neural nets can solve the overfitting problem. In: Proceedings of the Int. Joint Conference on Neural Networks 4: 4197-4201

31. Filippetti F, Franceschini G and Tassoni C (1995) Neural networks aided on-line diagnostics of induction motor rotor faults. IEEE Trans. on Industry Applications 31:892–899

32. Filippetti F, Franceschini G, Tassoni C and Vas P (2000) Recent developments of induction motor drives fault diagnosis using AI techniques. IEEE Trans. on Industrial Electronics 47: 994–1004

33. Fisher Controls, Control Valve Engineering.USA

34. Fogel DB (1990) Selecting an optimal neural network industrial electronics society. In: Proceedings of IEEE IECON'90,vol. 2, pp. 1211–1214

35. Fukuda T and Shibata T (1992) Theory and applications of neural networks for industrial control systems. IEEE Trans. on Industrial Applications 39: 472–489

36. Garcia FJ, Izquierdo V, Miguel L and Peran J (1997) Fuzzy Identification of Systems and its Applications to Fault Diagnosis Systems. In: Proceedings of the 3rd IFAC Symposium on Fault Detection, Supervision and Safety for Technical Processes – SAFEPROCESS'97, Hull, UK, vol. 2, August 26-28, pp. 705-712

37. Gorni AA (1997) The application of neural networks in the modeling of plate rolling processes. JOM-e 49(4) (electronic document)

38. Hashimoto H, Kubota T, Sato M and Harashima F (1992) Visual control of robotic manipulator based on neural networks. IEEE Trans. on Industrial Electronics 39: 490–496

39. Hayashi Y, Buckley JJ and Czogala E (1993) Fuzzy Neural Networks with Fuzzy Signals and Weights. International Journal of Intelligent Systems 8: 527-537

40. Haykin S (1999) Neural Networks – A Comprehensive Foundation (2nd Edition). Prentice-Hall, New Jersey

41. Horikawa S, Furuhashi T and Uchikawa Y (1992) On fuzzy modelling using fuzzy neural networks with the back-propagation algorithm. IEEE Trans. on Neural Networks 3:801-806

42. Huang CY, Chen TC and Huang CL (1999) Robust control of induction motor with a neural-network load torque estimator and a neural-network identification. IEEE Trans. on Industrial Electronics 46:990–998

43. Ikonomopoulos A, Uhrig RE and Tsoukalas LH (1992) Use of neural networks to monitor power plant components. In: Proceedings of American Power Conference, vol. 54-II, April, pp. 1132–1137

44. Ishibuchi H, Morioka K and Turksen IB (1995) Learning by fuzzified neural networks. International Journal of Approximate Reasoning 13(3):327-358

45. Ishibuchi H and Nii M (2001) Numerical analysis of the learning of fuzzified neural networks from if-then rules. Fuzzy Sets and Systems 120(2):281-307

46. Jang J-SR (1993) ANFIS: Adaptive-network-based fuzzy inference system. IEEE Trans. on Systems, Man and Cybernetics 23:665-684

47. Jung S and Hsia TC (1998) Neural network impedance force control of robot manipulator. IEEE Trans. on Industrial Electronics 45:451–461

48. Kavaklioglu K and Upadhyaya BR (1994) Monitoring feedwater flow rate and component thermal performance of pressurized water reactors by means of artificial neural networks. Nuclear Technology 107:112–123

49. Keller JM and Hunt D (1985) Incorporating Fuzzy Membership Functions into the Perceptron Algorithm. IEEE Trans. on Pattern Analysis and Machine Intelligence 7: 693-699

50. Khalid M and Omatu S (1992) A neural network controller for a temperature control system. IEEE Control Systems Magazine 12:58–64

51. Khalid M, Omatu S and Yusof R (1995) Temperature regulation with neural networks and alternative control schemes. IEEE Trans. on Neural Networks 6:572–582

52. Khotanzad A, Elragal H and Lu TL (2000) Combination of artificial neural-network forecasters for prediction of natural gas consumption. IEEE Trans. on Neural Networks 11:464–473

53. Kiguchi K and Fukuda T (1997) Intelligent position/force controller for industrial robot manipulators – application of fuzzy neural networks. IEEE Trans. on Industrial Electronics 44:753-761

54. Klir JG and Folger AT (1988) Fuzzy Sets, Uncertainty and Information. Prentice-Hall, New York

55. Koj J (1998) The Fault Sources of Pneumatic Servo-Motor-Control Valve Assembly. In: Proceedings of the III Polish National conference on Diagnosis of Industrial Processes, Jurata, Poland, pp. 415-419 (in Polish)

56. Koscielny JM and Syfert M (2000) Application of Fuzzy Neural Networks for Fault Isolation - Example for Power Boiler System. In: Proceedings of 6th IEEE International Conference on Methods and Models in Automation and Robotics - MMAR'2000, Miedzyzdroje, Poland, vol. 2, pp. 801-806

57. Kowal M, Korbicz J, Mendes MJGC and Calado JMF (2002) Fault Detection Using Neuro-Fuzzy Networks. Systems Science Journal 28(1):45-57

58. Lampinen J, Smolander S and Korhonen M (1998) Wood surface inspection system based on generic visual features. In: Fogelman-Soulié F and Gallinari P (eds) Industrial Applications of Neural Networks. World Scientific, pp. 35-42

59. Lee SC and Lee ET (1975) Fuzzy neural networks. Mathematical Biosciences 23:151-177

60. Leonhardt S and Ayoubi M (1997) Methods of fault diagnosis. Control Engineering Practice 5(5):683-692

61. Lewicki P, Hill T and Czyzewska M (1992) Nonconscious Acquisition of Information. American Psychologist 47(6):796-801

62. Lin C-T and Lee CSG (1996) Neural Fuzzy Systems: A Neuro-Fuzzy Synergism to Intelligent Systems. Prentice-Hall, Upper Saddle River, NJ

63. Lin FJ, Hwang WJ and Wai RJ (1999) A supervisory fuzzy neural network control system for tracking periodic inputs. IEEE Trans. on Fuzzy Systems 7:41-52

64. Lin FJ, Wai RJ and Hong CM (2001) Hybrid Supervisory Control Using Recurrent Fuzzy Neural Network for Tracking Periodic Inputs. IEEE Trans. on Neural Networks 12(1):68-90

65. Liu P (2000) On the approximation realization of fuzzy closure mapping by multilayer regular fuzzy neural network. Multiple Valued Logic 5(2): 463-480

66. Liu P and Wang H (1999) Research on approximation capability of regular fuzzy neural network to continuous fuzzy function. Science in China, Series E 41(2):143-151

67. Liu Y, Upadhyaya BR and Naghedolfeizi M (1993) Chemometric data analysis using artificial neural networks. Applied Spectroscopy. 47(1):12–23

68. Lopez-Toribio C, Patton R and Uppal F (1999) Artificial Intelligence Approaches to Fault Diagnosis for Dynamic Systems. International Journal of Applied Mathematics and Computer Science 9(3):471-518

69. Louro R (2003) Fault Diagnosis of an Industrial Actuator Valve. MSc Dissertation, Instituto Superior Técnico, Technical University of Lisbon, November

70. Marquardt D (1963) An Algorithm for Least-Squares Estimation of Nonlinear Parameters. SIAM Journal ofn Applied Mathematics 11:164–168

71. Martineau S, Gaura E, Burnham KJ and Haas OCL (2002) Neural network control approach for an industrial furnace. In: Proceedings of the 14th International Conference on Systems Science, Las Vegas, USA, pp. 227-233

72. McCulloch WS and Pitts W (1943) A Logical Calculus of the Ideas Immanent in Nervous Activity. Bulletin of Mathematics and Biophysics 5:115–133

73. Mendes MJGC, Kowal M, Calado JMF, Korbicz J and Sa da Costa JMG (2002) Fault Isolation Approach Using a Profibus Network: a case study. In: CONTROLO'2002, 5th Portuguese Conference on Automatic Control, pp. 525 – 530

74. Naidu SR, Zafiriou E and McAvoy TJ (1990) Use of neural networks for sensor failure detection in a control system. IEEE Control Systems Magazine 10:49–55

75. Ozaki T, Suzuki T, Furuhashi T, Okuma S and Uchikawa Y (1991) Trajectory control of robotic manipulators using neural networks. IEEE Trans. on Industrial Electronics 38

76. Patterson DW (1996) Artificial Neural Networks: Theory and Applications. Prentice-Hall

77. Patton RJ, Lopez-Toribio CJ and Uppal FJ (1999) Artificial Intelligence Approaches to Fault Diagnosis. International Journal of Applied Mathematics and Computer Sciences 9(3):471-518

78. Patton RJ, Frank PM and Clark RN (2000) Issues of Fault Diagnosis for Dynamic Systems. Springer, London

79. Payeur P, Le-Huy H and Gosselin CM (1995) Trajectory prediction for moving objects using artificial neural networks. IEEE Trans. on Industrial Electronics 42:147–158

80. Rahman MH, Fazlur R, Devanathan R and Kuanyi Z (2000) Neural network approach for linearizing control of nonlinear process plants. IEEE Trans. on Industrial Electronics 47:470–477

81. Rosenblatt F (1958) The perceptron: A probabilistic model for information storage and organization in the brain. Psychological Review 65:386–408

82. Rubaai A and Kotaru R (2000) Online identification and control of a DC motor using learning adaptation of neural networks. IEEE Trans. on Industry Applications 36:935–942

83. Rumelhart DE, Widrow B and Lehr MA (1994) The basic ideas in neural networks. Communications of the ACM 37(3):87–92

84. Rutkowska D and Hayashi Y (1999) Neuro-Fuzzy Systems Approaches. Journal of Advanced Computational Intelligence 3(3):177-185

85. Sardy S, Ibrahim L and Yasuda Y (1993) An application of vision system for the identification and defect detection on woven fabrics by using artificial neural networks. In: Proceedings of Int. Joint Conference on Neural Networks, pp. 2141–2144

86. Sorsa T, Koivo HN and Koivisto H (1991) Neural networks in process fault diagnosis. IEEE Trans. on Systems, Man and Cybernetics 21:815–825

87. Sun F, Sun Z and Woo PY (2001) Neural network-based adaptive controller design of robotic manipulators with an observer. IEEE Trans. on Neural Networks 12:54–67

88. Sundareshan MK and Askew C (1997) Neural network-assisted variable structure control scheme for control of a flexible manipulator arm. Automatica 33(9):1699–1710

89. Takagi H (1990) Fusion technology of fuzzy theory and neural networks – Survey and future directions. In: Proceedings of International Conference on Fuzzy Logic and Neural Networks (IIZUKA'90), Iizuka, Japan, July 20-24, pp. 13-26

90. Tsoukalas L and Reyes-Jimenez J (1990) Hybrid expert system-neural network methodology for nuclear plant monitoring and diagnostics. In: Proceedings of SPIE Applications of Artificial Intelligence VIII, vol. 1293, April 1990, pp. 1024–1030

91. Uhrig RE (1994) Application of artificial neural networks in industrial technology. In: Proceedings of the IEEE Int. Conf. Industrial Technology, pp.73–77

92. Vemuri AT and Polycarpou MM (1997) Neural-network-based robust fault diagnosis in robotic systems. IEEE Trans. on Neural Networks 8:1410–1420

93. Venayagamoorthy GK and Harley RG (1999) Experimental studies with a continually online-trained artificial neural network controller for a turbo generator. In: Proceedings of the International Joint Conference on Neural Networks, vol. 3, Washington, DC, July, pp. 2158–2163

94. Zurada JM (1992) Introduction to Artificial Neural Systems. West Publishing Company

95. Wang LX (1997) A Course in Fuzzy Systems and Control. Prentice-Hall, Englewood Cliffs, NJ

96. Wishart M and Harley RG (1995) Identification and control of induction machines using artificial neural networks. IEEE Trans. on Industry Applications 31:612–619

11. Causal Models for Distributed Fault Diagnosis of Complex Systems

Cosmin Danut Bocaniala and José Sá da Costa

This chapter describes a novel framework for using causal models in distributed fault diagnosis. The state-of-the-art distributed fault diagnosis methodologies lack a coherent partitioning methodology of the monitored system into a set of subsystems, such that the independence level of local diagnosis process for each subsystem is *maximal* and such that the communication between different subsystems, required for formulating global diagnosis, is *minimal*. The partitioning of the causal model is performed with regard to the *d-separation* property that renders each region of the partition causally independent from the rest of the model. This special property allows fault diagnosis to be performed locally, without the need of communicating with the rest of the model, as long as the border with the rest of the model is healthy, i.e., *maximum* independence level of local diagnosis processes. Moreover, the causal model is partitioned so that the regions of the partitions are separated by borders containing a minimal number of vertices. It follows that if communication with the neighbouring elements is needed, the computational complexity of the process is *minimal*.

11.1. Introduction

This chapter describes a novel approach regarding the use of causal models for performing distributed fault diagnosis of complex systems. The methodology has been introduced in (Bocaniala and Sa da Costa, 2004; 2005). Fault detection and isolation (FDI) methodologies use actuators and sensors measurements. When dealing with complex (large-scale) industrial installations, designing a fault diagnosis system becomes very difficult due to the large number of sensors and actuators. Moreover, any solution for this problem must take into account the fact that the practitioners prefer rather simplistic systems that use basic engineering fundamentals. This is due to the fact that, in practice, simple and verifiable principles always win the competition versus complex methods that are usually characterised by instability, unpredictable behaviour and large computational burden. The described distributed methodology is be able to achieve its goal using simple and verifiable principles coming mainly from causal modelling and distributed computing.

The common approach when designing a distributed fault diagnosis system is to define a partition on the system structure and to assign one agent to each region of the partition. The agents perform local diagnosis inside the area they are assigned to. Global diagnosis is obtained by defining a proper communication scheme among agents. Two implementations of this common approach are discussed in the following.

The first implementation of this approach is given in (Fabre *et al.*, 2002). A *system* is defined as a pair $S=(V,O)$, where V is the set of system variables and O is the set of possible states of S. A *partition* of system S represents a set of subsystems S_1, S_2, ..., S_m, such that $S_i=(V_i,O_i)$, $V_i \not\subset V_j$, $m \geq 2$, $1 \leq i \neq j \leq m$, $V=V_1 \cup V_2 \cup ... \cup V_m$. If each of the local states in O_i, $i=1,...,m$, represents the projection of at least one global state in O, then the obtained partition is unique and is called the *canonical* partition. Notice that, in this case, the information contained by the elements of the partition, i.e., the set of variables and the set of states, is the same information provided by the original system. The system S is now defined by smaller sets of local constraints on smaller subsets of variables. This kind of representation is very useful for complex systems for which the number of variables is very large and, thus, the number of possible states is enormous. Fabre *et al.* (2002) give an algorithm that computes the canonical partition starting from a given partition. The algorithm uses communication via common variables between different partition regions and it does not need to know in advance the set O of all possible states of the system. Notice that this implementation focuses on the system partitioning aspect. Similar implementations are given in (Albert *et al.*, 2001; Letia *et al.*, 2000).

The second implementation highlights the advantages of using more than one fault diagnosis methodology when diagnosing a complex system and it has been proposed in the framework of the recent MAGIC project (Köpen-Seliger *et al.*, 2003; Lesecq *et al.*, 2003). Isermann and Ballé (1997) underline the fact that a single diagnosis methodology is inadequate for matching all challenges posed by a complex system. Therefore, the main task is to decide, for each partition region, the available diagnosis methodologies that provide best results. Notice that in this case the implementation focuses on optimizing the local diagnosis results.

The two implementations mentioned above lack a coherent partitioning methodology of the monitored system into a set of subsystems such that the independence level of local diagnosis process for each subsystem is *maximal* and such that the communication between different subsystems, required for formulating global diagnosis, is *minimal*. The proposed partitioning methodology partitions the monitored system into fully independent subsystems, i.e., maximum independence level of local diagnosis processes. It also insures minimal borders between different subsystems, which imply minimal computational complexity for communication.

The complexity of a system resides in the number of its basic components, actuators and sensors. In this chapter, the causal model of a system is encoded as a directed graph (digraph) (Balakrishnan, 1997), where vertices represent the available actuators readings and sensors readings, and edges represent the causal links between these measurements. The complexity of the system is reflected in the complexity of the associated digraph. The described fault diagnosis methodology basically (i) considers the causal model of the system as a *map*, (ii) splits this map into edge disjoint *regions* separated by borders formed by vertices, and (iii) assigns a dedicated agent to each region (Figure 11.1). For step (ii), notice that each region may be treated recursively in the same manner as the initial map, therefore inducing a local hierarchy of agents. The local expertise of the agents, as well as the interaction between them is used to robustly detect and isolate the faults in the system. The use of this distributed scheme allows maintaining the focus only on those regions of the map that are affected by faults. Hence, monitoring a complex system becomes a tractable problem.

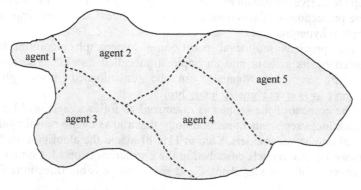

Figure 11.1.   The splitting of the causal model of a system.

In order to comply with the natural requirement for as small as possible a diagnosis computational time, the previous splitting is required to satisfy the next conditions: (i) the agents should be able to independently assess the state of the system in the assigned area, and (ii) the interaction between different agents should be kept as small as possible. The complexity of the interaction between two agents is given by the number of vertices located on the borders between the corresponding regions.

The first condition is met by using the d-separation criterion between each pair of neighbouring regions. The d-separation criterion, introduced in (Pearl and Paz, 1985), offers a parallel between causal independency and vertex separation in digraphs. If X, Y and Z represent three vertex subsets in a causal model, the d-separation criterion is able to determine if "knowing Z renders Y irrelevant to X." For the proposed partitioning, if X and Y represent the vertex subsets of two neighbouring regions, and if Z represents the vertex subset that constitutes the border between the two agents, then the d-separation criterion always holds.

Unfortunately, the d-separation criterion can be applied exclusively on acyclic digraphs (Neal, 2000; Pearl and Richter, 1996; Spirtes, 1995). Therefore, one of the main contributions of the chapter is a feedback loops replacement methodology that renders a cyclic causal model acyclic without actually losing the structural and behavioural information given by feedback.

The second condition is met by using the multilevel hypergraph partitioning (Karypis, 2002), which guarantees that a minimal number of vertices are located on the borders. The analysed causal model is transformed into a hypergraph, so that the following equivalence holds: the causal model has a minimal number of vertices on the partition borders if and only if the equivalent hypergraph has a minimal number of hyperedges cut by the partition borders. The multilevel partitioning paradigm is based on a very simple idea. First, the original hypergraph undergoes a sequence of successive approximations that represent smaller and smaller sized versions of the original configuration. The process of approximation continues until the hypergraph is reduced to a few tenths of vertices. At this point, some algorithms are used to compute a partitioning of the current form of the hypergraph. The final phase is to use the partitioning of the smallest hypergraph to derive the partitioning of the original hypergraph. This is achieved by successive projections of the current partition to the next level finer approximation of the original hypergraph.

The previous multilevel partitioning hypergraph algorithm has been implemented by its authors into an application called *hMeTiS*. The application, together with a User Manual, can be downloaded from http://www-users.cs.umn.edu/~karypis/hmetis/ index.html.

The content of the chapter is organized as follows. Section 11.2 presents the feedback loops replacement methodology that allows cyclic causal models to be transformed into acyclic models. Section 11.3 brings in the algorithm used to build the partitioned causal models described in the chapter. Section 11.4 summarizes the original contributions of this chapter and mentions possible directions for future work.

11.2. Feedback Loops Replacement Procedure for Obtaining Acyclic Causal Models

The section describes a methodology for replacing feedback loops in order to obtain acyclic causal models from causal models with feedback (Bocaniala and Sa da Costa, 2004; 2005). The most important property of the obtained acyclic causal model is that it reflects not only the structural properties of the original cyclic causal model, but also its behaviour in time. As mentioned in the chapter introduction, the considered system is modelled based on causality relationships between the available sensor readings. The *initial model* is represented as a digraph where vertices stand for the sensor measurements at the initial time-step of the analysis, and edges stand for cause-effect relationships between them. In order to reflect the behaviour of the system in time, this initial model is replicated at each time step, i.e., when new sensor measurements are available. The vertices of the replica correspond to the values of the sensor measurements at the current time-step. New edges, which reflect cause-effect relationships between vertices in the current replica of the model and vertices in the previous replicas, must be added. As detailed later in the section, adopting models built in the previous manner, offers the opportunity to replace a feedback loop of the system with an acyclic substructure by unfolding it in time. However, as shown later, *all* structural information and *all* temporal information given by feedback are preserved. It is to be noticed that, as the number of the considered time-steps increase, some vertices of aged replicas of the initial model become causally irrelevant to the other vertices in the model and, therefore, they can be eliminated. Thus, the model is dynamic in both positive and negative sense, i.e., vertices may be added and vertices may be eliminated as well.

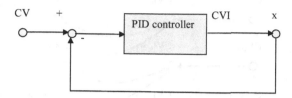

Figure 11.2. The control loop for the rod position of a valve.

In order to give a simple illustration of the reasons behind adopting this feedback replacement procedure let us analyze the system with feedback in Figure 11.2. The system in the figure is a flow control valve reduced to only three components: the control value (CV), the output of a PID controller (CVI) and the rod position (x). When a positioning command (CV) is issued, the controller uses the difference between CV and x in order to compute the control command CVI. The control commands are continuously issued on the basis of CV and x values in order to keep x as close as possible to CV. If one wishes to sketch the structural properties of the system in time, there are two possible situations to be analyzed: (i) the system is turned on at the initial time-step t of the analysis and (ii) the system is functioning at the initial time-step t of the analysis.

In the first case, the only causal relationships that are active at the initial time-step are those between CV and CVI and between x and CVI, i.e., the CVI value will be computed on the basis of CV and x. The causal relationship between CVI and x will become active after a very short interval of time d, $0<d<T$, while the output of the controller is computed. It is presumed that the sensor measurements are available periodically, at small interval of time of length T, i.e., its value represents the duration between two consecutive sensor measurements. The value of CVI_{t+d} will not affect the value of x_t but it will affect the value of x_{t+T}. Notice that, if it were possible to read the three sensors at time t', $t<t'<t+d$, only the ones corresponding to CV and x will provide values. The causal model for the first situation is depicted in Figure 11.3.

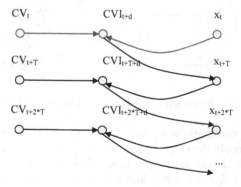

Figure 11.3. The system is observed when it is being turned on (the initial model is shown in red).

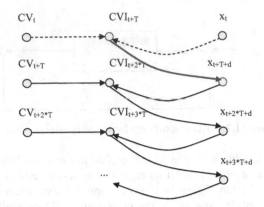

Figure 11.4. The system is observed when it is already turned on (the initial model is shown in red).

In the second case, the system is already functioning and, therefore, all three sensor measurements will provide values at the initial time-step. Still, neither CVI_t affects x_t nor x_t affects CVI_t. There are two possible initial models: (a) $CV_t \rightarrow CVI_{t+d}$ and $x_t \rightarrow CVI_{t+d}$, i.e., the value of CVI_t is neglected and (b) $CVI_{t+T} \rightarrow x_{t+T+d}$, i.e. the sensors are red during two time-steps and the values of x_t, x_{t+T}, CVI_t, CV_t, and CV_{t+T} are neglected. The first possible model is equivalent with the one in Figure 11.3. The second possible model is depicted by Figure 11.4. Notice that if we compensate the second model by adding edges $CV_t \rightarrow CVI_{t+T}$ and $x_t \rightarrow CVI_{t+T}$, then the structures of the two models are equivalent. The only difference is that after the initial moment t, the first computed value is CVI_{t+d} for (a) and x_{t+T+d} for (b).

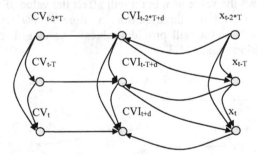

Figure 11.5. The system is observed inside the time window $[t-2*T,t]$.

There are two important observations to be made. First, notice that the causal model previously developed contains no feedback loops. Second, notice that the previous models do not reflect the causal links between the current value of a sensor measurement S_t and the previous values of the same sensor measurements, S_{t-i*T}, $i=1, 2, \ldots$. In practice, there is always a value $c>1$ for which all measurements at time instants $t-i*T$, where $i>c$, are causally irrelevant to the measurement at time instant t. It follows that all relevant causal relationships between S_t and its predecessors may be observed in the time window $[t-c*T,t]$. When dealing with more than one sensor measurement, as is the case for the system in Figure 11.2, then the time window that contains all relevant causal relationships inside the system is given by the largest value of the c parameters. This constant value is called the *relevant time-window span*. For instance, if the values of the c parameter for CV, CVI and x are $c_{CV}=1$, $c_{CVI}=2$, and $c_x=2$, respectively, the resulting causal model is shown in Figure 11.5. The model in the figure corresponds to the sensor measurements available in the time window $[t-2*T,t]$, where t is the current time instant.

Analysing the edge cut set that eliminates feedback from the structure, observe that, in the first case, the feedback loop between CVI and x *must* be cut on the edge $CVI \rightarrow x$, while, in the second case, the feedback loop of the system may be cut on any composing edge. The second case occurs much more often in practice and, therefore, the systems analysed in this section will be considered as already functioning. Thus, all feedback loops in the analysed system may be cut on *any* composing edge. This fact reduces the decisional effort when building the acyclic causal model of the system.

The example above and the accompanying discussion emphasised the fact that, in order to obtain the initial model of a system, an edge cut set that breaks all loops in the cyclic model of the system needs to be found first.

This section is structured as follows. The first subsection presents an algorithm that performs a partitioning of a causal model into a number of levels (Viswanadham *et al.*, 1987). The main property of the level partitioning is that each feedback loop in the model is assigned to a level in the partitioning. The second subsection proves that there is always an edge cut set for a cyclic causal model. The proof uses the distribution of feedback loops on levels given by the level partitioning. The third subsection presents, on the basis of the proof in the second subsection, the algorithm for building the acyclic causal model corresponding to a cyclic model using the feedback loop replacement procedure.

In order to facilitate the understanding of the theoretical concepts presented in the following, the digraph shown in Figure 11.6 is used.

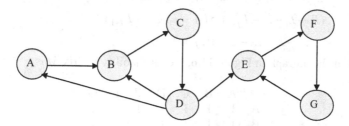

Figure 11.6. The digraph used to illustrate the theoretical aspects.

11.2.1. The Level Partitioning Algorithm of a Causal Model

Viswanadham *et al.* (1987) describe in their book an algorithm for structuring a digraph based on the *reachability* relation on the digraph vertex set. The reachability relation R is defined as follows. Given two vertices v_i and v_j, $v_i R v_j$ if and only if there is a directed path from v_i to v_j. Eventually, the reachability matrix M is defined as

$$m_{ij} = \begin{cases} 1, & v_i R v_j \\ 0, & \text{otherwise} \end{cases} \tag{1}$$

The reachability matrix M can be computed from the adjacency matrix A,

$$A = A^k = A^{k+1} = M \tag{2}$$

where A^k is computed using Boolean operations.

Structuring a digraph with respect to the reachability relation actually builds a partition on the vertex set into equivalence classes induced by this relation. These equivalence classes are called *levels*. The vertices found on a level have the next two properties.

(1) For $v_i, v_j \in L_k$ (the k-th level) there are only two possibilities:
   (a) v_i is reachable from v_j and v_j is reachable from v_i, i.e., the two vertices belong to the same feedback loop,
   (b) v_i is not reachable from v_j and v_j is not reachable from v_i, i.e., the two vertices are isolated one from each other.
(2) No vertex of L_j is reachable from any vertex of any following level L_{j+1} ($j=1,2,...,m\text{-}1$; m represents the number of levels), but there could be edges to L_j from any previous level L_k ($k=1,2,...,j\text{-}1$).

In order to build the levels, two sets of vertices are defined for each vertex v_i of the digraph. The *reachability set* R_i of v_i is formed by all the vertices that are reachable from v_i. The *antecedent set* A_i of v_i is formed by all the vertices from which v_i is reachable. The *level partitioning* of the digraph is built according to the definitions given by Eq. 4.

$$R_i = \left\{ v_j \in V : m_{ij} = 1 \right\}$$
$$A_i = \left\{ v_j \in V : m_{ji} = 1 \right\} \tag{3}$$

$$L_1 = \left\{ v_i : R_i \cap A_i = A_i \right\}$$
$$L_j = \{ v_i : v_i \in (V - L_1 - ... - L_{j-1}) \text{ and }$$
$$(R_i - L_1 - ... - L_{j-1}) \cap (A_i - L_1 - ... - L_{j-1}) \tag{4}$$
$$= (A_i - L_1 - ... - L_{j-1}) \}, j = 2,...,m$$

For the digraph in Figure 11.6, the reachability matrix M is

	A	B	C	D	E	F	G
A	1	1	1	1	1	1	1
B	1	1	1	1	1	1	1
C	1	1	1	1	1	1	1
D	1	1	1	1	1	1	1
E	0	0	0	0	1	1	1
F	0	0	0	0	1	1	1
G	0	0	0	0	1	1	1

The intersection $R_U \cap A_U$ equals A_U for $U \in \{A, B, C, D\}$. It follows, from Eq. 4, that $L_1 = \{A, B, C, D\}$. For the remaining vertices, $(R_U - L_1) \cap (A_U - L_1)$ equals $(A_U - L_1)$ for $U \in \{E, F, G\}$. It follows that the second and last level $L_2 = \{E, F, G\}$.

11.2.2. Finding a Minimal Edge Cut Set for the Feedback Loops

Balakrishnan (1997) defines a *strongly connected component* (SCC) of a digraph as a maximal set of interconnected feedback loops. It follows that the set of the SCCs of a causal model concentrates the whole feedback structure of the model. Notice from the description of the level partitioning algorithm that there can be only one SCC per level, i.e., the maximum possible number of SCCs equals the number of levels. Therefore, given the level partitioning of a cyclic causal model, the task of finding an edge cut set that breaks all loops in the system reduces to finding an edge cut set for each SCC given by the partitioning.

In the following, an algorithm that always provides an edge cut set for an SCC is given. The edge cut set will be required to be *minimal* in the sense that, if possible, each loop is cut on only one edge. Notice that there may be cut edges that break more than one loop. The most favourable situation is when the number of this kind of edges is maximal. The algorithm that computes the *minimal edge cut set* (MECS) for an SCC uses the breadth-first search (BFS) procedure when traversing the SCC. The formal description of the algorithm is given in the following. The MECS for the whole causal model is the reunion of the MECS computed for all its SCCs.

Algorithm 1 (The minimal edge cut set of an SCC)

Step 1. Choose randomly one vertex r in the SCC and consider it the root of the BFS tree. Build the BFS tree.
Step 2. An edge that does not belong to the BFS tree is called a *left-out* edge. For each layer of the BFS tree, for each vertex v on that layer, for each *left-out* edge e originating from v do the following.
Step 2.1. Check all directed paths containing v and e if they (i) do not contain any edge in the MECS, and if they (ii) contain at least an ancestor w of v in the BFS tree. If the previous two conditions are satisfied, then there is at least one loop, i.e., the loop containing v, e and w, which is not yet cut. By adding edge e to MECS, the loop containing v, e and w and possibly other loops will be cut by e.
Step 2.2. Check if MECS remains minimal after adding e and eliminate the redundant cut edges. An edge from MECS is called redundant if the loops that it cuts are already cut by other edges from MECS. See the proof of Theorem 1 for details.□

Theorem 1 *Given a cyclic causal model, Algorithm 1 always provides a minimal edge cut set for each SCC.*
Proof First of all, notice that each loop in the considered SCC contains at least one left-out edge. The justification is immediate. The BFS tree from Step 1 is acyclic. If

the left-out edges are added to this tree, then the obtained graph is the original SCC. The loops in the original SCC have been "restored" by adding the left-out edges. It follows that MECS represents a subset of the left-out edges set. What is left to be proven is that the MECS provided by Algorithm 1 really cuts all loops in the SCC and that it is minimal in the defined sense.

Let us denote by $BFS(t)$ the BFS tree with vertex t as root. Notice that, if the edge e in Step 2.1 of the algorithm is $v{\rightarrow}u$, all directed paths containing v and e represent directed paths in $BFS(u)$. Using this observation, Step 2 may be interpreted as follows: if there is an ancestor w of v in $BFS(r)$ from Step 1, such that w belongs to $BFS(u)$ and such that the directed path between root u and w in $BFS(u)$ does not contain any edge from MECS, then edge e is added to MECS. If each directed path in $BFS(u)$ between u and one of its ancestors w in $BFS(r)$ contains an edge f from MECS, then the loop containing v, e and w and possibly other loops are already cut by f. The previous discussion proves that, if there is any loop that contains edge e and that it is not yet cut by other edge in MECS, this loop will be cut by adding e to MECS in Step 2.1. It follows that MECS will cut all loops in the considered SCC. Moreover, MECS is already minimal in the sense that an edge enters MECS if and only if a loop not yet cut is detected. What is left to be investigated, so that MECS is minimal in the sense defined at the beginning of the subsection, is the elimination of redundant edges from Step 2.2.

Let us denote by $AN(v)$ the ancestors of v in $BFS(r)$ and by $EL(u)$ (from eliminated) all vertices s in $BFS(u)$ such that the directed path between u and s is cut by an edge from MECS. Then the condition for edge e to enter MECS may be expressed as

$$\forall e \text{ left-out edge from } SCC, e = v \rightarrow u, v \in BFS(r)$$

$$e \in MECS \Leftrightarrow AN(v) \cap \big(BFS(u) - EL(u)\big) \neq \varnothing \tag{5}$$

The redundant cut edges mentioned in Step 2.2 may appear in a $BFS(s)$ tree, $s \neq r$, as shown in Figure 11.7. The directed path from s to d contains both edges g and h. The condition $s \neq r$ is given as both g and h represent left-out edges and, by definition, $BFS(r)$ does not contain any left-out edge. As detailed above, edges g and h are cut with the purpose of disconnecting a and c respectively from the vertices in $AN(a)$ and $AN(c)$, respectively. When both g and h appear on the directed path from s to d in the $BFS(s)$ tree, $s \neq r$, the fact that they are cut may be interpreted as disconnecting a and c respectively from the vertices in $AN(a) \cap SubBFS(s,b)$ and $AN(c) \cap SubBFS(s,d)$ respectively, where $SubBFS(s,t)$ represents the subtree of $BFS(s)$ having the root t. If edge g is fixed and for any edge h and any vertex s

(1) g and h belong to the path between s and d in $BFS(s)$

(2) $AN(a) \cap SubBFS(s,b) \subseteq AN(c) \cap SubBFS(s,d)$ $\tag{6}$

then g may be eliminated from MECS in Step 2.2. It follows that MECS is minimal in the sense defined at the beginning of the subsection.□

An implementation of Algorithm 1 needs to administer the set of $BFS(s)$ trees, $s \neq r$, the $AN(s)$ sets, $s \neq r$, in the $BFS(r)$ tree, and the $EL(s)$ sets, $s \neq r$, of the $BFS(s)$ trees. The $AN(s)$ sets are static throughout the algorithm while the $BFS(s)$ trees and the $EL(s)$ sets are dynamic, depending on the edges that enter or leave

MECS. If l is the number of edges leftout after Step 1, the two main operations in Step 2 are performed for l times.

In the following, Algorithm 1 is applied for the SCC in the first level L_1 of the digraph in Figure 11.6. Let us assume r equals D. The $BFS(r)$ tree is shown in Figure 11.8. The left-out edges are displayed as dotted lines. The ancestors of the origins of the two left-out edges are $AN(A)=\{D\}$ and $AN(C)=\{B, D\}$. Initially, the $EL(s)$ sets, $s\neq D$, are void. For the left-out edge $A\rightarrow B$, the condition in Eq. 5 is true,

$$AN(A)\cap(BFS(B)-EL(B)) = \{D\}\cap(\{A,B,C,D\}-\varnothing) = \{D\} \qquad (7)$$

It follows that MECS = $\{A\rightarrow B\}$. Step 2.2 is not performed as MECS contains only one edge.

The second left-out edge, $C\rightarrow D$, points towards D that represents the root of the $BFS(D)$ tree considered in Step 1. Therefore, the edge is also added to MECS. Step 2.2 is performed by inspecting the $BFS(s)$ trees, $s\neq D$, from Figure 11.9. The only BFS tree that may contain a pair of redundant edges is $BFS(A)$. The first condition from Eq. 6 is fulfilled as edges $A\rightarrow B$ and $C\rightarrow D$ find themselves on the directed path from the root A to the vertex D. The second condition from Eq. 6 is false,

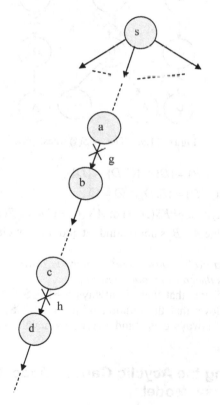

Figure 11.7. Two redundant edges in $BFS(s)$ tree.

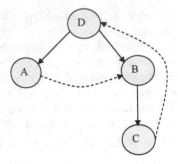

Figure 11.8.   The *BFS(D)* tree together with the left-out edges (dotted line).

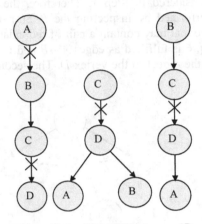

Figure 11.9.   The *BFS(s)* trees, *s≠D*.

$$AN(A) \cap SubBFS(A, B) = \{D\} \cap \{C, D\} = \{D\}$$
$$AN(C) \cap SubBFS(A, D) = \{B, D\} \cap \varnothing = \varnothing \qquad (8)$$
$$\{D\} \not\subset \varnothing \Rightarrow AN(A) \cap SubBFS(A, B) \not\subset AN(C) \cap SubBFS(A, D)$$

and, therefore, the edge $A \rightarrow B$ is not redundant and it is not eliminated from MECS.

Corollary 1 *Given a cyclic causal model, there is always a minimal edge cut set (MECS) that renders the causal model acyclic.*
Proof Theorem 1 insures that there is always a MECS for each SCC of a cyclic causal model. It follows that the reunion of these MECS, i.e., the MECS of the cyclic causal model, always exists and it renders acyclic the initial cyclic causal model.□

11.2.3. Building the Acyclic Causal Model Corresponding to a Cyclic Causal Model

Given the results in the previous subsection, it is now possible to give an algorithm that computes the acyclic causal model of a cyclic causal model by performing feedback loop unfolding in time. The formal description of the algorithm is given in the following. The algorithm must be provided with the relevant time-window span constant c_{max}, i.e., the maximum value of the c parameters (see the introductory part of the section).

Algorithm 2 (Feedback loops replacement for obtaining an acyclic causal model corresponding to a cyclic causal model)

Step 1. If the analysed causal model is cyclic, then first obtain the initial model (see the introductory part of this section) by eliminating the MECS from the cyclic causal model.
Step 2. Let t be the initial time-step. If S_t is an element of the initial model, then its instance at the i-th time-step, $i=1, \ldots, c_{max}$, is noted as S_{t+i*T}. The possible connections in the final acyclic model are detailed in the following.
Step 2.1. All vertices $S_{t+j*T}, 0 \leq j < i$, will have an outgoing connection with S_{t+i*T}.
Step 2.2. If U_t is another element of the initial model, $U_t \neq S_t$, so that S_t and U_t are connected in the initial model, then all pairs S_{t+i*T} and T_{t+i*T} will have the same type of connection.
Step 2.3. Finally, for each edge $U \rightarrow S$ or $S \rightarrow U$ in MECS, the connection $U_{t+(i-1)*T} \rightarrow S_{t+i*T}$ or $S_{t+(i-1)*T} \rightarrow U_{t+i*T}$ respectively is added to the model.□

Notice that Algorithm 2 represents a summary in a formalised manner of the discussion from the introductory part of the section. For examples, see also the introductory part of the section.

Theorem 2 *Each vertex in the acyclic causal model obtained by applying Algorithm 5 to a cyclic causal model, receives all input values that it is supposed to receive and provides all output values that it is supposed to provide.*
Proof The proof represents an analysis of Algorithm 2. First, the connections between vertices at the i-th step must be identical to the connections that exist in the initial model. This is insured by Step 2.2. The loss of connectivity information caused by the feedback loop replacement is recovered via unfolding in time, Step 2.3.□

Corollary 2 The acyclic causal model obtained by applying Algorithm 2 to a cyclic causal model preserves all structural information and all temporal information given by the initial cyclic causal model.
Proof It is an immediate consequence of Theorem 2.□

11.3. The Contributed Methodology of Partitioning Acyclic Causal Models Using d-Separation Criterion

This section first presents the algorithm that performs the proposed partitioning. The number k of size balanced regions and the value c of the overall imbalance tolerance between different regions (Karypis, 2002) are decided by the user. The decision must take into account the fact that the whole set of vertices is going to be distributed inside each region of the partition as well as on the borders of the partition. The goal is to obtain a partition that (i) has a minimal vertex-cut set and that (ii) has all pairs of neighbouring regions causally independent (d-separated). The uncertainty of this decision consists in the fact that the algorithm used guarantees minimal borders, but neither is it able to estimate the number of vertices located on them nor is it able to estimate how many vertices belong to each partition member. Future research needs to find methodologies able to eliminate this uncertainty. One possible direction is to insert principles from algorithms that provide minimal d-separation sets (Tian *et al.*, 1998) into multilevel partitioning algorithm.

The section also provides some general guidelines on how to use this partitioning to perform distributed fault detection and isolation. However, the purpose of the chapter is not to propose a distributed fault diagnosis methodology. The goal of the chapter is rather to describe a causal model-based framework for developing such methodologies.

Algorithm 3 (Partitioning a causal model into causally independent regions)

Step 1. If the input causal model *CM* contains feedback loops, use Algorithm 3 to perform feedback loops replacement in order to obtain the corresponding acyclic causal model (*ACM*).

Step 2. Compute the moral graph *MG* corresponding to *ACM*. The *moral* graph of a dag is built by connecting first all pairs of vertices that are parents of the same vertex and, then, giving up edge orientation (Lauritzen *et al.*, 1990). The "morality" of the obtained graph is insured by the fact that all vertices that share a child vertex are now "married" by connecting edges.

Step 3. Transform the *MG* graph into a hypergraph *HG* so that (i) the edges of *MG* represent the vertices of *HG* and (ii) each hyperedge *h* of *HG* corresponds to a vertex *v* in *MG* as follows,

$$h=\{e \in MG \, / \, e \text{ is an incoming/outgoing edge in/from } v\} \qquad (9)$$

Step 4. Use the *hMeTiS* application, with the *k* and *c* parameters decided by the user, to partition *HG* into *k* parts.

Step 4.1. The vertex-cut set in *MG* corresponds to the hyperedge-cut set of *HG*.

Step 4.2. The regions in the *MG* partition are delimited using the edge labelling of *MG* provided by the *HG* partition. The vertex-cut set on *MG* determines a partition of *ACM* into causally independent regions.□

Theorem 3 *Each hyperedge-cut set in HG has a correspondent vertex-cut set in MG of the same size.*

Proof When partitioning *HG* using *hMeTiS* in Step 4, each hyperedge *h* in HG may or may not be cut by the provided partition. In the following these two possible situations are analyzed.

If a hyperedge *h* in *HG* is cut by the *HG* partition provided by Step 4, this fact has the following interpretation. The elements in *h* span more than one region of the *HG* partition. But, the elements in *h* are all edges in *MG* with one end in a vertex *v* from *MG* (Eq. 8). Since the partition regions in *MG* are determined by the edge labelling provided for *HG* (Step 4.2), it follows that the edges in *MG* with one end in *v*, span more than one region of the *MG* partition. It follows that *v* represents a vertex located on the borders of the partition in *MG*.

If a hyperedge *h* in *HG* is *not* cut by the *HG* partition provided by Step 4, this fact has the following interpretation. The elements in *h* span one single region of the *HG* partition. But, the elements in *h* are all edges in *MG* with one end in a vertex *v* from *MG* (Eq. 8). Since the partition regions in *MG* are determined by the edge labelling provided for *HG* (Step 4.2), it follows that the edges in *MG* with one end in *v*, span one single region of the *MG* partition. It follows that *v* represents a vertex located inside one of the partition regions of *MG*.

From the previous two analyses, each hyperedge *h* in the hyperedge-cut set provided by Step 4 has a corresponding vertex *v* in the edge-cut set of *MG*. It follows that the claim in the theorem text is true, i.e., each hyperedge-cut set in *HG* has a correspondent vertex-cut set in *MG* of the same size.□

Corollary 3 *Given a causal model of a system, Algorithm 3 provides a partition of its acyclic form that (i) has a minimal vertex-cut set and that (ii) has all pairs of neighbouring regions causally independent, i.e., d-separated by the minimal vertex-cut set.*

Proof This corollary is an immediate consequence of Theorem 3. The hyperedge-cut set of *HG* provided by *hMeTiS* is minimal (Karypis, 2002). Theorem 3 proved that the vertex-cut set in *MG* induced by the hyperedge-cut set in *HG* has the same cardinal. It follows that the induced vertex-cut set in *MG* is also minimal.

One vertex set separating two regions in *MG* will d-separate the two regions in the acyclic form *ACM* of the original causal model *CM* (Lauritzen *et al.*, 2002). It follows that the vertex-cut set induced on *MG* by the hyperedge-cut set in *HG* will d-separate each pair of neighbouring regions in *ACM*.□

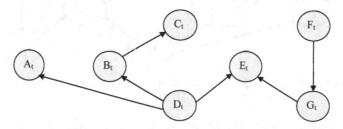

Figure 11.10. The initial model of the digraph in Figure 11.6.

In the following, it is presumed that the digraph in Figure 11.6 represents the causal model *CM* of a system, and Algorithm 3 is applied to provide the *CM* partitioning into causally independent regions. The MECS for the first level L_1 has already been computed in Section 11.2. The MECS for the second level L_2 contains one single edge, any of the three edges connecting *E*, *F* and *G*. Let us presume that $E \rightarrow F$ edge is chosen. Given the reunion of the two MECS, the initial model of the digraph in Figure 11.6 is shown in Figure 11.10. Let us presume that the relevant time-window span constant is 1, i.e., for all vertices the relevant past measurements are the ones taken at the previous time-step. The acyclic causal model *ACM* corresponding to *CM* (Step 1) is shown in Figure 11.11. The dashed edges are drawn in Step 2.1, Algorithm 2, while the dashed dotted edges are drawn in Step 2.3, Algorithm 2.

In practice, it is preferred sometimes to unfold in time only the pair of vertices disconnected by edges in MECS. If v is a vertex in *CM* whose all adjacent edges have not been selected for MECS, then v is not unfolded in time and all edges adjacent with v_{t+i}, $i=1,...,c_{max}$, become adjacent with v. All edges connected pairs of vertices from $\{v_i \ / \ i=0,...,c_{max}\}$ set are removed. The label used for the new vertex is "v" with no mention of time-step. This is done in order to reduce the complexity of *ACM* digraph and the obtained digraph is called the *reduced form* of ACM. In the case of the *CM* in Figure 11.11 there is only one vertex, *G*, whose all adjacent edges are not in MECS. It follows that the reduction is insignificant as the reduced form of this particular *ACM* has only one vertex, G_{t+1}, and one edge, $G_t \rightarrow G_{t+1}$, less than the original *ACM*.

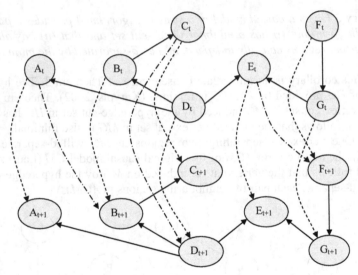

Figure 11.11. The acyclic causal model (*ACM*) corresponding to initial model in Figure 11.10.

The moral graph *MG* of *ACM* (Step 2) is shown in Figure 11.12. As mentioned in Step 2, the moral graph of *ACM* is built by first connecting ("marrying") all pairs of vertices that are parents of the same vertex and, then, giving up edge orientation (Lauritzen *et al.*, 1990). The dashed edges represents the edges added in order to insure the "morality" of the digraph.

The hypergraph *HG* corresponding to *MG* (Step 3) is obtained by considering the edges of MG as vertices in *HG*. Equation 8 is used to obtain the hyperedges of *HG*. For instance, the hyperedges corresponding to vertices A_t and A_{t+1} are

$$h_{A_t} = \{A_t \rightarrow A_{t+1}, A_t \rightarrow B_t, A_t \rightarrow B_{t+1}, A_t \rightarrow D_{t+1}\}$$

$$h_{A_{t+1}} = \{A_t \rightarrow A_{t+1}, A_{t+1} \rightarrow D_{t+1}\}$$

(10)

Notice that two hyperedges may share the same vertex (edge) in HG (MG). Hyperedges h_{A_t} and $h_{A_{t+1}}$ share the vertex (edge) $A_t \rightarrow A_{t+1}$ in HG (MG).

The number k of regions chosen is 2 and the overall imbalance tolerance chosen is 1% of the total number of vertices. The hyperedge-cut set of HG found by hMeTiS application (Step 4) is $\{h_{A_t}, h_{B_t}, h_{C_t}, h_{D_t}, h_{E_t}, h_{D_{t+1}}, h_{E_{t+1}}, h_{G_{t+1}}\}$. It follows that the vertex-cut set of MG is $\{A_t, B_t, C_t, D_t, E_t, D_{t+1}, E_{t+1}, G_{t+1}\}$. The two causally independent regions of the partition are $\{A_{t+1}, B_{t+1}, C_{t+1}\}$ and $\{F_t, G_t, F_{t+1}\}$. The partition is displayed in Figure 11.13.

Notice the large size of the border between the two regions, i.e., 8 out of 14 vertices. If the original digraph (Figure 11.6) would have represented the causal model of a real system, then the decrease of diagnosis complexity when using the obtained partition instead of using the original digraph would have proven insignificant, due to the large size of the border. The previous partition may be further refined using algorithms that provide minimal d-separation sets. One of these algorithms, introduced by Tian et al. (1998), is presented in the following.

Let us consider two vertices x and y in an acyclic digraph D. An algorithm is provided that finds a set Z such that Z, and no proper subset of Z, d-separates x from y.

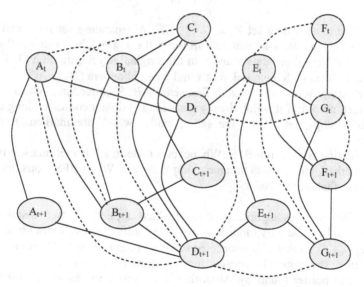

Figure 11.12. The moral graph MG of ACM in Figure 11.11.

Algorithm 4 (Minimal d-separation)

Step 1. Construct the subgraph corresponding to the ancestors of x and y, $D_{An(x \cup y)}$. A vertex w is called an *ancestor* of a vertex u in D if it is connected with u through a directed path, i.e., there is a set of vertices $\{v_1, v_2, ..., v_n\}$ so that $w=v_1$, $u=v_n$ and (v_i, v_{i+1}), $i=1,...,n-1$, is a directed edge in D.
Step 2. Construct the moral graph of $D_{An(x \cup y)}$, $(D_{An(x \cup y)})^m$.

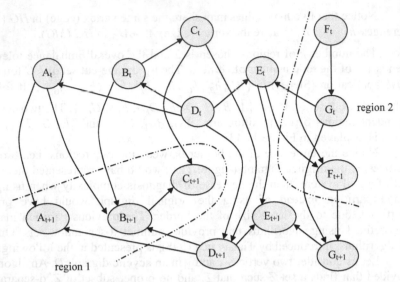

Figure 11.13. The partition into two causally independent regions of the *ACM* in Figure 11.11.

Step 3. Find a separating set Z' in $(D_{An(x \cup y)})^m$. A separating set for x and y in the moral graph represents a set that cuts all the paths in graph between x and y. Notice that the set Z' will d-separate x and y in the original acyclic digraph D. The set Z' may be initialized with the reunion of x and y neighbours in $(D_{An(x \cup y)})^m$.

Step 4. Starting from x, run breadth-first search (BFS) procedure. Whenever a node in Z' is met, mark it if it is not already marked, and do not continue along that path. When BFS stops, let Z'' be the set of nodes which are marked. Remove all markings.

Step 5. Starting from y, run BFS. Whenever a node in Z'' is met, mark it if it is not already marked, and do not continue along that path. When BFS stops, let Z be the set of nodes that are marked. □

The previous algorithm is valid when applied for two disjoint sets of vertices X and Y. The only modification is the addition of two extra vertices x' and y' to $(D_{An(X \cup Y)})^m$, so that x' is connected to all vertices in X and y' is connected to all vertices in Y. The minimal separator must be found for x' and y'.

The border found by Algorithm 3 is considered as set Z' from Step 3, Algorithm 4. Let $X = \{A_{t+1}, B_{t+1}, C_{t+1}\}$ and $Y = \{F_t, G_t, F_{t+1}\}$. The BFS tree for vertex x' added to *MG* (Step 4, Algorithm 4) is shown in Figure 11.14. The Z'' set is $\{A_t, B_t, C_t, D_{t+1}\}$ (the dashed circles in Figure 11.14). The BFS tree for vertex y' added to *MG* (Step 5, Algorithm 4) is shown in Figure 11.15. The Z set equals Z'' (the dashed circles in Figure 11.15). Notice that if $Z'-Z$ is added to Y, then Z d-separate X and Y. The new partition is shown in Figure 11.16. The new border is now half the size of the original border, i.e., 4 out of 14 vertices. The decrease of diagnosis complexity when using the new partition instead of using the original digraph is now significant, due to the small size of the new border. The new region 2 may be further partitioned using Algorithm 3.

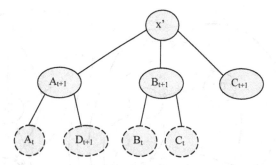

Figure 11.14. The BFS tree for Step 4 (left) and Step 5 (right), Algorithm 4.

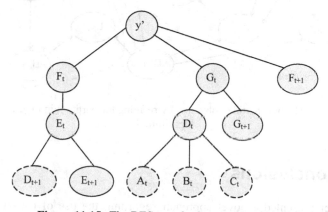

Figure 11.15. The BFS tree for Step 5, Algorithm 4.

One of the main properties of the previous partitioning is that, knowing the values of the vertices on its borders, each region becomes causally independent with regard to the rest of the causal model, i.e., d-separation criterion is "knowing Z renders Y irrelevant to X," where in this case X, Y are neighbouring regions, and Z the minimal vertex-cut set provided by Algorithm 4. From the fault diagnosis point of view, this suggests that the diagnosis of a region may be performed locally, knowing only the values of the vertices inside a region and the values of the vertices located on its border with the rest of the model. However, if one or more of the vertices located on the border become faulty, their values become unreliable and unusable. This may be interpreted as a break in the causality independence with regard to the rest of the model. In this case, some form of communication with neighbouring agents may be needed to compensate for the loss of causality independence. For instance, communication may have the purpose of recovering the correct value of a faulty sensor using redundancy relationships. However, the purpose of the chapter is not to propose a distributed fault diagnosis methodology. The previous remarks represent only some general guidelines on how to use this partitioning to perform distributed fault detection and isolation. Future research needs to concentrate on using the contributed causal model framework for developing such methodologies.

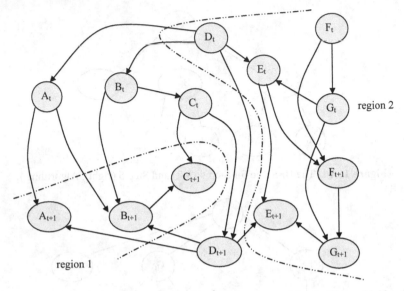

Figure 11.16. The new partition obtained by refining the partition in Figure 11.13 using Algorithm 4.

11.4. Conclusions

This chapter presented a novel approach regarding the use of causal models for performing distributed fault diagnosis of complex systems (Bocaniala and Sa da Costa, 2004; 2005). The described fault diagnosis methodology basically (i) considers the causal model of the system as a *map*, (ii) splits this map into edge disjoint *regions* separated by borders formed by vertices, and (iii) assigns a dedicated agent to each region. The main contribution of the chapter is the partitioning methodology that splits the causal model into causally independent (d-separated) regions, i.e., step (ii). The fact that each region is causally independent by the rest of the model allows performing the diagnosis of that region locally, without needing to communicate with the rest of the model. This property allows maintaining the diagnosis focus exclusively on those regions of the map that are affected by faults. Hence, monitoring a complex system becomes a tractable problem.

      The contributed work in this chapter has as support methodologies the multilevel hypergraph partitioning (Karypis, 2002) and d-separation theory (Pearl and Paz, 1985; Pearl and Verma, 1986). The original contributions are (i) the procedure for replacing feedback loops in cyclic causal models so that the resulting causal model is acyclic and so that no structural information or temporal information contained in feedback loops is lost, and (ii) the partitioning of causal models into causally independent regions using d-separation criterion.

Future research on this novel approach regarding the use of causal models for performing distributed fault diagnosis of complex systems needs to concentrate on two directions. The first direction is to eliminate the uncertainty when deciding the number k of size balanced regions and the value c of the overall imbalance tolerance (see Section 11.3). Currently these two values must be decided by the user. One possible solution is to insert principles from algorithms that provide minimal d-separation sets (Tian et al., 1998) into multilevel partitioning algorithm. The second direction is using the contributed causal framework to perform fault-tolerant control. Fault-tolerant control is concerned with making a controlled system able to maintain control objectives, despite the occurrence of a fault. The main challenge faced by the research in the field of fault-tolerant control systems is posed by practical applications to complex systems (Patton, 1997). For instance, one of the operations performed by fault-tolerant control systems is to accommodate faults that produce structural changes but do not require system shutdown. In this case, the causal model of the system and the associated distributed fault diagnosis system also suffer modifications and need to be updated. Reapplying the partitioning algorithm performs the updating.

Acknowledgements

This work was partially supported by Fundação para a Ciência e a Tecnologia, Minister of Science, Innovation and Technology, Portugal, grant number SFRH/BD/18651/2004.

References

1. Albert M, Längle T, Wörn H, Kazi A, Brighenti A, Senior C, Revuelta Seijo C, Sanz Bobi MA, Villar J (2001) Distributed architecture for monitoring and diagnosis. EU ESPRIT Project DIAMOND
2. Balakrishnan VK (1997) Graph theory, Schaum's Outlines. McGraw-Hill, New York
3. Bocaniala CD, Sa da Costa J (2004) Novel framework for using causal models in distributed fault diagnosis. In: Proceedings of Workshop on Advances in Control and Diagnosis, Karlsruhe, Germany, pp. 142-147
4. Bocaniala CD, Sa da Costa J (2005) Novel methodology for partitioning complex systems for fault diagnosis purposes. In: Proceedings of the 16th IFAC World Congress, Praha, Czech Republic
5. Fabre E, Benveniste A, Jard C (2002) Distributed diagnosis for large discrete events in dynamic systems. In: Proceedings of the 15th IFAC World Congress, Barcelona, Spain
6. Isermann R, Ballé P (1997) Trends in the application of model-based fault detection and diagnosis of technical processes. Control Engineering Practice 5(5):709-719

7. Karypis G (2002) Multilevel Hypergraph Partitioning. Technical Report 02-25, Department of Computer Science and Engineering, University of Minnesota, USA
8. Köpen-Seliger B, Marcu T, Capobianco M, Gentil S, Albert M, Latzel S (2003) MAGIC: An integrated approach for diagnostic data management and operator support. In: Proceedings of the IFAC Symposium SAFEPROCESS'03, Washington, USA, pp. 187-192
9. Lauritzen SL, Dawid AP, Larsen BN, Leimer HG (1990) Independence properties of directed Markov fields. Networks 20:409-505
10. Letia A, Craciun F, Kope Z, Netin A (2000) Distributed diagnosis by BDI agents. In: Proceedings of the OASTED International Conference on Applied Informatics
11. Lesecq S, Gentil S, Exel M, Garcia-Beltran C (2003) Diagnostic tools for a multi-agent monitoring system. In: Proceedings of IMACS IEEE CESA Multi-Conference on Computing Engineering in Systems Applications, Lille, France
12. Neal RM (2000) On Deducing Conditional Independence from d-separation in Causal Graphs with Feedback. Journal of Artificial Intelligence Research 12:87-91
13. Patton RJ (1997) Fault-tolerant control: The 1997 situation. In: Proceedings of the IFAC Symposium SAFEPROCESS'97, Hull, UK, pp. 1033-1055
14. Pearl J, Paz A (1985) Graphoids: A Graph-Based Logic for Reasoning about Relevance Relationships. Technical Report CSD-850038, Computer Science Department, Cognitive Systems Laboratory, University of California, Los Angeles, USA
15. Pearl J, Richter D (1996) Identifying Independencies in Causal Graphs with Feedback. In: Proceedings of the Twelfth Annual Conference on Uncertainty in Artificial Intelligence, August 1-4, Reed College, Portland, Oregon, USA
16. Pearl J, Verma T (1986) Formal Properties of Probabilistic Dependencies and their Graphical Representations. Technical Report CSD-860019, Computer Science Department, Cognitive Systems Laboratory, University of California, Los Angeles, USA
17. Spirtes P (1995) Directed Cyclic Graphical Representations of Feedback Models. In: Proceedings of the Eleventh Annual Conference on Uncertainty in Artificial Intelligence, August 18-20, Montreal, Quebec, Canada
18. Tian J, Verma T, Pearl J (1998) Finding Minimal d-Separators. Technical Report CSD-980007, Computer Science Department, Cognitive Systems Laboratory, University of California, Los Angeles, USA
19. Viswanadham N, Sarma VVS, Singh MG (1987) Reliability of Computer and Control Systems. North-Holland Systems and Control Series, Elsevier Science Publishers B.V., Amsterdam, Netherlands

Index